T0178646

Lecture Notes in Computer Science 14709

Founding Editors

Gerhard Goos
Juris Hartmanis

Editorial Board Members

The series Lecture Notes in Computer Science (LNCS), including its subseries Lecture Notes in Artificial Intelligence (LNAI) and Lecture Notes in Bioinformatics (LNBI), has established itself as a medium for the publication of new developments in computer science and information technology research, teaching, and education.

LNCS enjoys close cooperation with the computer science R & D community, the series counts many renowned academics among its volume editors and paper authors, and collaborates with prestigious societies. Its mission is to serve this international community by providing an invaluable service, mainly focused on the publication of conference and workshop proceedings and postproceedings. LNCS commenced publication in 1973.

Vincent G. Duffy

Editor

Digital Human Modeling and Applications in Health, Safety, Ergonomics and Risk Management

15th International Conference, DHM 2024
Held as Part of the 26th HCI International Conference, HCII 2024
Washington, DC, USA, June 29 – July 4, 2024
Proceedings, Part I

Editor
Vincent G. Duffy
Purdue University
West Lafayette, IN, USA

ISSN 0302-9743 ISSN 1611-3349 (electronic)
Lecture Notes in Computer Science
ISBN 978-3-031-61059-2 ISBN 978-3-031-61060-8 (eBook)
https://doi.org/10.1007/978-3-031-61060-8

This Springer imprint is published by the registered company Springer Nature Switzerland AG
The registered company address is: Gewerbestrasse 11, 6330 Cham, Switzerland

If disposing of this product, please recycle the paper.

Foreword

This year we celebrate 40 years since the establishment of the HCI International (HCII) Conference, which has been a hub for presenting groundbreaking research and novel ideas and collaboration for people from all over the world.

The HCII conference was founded in 1984 by Prof. Gavriel Salvendy (Purdue University, USA, Tsinghua University, P.R. China, and University of Central Florida, USA) and the first event of the series, "1st USA-Japan Conference on Human-Computer Interaction", was held in Honolulu, Hawaii, USA, 18–20 August. Since then, HCI International is held jointly with several Thematic Areas and Affiliated Conferences, with each one under the auspices of a distinguished international Program Board and under one management and one registration. Twenty-six HCI International Conferences have been organized so far (every two years until 2013, and annually thereafter).

Over the years, this conference has served as a platform for scholars, researchers, industry experts and students to exchange ideas, connect, and address challenges in the ever-evolving HCI field. Throughout these 40 years, the conference has evolved itself, adapting to new technologies and emerging trends, while staying committed to its core mission of advancing knowledge and driving change.

As we celebrate this milestone anniversary, we reflect on the contributions of its founding members and appreciate the commitment of its current and past Affiliated Conference Program Board Chairs and members. We are also thankful to all past conference attendees who have shaped this community into what it is today.

The 26th International Conference on Human-Computer Interaction, HCI International 2024 (HCII 2024), was held as a 'hybrid' event at the Washington Hilton Hotel, Washington, DC, USA, during 29 June – 4 July 2024. It incorporated the 21 thematic areas and affiliated conferences listed below.

A total of 5108 individuals from academia, research institutes, industry, and government agencies from 85 countries submitted contributions, and 1271 papers and 309 posters were included in the volumes of the proceedings that were published just before the start of the conference, these are listed below. The contributions thoroughly cover the entire field of human-computer interaction, addressing major advances in knowledge and effective use of computers in a variety of application areas. These papers provide academics, researchers, engineers, scientists, practitioners and students with state-of-the-art information on the most recent advances in HCI.

The HCI International (HCII) conference also offers the option of presenting 'Late Breaking Work', and this applies both for papers and posters, with corresponding volumes of proceedings that will be published after the conference. Full papers will be included in the 'HCII 2024 - Late Breaking Papers' volumes of the proceedings to be published in the Springer LNCS series, while 'Poster Extended Abstracts' will be included as short research papers in the 'HCII 2024 - Late Breaking Posters' volumes to be published in the Springer CCIS series.

I would like to thank the Program Board Chairs and the members of the Program Boards of all thematic areas and affiliated conferences for their contribution towards the high scientific quality and overall success of the HCI International 2024 conference. Their manifold support in terms of paper reviewing (single-blind review process, with a minimum of two reviews per submission), session organization and their willingness to act as goodwill ambassadors for the conference is most highly appreciated.

This conference would not have been possible without the continuous and unwavering support and advice of Gavriel Salvendy, founder, General Chair Emeritus, and Scientific Advisor. For his outstanding efforts, I would like to express my sincere appreciation to Abbas Moallem, Communications Chair and Editor of HCI International News.

July 2024   Constantine Stephanidis

HCI International 2024 Thematic Areas
and Affiliated Conferences

- HCI: Human-Computer Interaction Thematic Area
- HIMI: Human Interface and the Management of Information Thematic Area
- EPCE: 21st International Conference on Engineering Psychology and Cognitive Ergonomics
- AC: 18th International Conference on Augmented Cognition
- UAHCI: 18th International Conference on Universal Access in Human-Computer Interaction
- CCD: 16th International Conference on Cross-Cultural Design
- SCSM: 16th International Conference on Social Computing and Social Media
- VAMR: 16th International Conference on Virtual, Augmented and Mixed Reality
- DHM: 15th International Conference on Digital Human Modeling & Applications in Health, Safety, Ergonomics & Risk Management
- DUXU: 13th International Conference on Design, User Experience and Usability
- C&C: 12th International Conference on Culture and Computing
- DAPI: 12th International Conference on Distributed, Ambient and Pervasive Interactions
- HCIBGO: 11th International Conference on HCI in Business, Government and Organizations
- LCT: 11th International Conference on Learning and Collaboration Technologies
- ITAP: 10th International Conference on Human Aspects of IT for the Aged Population
- AIS: 6th International Conference on Adaptive Instructional Systems
- HCI-CPT: 6th International Conference on HCI for Cybersecurity, Privacy and Trust
- HCI-Games: 6th International Conference on HCI in Games
- MobiTAS: 6th International Conference on HCI in Mobility, Transport and Automotive Systems
- AI-HCI: 5th International Conference on Artificial Intelligence in HCI
- MOBILE: 5th International Conference on Human-Centered Design, Operation and Evaluation of Mobile Communications

List of Conference Proceedings Volumes Appearing Before the Conference

1. LNCS 14684, Human-Computer Interaction: Part I, edited by Masaaki Kurosu and Ayako Hashizume
2. LNCS 14685, Human-Computer Interaction: Part II, edited by Masaaki Kurosu and Ayako Hashizume
3. LNCS 14686, Human-Computer Interaction: Part III, edited by Masaaki Kurosu and Ayako Hashizume
4. LNCS 14687, Human-Computer Interaction: Part IV, edited by Masaaki Kurosu and Ayako Hashizume
5. LNCS 14688, Human-Computer Interaction: Part V, edited by Masaaki Kurosu and Ayako Hashizume
6. LNCS 14689, Human Interface and the Management of Information: Part I, edited by Hirohiko Mori and Yumi Asahi
7. LNCS 14690, Human Interface and the Management of Information: Part II, edited by Hirohiko Mori and Yumi Asahi
8. LNCS 14691, Human Interface and the Management of Information: Part III, edited by Hirohiko Mori and Yumi Asahi
9. LNAI 14692, Engineering Psychology and Cognitive Ergonomics: Part I, edited by Don Harris and Wen-Chin Li
10. LNAI 14693, Engineering Psychology and Cognitive Ergonomics: Part II, edited by Don Harris and Wen-Chin Li
11. LNAI 14694, Augmented Cognition, Part I, edited by Dylan D. Schmorrow and Cali M. Fidopiastis
12. LNAI 14695, Augmented Cognition, Part II, edited by Dylan D. Schmorrow and Cali M. Fidopiastis
13. LNCS 14696, Universal Access in Human-Computer Interaction: Part I, edited by Margherita Antona and Constantine Stephanidis
14. LNCS 14697, Universal Access in Human-Computer Interaction: Part II, edited by Margherita Antona and Constantine Stephanidis
15. LNCS 14698, Universal Access in Human-Computer Interaction: Part III, edited by Margherita Antona and Constantine Stephanidis
16. LNCS 14699, Cross-Cultural Design: Part I, edited by Pei-Luen Patrick Rau
17. LNCS 14700, Cross-Cultural Design: Part II, edited by Pei-Luen Patrick Rau
18. LNCS 14701, Cross-Cultural Design: Part III, edited by Pei-Luen Patrick Rau
19. LNCS 14702, Cross-Cultural Design: Part IV, edited by Pei-Luen Patrick Rau
20. LNCS 14703, Social Computing and Social Media: Part I, edited by Adela Coman and Simona Vasilache
21. LNCS 14704, Social Computing and Social Media: Part II, edited by Adela Coman and Simona Vasilache
22. LNCS 14705, Social Computing and Social Media: Part III, edited by Adela Coman and Simona Vasilache

47. LNCS 14730, HCI in Games: Part I, edited by Xiaowen Fang
48. LNCS 14731, HCI in Games: Part II, edited by Xiaowen Fang
49. LNCS 14732, HCI in Mobility, Transport and Automotive Systems: Part I, edited by Heidi Krömker
50. LNCS 14733, HCI in Mobility, Transport and Automotive Systems: Part II, edited by Heidi Krömker
51. LNAI 14734, Artificial Intelligence in HCI: Part I, edited by Helmut Degen and Stavroula Ntoa
52. LNAI 14735, Artificial Intelligence in HCI: Part II, edited by Helmut Degen and Stavroula Ntoa
53. LNAI 14736, Artificial Intelligence in HCI: Part III, edited by Helmut Degen and Stavroula Ntoa
54. LNCS 14737, Design, Operation and Evaluation of Mobile Communications: Part I, edited by June Wei and George Margetis
55. LNCS 14738, Design, Operation and Evaluation of Mobile Communications: Part II, edited by June Wei and George Margetis
56. CCIS 2114, HCI International 2024 Posters - Part I, edited by Constantine Stephanidis, Margherita Antona, Stavroula Ntoa and Gavriel Salvendy
57. CCIS 2115, HCI International 2024 Posters - Part II, edited by Constantine Stephanidis, Margherita Antona, Stavroula Ntoa and Gavriel Salvendy
58. CCIS 2116, HCI International 2024 Posters - Part III, edited by Constantine Stephanidis, Margherita Antona, Stavroula Ntoa and Gavriel Salvendy
59. CCIS 2117, HCI International 2024 Posters - Part IV, edited by Constantine Stephanidis, Margherita Antona, Stavroula Ntoa and Gavriel Salvendy
60. CCIS 2118, HCI International 2024 Posters - Part V, edited by Constantine Stephanidis, Margherita Antona, Stavroula Ntoa and Gavriel Salvendy
61. CCIS 2119, HCI International 2024 Posters - Part VI, edited by Constantine Stephanidis, Margherita Antona, Stavroula Ntoa and Gavriel Salvendy
62. CCIS 2120, HCI International 2024 Posters - Part VII, edited by Constantine Stephanidis, Margherita Antona, Stavroula Ntoa and Gavriel Salvendy

https://2024.hci.international/proceedings

Preface

Software representations of humans, including aspects of anthropometry, biometrics, motion capture and prediction, as well as cognition modeling, are known as Digital Human Models (DHM), and are widely used in a variety of complex application domains where it is important to foresee and simulate human behavior, performance, safety, health and comfort. Automation depicting human emotion, social interaction and functional capabilities can also be modeled to support and assist in predicting human response in real-world settings. Such domains include medical and nursing applications, work, education and learning, ergonomics and design, as well as safety and risk management.

The 16th Digital Human Modeling and Applications in Health, Safety, Ergonomics and Risk Management (DHM) Conference, an affiliated conference of the HCI International Conference 2024, encouraged papers from academics, researchers, industry and professionals, on a broad range of theoretical and applied issues related to Digital Human Modeling and its applications.

The research papers contributed to this year's volumes span across different fields that fall within the scope of the DHM Conference. The role of DHM in the design and evaluation of various technologies has been explored, emphasizing the importance of the field for personalized and useful systems and applications, that advance user experience and foster communication, collaboration and learning. A significant number of submissions addressed DHM in assistive technologies for older adults, individuals with impairments and persons suffering from injuries. Furthermore, contributions have brought to the foreground the significance of DHM in healthcare interventions, and in technologies to support mental health and well-being, bridging the gap between human physiology and technological innovation. Finally, ergonomics constituted a topic that received focus this year, elaborating on the impact of DHM on ergonomic solutions for safety in work environments and the design of smart technologies.

Three volumes of the HCII 2024 proceedings are dedicated to this year's edition of the DHM conference. The first focuses on topics related to Digital Human Modeling for Design and Evaluation; User Experience and Assistive Technologies; and User Experience, Communication, and Collaboration. The second focuses on topics related to Healthcare Design and Support; Technology in Mental Health and Wellbeing; and Artificial Intelligence and Health Applications. The third focuses on topics related to Work, Safety, and Ergonomics; Ergonomics, Artificial Intelligence and Smart Technologies; and Advanced Technologies for Training and Learning.

The papers of these volumes were accepted for publication after a minimum of two single-blind reviews from the members of the DHM Program Board or, in some cases, from members of the Program Boards of other affiliated conferences. I would like to thank all of them for their invaluable contribution, support and efforts.

July 2024   Vincent G. Duffy

15th International Conference on Digital Human Modeling and Applications in Health, Safety, Ergonomics and Risk Management (DHM 2024)

Program Board Chair: **Vincent G. Duffy,** *Purdue University, USA*

- Karthik Adapa, *UNC Chapel Hill, USA*
- Giuseppe Andreoni, *Politecnico di Milano, Italy*
- Pedro Arezes, *University of Minho, Portugal*
- Hasan Ayaz, *Drexel University, USA*
- Aydin Azizi, *Oxford Brookes University, UK*
- Angelos Barmpoutis, *University of Florida, USA*
- Simone Borsci, *University of Twente, Netherlands*
- Andre Calero Valdez, *University of Lübeck, Germany*
- Yaqin Cao, *Anhui Polytechnic University, P.R. China*
- Ignacio Castellucci, *Universidad de Valparaíso, Chile*
- Damien Chablat, *CNRS/LS2N, France*
- Karen Chen, *North Carolina State University, USA*
- Bong Jun Choi, *Soongsil University, Korea*
- Denis Coelho, *Jönköping University, Sweden*
- Clive D'Souza, *University of Pittsburgh, USA*
- H. Onan Demirel, *Oregon State University, USA*
- Yi Ding, *Anhui Polytechnic University, P.R. China*
- Manish Kumar Dixit, *Texas A&M University, USA*
- Ehsan Esfahani, *University at Buffalo, USA*
- Martin Fleischer, *Technical University of Munich, Germany*
- Martin Fränzle, *Oldenburg University, Germany*
- Afzal Godil, *National Institute of Standards and Technology, USA*
- Wenbin Guo, *University of Florida, USA*
- Sogand Hasanzadeh, *Purdue University, USA*
- Bochen Jia, *University of Michigan, USA*
- Genett Isabel Jimenez Delgado, *Institucion Universitaria de Barranquilla IUB, Colombia*
- Jari Kaivo-oja, *Turku School of Economics, University of Turku, Finland*
- Taina Kalliokoski, *University of Helsinki, Finland*
- Jeong Ho Kim, *Oregon State University, USA*
- Woojoo Kim, *Kangwon National University, Korea*
- Steffi Kohl, *Zuyd University of Applied Sciences, Netherlands*
- Richard Lamb, *East Carolina University, USA*
- Nicola Francesco Lopomo, *Università degli Studi di Brescia, Italy*
- Siu Shing Man, *South China University of Technology, P.R. China*
- Alexander Mehler, *Goethe University Frankfurt, Germany*

- Jörg Miehling, *Friedrich-Alexander-Universität Erlangen-Nürnberg (FAU), Germany*
- Salman Nazir, *University of Southeastern Norway, Norway*
- Peter Nickel, *Institute for Occupational Safety and Health of the German Social Accident Insurance (IFA), Germany*
- Ashish Nimbarte, *West Virginia University, USA*
- Joseph Nuamah, *Oklahoma State University, USA*
- Miguel Ortiz-Barrios, *Universitat Politecnica de Valencia, Spain and Universidad de la Costa (CUC), Colombia*
- Nicola Paltrinieri, *NTNU, Norway*
- Thaneswer Patel, *North Eastern Regional Institute of Science and Technology, India*
- Xingda Qu, *Shenzhen University, P.R. China*
- Qing-Xing Qu, *Northeastern University, P.R. China*
- Erwin Rauch, *Free University of Bolzano, Spain*
- Arto Reiman, *University of Oulu, Finland*
- Deep Seth, *Mahindra University, India*
- Fabio Sgarbossa, *NTNU, Norway*
- Jieun Shin, *University of Florida, USA*
- Thitirat Siriborvornratanakul, *National Institute of Development Administration, Thailand*
- Beatriz Sousa Santos, *University of Aveiro, Portugal*
- Hendrik Stern, *Universität Bremen, Germany*
- Lesley Strawderman, *Mississippi State University, USA*
- Youchao Sun, *Nanjing University of Aeronautics and Astronautics, P.R. China*
- Zhengtang Tan, *Hunan Normal University, P.R. China*
- Leonor Teixeira, *University of Aveiro, Portugal*
- Renran Tian, *IUPUI, USA*
- Joseph Timoney, *Maynooth University, Ireland*
- Vinay V. Panicker, *National Institute of Technology Calicut, India*
- Dustin Van der Haar, *University of Johannesburg, South Africa*
- Kuan Yew Wong, *Universiti Teknologi Malaysia (UTM), Malaysia*
- Shuping Xiong, *Korea Advanced Institute of Science and Technology, Korea*
- James Yang, *Texas Tech University, USA*

The full list with the Program Board Chairs and the members of the Program Boards of all thematic areas and affiliated conferences of HCII 2024 is available online at:

http://www.hci.international/board-members-2024.php

HCI International 2025 Conference

The 27th International Conference on Human-Computer Interaction, HCI International 2025, will be held jointly with the affiliated conferences at the Swedish Exhibition & Congress Centre and Gothia Towers Hotel, Gothenburg, Sweden, June 22–27, 2025. It will cover a broad spectrum of themes related to Human-Computer Interaction, including theoretical issues, methods, tools, processes, and case studies in HCI design, as well as novel interaction techniques, interfaces, and applications. The proceedings will be published by Springer. More information will become available on the conference website: https://2025.hci.international/.

General Chair
Prof. Constantine Stephanidis
University of Crete and ICS-FORTH
Heraklion, Crete, Greece
Email: general_chair@2025.hci.international

https://2025.hci.international/

Contents – Part I

User Experience and Assistive Technologies

User Experience, Communication, and Collaboration

Contents – Part II

Technology in Mental Health and Wellbeing

Artificial Intelligence and Health Applications

Contents – Part III

Ergonomics, Artificial Intelligence and Smart Technologies

Advanced Technologies for Training and Learning

Digital Human Modeling for Design and Evaluation

Bibliometrics-Based Analysis of Trends in Affective Design Evaluation Research

Ying Cao[✉] and Yonghong Wang

School of Mechanical Science and Engineering, Huazhong University of Science and Technology, Wuhan 430074, China
caoying@hust.edu.cn

Abstract. This paper aims to systematically understand the overall characteristics of emotional design evaluation research on a global scale, grasp the current research hotspots and knowledge evolution process of emotional design, and explore new future development trends based on current research hotspots. Taking the literature related to emotional design evaluation included in Web of Science as the data source, VOS viewer is used to sort out the research context from the annual output distribution of literature, country, research institution, author, and reference co-citation by scientific bibliometric method, and conduct visual analysis. The results showed that the number of literature within the search scope showed an overall upward trend, and in the field of affective design evaluation, the United States ranked first in the number of publications, followed by China, and the United Kingdom ranked third. The top three prolific authors are all scholars from China, namely Ding M, Guo F, and Liu WL; the journal with the most literature is FRONTIERS IN PSYCHOLOGY, the research hotpots are model, design, behavior, and quality. This paper visually analyzes the research status, development trend and research hotspots in the field of emotional design evaluation, which has corresponding guiding significance for relevant researchers.

Keywords: Affective design · Design evaluation · Bibliometrics · VOS viewer

1 Introduction

Emotional design is a product design concept and method that emerged in the late 1980s, and has not reached a consensus definition in the academic community. American scholars Norman and Drabble published in 1986 in the book "User-Centered System Design: New Perspectives on Human-Computer Interaction", for the first time proposed "user-centered design", which can be regarded as the original concept of emotional design. Emotional design mainly includes the acquisition, analysis and modeling of users' emotional factors, as well as the transformation of emotional factors in design [1, 2].

Emotion is very closely related to human life, and in product design, positive emotional feedback is also a key research direction for designers. Product design carries the user's needs, with the advent of the product design experience economy, "form follows

V. G. Duffy (Ed.): HCII 2024, LNCS 14709, pp. 3–15, 2024.
https://doi.org/10.1007/978-3-031-61060-8_1

function" began to "form follows emotion and fun" to change [3]. Since emotional design focuses on triggering human connection and imagination from sensory stimulation, thus generating positive emotions, and allowing people to obtain physical and psychological pleasure when using the product, which is different from the general design approach, the evaluation criteria also need to be adjusted accordingly.

Although there are many evaluation indexes in the design industry, and they are closely related to each other, the evaluation indexes may not necessarily be applicable to the emotional design of products because of the different evaluation perspectives and focuses. Summarizing the emotional evaluation indexes for products is of great significance to the emotional design of products, therefore, how to evaluate the emotion brought by products scientifically and effectively is the key issue of the emotional design of products.

2 Research Design

2.1 Research Methodology

Bibliometrics refers to the quantitative analysis of various types of literature, in a large number of literature data to find potential laws and information, was first proposed by Pritchard in 1969, bibliometric methods are currently one of the mainstream methods of literature research. VOS viewer was developed by VanEck and Waltman from the Center for Science and Technology Research at the University of Leiden, the Netherlands, in 2009, with a powerful user interface and mapping visualization features. It has a powerful user graphical interface and mapping visualization features [4, 5]. The scientific knowledge graph obtained by VOS viewer software through visualization is not only a visual knowledge graph, but also a serialized knowledge genealogy, which can intuitively and accurately display the evolution process and trend of the development of a discipline or knowledge field in a certain period of time, and has become an important tool widely used in bibliometric research at home and abroad.

In this paper, VOS viewer is used as the research tool platform, for the research literature on affective design evaluation published in the Web of Science database, the txt format file of the literature information is downloaded and exported from the Web of Science database, and the text is imported into the VOS viewer software in accordance with the needs of the research content, and then the data analysis is carried out.

2.2 Sources of Research Data

In this paper, VOS viewer is used as the research tool platform, for the research literature on affective design evaluation published in the Web of Science database, the txt format file of the literature information is downloaded and exported from the Web of Science database, and the text is imported into the VOS viewer software in accordance with the needs of the research content, and then the data analysis is carried out.

Since high-quality scientific literature is subject to rigorous peer review and strict scrutiny by the publication journals, its findings are more representative of the discipline. The following study chose to search in the Web of Science core database with the search strategy set to TS = (Emotional design) AND TS = (product design OR inter-action design OR user experience design) AND TS = (design evaluation OR user emotional experience evaluation OR user experience evaluation OR quality evaluation OR Design evaluation system), and select the commonly used WOS databases. SSCI, SCI-Expanded, A&HCI, CPCI-S and CPCI-SSH, which are the five major citation indexes commonly used in the WOS database, were selected as the search sources. In order to collect all the relevant articles, the search time span was set to the full year. A total of 673 documents were eventually obtained for further quantitative analysis.

3   Emotional Design Evaluation Bibliometric Results and Analysis

3.1   Essential Characteristics of Evaluative Research on Emotional Design

The pattern of change in the output of academic literature over time is an important measure of the trend of a research topic and allows for an effective assessment of the research dynamics of the discipline. According to the method described in the previous section, a total of 673 full-year literature (1998–2023) was retrieved. As shown in Fig. 1, in terms of the number of studies, the number of research publications related to affective design evaluation from 1985 to 2022 showed a rapid growth trend over time: 3 in 1998, 32 in 2013, and increasing to 90 in 2022; the number of citations also grew from 7 in 1999 to 1997 in 22 years. The research data indicate that the academic community's attention to the study of affective design evaluation is increasing day by day, and the research topic of affective design evaluation is also evolving and has been the focus of scholars' attention in recent years.

Since affective design is a complex cross-cutting theme, it involves knowledge from multiple disciplinary fields. According to the disciplinary statistical analysis of the WOS system, of the 673 documents, excluding those with a count of 10 or less, the remaining documents involve a total of 42 disciplines, with the top 10 disciplines being psychology multidisciplinary, business, ergonomics, computer science cybernetics, engineering electrical and electronics, computer science information systems, psychiatry, public environmental occupational health, computer science artificial intelligence, health care Science Services. Out of the 673 publications, 54 were from psychology multidisciplinary, 48 were from business, and 46 were from human engineering, representing 8.024%, 7.132%, and 6.835% of the total, respectively. These disciplinary topics are important research areas for affective design evaluation, which provide the theoretical foundation and tools and methods for affective design evaluation research. Meanwhile, the proposal of affective design evaluation also provides a good opportunity for the development of these disciplines.

3.2   Distribution of Literature by Country and Research Institution

The number of publications and the number of citations by country/region in the dataset depicts the high-producing countries in the research field and their impact. In terms of country/region output, a total of 66 countries/regions around the globe have contributed in this research area. Among them, the top 10 countries account for 90.936% of the total

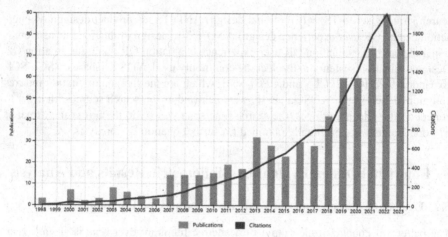

Fig. 1. Trends in Issues and Citations in the Emotional Design Evaluation Research Literature

number of publications. All of these countries have an output of more than 20 papers, which is an important source of output in affective design evaluation research worldwide. China is the second most productive country in affective design evaluation research, with 138 publications (20.525% of total publications). The top ranked country in terms of total number of publications is the United States (142, 21.1% of total publications), followed by the United Kingdom (80), Spain (49), Germany (41), Australia (40), South Korea (38), Canada (31), Italy (27), and the Netherlands (26). In terms of the number of articles, both China and the US have more than 100 articles, while other countries have much less in comparison.

Running the VOS viewer, selecting Organizations, and setting the minimum number of articles to 2, the 1076 global organizations get 161 nodes in total, which are divided into 18 clusters, and the number of cooperative relationships is 298, see Fig. 2. The size of the organization nodes in the figure indicates the article production, and the connecting lines between organizations indicate the strength of the cooperation, and the closer the cooperation is, the wider the connecting lines are between the organizations. From the distribution of the strength of cooperation relationships within each subnetwork, the international cooperation of affective design evaluation research is not close, showing a strong geographical characteristic, mainly between the country and region. Within the search, the University of London ranked first with 16 articles, followed by the University of California (11 articles), the University of Texas (11 articles), University College London (9 articles) and the University of Oxford (9 articles), among others.

3.3 Most Influential Journals and Authors

The articles within the search originated from 374 journals, listing the top ten most prolific journals in terms of number of articles published from 1998–2023, as well as their number of articles, which accounted for 16.64% of the total number of articles published, as shown in Table 1.The first place in terms of the number of articles published was FRONTIERS IN PSYCHOLOGY, with a total of 25 articles, the second

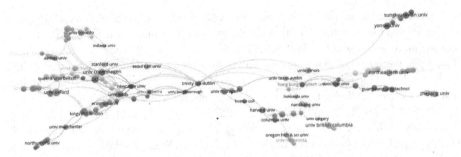

Fig. 2. Co-existing network of partner institutions

was INTERNATIONAL JOURNAL OF HUMAN COMPUTER INTERACTION and SUSTAINABILITY, both with a total of 13 articles, and the fourth place is INTERNATIONAL JOURNAL OF INDUSTRIAL ERGONOMICS. These four journals all have more than 10 articles, reflecting the fact that they are in the top position in the world. 10 articles or more, reflecting their influence in the field of affective design evaluation research.

Table 1. Leading Publishing Journals for Emotional Design Evaluation

Serial Number	Periodicals	Volume of Publications
1	FRONTIERS IN PSYCHOLOGY	25
2	INTERNATIONAL JOURNAL OF HUMAN COMPUTER INTERACTION	13
3	SUSTAINABILITY	13
4	INTERNATIONAL JOURNAL OF INDUSTRIAL ERGONOMICS	10
5	EUROPEAN JOURNAL OF MARKETING	9
6	IEEE ACCESS	9
7	SENSORS	9
8	APPLIED SCIENCES BASEL	8
9	IEEE TRANSACTIONS ON AFFECTIVE COMPUTING	8
10	INTERNATIONAL JOURNAL OF HUMAN COMPUTER STUDIES	8

Authors are the smallest unit of literature output and direct contributors to affective design evaluation research. By studying the authors' co-citations, it is possible to find out the more active scholars in this field in the world. Through the data statistics, it is found that there are not many authors with high output, Ding M from Hebei University of Technology, Guo F from Beijing University of Technology and Liu WL from Nanjing University have the highest number of publications, all with 5 publications. They were followed by Laine TH (Ajou University), Lee S (Hanyang University), Liu Y (Huazhong University of Science & Technology), Wang TX (National Center for Nanoscience & Technology, CAS). Nanoscience & Technology, CAS), Wang Y (East China University of Science & Technology), Boehner K (Georgia Institute of Technology) and Chen Y (Tsinghua University). (Tsinghua University). The collaboration between the authors is also not close, which also indicates the current status of the research on affective design evaluation: although more and more attention has been paid to the subject of affective design evaluation, and the research on it occupies a certain important position in the field of design, it has not been able to form a more systematic and mature theory, and the research on affective design evaluation is still in the stage of continuous exploration.

3.4 Analysis of Research Hotspots

The keywords of the literature are highly refined by the authors, and the high-frequency keywords reflect the research hotspots of emotional design in the long term. 673 documents include 3902 keywords, and the "Unit of analysis" is set to "AuThor". The "Unit of analysis" is set to "AuThor", and the frequency of keywords is set to 4. After screening and merging the synonyms, 69 keywords are formed into keyword co-occurrence clusters, which are shown in Fig. 3. Keywords with the same color in the figure are the same clusters, and there are 5 major clusters in total. From the analysis results, the keywords in descending order of frequency are Kansei engineering, User experience, Evaluation, Virtual reality, Affective computing, and Emotional design (see Table 2).

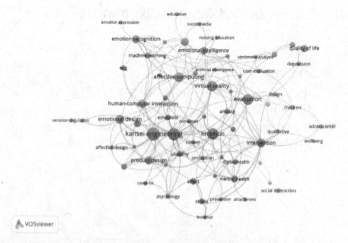

Fig. 3. Keyword co-occurrence clustering network

Table 2. Keywords and Word Frequency in the Emotional Design Evaluation Literature

Serial Number	Keyword	Word Frequency	Serial Number	Keyword	Word Frequency
1	Kansei engineering	26	11	Product design	12
2	User experience	23	12	Emotional intelligence	10
3	Evaluation	19	13	Product evaluation	10
4	Virtual reality	18	14	Quality of life	10
5	Affective computing	16	15	Mental health	9
6	Emotional design	14	16	Usability	8
7	intervention	13	17	Machine learning	8
8	Human-computer interaction	13	18	Design evaluation	8
9	Human-robot interaction	12	19	Affect	8
10	Emotion recognition	12	20	Anxiety	7

From the analysis results, there are five major clusters with more distinctive hot research themes for emotional design evaluation, which are 1-user experience, 2-human-computer interaction, 3-perceptual engineering, 4-user satisfaction, and 5-virtual reality.

Cluster 1 - user experience, which contains 21 cluster members, mainly contains keywords such as Affect, Emotional response, empathy, and user-centered design. User experience is the experience that users have when using a product or interacting with it, and a good user experience can effectively improve the satisfaction of using a product. Garrett proposed a "five-layer model of user experience elements", from abstract to concrete as the Strategy Plane: product goals, user requirements, etc.; The Scope Plane: functional specifications, content requirements, etc.; The Structure Plane: interaction design, information architecture, etc.; The Skeleton Plane -- elements of interface design, navigation design, information design, etc.; The Surface Plane --visual design related elements. Garrett also provides a set of user experience design methodology, which can effectively help product managers, UX designers and other roles to clarify the design thinking, and clearly access the internal logic of the design object [5]. Through the study of emotional design evaluation, it can well improve the user experience of products and deepen the emotional connection between users and brands.

Cluster 2 - Human-Computer Interaction, contains a total of 17 cluster members, mainly containing keywords such as Affective Computing, Collaborative learning, Deep learning, Emotion expression, Machine learning, User evaluation and other keywords. The keywords of this cluster all belong to the cutting-edge hot direction, which also shows the importance of affective design evaluation in cutting-edge design and the characteristic of the research object of design evaluation shifting to users.

Cluster 3 - Affective Engineering, contains 12 cluster members, including Aesthetics, Affective design, Arousal, Design evaluation, motivation, Usability, Product design and other keywords. Kansei Engineering, as a representative method of affective design, guides and evaluates the design process by obtaining users' perceptual imagery of product attributes and finding quantitative relationships between their subjective responses and design features [6]. The first research paper on PERCEPTUAL ENGINEERING was RESEARCH ON EMOTIONAL ENGINEERING by Prof. M Nagamachi of Hiroshima University, Japan, which was published in the journal Ergonomics in 1975, and this document was the beginning of the research on perceptual engineering [7]. Conference on Ergonomics held in Sydney in 1988, "emotional engineering" was formally named "Kansei Engineering", and since then the term "Kansei Engineering" has been officially launched. Since then, the term "emotional engineering" has been officially used.

Cluster 4 - User Satisfaction contains 10 cluster members, including Consumer Behavior, Customer Satisfaction, Qualitative, Social interaction, Children, and so on. User satisfaction is an important indicator of the success of a product, and the keywords in this cluster are mainly indicators of emotional design evaluation and key research objects, such as children and adolescents. Combined with the characteristics of the keywords, the research hotspot of this cluster can be summarized as follows: using the method of specific quantitative evaluation indexes to statistically analyze consumers' emotional preferences and reactions to product features, so as to adjust the design details or to identify and evaluate new design solutions.

Cluster 5 - Virtual Reality, contains a total of 9 cluster members, including Adolescence, Anxiety, Artificial intelligence, Emotional intelligence, Interaction design and so on. Keywords. This cluster focuses on describing the application of affective design evaluation in the field of innovation and why there is a need for the intervention of affective design evaluation in the field of innovation. The concept of affective design evaluation is constantly expanding, and the objects are transitioning from tangible physical objects to intangible virtual products and interactive processes.

In order to further investigate the cutting-edge themes and development trends of affective design evaluation research, the temporal relationship of the clusters is further observed, see Fig. 4. From the research hotspots summarized in the five clusters in Fig. 4, it can be found that Cluster 5 - Virtual Reality is the current cutting-edge theme of the affective design evaluation research, followed by Cluster 1 -User experience also remains the focus of current research on affective design evaluation.

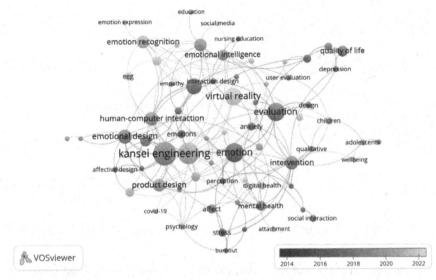

Fig. 4. Keyword clustering time

3.5 Theoretical Foundation

According to statistics, the 673 documents within the search cited a total of 31,550 valid references from 23,048 scholars. As some references were cited in pairs to form a co-citation relationship, the whole collection of references became a co-citation network. The co-citation network shows the evolution of affective design evaluation research at the basic knowledge level. Using VOS viewer to analyze the reference sources of all the literature in the sample, we screened out the literature with 8 or more co-citations and obtained the reference co-citation clustering network diagram, see Fig. 5. As seen in Fig. 5, the references form 45 nodes, which are divided into three major clusters. The key cited literature in the clusters and their main results are shown in Table 3.

Cluster 1 has the highest citation frequency (26) for the query "Development and Validation of Brief Measures of Positive and Negative Affect: The PANAS Scales" by DJ Watson et al. published in 1988, which is located in the co-citation network's Center. In this article, DJ Watson developed 2 emotion scales consisting of 10 items, including 2 dimensions of positive and negative (PANAS), which provide criterion data, convergent validity of the scales, and ordinal and extrinsic evidence of discriminant validity as a reliable, simple, and valid method to measure these 2 important dimensions of emotional factors [8]. In addition, a more frequently cited article in this cluster is DA Norman's 2004 article EMOTIONAL DESIGN: WHY WE LOVE (OR HATE) EVERYDAY THINGS, in which Norman mainly emphasizes the importance of the role of emotion in design and the fact that design should focus on the user's experience at the instinctual, behavioral, and reflective level [9]. In A CIRCUMPLEX MODEL OF AFFECT published by JA Russell in 1980, it was proposed that the interrelationships between different emotions can be represented by a spatial model, in which the concepts of emotion are organized according to pleasure (0°), excitement (45°), arousal (90°), pain (135°), unhappiness (180°), depression (225°), sleepiness (225°) and depression (180°).

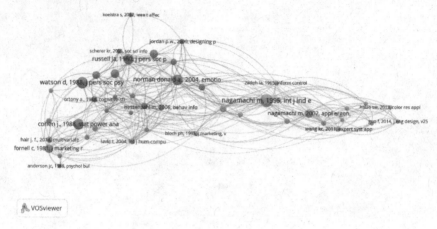

Fig. 5. Reference co-citation clustering

(225°), sleepiness (270°), and relaxation (315°). The model can be used to provide psychologists with expressions for representing and assessing the interconnectedness of affective dimensions, as well as expressions of cognitive structures used by laypersons in conceptualizing affect [10].

In Cluster 2, KANSEI ENGINEERING: A NEW ERGONOMIC CONSUMER-ORIENTED TECHNOLOGY FOR PRODUCT DEVELOPMENT, published in 1995 by Prof. M Nagamachi of Japan, is taken as a representative article, which categorizes perceptual engineering technologies into 3 classes: The paper classified perceptual engineering techniques into three categories: Category 1 is to classify the design elements of a new product in order to obtain a specific methodology; Category 2 is to utilize existing computer technologies, such as expert systems, neural network models, and genetic algorithms, so as to convey consumer feelings and intentions into design details; Category 3 is to obtain specific ergonomic conclusions through the establishment of mathematical structural models. This paper can be considered as far-reaching, establishing the research paradigm of perceptual engineering and attracting many followers, which is of great significance for the popularization of perceptual engineering in academia and industry [11, 12]. The second one is KANSEI ENGINEERING AS A POWERFUL CONSUMER-ORIENTED TECHNOLOGY FOR PRODUCT DEVELOPMENT published by Prof. M Nagamachi in 2022, which discusses the development of perceptual engineering in the last 20 years and proposes new concepts such as virtual perceptual engineering (VIKE) and The paper discusses the development of perceptual engineering in the last 20 years, proposes new concepts such as Virtual Perceptual Engineering (VIKE) and Collaborative Perceptual Design System, and introduces new application areas of perceptual engineering such as automobile, clothing, architectural products, and community design through concrete design cases [12].

In Cluster 3, C Fornell's article STRUCTURAL EQUATION MODELS WITH UNOBSERVABLE VARIABLES AND MEASUREMENT ERROR: ALGEBRA AND STATISTICS examines statistical tests for analyzing structural equation models with unobservable variables and measurement error [13]. The article USER EXPERIENCE

- A RESEARCH AGENDA by M Hassenzahl attempts to give an interim answer to the question of what is meant by "user experience". It provides a rough sketch of UX and what we think UX research will look like in the future [14].

The highly cited literature in the three clusters has a significant role to play in the development and refinement of research methods for evaluating affective design, and brings a lot of insights for subsequent research.

Table 3. Emotional Design Evaluation Major Clustering Highly Cited Literature

Cluster	Serial Number	Author	Literature Name	Citation Frequency
1	1	D Watson	DEVELOPMENT AND VALIDATION OF BRIEF MEASURES OF POSITIVE AND NEGATIVE AFFECT: THE PANAS SCALES	26
	2	DA Norman	EMOTIONAL DESIGN: WHY WE LOVE (OR HATE) EVERYDAY THINGS	25
	3	J Cohen	STATISTICAL POWER ANALYSIS FOR THE BEHAVIORAL SCIENCES	25
	4	JA Russell	A CIRCUMPLEX MODEL OF AFFECT	24
	5	MM Bradley	MEASURING EMOTION: THE SELF-ASSESSMENT MANIKIN AND THE SEMANTIC DIFFERENTIAL	20
2	1	M Nagamachi	KANSEI ENGINEERING: A NEW ERGONOMIC CONSUMER-ORIENTED TECHNOLOGY FOR PRODUCT DEVELOPMENT	31
	2	M Nagamachi	KANSEI ENGINEERING AS A POWERFUL CONSUMER-ORIENTED TECHNOLOGY FOR PRODUCT DEVELOPMENT	19
	3	CE Osgood	THE MEASUREMENT OF MEANING	14
	4	KC Wang	A HYBRID KANSEI ENGINEERING DESIGN EXPERT SYSTEM BASED ON GREY SYSTEM THEORY AND SUPPORT VECTOR REGRESSION	11
	5	HH Shang	A SEMANTIC DIFFERENTIAL STUDY OF DESIGNERS' AND USERS' PRODUCT FORM PERCEPTION	11
3	1	C Fornell .	STRUCTURAL EQUATION MODELS WITH UNOBSERVABLE VARIABLES AND MEASUREMENT ERROR: ALGEBRA AND STATISTICS	18
	2	M Hassenzahl	USER EXPERIENCE - A RESEARCH AGENDA	13
	3	JF Hair	MULTIVARIATE DATA ANALYSIS: A GLOBAL PERSPECTIVE	12
	4	AF Hayes	INTRODUCTION TO MEDIATION, MODERATION, AND CONDITIONAL PROCESS ANALYSIS: A REGRESSION-BASED APPROACH	11
	5	T Lavie	ASSESSING DIMENSIONS OF PERCEIVED VISUAL AESTHETICS OF WEB SITES	10

4 Conclusion

From the perspective of the number of papers issued, the number of papers issued in the field of affective design evaluation has shown a trend of rising year by year, and a trend of multidisciplinary integration in terms of issuing disciplines and journals. From the point of view of issuing countries and institutions, countries such as the United States, China, the United Kingdom, Spain, Germany and other countries are in the forefront of the world in the field of affective design research, presenting a strong geographical characteristic, mainly focusing on the cooperation between their own countries and regions. From the perspective of keyword clustering, there are five hot directions in the current research of emotional design evaluation, which are 1 user experience, 2 human-computer interaction, 3 perceptual engineering, 4 user satisfaction, and 5 virtual reality. It can be seen that emotional design evaluation is closely combined with cutting-edge technology, and artificial intelligence, virtual reality and other technologies complement each other and promote each other's development, and in the future user experience also remains the key direction of emotional design evaluation. From the perspective of reference clustering, the highly cited literature mainly includes some evaluation models, models of emotion measurement, etc., which provides better theoretical support for the research of emotional evaluation. In the future, the evaluation of affective design needs to pay more attention to the integration of multidisciplinary methods and the application of new tools and technologies, which also puts forward higher requirements on the learning ability, communication ability and innovation consciousness of researchers.

Acknowledgments. This study was funded by Teaching Reform and Practice of Design Discipline Basic Curriculum Group for Aesthetic Education (grant number 2021069).

References

1. Luo, S.J., Pan, Y.-H.: Research progress of perceptual image theory, technology and application in product design. J. Mech. Eng. **3**, 8–13 (2007)
2. Yan-zu, L.I.: New design concept: Kansei engineering. New Fine Arts **4**, 20–25 (2003)
3. Sweetf, F.: From Follows Emotion (Cutting Edge). Watson-Guptill, New York (1999)
4. Vaneck, N.J., Waltman, L.: Software survey: VOSviewer, a computer program for bibliometric mapping. Scientometrics **84**(2), 523–538 (2010)
5. Garrett, J.J.: Elements of user experience, the: user-centered design for the web and beyond. Interactions **10**(5), 49–51 (2011)
6. Lévy, P.D.: Beyond Kansei engineering: the emancipation of Kansei design. Int. J. Des. **7**(2), 83–94 (2013)
7. Li, Y., Liang, C.-H., Liu, X.-L.: Research status and enlightenment of Kansei engineering in China and Japan. Art and Design (6), 92–95 (2016)
8. Watson, D., Clark, L.A., Tellegen, A.: Development and validation of brief measures of positive and negative affect: the PANAS scales. J. Pers. Soc. Psychol. **54**(6), 1063–1070 (1988)
9. Norman, D.A.: Emotional Design: Why We Love (or Hate) Everyday Things (2004). https://doi.org/10.1111/j.1537-4726.2004.133_10.x
10. Russell, J.A.: A circumplex model of affect. J. Pers. Soc. Psychol. **39**(6), 1161–1178 (1980)

11. Nagamachi, M.: Kansei engineering: a new ergonomic consumer-oriented technology for product development. Int. J. Ind. Ergon. **15**(1), 3–11 (1995)
12. Nagamachi, M.: Kansei engineering as a powerful consumer-oriented technology for product development. Appl. Ergon. **33**(3), 289–294 (2002)
13. Fornell, C., Larcker, D.F.: Structural equation models with unobservable variables and measurement error: algebra and statistics. J. Market. Res. (JMR) **18**(1), 39–50 (1981). https://doi.org/10.2307/3151312
14. Hassenzahl, M., Tractinsky, N.: User experience - A research agenda. Behav. Inf. Technol. **25**(2), 91–97 (2006). https://doi.org/10.1080/01449290500330331

A Study on the Force Comfort of Over-Ear Headphones Based on 3D Anthropometric Data

Zihan Chen[1], Guangzheng Yu[1,2]([✉]), Tingting Wang[1], and Zhelin Li[1]

[1] School of Design, South China University of Technology, Guangzhou 510641, People's Republic of China
scgzyu@scut.edu.cn
[2] School of Physics and Optoelectronics, South China University of Technology, Guangzhou 510641, People's Republic of China

Abstract. The purpose of this study is to conduct a comprehensive study on the relationship between the dimensions of over-ear headphones, the dimensions of users' heads and ear anthropometric characteristic dimensions, and users' wearing comfort, to provide a practical design guidance program for the earmuff design of headphones. Initially, the head and ear anthropometric characteristic dimensions of 30 subjects (with balanced gender representation) were collected, measured, and statistically analyzed using a handheld 3D scanner. Additionally, four headphones were selected for the measurement and statistical analysis of their earmuff dimensions. Subsequently, experiments on headphone-wearing force comfort were designed and conducted. Preliminary results indicate that the size of the earmuff does not necessarily have an absolute effect on users' wearing force comfort and overall comfort. In the wearing comfort experience of headphones, the clamping force of the headphones does not directly affect wearing comfort. Furthermore, it is the force comfort of the headphones that determines the overall wearing comfort perception of the headphones, with a positive linear relationship between the two. This study can serve as a reference for the design and improvement of headphone earmuff size modeling.

Keywords: headphone · force comfort · anthropometric data

1 Introduction

With the improvement in living standards, users' requirements for products are increasing. Apart from meeting basic functional needs, users are increasingly concerned about product comfort. Headphones, during use, come into direct contact with the human external ear (composed of skin-soft tissue and complex surfaces of elastic cartilage) and its surrounding head surface. Given their large volume and weight, if the adaptability of the headphone earmuffs to the human body structure is not high, it may lead to problems such as auricular compression and uneven force distribution around the ear, affecting the comfort of use. This can result in ear pain or even injury, posing health risks to users. Anthropometrics in industrial product design is a highly effective approach for tailoring products to fit the contours and shapes of the user's body. Therefore, studying anthropometric data is crucial in the human factors design methodology of wearable products. Currently, ergonomic design for headphones has garnered significant attention from researchers. For instance, Hamamizadeh et al. [1]. Collected anthropometric dimensions of the external ear and head of Fars and Turk workers in Iran to inform the ergonomic design of earmuffs; Ban & Jung [2] analyzed and categorized the ear shapes of Koreans and Caucasians based on three-dimensional ear data and found that the depth, height, angle, and width of earmuffs are important design features; Stavrakos & Ahmed-Kristensen [3] defined six key 2D dimensions and two key angles for the design of headphones by scanning data from the heads of 200 people representing the Danish population. However, for the design of headphones that are in direct contact with human curved surfaces, it is necessary to be informed not only about the 2D dimensions that are compatible with the anatomy of the ear and head but also about the corresponding 3D shape information. For example, Lee et al. [4]. Utilized the curvature of the ear root to design the earband of ear-mounted headphones.

The main components of a headphone are the earmuffs and the headband. The earmuffs are important for the overall comfort of the headphones, and several studies have been conducted to optimize the design of the earmuffs (Gerges et al. [5]; Bhattacharyh et al. [6]). Yin [7], Cui [8] pointed out the most significant relationship between pressure and comfort. There are studies on earmuffs that show a lack of correlation between comfort and total force or average pressure on the headband (Lhuede [9]; Hsu et al. [10]; L.F. Kuijt-Evers [11]). The findings of Bhattacharya et al. [5] even showed the exact opposite of what was expected, i.e., stronger headband forces were more comfortable than weaker ones. This may be because a more uniform pressure distribution provides greater comfort, albeit at a higher total pressure. Hsu [10] designed an earmuff "comfort tester" to measure the comfort index, stating that the important design factors affecting earmuff comfort are airtightness, weight, heat dissipation ability, texture, and headband force band force.

Past research has demonstrated anthropometry to be a highly effective method in industrial product design for customizing products to fit the contours and shapes of the user's body. It has provided methodologies for designing wearable products for the head and ear based on the dimensions of key human features or feature curves. However, further research on ergonomic design methods for headphones is still necessary. For instance, compared with the headband, the earmuffs play a more crucial role in the comfort of headphones. Among the numerous parameters for evaluating headphone comfort, wearing force comfort is also a significant indicator. However, specific factors affecting wearing force comfort, such as the relationship between earmuff size and the characteristic dimension of the human ear, as well as the effect of clamping force, require further discussion. Therefore, this study aims to conduct in-depth research on the relationship between earmuff dimensions of headphones, the dimensions of anthropometric characteristic dimensions of the user's head and ear, and the user's wearing force comfort.

2 Methods

The overall process of this study was divided into four stages. First, the selection of experimental headphones involved creating a product list based on market research on headphones and selecting suitable headphones for experimentation according to research needs. Second, ear anthropometric dimensions were selected through a literature review related to ear dimension and headphone design, identifying head and ear landmarks, and characteristic dimension variables related to headphones. Third, subjects underwent wearing experiments to assess wearing comfort, and their heads were scanned to obtain head and ear dimensions before evaluation. Finally, a headphone earmuff pressure tester was used to obtain clamping force values for different subjects wearing different headphones.

2.1 Experimental Headphone

Headphones can be categorized into two types based on the way ear cups are worn: on-ear and over-ear types. On-ear headphones earmuffs are typically smaller, tightly compressing the auricle surface when worn. In contrast, over-ear headphones earmuffs are larger, encompassing the entire external ear and providing a higher level of comfort. Additionally, due to their larger ear shells, over-ear headphones offer a better sound field effect. Consequently, over-ear headphones are more favored by consumers, and the best-selling headphones in the market are primarily of the over-ear type. Therefore, this study focuses on over-ear headphones (referred to as headphones hereafter).

We investigated current products on the market, categorizing them according to product characteristics (open-back/closed-back) and earmuff appearance (orbicular/elliptical). Subsequently, we selected four products with broader coverage and stronger representation as experimental headphones, as shown in Table 1. We measured the earmuff dimensions of the four headphones using vernier calipers, as shown in Table 4.

Table 1. Specifications of experimental headphones.

	Sample1	Sample2	Sample3	Sample4
Product diagram				
Name	AKG-K702	Sennheiser-Moment-um4	Airpods Max	Sennheiser-HD660S
Type	Open-Back	Closed-Back	Closed-Back	Open-Back
Wight	294.84g	294.84g	385.55g	272.16g
Earmuff shape	orbicular	elliptical	elliptical	elliptical
Earmuff inner ring aspect ratio	1	1.5	1.4	1.6

2.2 Selection of Landmarks and Ear Dimensions

To define the characteristic dimensions related to headphones, we conducted a review of previous literature studies [2, 12–14]. We collected key landmarks and characteristic dimensions for head and ear measurements from these studies. Based on our research needs, we ultimately selected seven landmarks, as shown in Fig. 1, and five feature dimensions, as shown in Table 2.

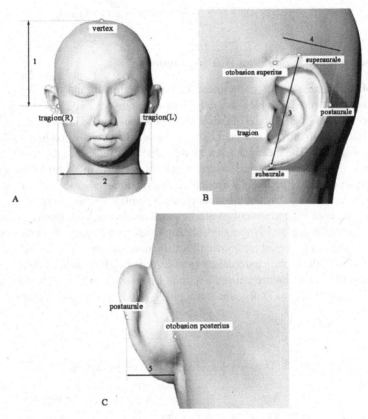

Fig. 1. Anthropometric landmarks and measurements of the ear

Table 2. Definition of anthropometric measurements of the ear.

Category	NO	Measurement	Description
Head dimensions	1	auricular height	vertex to tragion height
	2	bitragion breadth	distance between left and right tragion
Ear dimensions	3	auricle length	superaurale to subaurale length
	4	auricle width	distance between obs and pa in the direction of auricle length
	5	ear depth	distance between pa and obp

2.3 Experiment for Evaluating Wearing Comfort

A total of 30 Chinese adults participated in this experiment, and their demographic information is presented in Table 3. Initially, we used a Reeyee Pro (®Wiiboox) handheld 3D scanner to acquire a 3D model of the subjects' heads and ears. The selected landmarks and dimensions from the previous section were captured and measured in the 3D model processing software. The mean values were recorded after three measurements, and the 25th, 50th, and 75th percentile values were calculated as shown in Table 4. Subsequently, the subjects wore each experimental headphone in a randomized order for 3 min each. At the end of each wearing session, they completed a comfort evaluation questionnaire to assess the force comfort and overall comfort of each headphone. To eliminate bias based on brand perception, the brand logos of the headphones were masked. Specifically, force comfort was defined as the subject's overall satisfaction with the pressure exerted by the earmuffs on both sides of their external ears and surrounding head area while wearing the headphones. The questionnaire utilized a 7-point Likert scale, with the comfort variable coded as 1 (comfortable) to 7 (very uncomfortable), where higher scores indicated lower force comfort.

Table 3. Demographic information of the participants.

	Age	Height/cm	Weight/kg
Male (N = 15)	24.4 ± 2.5	173.9 ± 6.6	68.0 ± 10.6
Female (N = 15)	23.6 ± 1.5	163.5 ± 3.4	55.9 ± 8.2
Total (N = 30)	24.0 ± 2.1	168.7 ± 7.4	61.9 ± 11.2

Table 4. Ear dimensions with earmuff sizes

Ear dimensions	Headphone characteristics	Percentile (mm)		Earmuff sizes (mm)			
				1	2	3	4
auricle length	length of earmuff inner circle	25%	59.77	50	60	67	80
		50%	61.40				
		75%	64.75				
auricle width	width of earmuff inner circle	5%	31.65	50	40	48	50
		50%	33.99				
		95%	36.00				
ear depth	earmuff depth	5%	20.04	20	20	28	23
		50%	23.09				
		95%	26.36				

2.4 Evaluation of Clamping Force

In this experiment, the clamping force of different subjects wearing different headphones was measured as an objective index using an earmuff pressure tester designed for headphones. The tester comprises three main parts: the monitor, the adjustment frame, and the pressure sensor. The horizontal position of the red pressure sensor and the vertical height of the upper headband support frame are adjusted using bolts to simulate the pressure conditions experienced by subjects wearing headphones with varying auricular heights and bitragion breadths. This allows for the simulation of different head and ear dimensions when subjects wear different headphones. Based on the anthropometric dimensions of auricular height and bitragion breadth measured in the previous section, we obtained the clamping force values for 30 subjects wearing four types of headphones.

2.5 Data Analysis

The data were analyzed using SPSS software. To assess wearing comfort based on the subjects' ear dimensions, the ear dimensions were clustered using K-means cluster analysis. Each ear dimension was clustered into three categories: large, small, and medium sizes. One-way analysis of variance (ANOVA) and post hoc comparisons were then conducted to analyze the differences in comfort scores between the different size groups. Subsequently, the effects of the four different headphones on force comfort and overall comfort when worn by the subjects were analyzed. Descriptive statistics were used to illustrate the overall trends in force comfort, overall comfort, and clamping force. Additionally, correlation analyses were performed to examine the relationships between force comfort and overall comfort, as well as between force comfort and clamping force.

3 Results

3.1 Influences of Ear Dimensions on Force Comfort

The ear dimensions, including auricle length, auricle width, and ear depth, were categorized into three clusters, as illustrated in Fig. 2. One-way ANOVA was utilized to examine the differences in force comfort scores among the different size groups. The comparison results are presented in Table 5. Although the differences in force comfort scores among the four headphones across the three subgroups of ear dimensions were not significant, Fig. 3 demonstrates variations in force comfort scores among the four headphones within the same size subgroups. Particularly noteworthy is headphone No. 4, which consistently scored much higher in force comfort compared to the other three headphones within the subgroups of auricle length and auricle width.

3.2 Influences of Ear Dimensions on Overall Comfort

One-way ANOVA was employed to assess the differences in overall comfort scores among the different size groups. The results, as shown in Table 5, indicated that there

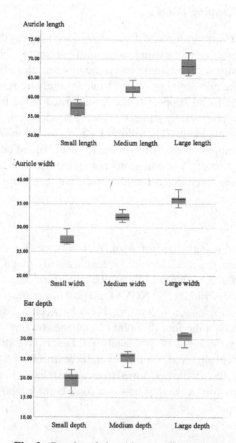

Fig. 2. Results of clustering ear dimensions.

were no significant differences in overall comfort scores across the three sizes of auricle length and ear depth for all four headphones. Similarly, most of the results for overall comfort scores did not show significant differences among the three levels of ear width, except for one case: participants with a large auricle width (Mean = 3.60, SD = 1.24) scored significantly higher in comfort than those with a medium width (Mean = 2.25, SD = 0.62) for headphone No. 2.

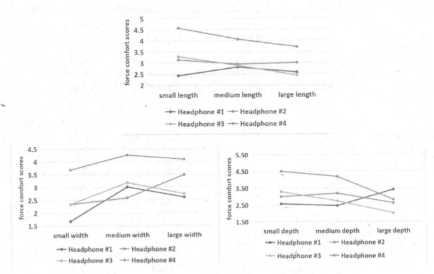

Fig. 3. Descriptive information of the force comfort scores by clusters.

3.3 Differences in Comfort Scores and Clamping Force Between Experimental Headphones

We used descriptive statistics to illustrate the overall trend of comfort scores and clamping force magnitude for the four headphones, as depicted in Fig. 4. Overall, regarding wearing comfort, headphone No.1 had the lowest score, indicating that it exhibited the best-wearing force comfort and overall comfort, as well as the lowest clamping force among the four headphones. Headphones No.2 and No.3 showed similar levels of wearing comfort, but there was a significant difference in their clamping force. Headphone No.4 demonstrated significantly different comfort scores compared to the other three headphones, indicating it was the least comfortable, and its clamping force was also significantly different from that of headphones No.1 and No.2, but closer to that of headphone No.3.

Correlation analysis was conducted to examine the relationships between force comfort and overall comfort, as well as clamping force and force comfort. The results are presented in Table 6, where "fc" represents force comfort, "oc" represents overall comfort, "cf" represents clamping force, and the numbers 1–4 correspond to headphone numbers. All four experimental headphones exhibited a significant positive correlation

Table 5. Results of ANOVA for wearing comfort difference according to ear dimensions clusters.

Dependent variable	Headphone	Mean	SD	Cluster	F	P
force comfort	#1	2.67	1.37	auricle length	.201	.819
				auricle width	1.182	.322
				ear depth	.870	.430
	#2	3.00	1.14	auricle length	.073	.929
				auricle width	2.881	.073
				ear depth	.426	.657
	#3	2.87	1.36	auricle length	.683	.514
				auricle width	.579	.567
				ear depth	1.845	.177
	#4	4.10	1.54	auricle length	.535	.592
				auricle width	.169	.845
				ear depth	2.508	.100
overall comfort	#1	2.77	1.45	auricle length	.978	.389
				auricle width	1.017	.375
				ear depth	.848	.439
	#2	2.93	1.17	auricle length	.440	.648
				auricle width	6.951	.004*
				ear depth	.010	.990
	#3	2.90	1.03	auricle length	.299	.744
				auricle width	1.626	.215
				ear depth	.034	.967
	#4	3.90	1.30	auricle length	.154	.858
				auricle width	.568	.573
				ear depth	.264	.770

between force comfort and overall comfort. However, there was no correlation between clamping force and force comfort (Table 7).

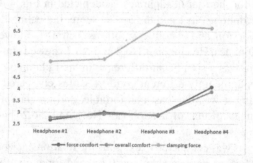

Fig. 4. Descriptive information of the comfort scores and clamping force.

Table 6. Matrix of correlation coefficients for comfort variables

Variable	1	2	3	4	5	6	7	8
fc1	1							
fc2	0.307	1						
fc3	0.068	0.177	1					
fc4	− 0.016	0.254	.700**	1				
oc1	.858**	0.311	0.071	-0.174	1			
oc2	0.2	.719**	0.059	0.08	0.294	1		
oc3	.366*	0.176	.755**	.464**	.376*	0.252	1	
oc4	0.155	0.349	.580**	.835**	0.042	0.245	.561**	1

*. $p < 0.05$. **. $p < 0.01$.

Table 7. Matrix of correlation coefficients for force comfort and clamping force variables

Variable	1	2	3	4	5	6	7	8
cf1	1							
cf2	.910**	1						
cf3	.865**	.912**	1					
cf4	.462*	.626**	.522**	1				
fs1	− 0.049	0.036	− 0.096	.379*	1			
fs2	0.199	0.228	0.177	.409*	0.307	1		
fs3	− 0.027	− 0.165	− 0.051	− 0.052	0.068	0.177	1	
fs4	− 0.172	− 0.209	− 0.09	− 0.108	− 0.016	0.254	.700**	1

*. $p < 0.05$. **. $p < 0.01$.

4 Discussion and Conclusion

In this study, an analysis of force comfort and overall comfort perception during head-phone wearing was conducted to quantify the relationship between anthropometric size, product size, and human perception, aiming to guide the design of related products. The findings revealed no significant difference in force comfort perception among different groups of auricle length, auricle width, and ear depth. In most cases, overall comfort scores also did not significantly differ among the various auricle length and ear depth groups. This suggests that subjects tended to have similar comfort perceptions regard-less of their auricular size. Further on, descriptive statistics were utilized to illustrate the overall trend of force comfort scores for the four headphones across different ear size groups. Under all groupings of auricle length and width, as well as the small and medium groupings of ear depth, headphone No. 4 consistently scored much higher in force comfort than the other three headphones. Among the four, headphone No. 1 performed the best in terms of comfort, while headphones No. 2 and No. 3 were relatively close to each other and slightly inferior to No. 1. However, a comparison of earmuff sizes revealed that headphone No.4 had the largest earmuff size, with an inner loop length of 20% to 60% larger than the other three headphones. This suggests that an increase in earmuff size does not necessarily lead to a better comfort experience. A larger size means more surface area in contact with the body, which may impact wearing comfort to some extent. Additionally, earmuff size may not be a critical factor in determining headphone comfort.

Moreover, an analysis of a question in the Comfort Evaluation Questionnaire regarding subjects' perception of pressure on the auricle when wearing headphones revealed that when the earmuff size was slightly smaller than the subject's auricle, the perception of compression was very insensitive. This may explain why the earmuffs of headphone No.1, the smallest among the four, performed the best in terms of comfort. Subjects were more receptive to slight pressure on the earmuffs, and it could even be argued that, within a certain range, users were not sensitive to this pressure. Another possible explanation is that the earmuffs of headphone No.1 have a more specific, rounded shape, which allows for a more even distribution of pressure when worn compared to the other models, thus providing better comfort.

Descriptive statistics were used to illustrate the overall trends in comfort scores and clamping force for the four headphones. In terms of wearing comfort, headphone No.1 received the lowest rating, indicating the best-wearing comfort. Headphones No.2 and No.3 had very similar comfort ratings, while headphone No.4 received the highest comfort rating, indicating the worst comfort, which was significantly different from headphones NO.1, 2, and 3. Regarding clamping force, headphone No.1 exerted the lowest clamping force of the four. Headphones No.1 and 2 had similar clamping force, whereas headphones No.3 and 4 exhibited relatively close clamping force. There was a significant difference in clamping force between headphones No.2 and 3. Notably, although there was no significant difference in comfort scores between headphones No.2 and 3, there was a significant difference in their clamping force. Similarly, while headphone No.4 was the least comfortable, it did not exhibit the greatest clamping force. This suggests that the relationship between clamping force and wearing comfort may not be linearly correlated. Correlation analysis was conducted to examine the relationship between force comfort, overall comfort, and clamping force, confirming this conjecture and aligning with previous findings [6]: no correlation was found between clamping force and comfort.

While the correlation between clamping force and force comfort was not significant, the analysis revealed a positive correlation between force comfort and overall comfort. This implies that higher force comfort when wearing headphones corresponds to better overall comfort perception. Hence, force comfort plays a critical role in evaluating the wearing comfort of headphones.

This study investigated headphone-wearing comfort through a wearing experiment, combining subjective perception with objective metrics. The findings suggest that earmuff size does not necessarily have a definitive impact on user-wearing force comfort and overall comfort. Moreover, in the headphone-wearing experience, the clamping force of the headphones does not directly impact wearing force comfort. Instead, comfort may be influenced by the uniformity of clamping force distribution on the body surface after transmission through the earmuffs. The study also found that headphone force comfort determines the overall perceived wearing comfort, exhibiting a positive linear correlation between the two. However, it's important to note that the four headphones used in this study did not control all variables, highlighting the need for further research to verify the relationship between earmuff size and wearing comfort. Additionally, exploring the impact of pressure distribution on wearing force comfort is a direction for future research.

Acknowledgments. This work was supported by the National Natural Science Foundation of China (grant number 12074129), the Fundamental Research Funds for the Central Universities (grant number 2022ZYGXZR104) and the National Key Research and Development Program of China (grant number 2022YFF0607000): Research and Applicati-on of Ergonomics Key Technical Standards for Elderly-oriented Community.

References

1. Hamamizadeh, E., Asilian-Mahabadi, H., Khavanin, A.: Evaluation of the external ear and head anthropometric dimensions among fars and turk workers for the ergonomic design of the earmuffs. Health Scope **11**(1) (2022)
2. Ban, K., Jung, E.S.: Ear shape categorization for ergonomic product design. Int. J. Ind. Ergon. **80**, 102962 (2020)
3. Stavrakos, S.K., Ahmed-Kristensen, S.: Methods of 3D data applications to inform design decisions for physical comfort. Work **55**(2), 321–334 (2016)
4. Lee, W., Jung, H., Bok, I., et al.: Measurement and application of 3D ear images for earphone design. In: Proceedings of the Human Factors and Ergonomics Society, vol. 60, issue 1, pp. 1053–1057 (2016)
5. Gerges, S.N.Y., Gerges, R.N.C., Dias, R.A.: Earmuff noise leakage measurements and evaluation. Arch. Acoust. **40**(1), 109–115 (2015)
6. Bhattacharya, S.K., Tripathi, S.R., Kasityap, S.K.: Assessment of comfort of various hearing protection devices (HPD). J. Hum. Ergol. **22**(2), 163–172 (1993)
7. Yin, H., Shen, X., Huang, Y., et al.: Modeling dynamic responses of aircraft environmental control systems by coupling with cabin thermal environment simulations. Build. Simul. **9**(4), 459–468 (2016)
8. Cui, W., Qin, O., Zhu, Y.: Field study of thermal environment spatial distribution and passenger local thermal comfort in aircraft cabin. Build. Environ. **80**, 213–220 (2014)
9. Lhuede, P.: Earmuff acceptance among sawmill workers. Egonomics **23**(12), 1161–1172 (1980)
10. Hsu, Y.L., Huang, C.C., Yo, C.Y., et al.: Comfort evaluation of hearing protection. Int. J. Ind. Ergon. **33**(6), 543–551 (2004)
11. Kuijt-Evers, L.F.M., Groenesteijn, L., de Looze, M.P., et al.: Identifying factors of comfort in using hand tools. Appl. Ergon. **35**(5), 453–458 (2004)
12. Lee, W., Jung, H., Bok, I., et al.: Measurement and application of 3D ear images for earphone design. In: Proceedings of the Human Factors and Ergonomics Society Annual Meeting, vol. 60(1), pp. 1053–1057. SAGE Publications, Los Angeles, CA (2016)

13. Alexander, M., Laubach, L.L.: Anthropometry of the human ear: a photogrammetric study of USAF flight personnel. Aerospace Medical Research Laboratories, Aerospace Medical Division, Air Force Systems Command (1968)
14. Alexander, K.S., Stott, D.J., Sivakumar, B., et al.: A morphometric study of the human ear. J. Plast. Reconstr. Aesthet. Surg. **64**(1), 41–47 (2011)

Manufacturing and Analysis of a Knee Ankle Foot Orthosis for Acquired Anisomelia by Using a Finite Elements Strategy

Emily Dávila[iD], Micaela Villa[iD], and Fabián R. Narváez[✉][iD]

GIB&B Research Group, Department of Biomedicine, Universidad Politecnica Salesiana, Quito, Ecuador
edavilat@est.ups.edu.ec, {mvilla,fnarvaeze}@ups.edu.ec

Abstract. Anisomelia is a leg length discrepancy and is an anatomical condition that can be caused by congenital or acquired disorders. A particular case of acquired severe anisomelia is caused by surgical treatment of femoral osteosarcomas, leading to a reduction in leg length. In this paper, we present and analyze a personalized ortheses manufacturing process (KAFO). To do that, the orthoses are designed based on biomechanical requirements for a particular case of severe anisomelia (more than 6 cm) caused by surgical treatment of femoral osteosarcoma. Then, custom-made KAFO is manufactured by a handcrafted process; thus a digitized 3D model of KAFO is carried out to optimize its thigh shell design using a numerical analysis based on the finite elements method. For this, a distribution of the weight force of 257.51 N in the ischial support is analyzed, obtaining a Von Mises criterion of 170, 15, the safety factor of 2, 03, a total deformation of 64,48, and an equivalent elastic strain of 0, 02, respectively. Finally, the design and manufacturing of KAFO are analyzed during the patient's gait. The results obtained report that the use of proposed KAFO reduces gait abnormalities, in contrast to the test without KAFO.

Keywords: Anisomelia · knee ankle foot orthosis (KAFO) · Finite Elements Analysis

1 Introduction

Anisomelia is well known as a leg length discrepancy (one leg shorter than the other) and is an anatomical condition that may be caused by congenital or acquired disorders [14]. Usually, acquired cases are caused by traumas or tumors that damage the bone growth plate, such as: bone tumors, fibrous dysplasia, neurofibromatosis, osteosarcomas, among others. Commonly, inequality in leg length produces an asymmetry in the body, gait abnormalities and this may cause lower back pain, hip pain, and other problems [23]. Patients with severe

V. G. Duffy (Ed.): HCII 2024, LNCS 14709, pp. 29–43, 2024.
https://doi.org/10.1007/978-3-031-61060-8_3

anisomelia (more than 2 cm) often create angular and torsional deformities of the ipsilateral or contralateral leg, including soft tissue contractures around the knee, hip, and ankle [21]. This severe condition affects functional leg lengths and loss of stability in both standing and walking, respectively. A particular case of acquired severe anisomelia is caused by surgical treatment of femoral osteosarcomas, which, in many cases, leads to reduced leg length and impaired functional mobility [17]. Thus, patients with this condition end up losing independence.

Lower limb orthoses, specifically Knee Ankle Foot Orthoses (KAFO), are commonly used to improve stability both in standing and walking when there is a severe leg length discrepancy [11,12]. These personalized mechanical supports allow the correction of lower limb deformities, stabilizing atrophied joints, and providing pain relief in the case of joint deterioration [11]. The KAFO's components include foot, thigh upright, a proximal thigh band, ankle, and knee joint. Usually, these are manufactured of metal-metal, polymer-metal, and composite metals, among others. These can be combined with other thermoplastic materials (ABS, PLA, PA) and natural polymers (hydrogels), among others. These materials are used due to their high strength-to-weight ratio specification [11]. However, the mechanical characteristics and performance of these materials are difficult to predict when concentrated loads or point loads are present on certain contact surfaces of the limb [22]. Therefore, the evaluation of its design is carried out by a trial and error strategy [6,22]. To improve the process of orthoses production, new manufacturing methods have been proposed, which are based on additive manufacturing (AM) technologies [2,20]. However, these methods require a 3D digitized anatomical model by using sophisticated scanner systems and different computerized tools for structural analysis. Today, there are standard off-the-shelf KAFOs or custom-made KAFOs. Standard KAFO is cheaper but might offer reduced comfort to a patient than a custom-made KAFO. In addition, a custom-made KAFO may allow for great comfort, but its manufacturing process is arduous and hand-crafted work. This is because the most common fabrication procedure used is mold, which may take several days to build. However, customization is essential for patients with a specific anatomical condition, which makes adaptation to morphological modifications to optimize its biomechanics functionality. Usually, these orthoses are not manufactured according to a computational analysis to estimate the behavior of their biomechanical structure and materials, respectively. For example, it is very important to determine the total deformation of materials and the safety factor when KAFO is used in patients with severe anisomelia, which release the weight load on the ischial support [3], but these structural analyzes of hand-made KAFO are difficult to carry out, which affect the ergonomics of the orthoses by disrupting the areas of support of the legs produced in the areas of unloading of weight. The orthoses.

2   Related Works

Today, finite element methods (FEM) are widely used in different fields of engineering and manufacturing science. It is recognized as one of the most powerful numerical methods in the area of solid mechanics due to its ability to analyze complex geometric surfaces and nonlinear material properties [4,9]. In the design and manufacturing process of orthoses, these analytical validations and numerical analysis have been included as computational tools to optimize their biomechanical functionality by applying simulated forces at different support points of the orthosis [4,9]. This computational analysis allows to identify some mechanical modifications of the orthoses design to obtain better manufacturing results and provide a good ergonomic patient experience, such as: viability, safety, and biomechanical functionality, among others [15]. In addition, this computational analysis optimizes the time and materials for manufacturing on the basis of the patient's condition and medical requirements. [11,18]. Despite the fact that the latest additive manufacturing process based on 3D printing technology has been used to construct orthoses, these design processes require a similar numerical analysis [11,20], which is used to evaluate the pressure produced by the limb in the areas of the load area of the orthosis. However, these approaches have been applied to orthoses with small mechanical structures, for example: ankle foot orthoses (AFO) [18], because these are printed in short time periods and using the same materials as thermoformable ones but in filaments (PLA, ABS, Nylon, Kevlar Fiber, and others). Similarly, some orthoses for upper limb segments have been constructed based on these approaches using numerical analysis [4,10].

On the other hand, previous works have shown that KAFO design and manufacturing are complex handcrafted work [7]. This is due to their mechanical structure, which is formed by different leg segments, which were joined with slide bars. In fact, each KAFO's element was constituted of different materials. Furthermore, the rest areas of the limb have been considered as weight discharge points, which were used to apply both point loads and distributed loads, respectively. For numerical analysis, the KAFO was manufactured using stainless steel, which was simulated by applying different force values to determine the presence of stress according to the Von Mises criterion. The computational analysis demonstrated that using a total load of 22,36 N in the upper calf for contact with the thigh generated a stress of 6,5153 MPa, considering this point as the most support area from the leg.

To evaluate the biomechanical performance of the KAFO, a dynamical analysis based on the FEM strategy has been proposed [16], which was based on a pressure measurement system to record the maximum and minimum values generated during the gait phases of a gait cycle (approximately 72 KPa), this value was used to apply the computational simulation. Thus, the upper socket of the KAFO was divided into 8 division regions of the pressure value obtained to measure stress under the Von Mises criterion with a structure of 3 Nylon+ 1 Carbon fyber + 3 Nylon layers, this process improves the method and design of the orthoses based on the 7,7872e8 MPa result.

In a similar way, FEM numerical analysis allows to evaluate the mechanical behavior of materials for orthoses structure. In a previous work [5], the behavior of materials was evaluated by dynamic analysis during gait cycles. To do that, a constant pressure of 51,87 MPa was applied to a KAFO over its entire mechanical structure, which reported a variable response during the gait. Then, the safety factor of the limb support areas were evaluated when these are composite of 3, 6 and 13 layers, respectively. The reported results shown safety factors of 0.41, 1.05 and 1.48 for composite material of 3, 9, and 13 layers, respectively, the latter being the better material for KAFO's structure. However, the KAFO's design and manufacturing process is directly dependent of anatomical condition of patients and require an essential numerical analysis to reduce the ergonomic effect of orthoses by disrupting the leg support areas produces in the weight unloading areas of the orthoses.

In this work, the manufacturing process of a personalized KAFO is presented and analyzed. Their design is based on biomechanical requirements for a particular case. This was caused by the reconstruction of the extracted femoral bone that placed a metal prosthesis. It has been shown that this implant may lose some components or sink stems, reducing the length of the limb (6 cm in the left leg), the functionality for standing and movement, and the weight overload [13]. As a consequence, orthoses have three principal functions: compensate for the length discrepancy, contain the knee joint, and discharge the weight with an ischial support toward the rest of the limb. [1,3,8] Thus, the KAFO's construction and operation of the KAFO are validated and analyzed using a finite element model, which was carried out in an iterative process using linear geometry [19]. Finally, the patient's gait patterns and their distributed load acting are used to calibrate the KAFO manufacturing process and compare the new patterns of mobility.

The rest of this paper is organized as follows: after this introduction and the related works, the next section presents the methods; then, results are shown, and the last section discusses the conclusions.

3   Materials and Methods

An overview of our proposed strategy is illustrated in Fig. 1. Firstly, KAFO was designed according to anthropometric measures extracted from a patient with severe anisomelia undergoing rehabilitation treatment. This information was provided by an expert orthotetics. The KAFO manufacturing process was carried out in accordance with the biomechanical recommendations used for constructing this kind of orthoses. This custom-made KAFO is manufactured by a hand-crafted process. To claim the biomechanical functionality of the proposed KAFO, specifically, for the weight unload during both standing and walking stance. Secondly, a digitized 3D model of KAFO is constructed. Then, its thigh shell design is optimized by a numerical analysis based on the finite elements method. Finally, the design and manufacturing of KAFO is analyzed during the patient's gait.

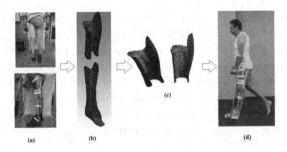

Fig. 1. Framework for KAFO's manufacturing and numerical analysis. Fig(a) illustrates the constructed KAFO for the acquired anisomelia case according to some biomechanical recommendations and materials, respectively. Fig(b) illustrates the digitalized 3D model of KAFO. Fig(c) illustrates the obtained results by applying our proposed finite elements approach. Fig(d) Illustrates gait analysis with KAFO

3.1   Design and Manufacturing of KAFO

The KAFO design process was carried out using anthropometric measures extracted from a 62-year-old man with a clinical history of limb salvage surgery applying metal prostheses caused by the presence of distal femur osteosarcoma. The alterations of these endoprostheses triggered: a severe anisomelia of 6 *cm* reflected in Fig. 2 caused by the sinking of the stem, periprosthetic fractures of the femur, and the loosening of the component. For this particular case, these symptoms repercusses in the biomechanical functionality of the body, causing pseudoarthrosis, scoliosis, overload weight in the right leg, instability in standing and a pathological gait. Therefore, the patient with this condition presents a loss of independence.

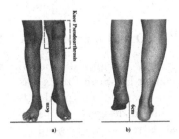

Fig. 2. Patient with severe left anisomelia of 6 cm. a) Frontal view in standing position b) Posterior view in standing stance.

The dimensions of the leg length discrepancy are measured manually to determine the KAFO structure. Therefore, a hand-craft process is used to construct each of the KAFO parts. For doing so, a negative plaster cast is obtained from the patient, for which the leg is positioned at the correct angles, obtaining a representation identical to the anatomical structure, then, a mould cast (positive) is constructed, which is used to obtain the thigh and leg shells from thermoformed polypropylene plates (of 4 mm thick). Therefore, in the thigh shell, the ischial area is located and corrected to support weight unload during both standing and walking stance, respectively. In addition, a plaster base is included to compensate the reduced leg length, which is replaced by a brick of heat-moldable foam. Finally, polypropylene shells are connected and supported by two aluminum side bars. These side bars reach from the femoral area to the foot base, respectively. The KAFO manufacturing process is illustrated in Fig. 3.

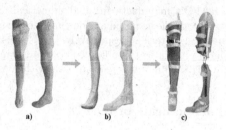

Fig. 3. Manufacturing process of KAFO. Fig a) illustrates a negative cast with plaster bandage front and side view. Fig b) Illustrates the positive plaster cast front and side view. Fig c) Illustrates the constructed KAFO in front and side views, respectively

The obtained mechanical structure provides an initial model of the KAFO (orthose), in which the ischial area is located and corrected to support the weight unload in bipedal-stance. This ischial area is contained in the thigh shell with a thickness approximately of 4 mm, however, the thickness varies in some of the curvatures of the structure due to the polishing process to achieve ergonomic adaptability.

3.2   3D Modeling of KAFO and Numerical Analysis

Once the KAFO is constructed, a digitized process is applied to obtain a 3D model. For doing that, a scanner Ein-Scan Pro 2x was used, for which each piece of the KAFO's structure was scanned, independently. Thus, each KAFO parts were exported to computer-aided design (CAD) software, named SolidWorks[1], in which a structural mesh is resized and assigned. Then, Ansys SpaceClaim software[2] is used to connect each generated element to the surface of the structural mesh. Finally, each surface is assigned a thickness on the final surface using SolidEdge[3] software. Finally, a 3D solid model is generated with suitable geometry and thickness. This workflow is illustrated in Fig. 4.

---

[1] https://www.solidworks.com/.
[2] https://www.ansys.com/products/3d-design/ansys-spaceclaim.
[3] https://solidedge.siemens.com/en/.

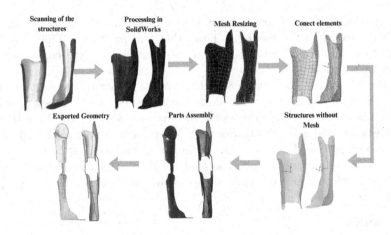

Fig. 4. 3D modeling process for our proposed KAFO

Once 3D models are obtained, the numerical analysis based on finite elements is carried out; for this, the manufacturing materials were characterized. So, the mechanical properties of polypropylene (PP) and aluminum (T4) were considered, which are described in Table 1, this information has been provided by the ANSYS Granta system.

Table 1. Mechanical properties of polypropylene and T4 aluminum.

Properties	Unit	Polypropylene	T4 Aluminum
Density	kg/m^3	9,02e−07	2,77e−06
Young Modulus	GPa	0,824−1,02	72−77
Poisson's ratio	−	0,422−0,465	0,325−0,344
Ultimate Tensile Strength	MPa	36,060	359−445
Yield Strength	MPa	24,1−28,4	248−330

Therefore, finite elements analysis (FEM) is performed on the assembled KAFO by using a parallel Y-vertical force at the ischial support. This applied force is calculated using the percentage of weight distribution (75 kg) in this limb, which corresponds to 35% and is equivalent to 257,51 N. This percentage is due to the displacement of the patient's center of gravity caused by anisomelia. The proposed finite elements analysis is implemented using the ANSYS software[4] (version 2021 R1), which is used as a numerical tool to determine the mechanical behavior in a structure element, which allows determining the maximum variation stress, total deformation and safety factor, respectively. The meshing

---

[4] https://www.ansys.com/.

process is generated by choosing the KAFO volume, and the shapes of the elements are selected as tetrahedrons. Thus, the total number of 15695 elements and the total number of 38773 nodes are established using the convergence of the optimal solution.

On the other hand, to determine the effect of the design and manufacturing of KAFO, a gait analysis was performed. This gait test consisted of measurements of different spatio-temporal parameters, such as: step length, stride length, step width, distance, and gait velocity. For that, gait parameters are measured during some gait cycles using Kinovea software[5] and with and without orthosis.

Therefore, the proposed numerical analysis allows to optimize the design of ischium support, in which the main thrust of the load falls on the KAFO.

4   Results

4.1   Experimental Setup

The KAFO device was manufactured for a male patient with a leg length difference of 6 cm. The manufactured materials include 4.8 mm thick natural polypropylene plates, while T4 Aluminum was used for the side bars, respectively. This KAFO was designed with an ischial support to distribute the patient's weight through the ischium from the pelvis in a curvature generated onto the polypropylene material, which was simulated as a chair support in resting stage, reducing the stress on this area. In addition, a compensatory heel (a brick of heat moldable foam) is included to match the existing asymmetry of the extremities. Then, a 3D model of KAFO is constructed and digitized by a scanner system.

4.2   Finite Elements Analysis

The proposed finite elements analysis was implemented in ANSYS software (version 2021 R1), running on a Windows PC with 2 Intel Quad Core i7 at 3.07 GHz and 24 GB of RAM, which is used to determine the mechanical behavior in a structure element. The shape of the element was selected as a tetrahedron. In this evaluation, the meshing process was generated by choosing the 3D model of KAFO. Then, the total number of 15695 elements with a total number of 38773 nodes were applied, respectively. In this evaluation, a constant force of 257,51N was applied to the ischial support, which was defined as 35% of the weight of the limb. So, a static analysis was simulated to identify: equivalent stress (according to the Von Mises criterion), safety factor, total deformation, and equivalent elastic strain of the KAFO.

The simulation was performed in two ways. Firstly, a constant force was applied as a point load on the ischial support area in the thigh shell. Second, the applied force was distributed in the ischial support area, respectively.

---

[5] https://www.kinovea.org/.

The obtained results report an equivalent stress of 170, 15 MPa, a safety factor of 2,03, a deflection of 64, 84 mm, and an equivalent elastic strain of 0,02 mm/mm. These values were obtained when a point load was applied to the ischial support area in the thigh shell. Similarly, the results obtained from the second simulation report an equivalent stress of 162.59 MPa, a safety factor of 2.47e−06, a deflection of 43.45 mm and an equivalent elastic strain of 0.014 mm/mm (1.4%). These values were obtained by applying the distributed load to the ischial support area in the thigh shell, respectively. These results show that the force distribution effect is small in the entire KAFO structure when different kinds of loads are applied to the ischial support area in the thigh shell and are considered to correct the curvature of the ischial support.

From Fig. 5, 6, 7 and 8, the graphical results are shown using the proposed FEM analysis. In these figures, the KAFO structure presents the distribution of the maximum stress based on the Von Mises criterion, the safety factor, the total deformation, and the equivalent elastic strain, respectively. In these figures, the proportional distribution of the weight through the surface curvature in the ischial support area is illustrated, which are distributed along the shells. In addition, these also provide evidence that some regions with pronounced curvatures undergo most of these mechanical factors along the orthoses. However, the concentration of these mechanical factors decreases when these come in contact and the foot base is in contact with the ground, reducing the weight load on the knee and ankle joints.

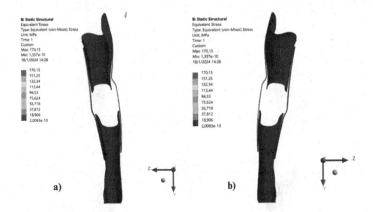

Fig. 5. Fig a) illustrates the behavior of equivalent stress (Von Mises) (front view) b) illustrates the behavior of equivalent stress (Von Mises) (posterior view)

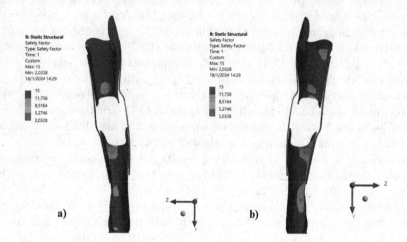

Fig. 6. Fig a) illustrates the behavior of the safety factor (front view). Fig b) illustrates the behavior of the safety factor (posterior view)

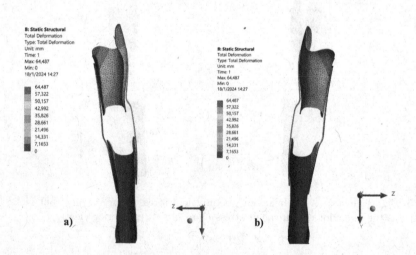

Fig. 7. Fig a)illustrates the behavior of total deformation (front view). Fig b) illustrates the behavior of total deformation (posterior view)

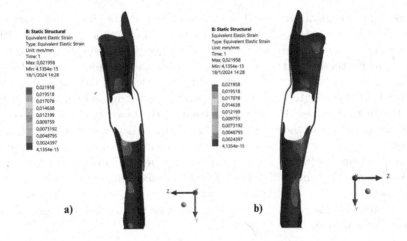

Fig. 8. Fig a) illustrates the behavior of equivalent elastic strain (front view). Fig b) illustrates the behavior of equivalent elastic strain (posterior view)

Table 2. Mechanical factors comparison of our proposed KAFO with KAFO reported in literature.

Author	Orthoses	Material	Load	Part	Von Mises Stress (MPa)	Security Factor
Kadhim et al. [7]	KAFO	Stainless Steel	22,36 N	Upper calf for thigh contact	6,5153	–
Salman et al. [16]	KAFO	3 Nylon+ 1 Carbon fyber + 3 Nylon	72 Kpa	All structure	7,7872	–
Hassan et al. [5]	KAFO	Composite 13 Layers	51,87 MPa	Sockets	–	1,48
Our proposal	KAFO	PP/Aluminum	257,51 N	All structure	170,15	2,03

Finally, the mechanical properties of our proposed personalized KAFO were compared with those of similar KAFO structures reported in the literature. The obtained results show that our KAFO's design is under suitable mechanical parameters, despite the different biomechanical requirements established by the anatomical condition of the patient. In Table 2 a comparison with KAFO structures manufacturing with different materials is shown.

4.3 Gait Analysis

The biomechanical functionality of our manufactured KAFO was evaluated by the patient undergo analysis. To do that, patient gait data were collected from a consecutive sequence of six gait cycles, walking a straight line about 8–10 m at normal speed, within and without KAFO, respectively. The gait parameters were recorded using the well-known for clinical applications and open source tool named Kinovea software. In particular, the clinical condition of the patient produces a pathological gait, which is caused by the affected limb that is kept in plantar flexion during the gait cycle. In contrast, the knee joint of the healthy leg is kept in constant hyperflexion. Therefore, the patient presents an uncertain step length. Furthermore, the step width exceeds the parameter value of 5–10 cm. Then, the gait analysis was carried out, for which gait data were collected using the KAFO and without KAFO. The gait spatio-temporal parameters were estimated in both cases. The obtained results are shown in Table 3, which is defined as an average of the experiment. In the particular case of the step length parameter, this value cannot be computed because it is considered a reflection by the severe anisomelia (6 cm). In contrast, the use of KAFO corrects the plantar flexion by supporting this with a brick of heat moldable foam, which is included on the foot-base. This mechanical support produces a step width parameter under suitable limits. Finally, the use of orthoses increased the stance phase, reducing the gait velocity.

Table 3. Reported results of gait analysis, with and without KAFO, respectively

Spatio-temporal gait parameters		
Parameter	without KAFO	with KAFO
Time (s)	05,12	05,70
Distance (m)	8	8
Gait Velocity (m/s)	15,625	14,03
Step Width (cm)	14	12
Step Length (cm)	Cannot be calculated	81,5
Stride Length (cm)	133	142,5

Additionally, a graphic analysis of the angles of the hip joint was also performed. For that, the angular trajectories of the leg joints were also recorded. The obtained results show relevant gait changes when the KAFO is to be used or not. Similarly, Fig. 10 (b) presents the angles ranges of the knee joints caused by the pseudoarthrosis affection. Finally, the angles of the ankle joint are presented in Fig. 10, in which the angles increased during the loading response. This is due to the constant position of plantar flexion during the gait. However, the hip joint shows values with slight deviations due to irregular rotation of the limb.

Therefore, fixed hyperflexion of the joint knee reduces overload weight, providing stability and support, reducing the compensatory mechanism of gait.

Finally, the reported results show that gait is abnormal, despite the considerable improvement caused by the application of the orthopedic device to stabilize the joint of the limb.

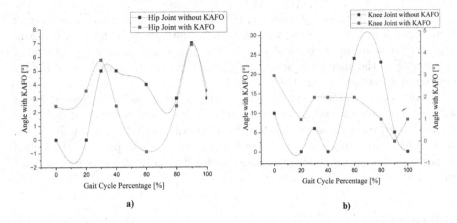

Fig. 9. Fig a) illustrates the Hip joint trajectories, without and with KAFO. Fig b) illustrates the Knee joint trajectories, without and with KAFO.

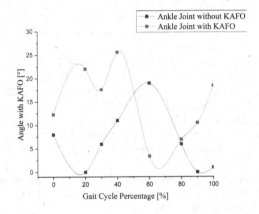

Fig. 10. Illustrates the Ankle joint trajectories, without and with KAFO.

5   Conclusions

The KAFO design and manufacturing process based on finite element analysis allow to correct some leg support areas to ensure patient comfort. In fact, the distribution of applied loads determines the mechanical behavior of their structure and materials, respectively. Despite the construction of handcraft based on molds and the thermoformed process, a numerical analysis of the digitized model is needed to detect some ischial curvatures required to support the weight of the patient for both the stance and the walking stage. Therefore, the use of a KAFO orthosis is capable of correcting and counteracting the biomechanical impact of anisomelia due to its ischial support. However, this orthesis manufacturing process with thermoformed materials or additive manufacturing requires both static and dynamic analysis strategies.

On the other hand, our proposed KAFO shows that gait abnormalities caused by anisomelia can be corrected with the good ischial support, fix, and compensation systems, respectively. Although the patient's gait can not be considered normal due to the knee joint being stabilized in hyperextension, generating different compensations during the gait cycle.

Finally, the obtained results report an equivalent stress, safety factor, factor of deflection, and equivalent elastic strain, according to materials used in the reported literature, showing that the force distribution effect is small on the whole KAFO structure when different kinds of loads are applied on the ischial support area in the thigh shell and is considered to correct the ischial support curvature.

References

1. Algabri, Y.A., Nouman, M.: The efficacy of ortho-prosthesis and knee ankle foot orthosis on functional Gait activities in pediatric congenital limb deficiency: a case report (2023). https://www.researchgate.net/publication/374506746
2. Alqahtani, M.S., Al-Tamimi, A., Almeida, H., Cooper, G., Bartolo, P.: A review on the use of additive manufacturing to produce lower limb orthoses. Prog. Addit. Manufact. **5**(2), 85–94 (2020). https://doi.org/10.1007/s40964-019-00104-7
3. España-Aguilar, J., Polanco-Aguilar, A., Yamhure-Kattah, G.: Prototype for knee-load relief through ischiatic support. Ingenieria y Universidad **25** (2021). https://doi.org/10.11144/JAVERIANA.IUED25.PKRT
4. Fuadi Emzain, Z., Qosim, N., Mufarrih, A.M., Hadi, S.: Finite element analysis and fabrication of Voronoi perforated wrist hand orthosis based on reverse engineering modelling method. J. Appl. Eng. Technol. Sci. **4**(1), 451–459 (2022). https://doi.org/10.37385/jaets.v4i1.1199
5. Hassan, S.S., Resan, K.K., Zeki Mahdi, A.: Design and analysis of knee ankle foot orthosis (KAFO) for paraplegia person. Eng. Technol. J. **31**(8), 1521–1533 (2013). https://doi.org/10.30684/etj.31.8A8
6. Kadhim, F.M., Hayal, M.S.: Analysis and evaluating of flexible ankle foot orthosis for drop foot deformity. Defect Diffus. Forum **398**, 41–47 (2020)
7. Kadhim, F.M.: Vibration measurement and analysis of knee-ankle-foot orthosis (KAFO) metal-metal type. Eng. Technol. J. **20**(2), 136–149 (2014). https://doi.org/10.31026/j.eng.2014.02.10
8. Meng, Z., Wong, D.W.C., Zhang, M., Leung, A.K.L.: Analysis of compression/release stabilized transfemoral prosthetic socket by finite element modelling method. Med. Eng. Phys. **83**, 123–129 (2020). https://doi.org/10.1016/j.medengphy.2020.05.007
9. Mian, S.H., Umer, U., Moiduddin, K., Alkhalefah, H.: Finite element analysis of upper limb splint designs and materials for 3D printing. Polymers **15**(14) (2023). https://doi.org/10.3390/polym15142993
10. Mian, S.H., Umer, U., Moiduddin, K., Alkhalefah, H.: Finite element analysis of upper limb splint designs and materials for 3D printing. Polymers **15**(14) (2023). https://doi.org/10.3390/polym15142993
11. Nouri, A., Wang, L., Li, Y., Wen, C.: Materials and manufacturing for ankle–foot orthoses: a review. Adv. Eng. Mater. **25** (2023). https://doi.org/10.1002/adem.202300238

12. Diaz-Hernandez, O., Santos-Borráez, A., Gómez Ruiz, A., Carrillo Gómez, C.F., Arellanes, I.G.R.: Automatic knee lock-release system for a knee-ankle-foot orthosis (KAFO) with IOT monitoring system in real time. In: IFMBE Proceedings, pp. 303–312 (2023)
13. Pennekamp, P., Wirtz, D., Dür, H.: Der proximale und komplette femurersatz. Operative Orthopadie und Traumatologie **24**, 215–226 (2012)
14. Perttunen, J., Anttila, E., Södergård, J., Merikanto, J., Komi, P.V.: Gait asymmetry in patients with limb length discrepancy. Scandivian J. Medicina Sci. Sports **14**, 49–56 (2004). https://doi.org/10.1046/j.1600-0838.2003.00307.x
15. Putra, A., Rahmatillah, A., Rodhiyah, N., Pujiyanto, Pawana, I.: Computational analysis of ankle-foot orthosis for foot drop case during stance phase in Gait cycle. J. Eng. Sci. Technol. **17**(2), 985–996 (2022), publisher Copyright: 2022 Taylor's University. All rights reserved
16. Salman, J.: Design, analysis and optimization of the knee-ankle-foot orthosis. Gulf Univ. J. **4**(1), 1–34 (2012). https://doi.org/10.12816/0011572
17. San-Julian, M., Vazquez-Garcia, B.: Biological reconstruction in bone sarcomas: lessons from three decades of experience. Orthopaedic Surgery **8**(2), 111–121 (2016). https://doi.org/10.1111/os.12243
18. Sarma, T., Pandey, D., Sahai, N., Prakash Tewari, R.: Material selection and development of ankle foot orthotic device. Mater. Today Proc. **18**(7), 2509–2514 (2019). https://doi.org/10.1016/j.matpr.2019.07.107
19. Sebastián Lasprilla, J., Ramírez, H.F., Mauledoux, M.: Preprocessing a static finite elements simulation for a transtibial prosthesis using CAE tools. Int. J. Mech. Eng. Technol. (IJM) **10**(12), 311–322 (2019)
20. Seo, K.J., Kim, B., Mun, D.: Development of customized ankle-foot-orthosis using 3D scanning and printing technologies. J. Mech. Sci. Technol. (2023). https://doi.org/10.1007/s12206-023-2406-1
21. Shi, Y., et al.: Effects of orthotic insole on gait patterns in children with mild leg length discrepancy. Gait Posture **93**(2021), 191–197 (2022). https://doi.org/10.1016/j.gaitpost.2022.02.003
22. Silva, R., Veloso, A., Alves, N., Fernandes, C., Morouço, P.: A review of additive manufacturing studies for producing customized ankle-foot orthoses. Bioengineering **9** (2022). https://doi.org/10.3390/bioengineering9060249
23. Vogt, B., Gosheger, G., Wirth, T., Horn, J., Rödl, R.: Leg length discrepancy-treatment indications and strategies. Deutsches Arzteblatt Int. **117**, 405–411 (2020). https://doi.org/10.3238/arztebl.2020.0405

Standardizing and Early Warning of Sewing Beginners' Posture Based on CNN Visual Recognition Technology

Zejun Huang, Zhen Qin[✉], and Hanze Ge

South China University of Technology, Guangzhou, Guangdong, China
sang2@163.com

Abstract. This study focuses on the posture problem in the sewing process and utilizes computer vision recognition technology to identify and warn the posture status of sewing workers, thereby reducing the risks and stress during the sewing process. By analyzing actual sewing scenarios, conducting questionnaires, summarizing expert opinions, and categorizing different sewing postures, the specific requirements and technical roadmap of computer vision recognition in sewing conditions are determined. OpenPose is used to extract the posture features of novice sewers in the sewing process, and then a deep learning network is built and trained using the PyTorch framework, enabling the model to provide early warnings for incorrect sewing postures of novice sewers.

Keywords: Sewing Posture · Early Warning · Computer Vision Recognition · OpenPose · PyTorch

1 Introduction

Sewing technology is essential to clothing design and production [1, 2]. The correctness of sewing posture affects the effectiveness of sewing production, the comfort of the body [3, 4], and the operator's safety [5]. Long-term incorrect posture also can lead to physical damage [6, 7]. Standardizing the posture of sewers in the early stages of learning can promote their development of good posture habits. Therefore, developing a system that can monitor and correct the posture of novice sewers in real time is of great significance.

In terms of sewing posture, it has always been a focus of research in human factors engineering. The literature [8] adjusted the sewing machine workstation, including table height, table tilt, and pedal position, to assess their impact on work posture and worker perception. The literature [9] used surface electromyography (sEMG) to investigate muscle load and activity patterns in the neck and shoulder muscles of female sewing machine operators and identified several key periods of muscle fatigue within 200 min of working time. The application of ergonomic interventions during these periods can help prevent sewing machine operators from developing work-related musculoskeletal disorders. Although this research did not directly involve the evaluation and correction of sewing posture using computer vision technology, they indirectly demonstrate the significance of this study.

V. G. Duffy (Ed.): HCII 2024, LNCS 14709, pp. 44–54, 2024.
https://doi.org/10.1007/978-3-031-61060-8_4

In terms of posture recognition, there are two types of pose recognition methods: hardware-based methods and image-based methods. Image-based methods have lower costs and are more efficient for multi-person recognition [10]. Therefore, image-based methods have been widely applied in industrial safety and human pose detection in recent years. The literature [11] identifies abnormal behaviors such as emergencies and machine failures in workers, and the literature [12] automatically evaluates hand postures of piano players to help beginners improve their performance skills. However, there is currently relatively little research on the use of this technology for posture regulation and early warning for beginners in sewing.

In this paper, OpenPose is utilized to extract posture features of novice sewers during the sewing process [13, 14]. The extracted feature maps, marked with skeletal nodes of the students, are used as the training dataset. Subsequently, a deep learning network is constructed using the PyTorch framework, and the network is trained using the dataset. This enables the model to provide early warnings for incorrect sewing postures of novice sewers.

2 Research Organization

The research mainly consists of four steps: scene and requirement analysis, collection and classification of postures, technology organization, and finally, experimental operations (Fig. 1).

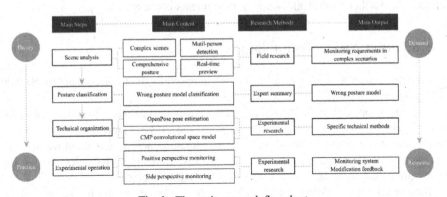

Fig. 1. The main research flowchart

2.1 Scene and Requirement Analysis

The sewing classroom or factory is a special and complex scene. Recognizing and alerting postures in this scene requires first understanding the various factors at play, such as the layout and methods of sewing machines, which contribute to the complexity of the recognition scene. It is also important to consider whether multiple individuals need to be identified, the comprehensive nature of the postures, and whether real-time feedback is necessary for monitoring. The main research method at this stage is to conduct on-site research of the sewing machine room, and ultimately summarize the specific requirements for identifying and warning sewing postures in complex scenarios.

2.2 Collection and Classification of Postures

To enable computers to recognize sewing postures more quickly and accurately, this study will collect and classify various postures that sewing beginners encounter during the sewing process. The main research methods at this stage are questionnaire surveys and expert summaries, mainly outputting various classified sewing postures.

2.3 Technical Organization

To meet the monitoring requirements in complex scenes for this research, technical selection and improvement are conducted. The main research method in this stage is experimental research, aiming to summarize specific technical methods suitable for this study.

2.4 Experimental Operation

Based on specific requirements and technological organization, this research conducted on-site monitoring and warning experiments in a sewing scene. The experiments were mainly divided into two monitoring perspectives: frontal and lateral, resulting in the development of a practical and operable sewing posture monitoring and warning system. Additionally, issues and requirements encountered during the practical operations were collected for further modifications and improvements in the next steps.

3 Computer Vision Technology

In computer vision technology, there are two main methods: top-down approach and bottom-up approach.

Top-down approach typically require early decisions between person detection and pose estimation, which can lead to incorrect allocation and pose prediction. After detecting a person, the algorithm immediately starts estimating their pose without waiting for the detection results of other people. This early decision-making can result in erroneous pose estimation, especially in cases of person overlap or occlusion.

Bottom-up approach first detect all the body key points in the image instead of detecting individuals one by one. Then, clustering techniques are used to group these key points into person poses. This approach has the advantage of robustness in multi-person scenes and can better handle cases of overlap and occlusion.

Additionally, the operational efficiency of the two algorithms in multi person recognition is different. By comparing the runtime of the two approaches using single-person Convolutional Pose Machines (CPM), the computational complexity of the top-down method increases linearly with the total number of people in the image, while the runtime of the bottom-up method increases relatively slowly with the number of people. This is because the top-down algorithm starts pose estimation immediately after detecting a person, so the runtime is directly proportional to the number of people in the image. The bottom-up algorithm first detects all the body key points in the image, decoupling the runtime from the number of people and making it dependent on the number of key points instead. The bottom-up algorithm has the potential to decouple runtime from the number of people in the image, allowing it to maintain relatively stable runtime even with an increasing number of people. This makes the bottom-up approach more advantageous in handling images with many people (Fig. 2).

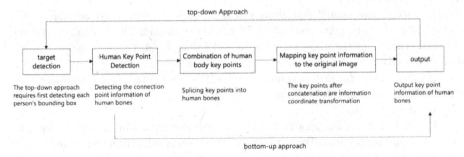

Fig. 2. The difference between top-down approach and bottom-up approach.

Based on these characteristics and factors, we consider Carnegie Mellon University's OpenPose technology for pose estimation. OpenPose is a bottom-up algorithm that first detects all the body key points in the image and then regresses all the key points using Convolutional Pose Machines (CPM), thus providing better robustness in multi-person scenes. The CPM model used in OpenPose employs large convolutional kernels to obtain a large receptive field, which can better handle the complexity and occlusion of sewing laboratory equipment and joints.

4 Experimental Research

4.1 Scene Requirement Analysis

Through specific visits to the research scene, this study summarizes the characteristics of the sewing process scene and the factors to consider in posture monitoring:

First, complex scene: Sewing areas are typically equipped with multiple sewing machines, and beginners operate around these machines. Multiple sewing equipment can cause occlusion of the human body, increasing the difficulty of computer recognition.

Second, multi-person environment: In a sewing scene, multiple individuals are usually operating multiple sewing machines simultaneously, so posture estimation needs to be able to recognize and track the poses of multiple individuals.

Third, comprehensive poses: Correct sewing poses involve not only hand and arm movements but also head, neck, and body postures. Therefore, in posture estimation, it is necessary to consider the key point information of the face and body comprehensively.

Fourth, real-time monitoring and warning: In the sewing scene, instructors of sewing techniques need observe and guide the postures and operations of beginners. Therefore, the posture estimation system needs to be able to monitor the postures of beginners in real-time and issue warnings when incorrect postures are detected, so that instructors can intervene and guide in a timely manner.

4.2   Collection and Classification of Postures

To collect and classify sewing postures, this study conducted a survey based on field investigations. The survey respondents were mainly beginners and experienced individuals who had been involved in sewing for more than 1 h per day on average, and 70 valid responses were collected.

The survey investigated dangerous situations and incorrect behaviors during the sewing process. Among the respondents, the behavior considered to be the most dangerous was needle pricks, accounting for over 80% of the total. The main factor causing dangerous behavior was found to be lack of concentration, accounting for 68.57%. The second factor was lack of skill, accounting for 24.29%. Therefore, it is important to maintain concentration, improve skill proficiency, avoid rushing, and reduce the likelihood of injury during sewing.

Moreover, respondents reported feeling eye fatigue or discomfort and muscle fatigue during long sewing sessions. The most common body parts to feel tired or uncomfortable during sewing were the neck and shoulders, followed by the waist and back. It is important to maintain good posture and take breaks and relax the relevant muscles to reduce fatigue and discomfort during sewing. Most respondents (92.86%) had not tried using tools or equipment to improve their working posture and reduce strain, indicating that they may not have paid enough attention to the impact of working posture and strain.

Furthermore, most participants (78.57%) had not received training or guidance on correct posture and ergonomics during sewing, which may increase the risk of incorrect postures and movements and lead to discomfort or injury during sewing.

To enable the computer to quickly recognize incorrect action patterns, this study also collected some common actions of novice sewers. These actions were rated and judged by instructors and individuals with extensive sewing experience. Based on these common actions, we classified them into three typical error types:

1. Lack of concentration during sewing operations.
2. Simultaneously holding or picking up other items during sewing operations.
3. Adopting incorrect postures such as bending, hunching, or lying down during sewing operations.

These movements can often cause physical harm and deviations in production for beginners. Therefore, based on these three common risky movements, an observation and warning program based on body posture recognition was designed and produced to observe the concentration level and behavior deviations of sewers.

4.3   System Design

Based on the causes of incorrect postures obtained from the survey and the common posture forms, we designed two monitoring perspectives: a frontal view and a side view. By simultaneously using information from multiple perspectives, we can obtain more comprehensive and accurate human posture estimation results. This provides valuable information and guidance for posture correction and danger warning applications.

Frontal View. The frontal view is better for recognizing the facial and hand postures of the operator and paying attention to issues such as lack of concentration and picking up other items during sewing. The frontal view involves more complex and varied movements. We considered using OpenPose to extract key points information to draw skeletal features and then train a deep learning network model based on PyTorch for judgment.

To determine lack of concentration, we use facial orientation. Instead of training a model, we calculate whether the x-axis distance between the two eyes and the nose is equal to determine if there is a perspective relationship on the face. If there is a perspective relationship, it indicates that the operator may have a lack of concentration.

Side View. The side view provides a better observation of the overall body posture, including the head, neck, torso, and legs. The side view directly uses the key points information extracted by OpenPose to calculate angles and provide real-time reminders for similar incorrect body postures. The calculation formula is as follows:

$$\tan \theta = \frac{|y_1 - y_2|}{|x_1 - x_2|}$$

In conclusion, we have developed a warning system that combines frontal and side views. The frontal view separates the facial and body parts for detection. The logic of the detection process is illustrated in Fig. 3.

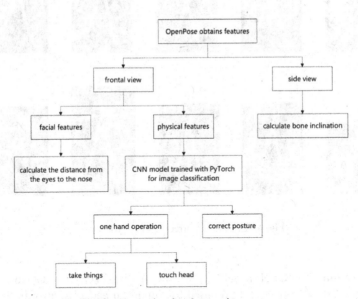

Fig. 3. The logic of early warning systems.

4.4 Construct the Convolutional Neural Network

Dataset Construction. During the construction of the dataset, we found that the number of captured photos was insufficient. Therefore, we exported each frame of the captured video as a jpeg format image. OpenPose was used to extract key points information from each image and draw skeletal features. To reduce redundant data, we made some adjustments to the images. The background of the images was set to black, and only the graphical information within the range of the minimum and maximum coordinates of x and y was retained. Partial datasets are shown in Figs. 4 and 5. Before applying the entire dataset to the training process, it was preprocessed with the following steps:

1. The images were divided into three categories: correct posture, take things, and touch head, and placed in three separate folders.
2. All images were resized to (224, 224) pixels, with black pixels added to the edges.
3. Data augmentation was applied to expand the dataset. Random horizontal flipping was applied to the images to increase the diversity of the dataset, improve the generalization ability of the model, make the model more robust, and reduce the risk of overfitting.
4. The images were normalized to have pixel values ranging from 0 to 1.

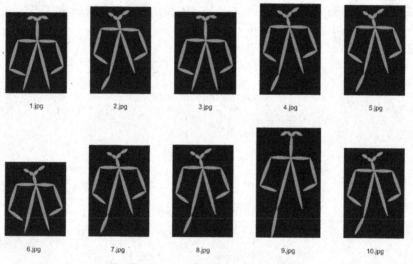

Fig. 4. Dataset of correct sewing posture.

Model Selection. The CNN model used for training was VGG16. VGG16 is a convolutional neural network model proposed by Simonyan and Zisserman in the paper "Very Deep Convolutional Networks for Large Scale Image Recognition". VGG16 has a simple structure, consisting of 13 convolutional layers, 3 fully connected layers, and 5 pooling layers. All convolutional layers in VGG16 use the same convolutional kernel parameters, with a kernel size of 3×3. All pooling layers use the same pooling kernel parameters, with a kernel size of 2×2. The pooling layers have a stride of 2 and use max pooling.

Model Training. We defined the loss function as the cross-entropy loss function and used the Adam optimizer to optimize the model's parameters. In the training loop, the

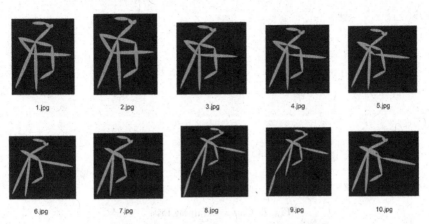

Fig. 5. Dataset of sewing while taking things.

number of epochs was set to 100. In each epoch, we first set the model to the training mode, then iterated through the training data loader, calculated the model's output and loss, and updated the model's parameters. At the same time, we calculated and recorded the loss value during the training process. Then, we set the model to the evaluation mode, iterated through the validation data loader, and calculated the accuracy of the model on the validation set. The accuracy was recorded in TensorBoard and the model with the highest accuracy on the validation set was saved. Finally, after training was completed, we printed out the best accuracy achieved during the training process and saved the model's parameters. The loss curve and accuracy curve are shown in Figs. 6 and 7.

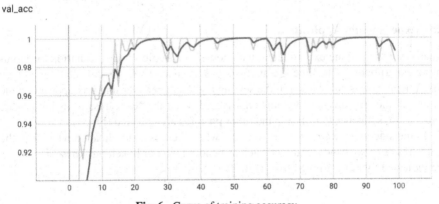

Fig. 6. Curve of training accuracy.

Attempt to input two bone images for testing, and the image classification results are shown in Fig. 8, indicating a high recognition accuracy.

loss

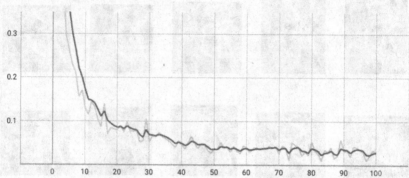

Fig. 7. Curve of training loss.

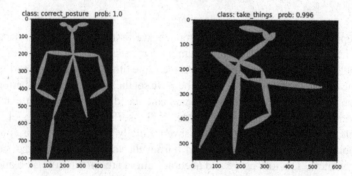

Fig. 8. Predicted Posture Results

4.5 Experimental Application

Finally, we applied the experimental techniques to specific sewing scenarios for monitoring experiments. When the seamstress's posture is correct, it is indicated by a green box. When there is a deviation in the sewing posture, a red warning box appears on the screen. In the frontal view, warnings are issued when the seamstress turns their head, reaches out, scratches their head, and other postures are detected (Fig. 9).

In the side view, warnings are triggered when there is a significant deviation in the seamstress's torso, hands, and feet, such as bending over or hunching. These deviations are indicated by red warning boxes (Fig. 10).

Fig. 9. Recognition and early warning from the frontal view.

Fig. 10. Recognition and early warning from the side view

5 Conclusion

By using computer recognition of beginners' facial and body data, we can effectively observe the behavioral states of sewing beginners during the sewing process. Compared to the traditional method of manual observation and intervention in sewing instruction, computer vision recognition is more comprehensive and timelier, and can simultaneously recognize multiple samples. Computer recognition also offers convenience and operability, as it can be implemented using a webcam. It can serve as an auxiliary means for practical teaching and risk control. However, during the experiment, some deviations were observed in the OpenPose recognition. In the future, with advancements in hardware technology and computing power, the accuracy of recognition can be further improved by considering multi-view 3D human pose estimation.

Acknowledgments. This study was funded by Guangzhou Municipal Bureau of Science and Technology, Guangzhou Basic Research Program Basic and Applied Basic Research Special General Project (SL2024A04J00955).

Disclosure of Interests. The authors have no competing interests to declare that are relevant to the content of this article.

References

1. Kim, S.Y.: A comparative study of contents of Korean basic sewing textbook. J. Korean Soc. Costume **62**(3), 73–83 (2012)
2. Jing-Bin, Y., Heng, L.: Comprehensive and innovative experimental teaching of industrial engineering based on sewing production. Res. Explor. Lab. (2013)
3. Vihma, T., Nurminen, M., Mutanen, P.: Sewing-machine operators' work and musculo-skeletal complaints. Ergonomics **25**(4), 295–298 (1982)
4. Tartaglia, R., Cinti, G., Carrara, S., et al.: Work posture and changes in the spine of sewing workers in the clothing industry. La Med. del lavoro **81**(1), 39–44 (1990)
5. Kirin, S., Šajatović, A.H.: Research of working postures in the technological sewing process using the REBA method. In: Sumpor, D., Jambrošić, K., Lulić, T.J., Milčić, D., Čubrić, I.S., Šabarić, I. (eds.) Proceedings of the 8th International Ergonomics Conference: ERGONOMICS 2020, pp. 111–119. Springer International Publishing, Cham (2021). https://doi.org/10.1007/978-3-030-66937-9_13
6. Jensen, B.R., Schibye, B., Søgaard, K., et al.: Shoulder muscle load and muscle fatigue among industrial sewing-machine operators. Eur. J. Appl. Physiol. **67**, 467–475 (1993)
7. Zhang, F., He, L., Wu, S., et al.: Quantify work load and muscle functional activation patterns in neck-shoulder muscles of female sewing machine operators using surface electromyogram. Chin. Med. J. **124**(22), 3731–3737 (2011)
8. Delleman, N.J., Dul, J.: Sewing machine operation: workstation adjustment, working posture, and workers' perceptions. Int. J. Ind. Ergon. **30**(6), 341–353 (2002)
9. Fei-ruo, Z., Li-hua, H., Shan-shan, W., et al.: Quantify work load and muscle functional activation patterns in neck-shoulder muscles of female sewing machine operators using surface electromyogram. Chin. Med. J. **124**(22), 3731–3737 (2011)
10. Chen, K.: Sitting posture recognition based on openpose. In: IOP Conference Series: Materials Science and Engineering. IOP Publishing, **677**(3), 032057 (2019)
11. Rijayanti, R., Hwang, M., Jin, K.: Detection of anomalous behavior of manufacturing workers using deep learning-based recognition of human-object interaction. Appl. Sci. **13**(15), 8584 (2023)
12. Johnson, D., Damian, D., Tzanetakis, G.: Detecting hand posture in piano playing using depth data. Comput. Music. J. **43**(1), 59–78 (2020)
13. Wei, S.E., Ramakrishna, V., Kanade, T., et al.: Convolutional pose machines.In: Proceedings of the IEEE Conference on Computer Vision and Pattern Recognition, pp. 4724–4732 (2016)
14. Cao, Z., Simon, T., Wei, S.E., et al.: Realtime multi-person 2D pose estimation using part affinity fields. In: Proceedings of the IEEE Conference on Computer Vision and Pattern Recognition, pp. 7291–7299 (2017)

The Use of Digital Human Modeling to Assess Vision Obstruction in Airport Taxi Operations

Gabrielle B. Joffe and H. Onan Demirel[✉]

Oregon State University, Corvallis, OR 97331, USA
{joffeg,onan.demirel}@oregonstate.edu

Abstract. The operation of ground support vehicles in busy airport taxiways and runways is a growing concern, especially when the driver does not have an adequate field of view (FoV). Airport ground vehicle accidents due to vision obstruction have resulted in loss of revenue, injuries, and fatalities. The research presented in this paper examines and quantifies vision obstruction in airport ground support vehicles using an early design methodology based on digital human modeling (DHM). The methodology is presented through investigating two case studies based on actual airport accidents influenced by vision obstruction, involving pushback tractors and an aircraft refueling truck. Each study comprises three-dimensional (3D) computer-aided design (CAD) models of the vehicles and four DHM manikins with varying anthropometries. Obstruction-causing vehicle elements are identified, and then the CAD models are redesigned to improve the driver's forward FoV. Results from this study show that DHM can facilitate a proactive design approach by pinpointing potential hazards in the design of ground vehicles by retrofitting changes during early-phase design via digital models to reduce the risk of driver vision obstruction.

Keywords: Digital Human Modeling · Human Factors Engineering · Ergonomics · Vision Obstruction · Aviation · Engineering Design

1 Introduction

Investigations have revealed that accidents involving airport ground support vehicles, such as pushback tractors [3,17,37], aircraft refueling trucks [26,39], and shuttle buses [25], are influenced by the operator having an inadequate field of view (FoV). In such cases, drivers experience vision obstruction due to protruding structural elements of the vehicle they operate, poor weather conditions, or other stationary and moving vehicles on taxiways and runways, such as aircraft. According to the Federal Aviation Administration (FAA), between 1985 and 2000, eight ground crew workers were killed at various airports across the United States upon being struck by a ground support vehicle on the apron [18]. More than half of these accidents were due to the vehicle operator having a

© The Author(s), under exclusive license to Springer Nature Switzerland AG 2024
V. G. Duffy (Ed.): HCII 2024, LNCS 14709, pp. 55–68, 2024.
https://doi.org/10.1007/978-3-031-61060-8_5

limited FoV of their surroundings [18]. In addition to that, globally, it is estimated that airlines spend around $10 billion USD each year on damage incurred by ground support equipment, including destruction of aircraft, interruptions to departures, and injuries to airport personnel [19]. Greater attention must be given to the driver's FoV during the design of ground support vehicles.

This paper focuses on assessing the risk of vision obstruction related to the design of ground support vehicles. We propose an early design methodology that injects digital human modeling (DHM) to evaluate the percent obstruction in different scenarios that involve pushback tractors, refueling trucks, and aircraft during taxi operations. DHM is a computational technique that uses digital manikins to represent humans in a computer-aided engineering (CAE) or virtual reality (VR) environment to facilitate the prediction of human performance and safety [2]. It allows designers to simulate human interactions with products and environments, evaluate ergonomics, and consider user abilities and limitations before physical prototyping begins [9,11]. In addition to reducing design time, DHM has also been shown to reduce costs related to the design process [9,12].

While vision obstruction accidents have not been extensively researched on airport vehicles, there have been studies conducted on automobiles [4,10,28]. For example, Mellon [24] and Srinivasan et al. [35,36] demonstrated the development of early design frameworks concerning automotive A-pillar geometry and Formula One halo concepts, which illustrated alternative strategies for how designers can evaluate and potentially improve driver vision through the use of DHM. In a similar fashion, this paper introduces a framework that will allow designers to incorporate obstruction-related early design decision-making targeted to airport ground operations. The early design approach we propose allows for a rapid and approximate evaluation of the blind spots experienced by the driver, which will lead to a better understanding of how vehicle design and the operator's outside environment contribute to this type of accident.

2 Background

2.1 Vision Obstruction in Airport Ground Support Vehicles

Vision obstruction accidents involving airport ground support vehicles during ground and taxi operations are a concern, leading to extensive damage, injuries, and casualties. Mainly, pushback tractors and aircraft refueling trucks are two common airport ground vehicles associated with accidents influenced by vision obstruction. This section briefly overviews the literature on vision obstruction accidents involving pushback tractors and aircraft refueling trucks.

Pushback Tractors. Pushback, also referred to as towing, is the process of moving a parked aircraft, most often onto the taxiway in preparation for take-off, when it is unable to move under its own power [34]. The operation is often carried out by pushback tugs, which are large tractors designed for this purpose.

Moreover, many pushback accidents are influenced by obstructions to the tractor driver's FoV. A study conducted on the risks associated with the pushback process pointed out that towing can be a risky procedure due to the inadequate visual angle the driver has inside the tractor cab [16]. This makes it difficult for the operator to see important markings on the taxiway, such as centerlines, potentially leading to accidents. Most notably, 35.1% of the studied pushback collision scenarios involved an aircraft being pushed back into another aircraft, often due to the obstruction of critical markings on the ground [16].

For instance, an accident in 2019 involved a Boeing 747-400 being backed into a Boeing 787-9 at Amsterdam Airport Schiphol in the Netherlands during pushback. The investigation found that visual obscuration contributed to the event as the driver of the 747 tractor failed to see the 787 due to his vision being obstructed by the 747's engines [17]. Another example is an accident at Ben Gurion International Airport in Tel Aviv, Israel, which occurred in 2018, involving a Boeing 767-300 colliding with a Boeing 737-700 on pushback. The report revealed that the pushback drivers' fields of view were limited by the aircraft they were pushing back, and rainy conditions further impeded their abilities to see the other aircraft [37].

Aircraft Refueling Trucks. Many conventional aircraft refueling trucks are designed with an elevating platform that is placed to the driver's right side of the cab. This platform provides the operator with a surface to stand on, allowing them to reach the wings and refuel the aircraft [23]. However, when it is not in use, it becomes a protruding structural member that has the potential to block the driver's right-side view and lead to the creation of blind spots.

For example, in 1998, an accident occurred at Philadelphia International Airport in which a taxiing Douglas DC-9 aircraft collided with an aircraft refueling truck, resulting in substantial damage to both vehicles [26]. It was discovered that the driver was unable to see the approaching DC-9 due to another stationary aircraft that was on his right, as well as fueling equipment that sat adjacent to the right window of the cab [26]. Another accident involving vision obstruction, in which a fuel truck collided with a DHC-8 aircraft during taxi operations, occurred in 2019 at Toronto Pearson International Airport [39]. This led to the aircraft sustaining irreparable damage, as well as severe panic and a total of 15 injuries onboard the aircraft [39]. The driver's vision was significantly obstructed by the service platform to his right, in addition to condensation that covered the truck's windows [39]. The report concluded that the occurrence of a collision was nearly inevitable due to his inadequate FoV [7, 8, 39].

2.2   Analyzing Driver Vision with Digital Human Modeling

DHM has been shown to be beneficial to early-phase design, especially in vehicle design and manufacturing [13, 27, 31]. One of the most critical aspects when undertaking the design of a vehicle is ensuring that the driver has an unobstructed FoV [6]. With the use of DHM, designers are able to identify hazardous occluding structural vehicle components before the start of physical prototyping. For example, a study by Reed et al. [30] explored the use of DHM for designing a new postal delivery truck. Using Siemens Jack software, the designers conducted thorough FoV analyses in order to place the vehicle's mirrors in locations that would minimize obstructions. With this proactive DHM-based approach, the direct and indirect fields of view in the truck were improved substantially over the previous mail delivery vehicle design [30]. Another example of the benefits of DHM in vehicle design is a research study by Demirel et al. [14], which coupled DHM with image processing to quantify vision obstruction caused by halo crash-protection equipment in Formula One race cars. In that study, the authors used DHM to produce snapshots of the driver's forward FoV to compare and evaluate the percent obstruction associated with multiple halo concept variants [14]. Another study by Summerskill et al. [38] used DHM to assess dangerous blind spots in heavy goods vehicles (HGVs). Their work highlighted the necessity for direct vision regulations to be established for HGV cabs [38].

3   Methodology

This research work delves into two unique case studies representing airport vehicle accidents. The case studies are not direct accident reconstructions, but they are based on the aforementioned pushback and fuel truck events in Tel Aviv and Toronto, both accidents in which vision obstruction played a significant role. The case studies are as follows:

1. Two aircraft collide with each other during the pushback process.
2. An aircraft refueling truck collides with a taxiing aircraft.

Although both case studies are unique regarding the specific vehicles involved, the DHM-integrated methodology we implemented to assess how the vision obstruction impacted the driver's performance is the same. First, our methodology starts with an in-depth review of the accident reports, which allows us to understand the path the vehicles traveled and the factors that influenced vision obstruction. Next, we build representative computer-aided design (CAD) (e.g., Siemens NX [32]) models of airport vehicles and aircraft. The CAD models are then imported into the DHM software, Siemens Jack [33], where vision obscuration analysis is performed based on each case study. The vehicles are arranged in a manner similar to the actual accidents, and four manikins of varying anthropometries (5th percentile female, 5th percentile male, 95th percentile female, and 95th percentile male) from the Anthropometric Survey of U.S. Army Personnel (ANSUR II) database are placed inside the vehicles as drivers with a neutral driving posture, which is based on photographs and videos of pushback and fuel truck drivers. The neutral driving posture in this study assumes that the manikins maintain a straight head position and there is no change in their head angles at any point in the scenarios. Varying the anthropometries helps assess how different anthropometric parameters influence the vision obstruction.

The steering wheel and driver's seat are given respective adjustability allowances of 10.0 cm and 25.4 cm in order to accommodate each anthropometry properly.

Both case studies are separated into "frames", which represent moments in time leading up to the occurrence of the accidents. This approach provides a visualization of the drivers' fields of view in time, typical of how they operate the vehicle. Siemens Jack's Coverage Zone tool is then utilized to quantify how much of the target object (e.g., an aircraft) is visible to the manikin at that time. Coverage Zone analysis uses a ray-casting approach, emitting rays from the manikin's eyes onto a target plane that represents the target object's overall bounding area, to measure percent visibility (see Fig. 1) [15].

The CAD models of the ground support vehicles are redesigned based on the results. Later, we rerun the Coverage Zone analyses to determine whether the drivers' vision had improved as a result of the design changes. This approach

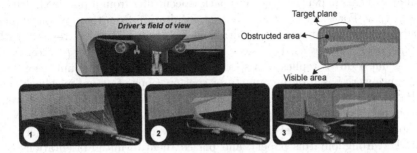

Fig. 1. 1: The rays are emitted from the manikin's eyes; 2: The rays are projected onto the target plane; 3: Visible area (green) and the obstructed area (red). (Color figure online)

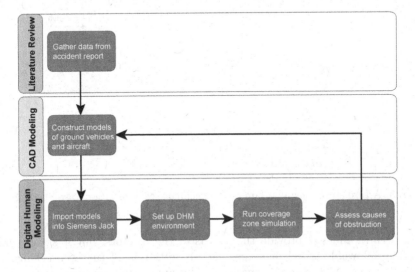

Fig. 2. The data flow includes the literature review, CAD, and DHM.

helps designers understand obstruction-causing vehicle segments early in the design process. Figure 2 illustrates the data flow in the proposed methodology.

4   Case Studies

The case studies presented in this paper analyze the FoV of a pushback tractor driver and a fuel truck driver in the moments leading up to two accidents. In this section, we explain how we implemented the methodology in each study.

4.1   Case Study 1 - Pushback Accident

This case study explores the moments leading up to a collision of two aircraft, a Boeing 737-700 and a Boeing 767-300 (referred to as "737" and "767" for the remainder of this paper), during pushback, specifically from a pushback driver's point of view. For this case study, we took inspiration from the previously mentioned pushback accident that occurred in Tel Aviv [37]. After reviewing the accident report, we modeled a generic pushback tractor in CAD software. While this was not a direct replica of a specific pushback tractor, the dimensions and appearance were based on manufacturer specifications of actual pushback vehicles [5, 21]. Further, we constructed CAD models of the 737 and 767 by referencing existing models from an open-source CAD file-sharing repository [22]. Next, we imported all CAD models into the DHM software, Siemens Jack (referred to as "Jack" throughout this paper), and placed them in initial orientations that were similar to diagrams provided in the accident report (Fig. 3).

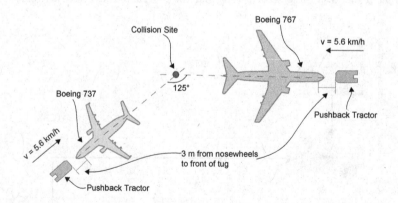

Fig. 3. A bird's-eye view diagram of the accident scene used for Case Study 1.

The report did not provide the speeds of the tractors, but it stated their maximum allowable travel distances and the duration of the event. Thus, we were able to create the three time frames by approximating a speed from the velocity equation

$$v = \frac{d}{t} \tag{1}$$

where v is the velocity of the tractors, d is the allowable travel distance of the aircraft (75 m), and t is the total amount of time over which the event occurred (48 s). Due to a lack of available data, we assumed equal velocities for both pushback tractors and that there was no acceleration at any point in the scenario. Employing this equation yielded a speed of 5.6 km/h. Figure 3 displays the diagram we used to position the vehicles in the first time frame.

This case study examines three time frames leading up to the collision, split into five-second intervals (t = 0, 5, 10). To create the frames, we made a copy of the initial Jack simulation environment (at t = 0) and moved the vehicles forward in the following simulation setup (at t = 5 and 10), using the derivation of the velocity equation, $d = vt$ where d is the distance traveled by the vehicles, v is the previously-calculated velocity, and t is the moment in time, which yielded that the vehicles moved 7.8 m in every frame. Later, we placed manikins inside the pushback tractor in the neutral driving position (see Fig. 4). We analyze the FoV of the 737 pushback tractor driver as the accident report [37] stated that aircraft with lower bellies have the potential to cause more obstruction to operators. Finally, we ran Coverage Zone simulations in Jack. The target plane was dimensioned to represent the overall bounding area of the 767 since it is the critical object for the 737 pushback driver to see in this event. After we ran the simulations with the original vehicle design, we redesigned the CAD model of

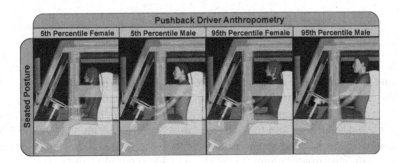

Fig. 4. The neutral driving posture of the manikins in the pushback tractor cab.

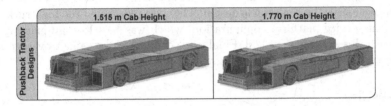

Fig. 5. Pushback tractor models used in the Case Study 1 Coverage Zone simulations.

the tractor, eliminating the principal obstructing elements, and then we ran the same simulations to assess improvements to driver vision (Fig. 5).

4.2   Case Study 2 - Fuel Truck Accident

Case Study 2 examines an accident scenario in which a fuel truck collides with a taxiing DHC-8 aircraft based on the 2019 accident that happened in Toronto [39]. We modeled a generic aircraft refueling truck with a similar design to the one in the collision, and we also created a model of a DHC-8 aircraft. Following the CAD modeling, the fuel truck and aircraft models were imported into Jack and placed in positions approximated from the accident report (Fig. 6).

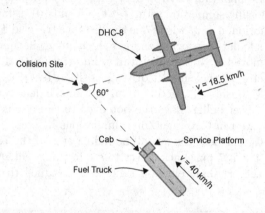

Fig. 6. Depiction of the top-view sketch used for the scene setup in Case Study 2.

Since the report provided the speeds of the vehicles—40 km/h for the fuel truck and 18.5 km/h for the aircraft—we used the distance equation to determine the distance both vehicles would move in each frame. We split this case study into three half-second intervals (t = 0, 0.5, 1) due to the vehicles' faster speeds. Thus, the DHC-8 and fuel truck traveled approximately 2.57 m and 5.5 m, respectively, in each subsequent frame. Next, we positioned the manikins into the neutral driving posture and placed them inside the fuel truck cab (see Fig. 7). Later, we created a target plane that assumed the overall longitudinal width and height of the DHC-8. We ran the Coverage Zone analyses and assessed the vision obstruction caused by the vehicle design. Then, we redesigned the fuel truck with a different service platform configuration, which was based on an existing fuel truck with this arrangement [29]. Finally, we conducted the same Coverage Zone simulations with the new design (Fig. 8).

5   Results

This research was comprised of a total of 48 Coverage Zone simulations in Jack DHM software. These 48 vision obstruction analyses consisted of 24 simulations

Fig. 7. The neutral driving posture of manikins in the fuel truck cab.

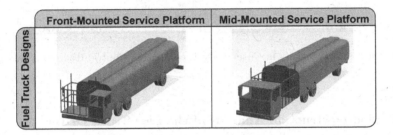

Fig. 8. The two fuel truck designs used in the Case Study 2 vision analyses.

per case study, which included four manikins, two vehicle design variants, and three time frames. The outcome of this study examines the connections between driver anthropometry and visibility as the vehicles approach the collision site.

5.1   Vision Obstruction Analysis of the Pushback Tractor Driver

Results from the initial 12 simulations conducted in Case Study 1 showed that the manikins of taller heights had a much more limited FoV than the shorter manikins. For instance, at t = 5 s, when the airplanes were 28 m apart, the 5th percentile female was able to see greater than 20% more of the target plane than the 95th percentile male manikin. This is attributed to the taller manikins sitting closer to the roof of the vehicle, blocking their line of sight. Additionally, target plane visibility tended to decrease for the larger drivers as the aircraft approached collision. For the smaller manikins, the majority of the vision obstruction was a result of the target plane being obscured by the 737 they were pushing back.

Since the main contributing factor to the vehicular obstruction was the height of the cab, we increased the height by 25.5 cm, which falls within the range of existing cab heights [1]. We ran 12 more simulations on the redesigned cab, which showed that the target plane visibility remained similar for the shorter manikins but increased for the taller manikins. For example, in the final frame, at t = 10 s, the target plane visibility increased from 19.15% to 53.83% for the 95th percentile male manikin, as a result of the taller cab height. Further, the difference between the visibility values for the different anthropometries became minute. Figure 9 demonstrates the results of Case Study 1.

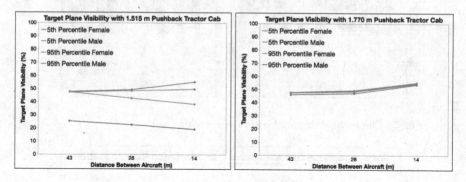

Fig. 9. The visibility results in Case Study 1, comparing the two tractor cab designs.

5.2 Vision Obstruction Analysis of the Fuel Truck Driver

Findings from the 12 simulations with the original fuel truck design did not show a clear trend between anthropometry and visibility. The visibility scores were similar for all of the manikins at each time frame, except for a few data points. The target plane visibility tended to increase from the first to second frame for all manikins. On the contrary, the largest difference in visibility occurred in the third frame for all anthropometries. An example of this is the percent visibility decreasing from 59.02% in Frame 2 to 43.91% in Frame 3 for the 95th percentile male manikin. Further, most of the obstruction came from the structural elements of the loading platform.

We then redesigned the fuel truck so that the service platform sat behind the cab. Results from the 12 simulations with the new fuel truck design displayed

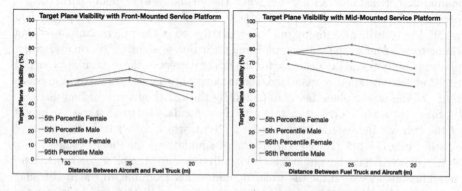

Fig. 10. The visibility results in Case Study 2, comparing two fuel truck configurations.

significant increases in visibility scores for all anthropometries. Shorter manikins saw larger increases in visibility, up to nearly 30%. For example, the second frame target plane visibility increased from 57.05% to 83.54% for the 5th percentile female. The results of Case Study 2 are displayed in Fig. 10.

6 Discussion

The methodology presented in this paper allows designers to proactively examine driver vision in airport ground support vehicles using digital manikins. This approach has the potential to assist designers in early-phase design and provide a method to reduce the risk of future accidents in which vision obstruction is a contributing factor. The results indicated that the design of airport ground vehicles can contribute to the obstruction of the driver's FoV. For example, a low cab roof height proved to be a significant contributor to the vision obstruction in the pushback tractor. Likewise, front-loading fueling utilities found in fuel trucks contribute to vision obstruction. These findings can help designers decide how to lessen vision-related concerns during the conceptual design and evaluation.

Although DHM vision obstruction analyses illustrated in this study supplied valuable insight into the FoV of airport ground vehicle drivers, there were multiple shortcomings in this research. First, the manikins' postures were adjusted manually and, therefore, are subjective. It is known that manual posture adjustment in DHM simulations is prone to error and introduces designer bias into the study [20, 40]. Further, it was difficult to maintain consistency in the manikins' postures between frames, which had the potential to lead to errors in the visibility scores. Also, assuming the head remained straight did not accurately depict the drivers' postures since they would likely turn their heads to scan their surroundings as they drove the vehicle. This study also assumed clear weather conditions, as it is challenging to simulate rain or fog in a DHM environment. Additionally, the case studies in this research were low-fidelity representations of the drivers' fields of view since the CAD models of the ground vehicles were proof-of-concept models and, thus, were not exact replicas of the vehicles that were involved in the accidents. Moreover, since the target planes must be rectangular, their total length and width were much larger than the actual length and width of the aircraft. As the target plane positioning was subjective, alternate methods of placing them would produce differing results. Therefore, the generated visibility scores provide a low-fidelity representation of how much of the aircraft the manikin was able to see at the given moments in time. One final limitation of this research is the lack of cognition in DHM simulations. Since manikins do not perceive what they are seeing, one cannot make conclusions from this study about the cognitive aspects of driver vision in airport ground support vehicles.

7 Conclusion and Future Work

This paper proposed a DHM-based design methodology that evaluates and quantifies vision obstruction in airport ground support vehicles. It presents two case studies involving a pushback tractor and a refueling truck. The method illustrated in this paper offers an alternative early-design approach to how designers can address and mitigate risks early in the design process.

Future work will include incorporating techniques that target this study's limitations. Since this research did not consider the poor weather conditions that compounded visibility issues in the two accidents, it would be valuable to simulate rainy and foggy conditions to evaluate how they impact driver vision in the airport environment. Further, using motion capture with human test subjects in a laboratory environment would allow for more accurate driving postures that are less prone to error. Finally, immersing human participants in a virtual reality (VR) environment consisting of a full-scale virtual airport taxiway scene and employing mental workload (MWL) assessment techniques would allow us to inject cognition into the research and understand what drivers see when operating an airport ground vehicle.

Disclosure of Interests. The authors have no competing interests to declare that are relevant to the content of this article.

References

1. Aero Specialties: TLD TMX-150-9/12/15/16 Pushback & Tow Tractor. https://www.aerospecialties.com/aviation-ground-support-equipmentgse-products/tow-tugs-pushback-tractors/large-20000-dbp/tld-tmx-150-9121516-pushback-tow-tractor/. Accessed 11 Jan 2024
2. Ahmed, S., Irshad, L., Gawand, M.S., Demirel, H.O.: Integrating human factors early in the design process using digital human modelling and surrogate modelling. J. Eng. Des. **32**, 1–22 (2021). https://doi.org/10.1080/09544828.2020.1869704
3. Air Accident Investigation Sector: Incident final report. Technical report AIFN/0011/2013, Air Accident Investigation Sector, Dubai, United Arab Emirates (2016)
4. Baysal, D.N.: Assessment of vehicular vision obstruction due to driver-side B-pillar and remediation with blind spot eliminator. In: Automotive Technical Papers. SAE International (2023). https://doi.org/10.4271/2023-01-5056
5. BEML: A Multi Role GSE From BEML Model BA10G40. https://alumni.bemlindia.in/writereaddata/Downloads/20170905133400Aircraft%20Towing%20Tractor.pdf. Accessed 11 Jan 2024
6. Bhise, V.D.: Ergonomics in the Automotive Design Process. CRC Press, Boca Raton (2011)
7. Canadian Owners and Pilots Association: Poor fuel truck design and weather cited in dash-8 collision report - TSB. https://copanational.org/poor-fuel-truck-design-and-weather-cited-in-dash-8-collision-report-tsb/. Accessed 21 Dec 2023
8. CBC News: 'incredibly scary': air canada plane, fuel tanker collide at Toronto's Pearson airport. https://www.cbc.ca/news/canada/toronto/air-canada-jazz-fuel-tanker-truck-pearson-collision-1.5130624. Accessed 21 Dec 2023

9. Chaffin, D.B.: Digital Human Modeling for Vehicle and Workplace Design. SAE International, Warrendale (2001)
10. Cho, Y., Han, B.: Application of slim A-pillar to improve driver's field of vision. Int. J. Automot. Technol. **11**, 517–524 (2010)
11. Demirel, H.O., Ahmed, S., Duffy, V.G.: Digital human modeling: a review and reappraisal of origins, present, and expected future methods for representing humans computationally. Int. J. Hum.-Comput. Interact. **38**(10), 897–937 (2022)
12. Demirel, H.O., Duffy, V.G.: Applications of digital human modeling in industry. In: Duffy, V.G. (ed.) ICDHM 2007. LNCS, vol. 4561, pp. 824–832. Springer, Heidelberg (2007). https://doi.org/10.1007/978-3-540-73321-8_93
13. Demirel, H.O., Duffy, V.G.: Digital human modeling for product lifecycle management. In: Duffy, V.G. (ed.) ICDHM 2007. LNCS, vol. 4561, pp. 372–381. Springer, Heidelberg (2007). https://doi.org/10.1007/978-3-540-73321-8_43
14. Demirel, H.O., Jennings, A., Srinivasan, S.: An early design method to quantify vision obstruction: formula one (F1) halo case study. In: Duffy, V.G. (ed.) HCII 2022. LNCS, vol. 13319, pp. 32–44. Springer, Cham (2022). https://doi.org/10.1007/978-3-031-05890-5_3
15. Demirel, H.O., Srinivasan, S.: A proactive ergonomics framework to assess a-pillar vision obstruction. Digit. Hum. Model. Appl. Optim. **46**, 16 (2022)
16. Dieke-Meier, F., Fricke, H.: The need for a collision prevention system for the pushback of aircraft. In: 28th International Congress of the Aeronautical Sciences (ICAS), Brisbane (2012)
17. Dutch Safety Board: Collision during pushback. Technical report, Dutch Safety Board, Amsterdam, Netherlands (2022)
18. Federal Aviation Administration: Injuries and fatalities of workers struck by vehicles on airport aprons. Technical report, Federal Aviation Administration, United States (2002)
19. Flight Safety Foundation: Covering the ground. https://flightsafety.org/asw-article/covering-the-ground/. Accessed 22 Sept 2023
20. Gawand, M.S., Demirel, H.O.: A design framework to automate task simulation and ergonomic analysis in digital human modeling. In: Duffy, V.G. (ed.) HCII 2020, Part I. LNCS, vol. 12198, pp. 50–66. Springer, Cham (2020). https://doi.org/10.1007/978-3-030-49904-4_4
21. Goldhofer: AST-1X. https://www.goldhofer.com/en/towbarless-tractors/ast-1x. Accessed 11 Jan 2024
22. GrabCAD: Grabcad community. https://grabcad.com/library. Accessed 22 Dec 2023
23. Joshi, G.: How is an aircraft refueled? https://simpleflying.com/how-is-an-aircraft-refueled/. Accessed 21 Dec 2023
24. Mellon, T.R.P.: Using digital human modeling to evaluate and improve car pillar design: a proof of concept and design of experiments. Master's thesis, Oregon State University, Corvallis, OR (2021)
25. National Transportation Safety Board: Aviation accident final report. Technical report FTW98FA001, National Transportation Safety Board, Denver, Colorado (1998)
26. National Transportation Safety Board: Aviation investigation final report. Technical report NYC98LA177, National Transportation Safety Board, Philadelphia, Pennsylvania (2000)
27. Naumann, A., Rötting, M.: Digital human modeling for design and evaluation of human-machine systems. MMI-Interaktiv **12**, 27–35 (2007)

28. Quigley, C., Cook, S., Tait, R.G.: Field of vision (a-pillar geometry) - a review of the needs of drivers: final report. https://api.semanticscholar.org/CorpusID: 106615924. Accessed 29 Sept 2023

29. Rampmaster: 10,000 gallon WD exchange rampmaster jet refueler. https://www.rampmasters.com/refueler-solutions/10000-gallon/10000-gallon-wd-exchange/. Accessed 27 Dec 2023

30. Reed, M.P., Satchell, K., Nichols, A.: Application of digital human modeling to the design of a postal delivery vehicle. Technical report, SAE Technical Paper (2005)

31. Scataglini, S., Paul, G.: DHM and Posturography. Academic Press, Cambridge (2019)

32. Siemens PLM Software: NX. https://plm.sw.siemens.com/en-US/nx/cad-online/. Accessed 22 Dec 2023

33. Siemens PLM Software: Tecnomatix Jack. https://www.plm.automation.siemens.com/media/store/en_us/4917_tcm1023-4952_tcm29-1992.pdf. Accessed 23 Dec 2023

34. Skybrary: Pushback. https://skybrary.aero/articles/pushback. Accessed 28 Dec 2023

35. Srinivasan, S.: Early design evaluation of see-through automotive A-pillar concepts using digital human modeling and mixed reality techniques. Master's thesis, Oregon State University, Corvallis, OR (2022)

36. Srinivasan, S., Demirel, H.O.: Quantifying vision obstruction of formula one (F1) halo concept variants. In: Proceedings of the 7th International Digital Human Modeling Symposium, vol. 7. University of Iowa (2022)

37. State of Israel Ministry of Transportation and Road Safety: Safety investigation report - final. Technical report 31-18, State of Israel Ministry of Transportation and Road Safety, Tel Aviv, Israel (2019)

38. Summerskill, S., Marshall, R., Paterson, A., Reed, S.: Understanding direct and indirect driver vision in heavy goods vehicles. Technical report, Loughborough University, Loughborough, UK (2015)

39. Transportation Safety Board of Canada: Air transportation safety investigation report A19O0063. Technical report, Transportation Safety Board of Canada, Toronto, Canada (2020)

40. Ziolek, S.A., Nebel, K.: Human modeling: controlling misuse and misinterpretation. Technical report, SAE Technical Paper (2003)

Improving Welding Robotization via Operator Skill Identification, Modeling, and Human-Machine Collaboration: Experimental Protocol Implementation

Antoine Lenat[1,2], Olivier Cheminat[2], Damien Chablat[1(✉)], and Camilo Charron[1,3]

[1] Nantes Université, École Centrale Nantes, CNRS, LS2N, UMR 6004, 44000 Nantes, France
{Antoine.Lenat,Damien.Chablat,Camilo.Charron}@ls2n.fr
[2] CETIM, 74 Rte de la Jonelière, 44300 Nantes, France
Olivier.Cheminat@cetim.fr
[3] Université Rennes 2, Rennes, France

Abstract. The industry of the future, also known as Industry 5.0, aims to modernize production tools, digitize workshops, and cultivate the invaluable human capital within the company. Industry 5.0 can't be done without fostering a workforce that is not only technologically adept but also has enhanced skills and knowledge. Specifically, collaborative robotics plays a key role in automating strenuous or repetitive tasks, enabling human cognitive functions to contribute to quality and innovation. In manual manufacturing, however, some of these tasks remain challenging to automate without sacrificing quality. In certain situations, these tasks require operators to dynamically organize their mental, perceptual, and gestural activities. In other words, skills that are not yet adequately explained and digitally modeled to allow a machine in an industrial context to reproduce them, even in an approximate manner. Some tasks in welding serve as a perfect example. Drawing from the knowledge of cognitive and developmental psychology, professional didactics, and collaborative robotics research, our work aims to find a way to digitally model manual manufacturing skills to enhance the automation of tasks that are still challenging to robotize. Using welding as an example, we seek to develop, test, and deploy a methodology transferable to other domains. The purpose of this article is to present the experimental setup used to achieve these objectives.

Keywords: Skills · Scheme · Cognition · Welding · Robotics

1 How to Analyze Skills with Psychology

Skills are critical for problem resolution, this explains why literature about this subject is abundant, notably in psychology. We can find lots of definitions about

V. G. Duffy (Ed.): HCII 2024, LNCS 14709, pp. 69–88, 2024.
https://doi.org/10.1007/978-3-031-61060-8_6

skills, but they each share four mainstays that are well summarized in Vergnaud theory [27, p. 88]. Skills are based on goals, rules to generate activity, operational invariants, and inference. When an operator, as a welder, is resolving a situation he is anticipating the evolution of the situation with and without his intervention, this is a goal. To interact with the situation, he does some action, gathers information, and controls, these rules generate an activity. He has to decide which information is pertinent and/or true, this is based on beliefs and implicit knowledge. These is operational invariants. All of this needs a computational activity from the brain to adapt to the situation, which we will name inferences. When some of these pillars are consistent from one situation to another, we obtain a scheme. Schemes are, in Vergnaud own words, *"the invariant organization of activity for a certain class of situations"* (p. 88). Hoarau [11] gives examples of activity analyses made with scheme framework, where strategies used by operators are revealed by identifying consistent control loops from one situation to another. Moreover, the scheme can be adapted for specific fields like mathematics [3].

The four elements of the scheme require consistent regulation to facilitate adaptation by the operator. Welders, for instance, must actively gather information on the current situation, enabling them to compare it with the predicted scenario. Any mismatch will trigger a need for immediate adaptive measures; cognitive or physical ones. We can observe that an operator evolves in a situation to resolve a problem, having a productive impact. At the same time, the ability to adapt to various situations while performing tasks contributes to a valuable experiential learning process, making constructive growth for the individual. These regulations can operate in a closed loop for action or a longer loop in planning, for example. Finally, a scheme can be a good way to understand skills, giving an opportunity to have a modus operandi transferable from one field to another. This modus operandi began by understanding the profession's analysis. In doing so, we can propose a set of variables and situations to analyze the four fields of the scheme. When we have measured variables in these situations, we can search for invariant organization that are schemes. These schemes are a good way to analyze and describe skills, abilities and competencies. Each of this terms describe one part of the schemes while the latter include dynamical organization and adaptation to a specific class of situations. This is why we will use the term of schemes in a way that incorporate skills, abilities and competencies.

2   Welding Variables

Studying welding revealed many parameters, around sixty, that can directly influence the bead or have an impact on the welder. We propose here a classification of these variables into the following categories: Human factors, Physico-chemical forces, Process control parameters (electrical and shielding gas), Workpiece parameters, Manipulation parameters, Filler metal parameters, and Ergonomic parameters.

The choice of current, a critical parameter in welding, significantly influences welding energy, alongside welding speed and voltage. Manually selected by the welder, it becomes our first variable to consider. However, this setting is subject to variation based on the distance between the electrode (torch) and the workpiece to be assembled, which we refer to as stick out. Similarly, the torch angle impacts the distribution of this energy. Therefore, we need to have an estimation of the torch's position and orientation concerning the workpiece.

This orientation and position are directly influenced by the welder's choices and manipulation, notably via sick-out. Estimating how the latter is precisely carried out is crucial to understanding the human-specific aspect. That's why we need to focus on the complete body movement of the welder to estimate the welding speed and the variations that may be imposed. Moreover, good welding can be obtained with several combinations of parameters since they synergize.

A major difference exists between the two welding processes we intend to study (GMAW and GTAW): the filler material deposition. In the first one, the filler metal is supplied by a melting electrode. Therefore, deposition quantity is directly linked to the welding current, nature of the filler material, and wire diameter. In GTAW, the welder manually introduces the filler metal with a filler rod: hence, they must manage the feed rate, deposition quantity, and the location of deposition (in the weld pool, in the arc, etc.).

Other choices are left to welders, although these choices are guided by standards regarding the dimensions of the parts and other constants. We particularly consider the choice of the number of passes, stops (stopping the bead and then restarting), length of filler metal exiting the GMAW nozzle before welding, and the precision applied to the preparation of parts like chamfering and grinding.

The human factor is thus crucial: an analysis of it seems relevant. We can explore the degree of investment, physical or cognitive fatigue, adaptation to discomfort related to posture or welding fumes, eye position, and reaction time.

The piece to be assembled will govern the welding parameters; therefore, the dimensions and nature of the piece materials must be specified. Among these parameters, we can also look into shielding gas, especially the nature of the gas and its flow rate. The welding to be performed will depend on the position of the two pieces to be assembled. If welding vertically, we must consider the variation of forces at play, including conduction in the metal pieces and gravity on the weld pool. All these variables are shown in Fig. 1.

The next section will introduce the measurement tools that we are considering for the study of these parameters.

3   Measuring Instruments

After defining relevant parameters, we must choose measurements guided by the question: how can a welder achieve a weld that a robot cannot?

Among the various measurement systems, we find those associated with electrical parameters. These parameters govern the supply of energy necessary for

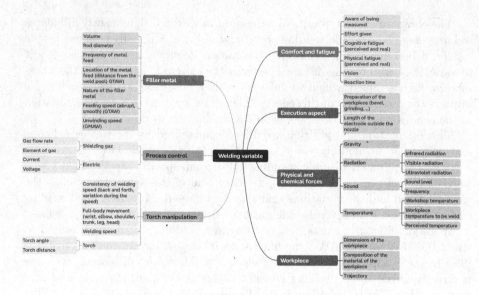

Fig. 1. Mind map of welding parameters to study

melting the edges and creating the weld: (i) Welding generator display, (ii) Voltage (as a measure of the torch/workpiece distance), and (iii) Multimeter (for current and voltage).

Welding relies on the supply of energy and, in some cases, on the supply of metal. To analyze the volume of metal supplied in GTAW, we plan to graduate the metal rods to have reference points when filming. The dimensions of the GTAW filler rod must also be documented, especially its diameter. The analysis of the filler metal can thus be carried out using: (i) Welding camera (Cavitar©[1]), (ii) Measuring wire-feed roller, and (iii) Ruler.

Next, we have a set of measurements related to the workpieces to be assembled; the dimensions of these are taken into account to define the parameters. Additionally, we can verify pre-welding modifications (chamfering, grinding), and finishing touches: (i) Surface condition (roughness), (ii) Angle protractor or Goniometer, and (iii) Ruler/caliper.

Measurements of the human body can be used for two purposes: Tracking movement and analyzing physiological functions: (i) Inertial sensors, (ii) Stopwatch (for welding speed), (iii) EEG (Electroencephalogram), (iv) ECG (Electrocardiography, (v) EMG (Electromyography), (vi) Eye-tracking, (vii) Optical motion capture, and (viii) VO2 (Oxygen consumption).

Finally, we can analyze the weld pool during welding to obtain, notably, its dimensions (width and/or thickness). Sound analysis of welding is also relevant: (i) Welding camera (Cavitar©), (ii) Laser, (iii) Microphone/acoustic sensor, and (i) Ultrasound.

---

[1] https://www.cavitar.com/applications/welding-imaging/.

Video capture can be valuable for several reasons, particularly to easily visualize information in a qualitative manner. This allows us to analyze the addition of filler metal in GTAW [17], observe variations in torch manipulation, identify body segments involved during welding, estimate arc length, and more.

To complete these measurements, a survey or interview can be developed to understand the welder's choices and gain insights into how they justify their actions and decisions.

4 Analysis of Measurement Tools

We do not intend to delve into an analysis involving machine learning or neural networks. These techniques require extensive training and, thus, a large database that we do not possess. Conversely, we prefer to focus on a detailed understanding of a small sample and describe their skills within the schemes framework.

4.1 Electrical Parameters: Process Control

Arc welding is governed by its electrical parameters, particularly current and voltage. These two parameters, combined with welding speed, allow the calculation of welding energy, an interesting indicator to understand the process evolution.

The set current is directly adjusted by the operator in the generator; however, this value fluctuates with the distance between the welding torch and the workpiece. Some welding machines offer the capability to measure this physical quantity and store it in memory, enabling precise post-analysis. This measurement can be made with a multimeter, Hall effect [17] or WeldQAS.

Voltage is in synergy with current and also varies depending on the distance between the torch and the workpiece (stick-out). Thus, this distance can be used as a control parameter on voltage by the welder during the process. Multimeter and WeldQAS can also be used to measure these quantities, especially voltage [17].

4.2 Filler Metal: A Critical Process Difference

For GMAW welding, using a consumable electrode, the filler metal's direct dependence on current ensures consistent wire feed rate. Analyzing it involves using a measuring roller integrated with the generator's unwinding rollers to derive the feed rate. Coupled with wire diameter, this yields feed volume. However, data gaps persist, notably the wire feed angle, obtainable through motion capture leveraging IMUs (Inertial Measurement Unit). Zhang [33] used IMUs to measure the inclination of GTAW's torch, but the same idea can be used in GMAW for torch and filler metal.

In GTAW, the welder manually holds the filler rod, rendering measuring roller use impractical. Some motion capture methods are disqualified as they disrupt the filler rod's weight and the welder, presenting challenges for analysis. However, nearby cameras can effectively capture filler metal angle and frequency. Although the uniform filler rod makes added metal volume inconspicuous, graduation is considered for visual assistance in video, aiding feed volume calculation.

We will use a welding camera to measure these angles based on [17] and more parameters such as frequency or transfer mode [23, 24].

4.3   Sound: A Characteristic Emission

The welding process produces noise during the operation, dependent on numerous parameters, both in the audible range and inaudible acoustic emissions, as reported by [30]. Some welders seem to use this sound as an indicator [17, 22, 29]. Although the sound may vary significantly based on the nature and thickness of the workpieces to be welded, the welder may adapt and use it as an indicator to regulate the process. [30], particularly caution on the microphone angle and gas flow. Therefore, we consider the study of sound relevant and will use a microphone during our experiments. The parameters studied will include the frequencies and amplitudes of the sound signal; frequency domain analysis using a Fourier transform is also relevant, as shown by [22, 30].

Some people propose estimating the depth (penetration) of the weld pool based on sound, as demonstrated by [21]. Sound appears to be an interesting possibility for real-time control of the welding process [16]. Sound offers valuable characteristics for studying the welder's schemes, dimensions of the weld pool, and has a high potential for automating certain tasks currently not feasible for robots. Therefore, sound analysis is highly recommended.

4.4   Temperature: Anticipating Cooling

The workpiece temperature, coupled with the cooling time, governs the metallurgical structure of the weld bead; these details can be found in phase diagrams. These diagrams predict the phases obtained after thermodynamic equilibrium based on temperature and the chemical composition of the alloy. Temperature is a critical parameter depending on the welding energy supplied, material nature, and the environment.

The measurement of temperature in welding is described in the standard ISO 13916 [12], which mandates measuring the temperature at a specific distance from the weld bead. Various measurement tools are available with different levels of precision, including: (i) Thermosensitive products (e.g., pencils or paints) (TS), (ii) Contact thermometer (CT), (iii) Thermocouple (TE), and (iv) Optical or electrical devices for non-contact measurements (TB).

In our case, the electric arc in the GTAW process reaches 3000 °C in a room temperature environment; metals will rise to around 300 °C. With such a wide measurement range, we cannot expect high precision. We can still measure the temperature of the bead for some information with optical measurement. Temperature can, indeed, be a way for an operator to analyze the welding process (directly or indirectly).

5   Weld Pool Dimensions: A Visible Factor for the Welder

The weld pool represents the liquid part of the workpieces being assembled, with a very high light intensity; it is the most visible element, perhaps the only one, that the welder sees during the process. Its dimensions directly influence the shape of the weld bead since it's forming during its cooling.

Dimensions include the visible surface and the penetration depth. Applying too much energy in one area risks melting the piece throughout its thickness and creating a hole. It can be an interesting element to measure. However, the strong contrasts imposed by the weld pool and ambient lighting make video measurements challenging. We will explore different approaches.

5.1   Laser Measurements

Laser techniques analyze light diffraction to measure the surface dimensions of a weld pool [2,14]. However, articles often neglect weld pool penetration analysis. Ensuring data continuity, particularly in-depth, is challenging; analyzing weld bead thickness is feasible, but penetration rate assessment remains elusive. The technique lacks portability and exhibits variable performance. This method is expensive, complex to implement, and appears irrelevant to our study, considering its drawbacks.

5.2   Ultrasonic Measurements

Ultrasonics can be used to determine weld pool dimensions, especially its depth [2,10] mention several articles using this technique, particularly to obtain weld pool depth. However, the heating of the workpiece and sensors limits the use for real-time (in-line) process control. Ultrasonics are effective in determining boundaries between states of matter in a welding process. Ultrasonics can also be coupled with a laser system described earlier [18], or with data such as intensity, voltage, or sound. Finally, studies on weld beads using ultrasonic techniques are generally proposed to detect common defects.

5.3   Camera Measurements

Cameras are very sensitive to strong contrasts, as mentioned; however, it is interesting to note that image processing can be used to obtain weld pool images. We mentioned Weez-U Welding©, which use a camera mounted on the robot to capture multiple successive images with different intensity filters before compiling them. Some authors use high-speed cameras with significant magnification to observe weld pool solidification [4,5]. Some cameras offer direct filtering to observe through the arc radiation; this is notably the case with the Cavitar ©, which can help measure the dimensions of the weld pool. Since we can use Cavitar to measure the angle of the filler rod and torch with the workpiece, we can use it to measure the dimensions of the weld pool.

6   Operator Motion Capture

We aim to compare two elements: what the welder precisely executes and what justifies their actions. This involves studying the welder's movements to understand the welding speed, selected intensity, regularity of the motion, etc. These details are then compared with the reasons behind the actions, exploring why a variation in movement occurs at a specific moment and what information is perceived. Analyzing the operator's beliefs and knowledge is crucial, considering both implicit and explicit dimensions.

Among the various measurement instruments, we have particularly focused on motion capture. The welder's movements reflect decisions, personality, and the ability to interact with the environment to adapt to a situation. In our case, the situation involves performing an electric arc weld, a specialized process where the quality of the result is not directly observable. Moreover, the electric arc produces intense visible radiation and electromagnetic disturbances. It is essential to keep this in mind when analyzing measurement tools.

To capture human body movement, we need the orientation and position of different body segments to estimate joint angles. Tools considered for this purpose include:

- Optical motion capture: the reflection of infrared light (wavelength greater than 800 nm) on passive markers to calculate the spatial position of markers. This system ensures high precision.
- IMU: a system consisting of an accelerometer and a gyroscope to measure acceleration and angular velocity, respectively. These data are then used to calculate the spatial position and orientation of a segment to which the IMU is attached. They are known for their high acquisition frequency and reasonable cost.
- RGB video: standard color video (Red Green Blue) that can be used to define the outlines of a subject. It can be coupled with an infrared camera to provide more information on the distance between a subject and the camera; this is then referred to as a depth camera. It combines ease of implementation and reasonable cost.
- Depth camera: estimation of the distance to an object using stereographic vision (double camera). Some depth cameras use infrared radiation, similar to optical motion capture. It allows reproducing movement in a three-dimensional environment.

6.1   Optical Motion Capture

Motion capture involves a set of cameras (transmitter/receiver) emitting light in near-infrared (IR) (wavelength 820 nm). The arc welding radiation spectrum is primarily in the visible range and extends into the UV. However, there are emissions in the IR range, with a peak observed at 817 nm, which may introduce noise into our tools. More information on radiation is available in articles by [8, 25, 31].

Optical motion capture is currently used in welding with virtual or augmented reality environments [19, 20]. The limitation we can highlight is the virtual aspect of welding, relying on models that may not be as precise as reality. An article by [6] proposes performing this measurement by creating occlusion between the cameras and the arc using an opaque box based on measurements made by [7]. However, these measurements suffer from data loss and noise due to radiation.

We conducted experiments to observe the impact of the welding process on optical motion capture measurements with a SmartTrack 3/M from ART. This tool is a portable motion capture camera, easily transportable in a workshop. The major drawback of this tool is its limit to 4 markers.

We tried to estimate the noise made by the electric arc on motion and IMU. Therefore, we decided to place two markers as fixed references on a linear support on the table. These two markers will be named body #0 and #1. Another one was used for measure and get placed on the Weez-U© robot arm. This one will be named body #2. The experiment involved linear motion with torch ignition at the midpoint and a constant speed. The aim was to confirm data linearity by monitoring any mid-displacement variations, ensuring no interference from the electric arc. Moreover, our fixed reference (body #0 and body #1) should be measured during the whole welding process.

Figure 2 illustrates the position according to a Cartesian coordinate system located at the center of the camera for the three present references. The trials measure the robot's positioning throughout the trajectory, unaffected by torch ignition. However, for the two fixed bodies, we observe a loss of vision (characterized by the return of positions to 0). This effect is not systematic during the trials.

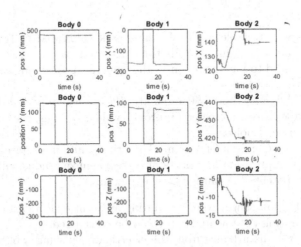

Fig. 2. Welding arc noise test measurements on optical motion capture

In conclusion, these trials indicate good measurement stability after arc ignition if detection is ensured. However, some markers may experience occlusion if close to the axis between the camera and the electric arc, with the arc's radiation hindering marker detection. The solution appears viable, but careful attention should be paid to the camera's placement relative to the welder.

A new trial was conducted to measure the welder's arm movements. We placed a marker on the forearm and another on the same arm of the operator. We calibrated a new sensor, placing it out of the field of vision to check for possible spurious detection.

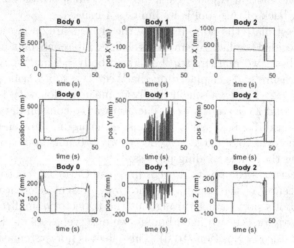

Fig. 3. Results of capturing the movement of a welding arm

The results are available in Fig. 3. The absent calibrated body is body #1; we observe its detection due to radiation produced by the electric arc. This emphasizes the need to pay attention to the camera's positioning relative to the welder and the workpiece.

The other two bodies (body #0 and body #2) are generally well-detected, but body #0 is temporarily undetected (approximately 5 s). Thus, the arc introduces a significant source of noise.

Combined with the limit of four markers, this solution, despite its considerable advantages in precision and portability, seems incongruous with our objectives. However, potential avenues can be explored:

1. To address the low sensor count, acquiring an additional SmartTrack camera and synchronizing data acquisition could be considered.
2. To mitigate the disturbance from the electric arc, placing a band-pass filter in front of the lenses is an option. However, this may introduce optical path drift and data blurring. Additionally, as the arc and camera radiation are close, the band-pass filter doesn't guarantee satisfactory results.

6.2   Inertial Measurement Units (IMUs)

Inertial Measurement Units employ a gyroscope and an accelerometer to provide angular velocity and acceleration of a body. This theoretically enables obtaining a segment's position through double integration of accelerometer data and its orientation through gyroscope data integration. However, the high sensibility of IMU makes acceleration data subject to noise. IMU are also used to obtain angle by measuring the acceleration of gravitation and coupling with data from the gyroscope by signal processing.

Some researchers utilize these measurement tools in welding, including [32,33]. To assess IMU immunity to the measurement environment, we coupled the SmartTrack experiment with an inertial sensor attached to the Weez-U© arm. The sensor is positioned on a segment further from the torch for ease of implementation using an existing strap.

Similar to the initial observation with optical motion capture, no variations are observed during arc ignition. Although the trajectory is coded for constant speed, we note jerks attributed to the robot's architecture.

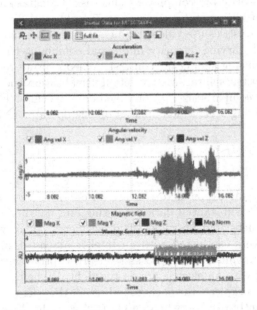

Fig. 4. Inertial measurements with acceleration, angular velocity, and magnetic field according to a Cartesian reference.

On Fig. 4 we observe significant angular velocity and acceleration noise when the torch ignites, initially attributed to the magnetic field, but now believed to be the robot's vibrations during welding.

A follow-up experiment with the IMU on both a table and the floor aimed to confirm this hypothesis. The goal was to check if displacement was measured while the sensor was stationary. On the table, during arc ignition (identified by the magnetometer), the accelerometer displayed a highly noisy signal. On the floor, these signals were absent, demonstrating the sensor's immunity to disturbances from the electric arc.

Inertial Measurement Units appear promising for capturing human body movement. For a complete body, 15 sensors are necessary (head, neck, lumbar, two arms, two forearms, two hands, two thighs, two shins, two feet). Manufacturers offer suits providing joint data directly from these measurements, such as Movella© (with Xsens IMUs) or Teslasuit©, the latter potentially suitable for comprehensive testing.

6.3   RBG Video

Traditional camera video is qualitatively valuable and can be used quantitatively by outlining the operator's contour for posture analysis, especially with a depth camera. However, this application is usually used in classification more than precise measurement of articulation's angle. Moreover, the intense light interference from the electric arc complicates this task. Cameras can provide additional insights into filler metal management or weld pool dimensions. Despite challenges, some industries use videos with extensive processing, capturing successive images with varying intensity filters and combining them to retain relevant portions, reducing significant contrast. Video capture remains beneficial for qualitative aspects, facilitating easy action visualization and data processing validation through comparisons with obtained data graphics. They can be used to take all the working scenes or be placed on the operator to have his field of view.

6.4   Depth Camera

The depth camera was explored to capture an operator's contours and movements. This involves substantial data processing and multiple cameras to estimate the three-dimensional positions of all segments, along with the risk of occlusions. Tests were conducted with an Intel RealSense D400 camera using stereoscopy. The two images in Fig. 5 show depth capture without an electric arc on the left and with an electric arc on the right. While the quality is good, distinguishing the workpiece, the background robot, the operator, and the torch, the image significantly distorts when an electric arc is lit. Despite its interest, this technology lacks precision and is affected by electric arc noise, rendering it unsuitable for our study.

6.5   Measurement by Force Sensors/Pressure Plate

A force plate is a tool in the form of a thin platform placed on the ground. It provides information on the distribution of forces and moments applied to support surfaces, offering an estimate of the subject's center of gravity changes while moving on it. Mainly used in gait analysis, these plates show the temporal

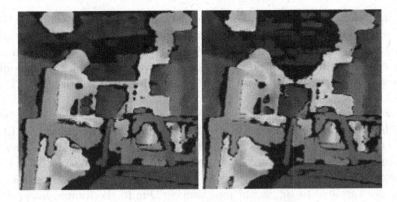

Fig. 5. Depth camera scan difference with (left) and without (right) electric arc

evolution of vertical forces, providing insights into gesture deviation, direction, and balance. While redundant if we have access to the welder's complete motion, these plates can offer valuable information about the welder's balance and positional changes during welding but the welder needs to get on it during the process.

6.6   Summary of Motion Capture Measurements

Motion capture is dominated by optical techniques with passive markers. While highly precise, this technology requires large spaces with numerous cameras. The arc's radiation interferes with measurement wavelengths, introducing noise and occluding markers despite precautions [6,7]. We utilized a portable Smart-Track 3 motion capture; despite its precision, the limitation to four markers is a significant drawback. If access to a complete room becomes available, we may reconsider this solution; currently, it is not feasible. Inertial sensors are cost-effective and offer high acquisition frequency and sensitivity. Though susceptible to noise, they provide precise data, making them relevant for our study [1,9]. Additional force plates can complement the setup. These techniques can also yield information on the torch's orientation and position.

7   Physiological Measurements: The Body's Response

Physiological measurements encompass signals from the body's electrical activity (muscles – EMG, heart – ECG, brain – EEG), eye movements (gaze tracking), oxygen consumption, emotional responses, etc. While some are valuable for user interface development, in our context, most won't provide significant information.

7.1   Measurements of Physiological Electrical Signals

The analysis of muscular activity helps determine the muscles used in a gesture, providing a more detailed analysis of the movement and revealing associated muscle fatigue. Brain activity reveals cognitive load and the regions involved during an action, highlighting the preferential processing of one piece of information over another (approximately). Heart activity provides information on a person's stress; being also linked to physical activity, this complex data requires correlation with other information. Although it offers relevant details, it is not essential.

These three activities can be measured using the electrical signals produced by the human body: (i) EEG: Electroencephalogram for the brain, (ii) ECG: Electrocardiogram for the heart, and (iii) EMG: Electromyogram for the muscles.

However, the generated intensities are low and highly influenced by the sensor's proximity to the skin. Additionally, electromagnetic disturbances from the welding arc can lead to significant interference. Due to the limited information provided by physiological measurements, their sensitivity to noise, and the substantial data processing required, we believe their use is not necessary.

7.2   Gaze Tracking

The gaze tracking system, utilizing infrared oculometry, recalibrates the gaze direction on a video obtained from a camera located on the nose's edge. Some glasses supplement these data with a gyroscope to provide head orientation. Gaze tracking can offer valuable insights into an operator's behavior, revealing visual cues in the environment and providing information on cognitive information processing through fixation duration and gaze scanning rate. In our case, we aim to determine the gaze position concerning the weld pool's location, understanding whether the operator looks before or after the pool, fixates on it, or maintains a constant scan. However, the protective hood against the welding arc's light poses a challenge to using this technology, limiting its application in our study. Despite having oculometric data, we lack a detailed image, only obtaining a luminous point surrounded by darkness.

An attempt was made using Tobii Proglasses 2, provided by the University of Nantes. The camera quality remains good until the welding hood is worn. At that moment, the video becomes less usable and completely unworkable when the electric arc is initiated. Several possibilities could enable the use of this technique:

1. Modify the protective glass: Creating a protective glass with two different filter intensities, a weaker filter in front of the camera and a standard one for the eyes.
2. Utilize the gyroscope: Before initiating the arc, the trajectory can be identified based on the gap between the parts to be welded. Head tilt variations can be used to align the trajectory, considering the weld pool at the center of this line.
3. Move the camera: Placing the camera on the other side of the filtering glass may provide a clearer image; additional video processing might make the video usable.

The first hypothesis poses safety risks if not executed correctly, and video quality might not guarantee to observe part positions. The second hypothesis is sensitive to gyroscope data drift. The third hypothesis involves challenges such as the difference in the field of view between the camera and eyes, along with data processing difficulties.

Eye tracking is used in welding, especially in conjunction with virtual reality. Despite the potential benefits of eye-tracking measurements, ensuring effective utilization of this measurement tool cannot be guaranteed.

8   Summary and Conclusion of the Measurement Tools

In summary, considering all the measurement tools mentioned here and their potential use for studying the welder's schemes, we propose a matrix of possible utilization (see Table 1). This matrix indicates whether a measurement tool is applicable (yes or no) in our case. If a tool is considered feasible under certain conditions, we may note "perhaps" with an explanation.

Within these parameters, we can identify which one matches with a cognitive aspect of skills, meaning one pillar of the scheme. Consider, for instance, the electric parameters that an operator can set, embodying a prescribed rule of action. By examining the correlation between a torch manipulation reaction and the weld pool dimension, we identify an inference mechanism at play. Time reaction being unknown, we have to be careful when we analyze data. Through collaborative discussions with the operator and meticulous comparisons with other parameters, we can find and derive goals and operational invariants. This intricate analysis provides valuable insights into the interplay of cognitive skills and their manifestation within the defined framework.

9   Survey and Interview: A Subjective Measure of the Rationale of the Operator

To gather the operator's insights, especially to understand the rationale behind their actions, we can utilize a survey or conduct an interview. However, a drawback of using a survey is its restrictive nature, providing limited freedom for the operator's responses and potentially directing them in a particular direction. This limitation could subsequently constrain the depth of the analysis we can perform.

Several interview techniques are available. Our objective is to comprehend the reasons behind specific actions, and for this purpose, Pierre Vermersch's explicitation interview appears most suitable [28]. However, this method is acknowledged for its complexity in implementation, requiring training in interview techniques. Another equally interesting and easier-to-implement method is autoconfrontation.

Autoconfrontation, a commonly used technique, involves using traces, including videos, to place an operator back into the action situation, allowing them to

Table 1. Summary of the measurement tools applicability in our study

Measurement Tool	Applicable in our study	Under conditions	Not applicable	Comments
Welding display	X			
Cavitar©	X			
Non-contact thermometer	X			
ECG			X	
EEG			X	
EMG			X	
Eye tracking		X		Maybe with adaptation of the protective glass
Measuring roller	X			Applicable in GMAW, not in GTAW
IMU	X			
Laser		X		Expensive
Micro/acoustic sensor	X			Noise and risk of occlusion
Motion capture		X		
Multimeter	X			
Oscilloscope	X			
Pressure platform		X		Accurate measurements would require coverage over a substantial area.
Thermosensitive product	X			Not very precise
Survey	X			
Ruler/caliper	X			
Thermocouple		X		Can be done if pre-welded
Contact thermometer		X		Does not allow real-time study
Ultrasonics		X		
Video	X			Caution about what is intended to be measured
Welding speed	X			
VO2			X	Little interest

explain their gestures [26]. Another method is the double instruction, aiming to prompt individuals to assume the role of an instructor to explain their profession [15].

Interview techniques focus the interviewee's attention on specific aspects, such as action realization with video support in autoconfrontation, precise and non-generalized actions in the explicitation interview, and pedagogical debate in the case of double instruction. The importance of pauses remains central in these techniques. As this report concentrates on objective measurements, we won't delve further into these interview techniques.

10 Proposed Experimental Protocol

We propose creating a reference piece for a group of welders. This piece should encompass various situations, easily adaptable into a few variants (thickness and material), and representative of many mechanized welding production processes. To achieve this, we present the piece in Fig. 6.

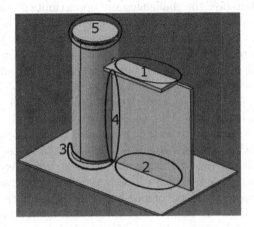

Fig. 6. Reference piece to be used in the experimental protocol

This part incorporates the following situations (positions according to ISO 6947 [13]:

1. Angle at the ceiling – plate against plate (position PD)
2. Flat angle – plate against plate (position PB)
3. Flat angle – tube against plate (position PB)
4. Vertical ascending angle – tube against plate (position PF)
5. Flat angle – tube against tube (position PB - external)

The welder will have at his disposal all the necessary sheets and tubes accompanied by the technical drawing of this reference part. We propose to manufacture this piece with three different thicknesses: 2 mm, 4 mm, and 6 mm. A second piece may be produced in a subsequent trial to analyze edge-to-edge welds, especially in GTAW welding, to observe a task that is challenging for automation.

Before carrying out the welds, we will equip the welders with a set of inertial sensors to obtain the orientation of body segments (arms, forearms, torso, etc.). These inertial sensors can be incorporated into a suit (Teslasuit© or Movella©, or using IMUs with custom coding). We will focus on joint amplitudes, particularly those of the upper limbs, directing our attention to torch manipulation speed, pause times, and back-and-forth movements.

We will add a set of sensors to the work environment: (i) Non-contact thermometer (infrared) to measure temperature, (ii) A microphone to analyze sound,

(iii) A welding camera (Cavitar©) to analyze the fusion pool with filler metal and stick-out, (iv) An RGB camera to qualitatively analyze the complete body movement and provide a record of the activity, (v) Inertial measurement units to capture movements.

After completing the weld, we suggest conducting an exchange with the welder in the form of an interview to analyze the reasons behind their actions and understand their activity.

This article underscores the challenges and opportunities related to assessing welders' schemes in a welding environment. The interference of the electric arc (light, electromagnetic field, etc.) on most measurement tools justifies comparing objective indicators, such as sound and temperature, alongside subjective evaluations through self-confrontation interviews [26]. Our proposed approach involves analyzing welders' movements and reactions using objective measures like sound and temperature in various representational situations provided in a reference workpiece (see Fig. 6). Our analysis will focus on identifying the control loop made by welders to operate a regulation during the welding process. The goal is to identify invariant organizational aspects across multiple situations, reflecting their schemes. By examining welders' movements and reactions with objective data, we aim to gain a comprehensive understanding of their schemes and develop a model encompassing all facets of their expertise. This model aspires to address current technical limitations faced by robots in specific tasks by incorporating human gestures and cognitive aspects of skills.

11   Conclusions and Future Work

The workforce in industries, including welders, constitutes the core of Industry 5.0, yet understanding the principles behind their skills poses challenges. In this article, we propose a set of measures to explore the reasoning behind each decision made by welders. Acknowledging the numerous variables influencing the welding process, we aim to identify critical ones used by welders, recognizing the presence of implicit skills, described within schemes framework.

Measuring a welder's movement is crucial but is a time-consuming step. Inertial Measurement Units (IMUs) offer a suitable compromise, despite requiring signal processing. While the weld pool dimensions are critical, measuring them poses challenges.

This article primarily centers on welding, yet the methodology employed here can be applicable to various professions. In summary, individuals seeking to analyze schemes must comprehend the intricacies of the job to determine multiple representative situations. Within these scenarios, it is imperative to select variables relevant to the operator. Then we have to measure them. Throughout the data analysis process, emphasis should be placed on identifying control loops that connect perception and action. Upon identification of these loops, it is crucial to verify their consistency across different situations. The organizational constants revealed through this process are indicative of the skills.

References

1. Ahmad, N., Ghazilla, R.A.R., Khairi, N.M., Kasi, V.: Reviews on various inertial measurement unit (IMU) sensor applications. Int. J. Signal Process. Syst. **1**(2), 256–262 (2013)
2. Alvarez Bestard, G.A., Absi Alfaro, S.C.: Measurement and estimation of the weld bead geometry in arc welding processes: the last 50 years of development. J. Braz. Soc. Mech. Sci. Eng. **40**(9), 444 (2018)
3. Charron, C.: Conceptualization of fractions and categorization of problems for adolescents. Eur. J. Psychol. Educ. **17**(2), 115–128 (2002)
4. Chiocca, A.: Etude de l'influence des écoulements dans le bain de fusion sur les mécanismes de solidification en soudage sur l'alliage Cu30Ni. Ph.D. thesis, Université Montpellier (2016)
5. Delapp, D., Cook, G., Strauss, A., Hofmeister, W.: Quantitative observations of surface flow and solidification on autogenous GTA weld pools. In: ASM Proceedings of the International Conference: Trends in Welding Research, vol. 2005, pp. 97–102 (2005)
6. Erden, M.S., Tomiyama, T.: Identifying welding skills for training and assistance with robot. Sci. Technol. Weld. Joining **14**(6), 523–532 (2009)
7. van Essen, J., et al.: Identifying welding skills for robot assistance. In: 2008 IEEE/ASME International Conference on Mechtronic and Embedded Systems and Applications, pp. 437–442 (2008)
8. Gourzoulidis, G.A., et al.: Photobiological hazards in shielded metal arc welding. Physica Med. **106**, 102520 (2023)
9. Gu, C., Lin, W., He, X., Zhang, L., Zhang, M.: IMU-based motion capture system for rehabilitation applications: a systematic review. Biomimetic Intell. Robot. **3**(2), 100097 (2023)
10. Hardt, D., Katz, J., et al.: Ultrasonic measurement of weld penetration. Weld. J. **63**(9), 273s–281s (1984)
11. Hoarau, M., Charron, C., Mars, F.: Revealing misleading schemes through operator activity analysis: a factory case study. Hum. Factors Ergon. Manuf. Serv. Industr. **28**(6), 360–371 (2018)
12. ISO 13916: Soudage—Mesurage de la température de préchauffage, de la température entre passes et de la température de maintien du préchauffage (2018)
13. ISO 6947: Soudage et techniques connexes—Positions de soudage (2019)
14. Kovacevic, R., Zhang, Y.M.: Sensing free surface of arc weld pool using specular reflection: principle and analysis. Proc. Inst. Mech. Eng. Part B: J. Eng. Manuf. **210**(6), 553–564 (1996)
15. Lainé, A., Mayen, P.: Chapitre 9 - L'instruction au sosie. In: Valoriser le potentiel d'apprentissage des expériences professionnelles, pp. 103–120. Praxis (Eduter Ingénierie), Éducagri éditions, Dijon cedex (2019)
16. Lv, N., Chen, S.: Investigation on acoustic signals for on-line monitoring of welding. In: Tarn, T.J., Chen, S.B., Fang, G. (eds.) Robotic Welding, Intelligence and Automation. Lecture Notes in Electrical Engineering, vol. 88, pp. 235–243. Springer, Heidelberg (2011). https://doi.org/10.1007/978-3-642-19959-2_29
17. Manorathna, P., Marimuthu, S., Justham, L., Jackson, M.: Human behaviour capturing in manual tungsten inert gas welding for intelligent automation. Proc. Inst. Mech. Eng. Part B: J. Eng. Manuf. **231**(9), 1619–1627 (2017)
18. Mi, B., Ume, C.: Real-time weld penetration depth monitoring with laser ultrasonic sensing system. J. Manuf. Sci. Eng.-Trans. Asme **128** (2006)

19. Mueller, F., Deuerlein, C., Koch, M.: Intuitive welding robot programming via motion capture and augmented reality. IFAC-PapersOnLine **52**(10), 294–299 (2019)
20. Ong, S.K., Yew, A.W.W., Thanigaivel, N.K., Nee, A.Y.C.: Augmented reality-assisted robot programming system for industrial applications. Robot. Comput.-Integr. Manuf. **61**, 101820 (2020)
21. Pal, K., Pal, S.K.: Monitoring of weld penetration using arc acoustics. Mater. Manuf. Process. **26**(5), 684–693 (2011)
22. Saini, D., Floyd, S.: An investigation of gas metal arc welding sound signature for on-line quality control. Weld. J.-New York **77**, 172–s (1998)
23. Gonçalves e Silva, R.H., Correa Riffel, K., Pompermaier Okuyama, M., Dalpiaz, G.: Effect of dynamic wire in the GTAW process. J. Mater. Process. Technol. **269**, 91–101 (2019)
24. Silwal, B., Santangelo, M.: Effect of vibration and hot-wire gas tungsten arc (GTA) on the geometric shape. J. Mater. Process. Technol. **251**, 138–145 (2018)
25. Tenkate, T.D.: Optical radiation hazards of welding arcs. Rev. Environ. Health **13**(3), 131–146 (1998)
26. Theureau, J.: Les entretiens d'autoconfrontation et de remise en situation par les traces matérielles et le programme de recherche cours d'action. Rev. d'anthropologie connaissances **4,2**(2), 287–322 (2010)
27. Vergnaud, G.: The theory of conceptual fields. Hum. Dev. **52**(2), 83–94 (2009)
28. Vermersch, P.: L'entretien d'explicitation. Psychologies & psychothérapies, ESF sciences humaines, Paris, 9e éd. 2019 edn. (2019)
29. Wang, J.F., Yu, H.D., Qian, Y.Z., Yang, R.Z., Chen, S.B.: Feature extraction in welding penetration monitoring with arc sound signals. Proc. Inst. Mech. Eng. Part B: J. Eng. Manuf. **225**(9), 1683–1691 (2011)
30. Wang, J., Chen, B., Chen, H., Chen, S.: Analysis of arc sound characteristics for gas tungsten argon welding. Sens. Rev. **29**(3), 240–249 (2009)
31. Weglowski, M.: Investigation on the electric arc light emission in TIG welding. Int. J. Comput. Mater. Sci. Surf. Eng. **1** (2007)
32. Zhang, G., Shi, Y., Gu, Y., Fan, D.: Welding torch attitude-based study of human welder interactive behavior with weld pool in GTAW. Robot. Comput.-Integr. Manuf. **48**, 145–156 (2017)
33. Zhang, W., Xiao, J., Chen, H., Zhang, Y.: Measurement of three-dimensional welding torch orientation for manual arc welding process. Meas. Sci. Technol. **25**(3), 035010 (2014)

Measuring Fatigue Dynamics of Augmented Reality in the Digital Learning Era Using Motion Capture Data

Varun Pulipati[1], Jung Hyup Kim[2(✉)], Fang Wang[3], Siddarth Mohanty[2], Danielle Oprean[4], Madeline Easley[2], and Kangwon Seo[2]

[1] Department of Electrical Engineering and Computer Science, University of Missouri, Columbia, MO 65211, USA
vpccn@umsystem.edu

[2] Department of Industrial and Systems Engineering, University of Missouri, Columbia, MO 65211, USA
{kijung,smdqv,mge6pp,seoka}@missouri.edu

[3] Department of Engineering and Information Technology, University of Missouri, Columbia, MO 65211, USA
wangfan@missouri.edu

[4] Schoolof Information Science Learning Technologies, University of Missouri, Columbia, MO 65211, USA
opreand@missouri.edu

Abstract. In this digital learning era, Augmented Reality (AR) has become a significant driver of innovative user experience. However, the ergonomic implications of AR, particularly regarding the postural fatigue dynamics, have not been comprehensively addressed. This study investigates the correlation between prolonged AR engagement and the onset of postural fatigue, characterized by a backward shift in the center of mass (COM). Employing motion capture technology alongside cognitive load assessment tools such as the NASA Task Load Index and HoloLens eye-tracking, we seek to quantify the relationship between user posture, engagement duration, and perceived workload. We hypothesize that an observable rearward displacement of COM signifies escalating fatigue levels. The methodology integrates ergonomic analysis, biomechanics, and predictive modeling. Preliminary findings indicate a decline in postural stability with increased AR exposure, reinforcing the need for ergonomics interventions. This study underscores the necessity of ergonomic consideration in the design and use of AR systems to safeguard user well-being in educational settings.

Keywords: Augmented Reality · Motion Capture · Predictive Analysis · Data Analysis

1 Introduction

The ascent of AR as a cornerstone of modern technological advancement is rooted in its rich history of development. From its early inception as a novel concept in the 1960s to its sophisticated implementation in contemporary devices [1], AR has consistently

V. G. Duffy (Ed.): HCII 2024, LNCS 14709, pp. 89–100, 2024.
https://doi.org/10.1007/978-3-031-61060-8_7

expanded the horizons of user interaction. Despite its prolific growth, the intersection of AR and ergonomics [2] and workload remains a nascent area of inquiry. The implications of AR on society are manifold. In educational settings, AR presents opportunities for immersive learning [3] but also poses possible workload effects during prolonged use [4]. In healthcare, AR can transform patient care yet may also contribute to professional fatigue if ergonomic risks are not mitigated. The entertainment industry, meanwhile, thrives on the allure of AR's immersive experiences but seldom acknowledges the potential for user discomfort and strain. It is within this broader societal context that our research acquires its urgent relevance.

Our hypothesis posits that prolonged engagement with AR technology induces fatigue and tiredness in users, a phenomenon that can be observed and quantified through motion capture data. We theorize that as users interact with AR over extended periods, there will be discernible changes in their physical movements and postures, indicative of increasing fatigue levels. Our study aims to thoroughly test this hypothesis, seeking to establish a clear link to the ergonomic behavior of AR exposure.

Our approach to studying fatigue dynamics in AR involves drawing from deep interdisciplinary knowledge. We apply biomechanical principles to analyze the subtle nuances of human movement within AR environments. Through motion capture technology, we glean high-fidelity data that reveal the intricacies of human posture as users engage with AR. Concurrently, physical load informs our use of the NASA TLX [5], allowing us to map the workload placed on users during AR tasks [6]. The inclusion of eye-tracking data from HoloLens devices adds a layer of depth to our understanding of user engagement, enabling us to correlate visual attention to direction with postural changes.

Our initial findings show the trend toward decreased postural stability during AR learning. This study enables us to quantify the dynamics of fatigue experienced during AR learning by utilizing motion capture data. Through this approach, our objective is to concentrate on significantly enhancing user comfort and safety in the development of upcoming AR learning settings.

2 Methodology

2.1 Experimental Design

In this study, a quasi-experimental design [7] was utilized to assess an Augmented Reality (AR)-based interactive learning system, specifically tailored to augment engineering education [8–11]. This innovative system comprised fifteen 3D scenes, thoroughly crafted in Unity. These scenes were split across two biomechanics lectures, with seven scenes in the first lecture and eight in the second. Intriguingly, the lectures were displayed on Microsoft HoloLens 2, where scenes would dynamically pop up based on the participant's location, pre-configured with a naming convention numbered from 1 to 8 to facilitate easy navigation and association. They were presented on a semi-circular virtual blackboard, forming part of an immersive learning environment. This environment was organized into five distinct panels: Central, Left-central, Right-central, Left, and Right. Each panel displayed unique information, contributing to a comprehensive educational experience, encompassing teaching methodologies, problem-solving techniques, and visual representation of concepts as shown in Fig. 1.

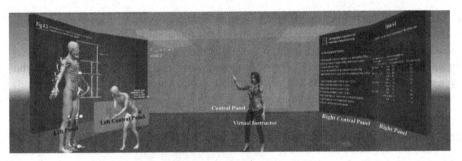

Fig. 1. Labelled 3D scene of an AR module built with unity.

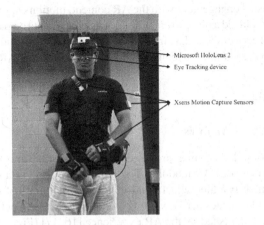

Fig. 2. Equipped Hardware components.

Participants in the study were equipped with advanced technological tools, including the Microsoft HoloLens 2 [12], Xsens Motion Capture sensors [13], D-lab Eye Tracking (see Fig. 2), and a screen to display questionnaires. The experiment also featured Location Tracking, which was attached to the participants' tables. These tables are designated for placing laptops that contain experimental questionnaires. Prior to the commencement of the experiment, participants underwent a thorough orientation session, which involved a training module designed to acquaint them with the experiment's components and processes.

The AR system's features were notably advanced. A 3D animated virtual instructor, powered by the Xsens motion capture system and Murf AI, facilitated realistic movements and natural-sounding voice synthesis. The Microsoft HoloLens 2, enhanced with the Microsoft Mixed Reality Toolkit 3, enabled spatial interactions and eye-tracking, capturing crucial data like user gaze points and interaction times with virtual objects. Spatial navigation and AR scene activation were adeptly managed using the Q-Track NFER system [14], which included a router, locator receiver, positioning sensor, and software. This setup allowed the system to respond dynamically to the user's real-time location. In place of traditional paper-based methods, an online questionnaire system was integrated into the AR environment, ensuring an uninterrupted user experience.

The study's participants consisted of 21 undergraduate engineering students. They received comprehensive training on using the HoloLens and navigating the AR environment. Each Unity scene, corresponding to a specific lecture segment, was deployed as an independent AR application. Participants navigated through these scenes, with the system tracking their location and gestures (recognized via Xsens motion capture data) used for system navigation and interaction.

2.2 Data Collection

This section details the collection of various types of data essential for the study. It includes the process of capturing eye-tracking data using Microsoft HoloLens 2 to analyze participants' visual engagement with the AR content, motion capture data using the Xsens system, which played a pivotal role in collecting precise data on participants' physical movements, and performance data from the post-assessment questionnaire providing critical insights into the learning outcomes and effectiveness of the AR system.

3 Data Analysis

3.1 Postural Dynamics Analysis

The Analysis of Postural Dynamics provided a detailed insight into how participants physically interacted with the AR modules. Through the detailed visualization of Center of Mass (COM), which is a theoretical point where the total mass of the body is concentrated [15], and coordinates across various modules, we could discern the subtleties of balance and stability affected by the AR experience [16, 17] (Fig. 3).

Utilizing the motion capture data, we plotted the deviations of the individual's COM positions (x, y, z) from the overall average for each module. Plots (see Fig. 4) illustrated these deviations, showing a clear variance in participant postures across different modules. For instance, the deviations in the 'COM pos x' occasionally showed a substantial divergence from the average, suggesting lateral shifts in balance that could indicate a reaction [18] to the content or an ergonomic response to the AR environment. Additionally, we plotted the COM position against time for each axis (x, y, z) in a series of line graphs. These plots revealed patterns over time, such as whether there was a trend towards increased deviation, which might be associated with fatigue or discomfort as the participants progressed through the modules.

To explore the link between physical demand and variations in the COM, the study compared the deviations of the COM from a baseline posture for each module. This baseline posture refers to the initial stance of the participant when they begin interacting with the AR module. It supported a deeper analysis of postural dynamics, offering quantifiable evidence of how the AR system impacted physical engagement. Variations in COM deviations suggested that certain modules may impose more physical demands on participants, leading to more pronounced postural adjustments.

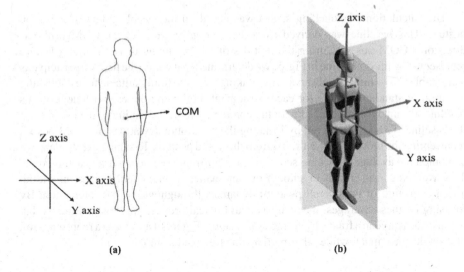

(a) A figure showing the position of the COM   (b) Three anatomical planes of the human body

Fig. 3. Demonstration of COM.

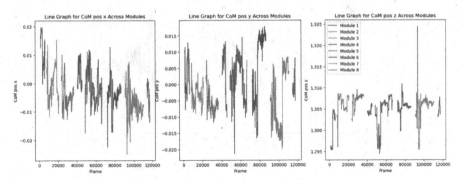

Fig. 4. Initial COM analysis Visualizations in three axes of moment.

3.2 Slouching Scores Analysis

In this study, we implemented slouching scores as a quantitative method to assess fatigue dynamics within AR environments. This metric was designed to evaluate the postural changes experienced by participants engaged during the experiment (Eq. 1). The slouching score is a numerical indicator ranging from 0 to 100, which calculates the extent of a participant's postural deviation from an initial posture. If a slouching score is 100, it means that no deviation from the initial posture, representing no physical fatigue, whereas lower scores indicate higher physical fatigue.

$$Slouching\ score = 100 \times (1 - (\frac{abs(COM\_pos\_X - Global\_Baseline)}{Maximum\_Deviation})) \quad (1)$$

The calculation of slouching scores was based on the establishment of an initial posture. This baseline was derived from the average position of the COM in the x-direction ('COM pos x') during the first 4 s of the beginning of AR learning lecture represented by the dotted line in Fig. 5. We determined that within the first 4 s, participants were stable across multiple observations, making this time frame suitable for establishing a neutral or standard posture for each participant. Following the establishment of this baseline, the analysis proceeded with the computation of the maximum deviation from the baseline. This was achieved by isolating the maximum deviations in 'COM pos x', representing the most significant shifts from the initial posture. To synthesize the data, we computed the average slouching score for each 60-frame segment within each module. This averaging was crucial to smooth out anomalies in individual frames, providing a clearer picture of the overall postural dynamics throughout the AR interaction. By focusing on these averages, the analysis could reveal broader patterns and trends that might be obscured in a frame-by-frame examination. Figures 4 and 5 was a representation of a single participant, while other participants followed a similar trend.

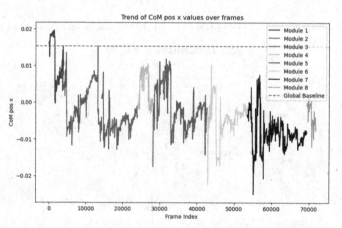

Fig. 5. Frame-by-Frame COM pos X Trajectory Across Modules

To confirm the relationship between these average scores and the physical demand experienced by participants, we planned to compare them with the NASA TLX Physical Demand (PD) values. The NASA TLX is a subjective assessment tool that measures the perceived physical strain and workload experienced by an individual. Each subscale in the NASA TLX, including the PD, is rated on a scale from 0 to 100, where 0 indicates very low demand, and 100 indicates very high demand. This comparison is aimed at establishing a correlation between the objective postural data (quantified by slouching scores) and the subjective perception of workload and physical demand (as measured by NASA TLX). For instance, a high slouching score, close to 100, would typically be expected to correspond to a lower NASA TLX PD value, indicating minimal perceived physical strain. This is because a slouching score of 100 signifies no deviation from the baseline posture, implying an ergonomically sound and comfortable position for the participant. Conversely, a lower slouching score, indicating a greater deviation from the baseline posture and potentially more ergonomic strain, would correspond to a higher NASA TLX PD value. This correlation would suggest that as participants experience more significant postural changes (as reflected in lower slouching scores), they also perceive a higher level of physical demand and strain during their interaction with the AR system.

4 Results

4.1 Slouching Scores

Our findings demonstrated a consistent trend across the participant group – a gradual decline in slouching scores calculated by using COM pos X values across all modules. According to our Hypothesis, this declining trajectory of scores suggests an escalation in postural deviation, due to increasing fatigue and physical demand experienced by participants as they engaged more extensively with the AR modules. For example, observing a participant's slouching score decrease from 100 in the first module to 70 in the last module illustrates a significant 30-point reduction. This reduction aligns with a corresponding 30% increase in perceived physical demand, as reflected in their NASA TLX Physical Demand (PD) values. A critical observation from our analysis was the alignment of data from 11 out of 16 participants with the hypothesized model. This alignment indicates a notable correlation between the decrease in slouching scores and an increase in physical demand over the progression of modules as shown in Table 1.

Table 1. Table showing Data of Average slouching scores across modules and NASA TLX PD values of participants.

1	2	3	4	5	6	7	8	NASA TLX PD	Approx Difference
63	65	48	53	30	25	35	29	70	71
69	64	71	84	67	77	60	67	1	33
92	96	89	62	64	85	58	67	40	42
83	88	86	87	86	83	69	92	60	32
94	84	88	74	86	83	91	89	10	11
95	80	72	76	72	59	66	61	10	39
97	91	83	87	90	84	88	81	60	19
85	84	86	87	80	62	44	60	50	55
94	80	58	53	66	64	63	76	10	24
89	87	87	76	86	87	78	76	20	24
86	81	62	46	50	48	65	54	55	46
89	83	89	77	85	78	71	79	1	21

(continued)

Table 1. (*continued*)

1	2	3	4	5	6	7	8	NASA TLX PD	Approx Difference
97	96	92	97	90	95	94	66	60	34
82	63	62	67	58	59	53	26	10	75
91	89	88	89	90	89	87	87	80	13
82	57	41	67	53	44	34	47	50	53

The data in Table 1 delineates the average slouching scores across eight modules for selected participants, along their corresponding NASA Task Load Index Physical Demand values. The 'Approx Difference' column calculates the deviation of the last module's slouching score from the maximum possible score of 100, providing an indicator of the change in posture over the course of the modules.

4.2 Regression Model

The linear regression model allowed us to predict Physical Demand (PD) values for each participant, based on their slouching scores across AR modules. This led us to a comparison between the actual NASA TLX PD values and the predicted PD values obtained from the regression model.

Table 2. Tabular chart showing Regression Coefficients for slouching scores by AR modules.

Slouching scores	Regression Coefficients	Std Error	t Ratio	Prob > |t|
Intercept	−22.70897	50.14632	−0.45	0.6595
Module 1	−2.034923	0.752309	−2.70	0.0205*
Module 2	4.3616112	1.018101	4.28	0.0013*
Module 3	−2.883978	0.779677	−3.70	0.0035*
Module 4	1.3736066	0.502748	2.73	0.0195*

Table 2 reveals that the slouching scores for the first four AR modules (1, 2, 3, 4) are significantly correlated with the NASA TLX Physical Demand (PD) values. For modules 1 and 3, the negative coefficient suggests that increased physical demand leads to higher postural deviation. Conversely, for modules 2 and 4, the high physical demand results in lower postural deviation.

The scatter plot shown in Fig. 6 compares the actual NASA TLX Physical Demand (PD) scores with the PD scores predicted by our regression model. Each point in the graph corresponds to a pair of actual and predicted PD scores for an individual participant. R-squared value is 0.64. It means that approximately 64% of the variability in actual NASA TLX PD scores can be explained by our linear regression model. Also, the P-value is

0.0166. It implies that the model has a good predictive power and that the relationship between the actual and predicted values is statistically significant.

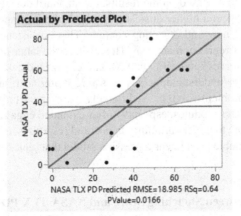

Fig. 6. A Scatter plot comparing actual NASA TLX PD values against predicted PD values.

From all the above results we can understand this is a good fit model and demonstrates robust performance. To support this analysis, we did correlation analysis between NASA TLX PD values and the Predicted PD values. The result shows 0.8114 (see Table 3), which is a high correlation between them. It suggests that the model's estimates are closely aligned with actual data. A correlation above 0.8 is considered indicative of a strong relationship, meaning that the model's predictions are likely to be consistent and reliable.

Table 3. Correlation Matrix of Actual vs. Predicted Nasa TLX PD Scores.

	NASA TLX PD	Predicted PD
NASA TLX PD	1.0000	0.8114
Predicted PD	0.8114	1.0000

5 Discussion

While AR's potential for creating immersive and interactive experiences is widely recognized, there is a growing imperative to address the ergonomic challenges associated with its prolonged use. The need for ergonomic consideration in AR design is crucial to mitigate the risks of postural fatigue and ensure that advancements in AR contribute positively to user well-being. Our analysis of motion capture data has provided pivotal insights, affirming the connection between escalating physical demand and changes in body posture.

5.1 Regression Model

Table 2 indicates that modules 5 to 8 were omitted from the regression model, which only comprises modules 1 to 4. Based on the results, the standard deviation values, ranging between 10 and 15, reflect a higher consistency in participant responses, likely driven by the introduction of new and engaging content. This consistency provides a more reliable basis for linear regression analysis. However, in the latter modules (5 to 8), the standard deviation increases between 17 and 20. This change indicates altered participant learning behavior from understanding new learning material to applying previously learned concepts in problem-solving. Additionally, participant fatigue becomes more pronounced in these later modules, especially after extended engagement periods [19]. These factors contribute to larger variability in postural responses, making the data from these modules less suitable for a linear regression model that seeks to capture consistent patterns.

5.2 Relationship Between Slouching Score and NASA TLX PD

The relationship between slouching scores and NASA TLX PD values revealed a proportional link. As users progressed through AR modules, a decrease in slouching scores was associated with an increase in perceived physical demand, according to NASA TLX PD values. This correlation highlights the slouching scores as a viable measure for assessing the ergonomic impact of AR interfaces, emphasizing the importance of considering physical demand in the design and assessment of AR experiences.

The linear regression analysis produced a combination of positive and negative coefficients. Notably, Modules 1 and 3 exhibited negative coefficients, implying that higher average slouching scores, indicative of more relaxed postures, were associated with lower predicted physical demand values. In contrast, Modules 2 and 4, characterized by positive coefficients, suggested an inverse relationship; higher average slouching scores indicated an increase in the predicted physical demand. This pattern is attributed to the content and complexity of these modules: Modules 1 and 3 were less challenging and physically demanding, allowing participants to adopt more relaxed postures and perceive lower physical demands. Conversely, Modules 2 and 4, involving new, complex information and problem statements, required heightened attention from participants. This increased engagement led to less relaxed postures, as detected by our motion capture sensors, and a consequent rise in physical demand.

5.3 Explain the Correlation of Both Predicted and Actual NASA TLX PD

The correlation analysis between predicted and actual NASA TLX PD values demonstrated a significant positive relationship, affirming the predictive strength of our regression model. A strong correlation indicates that the slouching scores are dependable indicators of perceived physical demand in AR environments. This finding supports our decision to focus on the first 4 modules of the lecture for more accurate prediction. Which explains that the hypothesis of fatigue influence in AR environments can be observed and influential.

6 Conclusion

Our study embarked on a significant exploration into the ergonomic implications of Augmented Reality (AR). The findings revealed critical insights into the effects of prolonged AR engagement on user posture and fatigue, highlighting the necessity for ergonomic considerations in AR systems. In our research, we successfully identified delicate physical demand variations in body movement within augmented reality (AR) settings. Our results, especially those related to the 'slouching scores' obtained from motion capture data, showed a clear change in postural stability associated with prolonged exposure to AR.

Our analysis concluded a significant correlation between our slouching scores and the NASA TLX Physical Demand (PD) values, suggesting that as participants reported higher physical demand, their postural stability decreased accordingly. This correlation underpins the importance of detecting user comfort and fatigue in the design of AR systems, especially in educational and training contexts where prolonged use is common. However, our research is not without limitations. The data was drawn from a small sample size, and the study's scope was confined to specific AR modules in an educational setting. Future research should thus aim to expand the sample size and diversify the AR content to further validate and generalize our findings. Also, the integration of machine learning and advanced predictive models stands out as a promising avenue for enhancing real-time analysis and intervention strategies in AR systems. Technologies could enable the development of adaptive AR systems that dynamically adjust content presentation based on real-time assessments of user fatigue and engagement.

Acknowledgments. This study was funded by the National Science Foundation (NSF).

References

1. Rampolla, J., Kipper, G.: Augmented reality: an emerging technologies guide to AR. Elsevier (2012)
2. Aukstakalnis, S.: Practical augmented reality: a guide to the technologies, applications, and human factors for AR and VR. Addison-Wesley Professional (2016)
3. Kim, J.H., Chan, T., Du, W.: The learning effect of augmented reality training in a computer-based simulation environment. In: Zaphiris, P., Ioannou, A. (eds.) LCT 2015. LNCS, vol. 9192, pp. 406–414. Springer, Cham (2015). https://doi.org/10.1007/978-3-319-20609-7_38
4. Guo, W., Kim, J.H.: How augmented reality influences student workload in engineering education. In: Stephanidis, C., Harris, D., Li, W.-C., Schmorrow, D.D., Fidopiastis, C.M., Zaphiris, P., Ioannou, A., Fang, X., Sottilare, R.A., Schwarz, J. (eds.) HCII 2020. LNCS, vol. 12425, pp. 388–396. Springer, Cham (2020). https://doi.org/10.1007/978-3-030-60128-7_29
5. Hart, S.G.: NASA-task load index (NASA-TLX); 20 years later. In: Proceedings of the Human Factors and Ergonomics Society Annual Meeting. Sage Publications Sage CA: Los Angeles, CA (2006)
6. Guo, W., Kim, J.H.: How Metacognitive Monitoring Feedback Influences Workload in a Location-Based Augmented Reality Environment. In: Harris, D., Li, W.-C. (eds.) HCII 2021. LNCS (LNAI), vol. 12767, pp. 163–171. Springer, Cham (2021). https://doi.org/10.1007/978-3-030-77932-0_14

7. White, H., Sabarwal, S.: Quasi-experimental design and methods. Methodol. Briefs Impact Eval. **2014**(8), 1–16 (2014)
8. Yu, C.-Y., et al.: Developing an augmented reality-based interactive learning system with real-time location and motion tracking. In: International Conference on Human-Computer Interaction. Springer (2023). https://doi.org/10.1007/978-3-031-34550-0_16
9. Guo, W., Hyup Kim, J.: Investigating academic performance using an ar-based learning environment with retrospective confidence judgments. In: Proceedings of the Human Factors and Ergonomics Society Annual Meeting. SAGE Publications Sage CA: Los Angeles, CA (2022)
10. Guo, W., Kim, J.H.: Designing augmented reality learning systems with real-time tracking sensors. In: Advances in Neuroergonomics and Cognitive Engineering: Proceedings of the AHFE 2021 Virtual Conferences on Neuroergonomics and Cognitive Engineering, Industrial Cognitive Ergonomics and Engineering Psychology, and Cognitive Computing and Internet of Things, July 25–29, 2021, USA. Springer (2021). https://doi.org/10.1007/978-3-030-80285-1_32
11. Kim, J.H., et al.: The effect of virtual instructor and metacognition on workload in a location-based augmented reality learning environment. In: Proceedings of the Human Factors and Ergonomics Society Annual Meeting. SAGE Publications Sage CA: Los Angeles, CA (2023)
12. Kapp, S., et al.: ARETT: augmented reality eye tracking toolkit for head mounted displays. Sensors **21**(6), 2234 (2021)
13. Roetenberg, D., Luinge, H., Slycke, P.: Xsens MVN: Full 6DOF human motion tracking using miniature inertial sensors. Xsens Motion Technologies BV, Tech. Rep. **1**, 1–7 (2009)
14. Schantz, H.G.: A real-time location system using near-field electromagnetic ranging. In: 2007 IEEE Antennas and Propagation Society International Symposium. IEEE (2007)
15. Stapley, P.J., et al.: Does the coordination between posture and movement during human whole-body reaching ensure center of mass stabilization? Exp. Brain Res. **129**, 134–146 (1999)
16. Granata, K., Gottipati, P.: Fatigue influences the dynamic stability of the torso. Ergonomics **51**(8), 1258–1271 (2008)
17. Schütte, K.H., et al.: Wireless tri-axial trunk accelerometry detects deviations in dynamic center of mass motion due to running-induced fatigue. PLoS ONE **10**(10), e0141957 (2015)
18. Patrona, F., et al.: Motion analysis: action detection, recognition and evaluation based on motion capture data. Pattern Recogn. **76**, 612–622 (2018)
19. Halim, I., et al.: Assessment of muscle fatigue associated with prolonged standing in the workplace. Saf. Health Work **3**(1), 31–42 (2012)

Human Ergonomic Analysis for Car Seating Safety Using RAMSIS Software

Pranati Somaraju, Sayali Sanjay Kulkarni, Vincent G. Duffy,
and Sameeran Kanade[✉]

Purdue University, West Lafayette, IN 47906, USA
{psomaraj,kulka121,duffy,kanade}@purdue.edu

Abstract. Vehicle seating safety is critical to vehicle design and development. The ergonomics of the seat design in a vehicle can enhance human comfort and system performance, adding to a safe and comfortable driving experience. This research focuses on improving automobile seating safety through an ergonomic analysis of seat safety using human modeling in RAMSIS software. RAMSIS is a popular software tool in the automotive industry for human modeling and ergonomics analysis. The software can evaluate the performance of seat belts, airbags, and other safety features and can give advice on where these features should be placed. RAMSIS is an important tool in designing cars that are safer and more comfortable, improving the overall security and wellbeing of passengers. This report also highlights the usage of RAMSIS software for Manikins creation. It helps in creating a virtual human model that can be used to evaluate the ergonomics of a car seat's design. The study emphasizes the importance of human modeling and ergonomics analysis in automotive design and development. Overall, this study provides the significance for using RAMSIS software to design a secure and comfortable car seat.

Keywords: RAMSIS Software · Seat safety analysis · Vehicle Ergonomics · Human-Modeling simulation · Minikins creation · Safety · Comfort · Vehicle Crash

1 Introduction and Background

1.1 RAMSIS Software Introduction

The vehicle seat safety is critical for the protection and well-being of passengers. The primary component of a vehicle that comes into contact with passengers during a collision is the seat, and it is critical that the seat should be designed in such a way that it should provide the best possible protection against injury.

The ergonomics of the vehicle seat are crucial aspects of safety. Ergonomics is the science of designing products, systems, or processes to improve human well-being and overall system performance. In the context of vehicle seats, ergonomics entails designing seats that provide optimal support and comfort to passengers while minimizing the risk of injury in the case of an accident.

© The Author(s), under exclusive license to Springer Nature Switzerland AG 2024
V. G. Duffy (Ed.): HCII 2024, LNCS 14709, pp. 101–112, 2024.
https://doi.org/10.1007/978-3-031-61060-8_8

RAMSIS is a computer-aided design software program that focuses on examining and improving the anthropometry and ergonomics of vehicle interiors. RAMSIS develops virtual human models that can be altered to replicate various postures, movements, and activities and assess the ergonomic and safety performance of the vehicle design using a database of human body measurements and anthropometric data. In order to provide drivers and passengers of all sizes and shapes with the optimum comfort, safety, and usability, RAMSIS software is widely used in the automotive sector. To evaluate vehicle ergonomics RAMSIS software considers factors like Occupant size and shape, Posture, Seat shape and contours, Reachability & visibility, seating position, vibration and noise. By taking into account these factors, RAMSIS software can provide a thorough evaluation of vehicle ergonomics, assisting manufacturers in designing seats that offer the best support, comfort, and accessibility to passengers while also lowering the risk of pain or injury.

The RAMSIS software program enables customization depending on certain design requirements and parameters while also offering a more affordable and time-efficient alternative to real prototypes and crash testing. RAMSIS software can ultimately assist manufacturers meet regulatory and safety criteria while also enhancing product quality and customer satisfaction. RAMSIS software is, in a nutshell, a vital tool for guaranteeing the security and comfort of car occupants.

1.2   RAMSIS Software Background

The RAMSIS software was designed to provide a thorough analysis of vehicle seat ergonomics and safety. Its objective was to develop techniques for anticipating driver postures and comfort while also overcoming the constraints of two-dimensional human templates. RAMSIS' main component is a highly accurate three-dimensional human model based on anthropometry databases from around the world that can be used to simulate occupants with a wide range of body measurements. The RAMSIS software's initial focus was on assessing seat designs for comfort and safety, but as time has gone on, its capabilities have grown to cover full-body ergonomics and car interior design. The software uses a huge database of anthropometric data to create unique manikins that may mimic real-world situations. The manikins can be adjusted based on a range of factors, including age, gender, weight, and height. This flexibility makes it possible to analyze a wide range of occupant sizes and forms, ensuring that vehicle designs satisfy the requirements of a diverse range of people.

To improve vehicle designs for safety, comfort, and accessibility, RAMSIS software program is now widely used by manufacturers, designers, and researchers worldwide. The RAMSIS software's capacity to assess vehicle designs for safety, comfort, and accessibility has made it a crucial tool for the automobile industry. RAMSIS offers manufacturers detailed feedback on how various design elements affect occupant safety and comfort, which is one of the system's key benefits in helping them improve their designs for better performance. With the help of this feedback, automobiles that adhere to industry standards and regulation can be made safer and more comfortable.

1.3 RAMSIS and How It is Used

A key component of car design that guarantees passenger comfort and safety is seat safety. Inconvenience, weariness, and injury may result from the seat's design having an effect on the user's posture, reach, and grip power. To improve sitting safety in cars, possible dangers can be found and solutions can be developed with the aid of an ergonomic analysis of seat design. This research examines the application of human modeling to the RAMSIS software's ergonomic investigation of car seat safety.

RAMSIS is frequently used in many different industries to evaluate ergonomic concerns and improve designs for human factors. Users using RAMSIS can generate 3D models of human bodies that can be used to replicate a variety of bodily functions and interactions with tools. By examining elements including posture, reach, and grip strength, RAMSIS can assist in finding potential ergonomic problems. The automobile sector has used RAMSIS to design and enhance car interiors for better safety and ergonomics. RAMSIS can also be used to examine the ergonomic problems with car seat design.

1.4 Review of Human Modeling Ergonomics Methods

Computer simulation is used in the field of study known as "human modeling ergonomics" to examine how people behave and interact with their surroundings. The method involves simulating numerous physical activities and interactions using digital human body models created by software. Human modeling ergonomics can assist in identifying potential ergonomic problems and creating solutions to enhance productivity and safety.

Human modeling ergonomics can assist in identifying potential risks associated with the design and use of equipment. The program can measure elements like posture, reach, and grip strength to spot possible problems with pain, exhaustion, and injury. Human modeling ergonomics can also be used to create improvements to work processes or equipment design in order to increase safety and productivity.

Making a 3D model of the human body is the first stage in human modeling ergonomics. The model needs to be precise and accurate for the population under investigation. Any pertinent anthropometric information, such as height, weight, and body measurements, should be included in the model. Once the model has been developed, it can be used to replicate a variety of bodily functions and equipment interactions.

1.5 Making Use of RAMSIS for Automotive Seat Ergonomic Analysis

Automobile seats can be ergonomically analyzed using RAMSIS. To investigate ergonomic concerns, RAMSIS enables users to model the seat and the occupant in 3D and simulate numerous scenarios. RAMSIS can assist in identifying potential seat design risks like discomfort, fatigue, and injuries. RAMSIS can also be used to create improvements to sitting safety, such as better lumbar support, height-adjustable seats, and improved seat back angles.

2 Review of Conducted Studies

2.1 Problem Statement

The goal of performing an ergonomic analysis of automobiles using RAMSIS is to enhance interior design to maximize passenger comfort, safety, and use. A human modeling program called RAMSIS enables virtual testing and prototyping of vehicle interiors, allowing designers to assess the design's fit and comfort, recognize potential ergonomic hazards and areas for development, and make interiors for vehicles that are safer and more comfortable.

Poor ergonomic design in the past has created possible safety risks for passengers as well as discomfort and even pain. As a result, manufacturers now face additional regulatory obligations, lower productivity, and rising healthcare expenses. As a result, the field of ergonomics has grown as people are becoming more aware of the detrimental effects that bad ergonomic design has on passenger health and safety.

RAMSIS is an effective method for ergonomic study since it enables virtual evaluation of car interiors, eliminating the requirement for manual testing and actual prototypes. Also, the usage of RAMSIS can record a wider variety of human movement and behavior, resulting in a more cozy and secure interior design for vehicles.

In conclusion, the goal of ergonomic study of automobiles using RAMSIS is to enhance interior design of vehicles by maximizing passenger comfort, safety, and use. The use of RAMSIS in this research has the potential to lower costs, enhance the passenger experience, and lessen manufacturers' possible legal exposure.

2.2 Literature Review

Ergonomic analysis of seat safety using human modeling in RAMSIS has been the topic of several studies. In this literature review, four papers that have used the RAMSIS software for ergonomic analysis of seat safety in automobiles are reviewed, and their unique findings are discussed.

According to the findings of a study conducted by Peter van der Meulen & Andreas Seidl [1], RAMSIS' development and evolution, key features, and application in various stages of the vehicle design process were all discussed. The authors emphasize the value of ergonomic analysis in vehicle design because it can improve safety, comfort, and overall user experience. Overall, the paper provides an excellent overview of RAMSIS's capabilities and applications in the automotive industry, emphasizing the importance of ergonomic analysis in vehicle design.

In another study conducted by Yang, J., Xu, B., Liu, M., & Zhu [2], Y., RAMSIS was used to evaluate the occupant safety of vehicle seats, including the effectiveness of headrests and the impact of different seat belt configurations. They also simulated different crash scenarios to evaluate the safety of various seat designs. Their study also demonstrated that RAMSIS can effectively simulate and analyze the impact of various seat designs on occupant safety, providing valuable insights into the optimization of seat structures and restraint systems. The authors conclude that RAMSIS can be a powerful tool in the planning, design and optimization of seat structures and restraint systems, but it should be used in conjunction to the real-world testing scenarios and validation to achieve maximum safety for vehicle occupants.

The study conducted by Min, Y., Kim, H., & Lee, J. [3], the authors used RAMSIS to create virtual human models of various sizes and shapes. After creating appropriate manikins, they assessed their reachability of the center console. The authors discovered that the center console design had a significant impact on driver ease of use and accessibility. They also discovered that the reachability of the center console varies depending on the driver's size and shape, and that the optimal design could be achieved by accommodating different body types. The study demonstrates that RAMSIS can be a useful tool for analyzing the ergonomics of center console design in the automotive industry, improving the overall user experience of drivers.

When designing seats for vehicle safety, there is also a possibility that a crash might occur from the rear end of the car. So, its important to consider factors for seat safety when a rear end collision occurs. In the study conducted by Li, Y., Yan, L., Chen, T., Zhang, J., & Fan, W. [4], the authors explore the use of RAMSIS software to evaluate occupant position and injury risk in rear-end collisions. They conducted Rear-end collision simulations and the study assess occupant position and injury risk. They compare the simulation results to real-world crash test data and discover that RAMSIS accurately predicts occupant position and injury risk in the majority of scenarios. They also mentioned RAMSIS' limitations, such as the need for precise input data and the lack of consideration for factors like vehicle structure and occupant behavior during collisions.

Each of these studies used the RAMSIS software for a specific purpose related to enhancing seating safety in automobiles. They indicate the efficacy of RAMSIS in predicting the effectiveness of seat structures, restraint systems, and occupant safety during different crash scenarios. RAMSIS has proven to be accurate in predicting occupant position and injury risk in various crash scenarios, which highlights the importance of using such simulations in vehicle design. However, it should be noted that RAMSIS has limitations, such as the need for precise input data and the lack of consideration for factors like vehicle structure and occupant behavior during collisions. Therefore, RAMSIS should be used in conjunction with real-world testing and validation to achieve maximum safety for vehicle occupants.

2.3 Citation Trends: Trend Analysis for Vehicle Safety Using RAMSIS

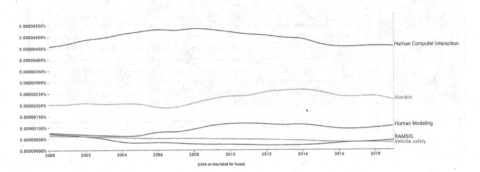

The above graph shows Google ngram results for the words usage of RAMSIS, Human Modeling, Manikin, Human Computer Interaction and Vehicle safety.

According to the graph, from 2000–2019 usage of the word "human modeling" increased gradually, with a slight decline in the mid-2000s. With a modest increase in the early 2000s and a slight fall in the middle of the 2010s, usage of the term RAMSIS has stayed largely consistent from 2000 to 2019. The usage of the term Human Computer Interaction has increased significantly from 2000 to 2019, with a consistent upward trend throughout the period. With a minor increase in the early 2000s, this term Vehicle Safety's usage has stayed relatively consistent from 2000 to 2019. From 2000 to 2019, this term Manikin usage increased dramatically, with a sharp rise trend in the middle of the decade and a modest downward trend in the middle of the next.

3 Procedure

The first step in performing ergonomic analysis with RAMSIS is to create a digital model of the vehicle's interior. This model includes the seat, steering wheel, pedals, and other relevant components for the analysis. Following the creation of the model, a digital human model is added to simulate interactions between the occupant and the vehicle. The model is tailored to the occupant's size, weight, and posture.

The simulation is then run to evaluate the design's ergonomics. RAMSIS considers factors such as the occupant's head, neck, and back position in relation to the seat, the seat angle, and seatbelt placement. RAMSIS can also simulate crash scenarios to determine how effective the seat design is at preventing injuries.

Statement of work	Tasks
Step 1	Open the RAMSIS application, then pick the appropriate automobile.

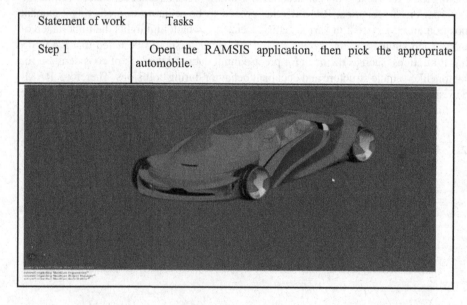

Step 2	Create a Manikin human model in order to simulate and act as a simulation's resident.

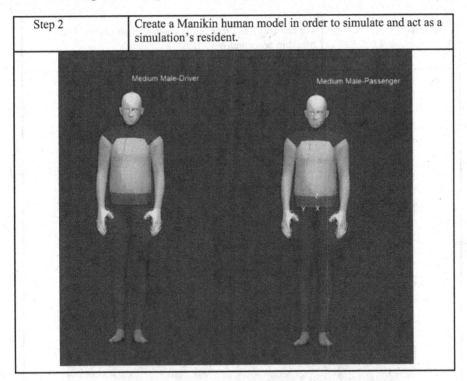

Step3	Specify posture of Manikin; in this step we are trying to define a specific seating posture in order to analyze and make appropriate changes and adjustments in the positioning of the human model.

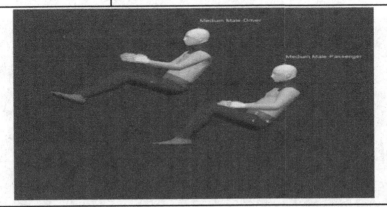

Step 4	We can make changes to the posture/positioning of the Manikin accordingly.

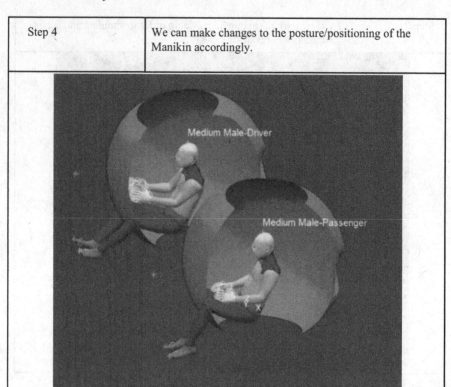

Step 5	Define the manikins' start joints and make sure that the Mankin is positioned in a comfortable position.

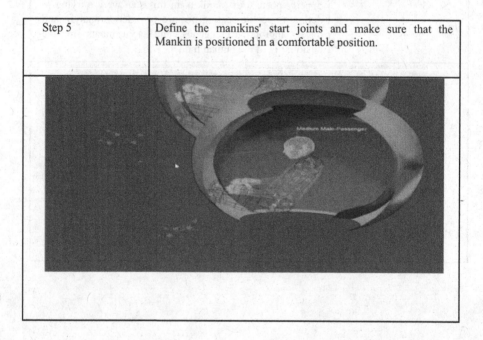

Step 6	Insert manikins, load the necessary automobile geometry, and specify endpoints for seat analysis.

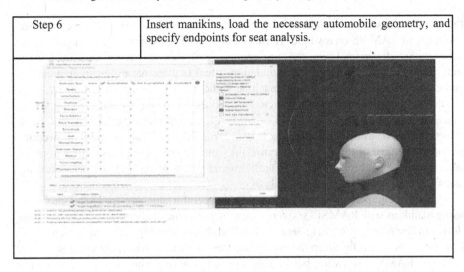

Step 7	Examine the safety and comfort of the seating position. verify Steering wheel distance, roofing height, manikin seating position to assess the comfort of the seating position in the car. Make note of any issues or problems leading to difficulty in vehicle safety

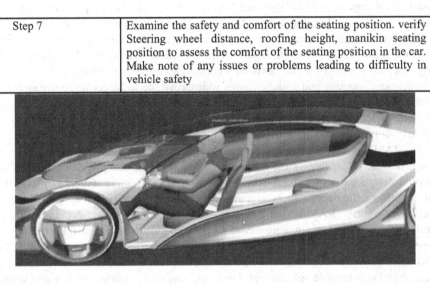

4   Analysis and Discussion

Being an avid mac user, one of the major issues with running RAMSIS on a Mac is that the software does not natively support the mac operating system. Since RAMSIS is a windows-based software, I had to spin up a virtual machine in my mac using software called VMware to run a windows operating system. Inside my virtual machine, I ran RAMSIS inside the VM container. And, another problem involved here was running RAMISIS on a virtual machine resulted in performance issues like lower processing speed, limited RAM and graphic card issues. I encountered compatibility issues between the Windows operating system and the Mac hardware, which further hindered the performance of RAMSIS on my mac. These performance issues may have an impact on the accuracy and dependability of the simulation results. This caused the software to crash multiple times while building the simulation. I had to clear out my open applications and cache in mac to run the virtual machine without any problems. Additionally, I had to allocate maximum possible resources like processing speed and RAM to my virtual machine. Overall, running RAMSIS on a Mac presented major difficulties, but. I followed the above-mentioned solutions to overcome these difficulties and it allowed me to take advantage of the software's powerful features and capabilities. Apart from the demo lectures, I referred to numerous articles and videos on the internet to simulate my steps and conduct my seat safety analysis.

A crucial component of designing a safe and comfortable seat for an automobile is using manikins with RAMSIS software. Designers can make alterations to the car seat's design to best suit passengers of various sizes and shapes by using manikins, which mimic how the seats would fit different body types. Designers must first input anthropometric data into RAMSIS software, before they may employ manikins. In order to test how passengers of various sizes and shapes will fit in the automobile seat design, the software creates a virtual manikin that mimics the human body. By moving the manikin into a different position and measuring the space between it and the various components of the car seat, designers can then assess how well the car seat design fits the user. By doing so, designers can spot possible problems with comfort and safety, including pressure areas or insufficient support, and make changes to improve the fit.Moreover, designers can test the comfort of a vehicle seat's design in various driving scenarios using a manikin to imitate various seating positions, such as erect or reclined. This enables designers to maximize comfort and support in the car seat.

The RAMSIS simulation results provide valuable insights into the ergonomic aspects of seat design. By analyzing the occupant's body position, the software can identify potential design flaws that could cause discomfort or even injury. For example, if the seat is too high, the occupant's head may strike the roof during a collision, resulting in severe head injuries. RAMSIS can also assess the seatbelt's effectiveness in preventing injuries. The software can simulate various crash scenarios to determine if the seatbelt is properly positioned and will keep the occupant from being ejected from the vehicle. In conclusion, the usage of manikins in RAMSIS software is a crucial element for creating a secure and comfortable vehicle seat. Designers can find possible comfort and safety problems and make changes to the vehicle seat design to improve the fit and support by simulating how the seat would fit passengers of various sizes and shapes.

5 Future Work

While RAMSIS is a useful tool for evaluating the ergonomic aspects of seat design, much work remains to be done to improve occupant safety. Future research could concentrate on creating more sophisticated human models that better represent the variability in human body types and postures. Moreover, new materials and technologies to improve the effectiveness of seatbelts and other safety features could be developed.

5.1 Integrating IOT Sensor Data with RAMSIS for Accurate Analysis

The testing of vehicle seats for safety is an important aspect of automotive design and development. Automobile manufacturers typically conduct a variety of tests to ensure that their vehicle seats meet safety standards and provide adequate protection to occupants in the event of a collision. Companies simulate real world crash situations using a dummy manikin inside a real vehicle developed by them. IOT sensors can be integrated inside such cars to capture different data points like the weather conditions, minikin posture, movement analysis, vehicle condition analysis during different crash position. These datapoints can help to simulate more realistic scenarios and provide better insights into the impact of different design features on occupant safety.

5.2 Investigating Various Types of Crash Scenarios Using RAMSIS

Previous works and literature review mentioned seat safety during different types of crash scenarios like rear end collision and front-end collision. It is also important to explore different crash situations like a side roll over, a massive object falling on top, to evaluate the effectiveness of seat safety. This can aid in the identification of design elements that can improve occupant safety in a broader range of crash scenarios. Using the above methodology, we can collect data points and provide a future update in RAMSIS which can help us in investigation crash scenario of our choice. The automobile industries can define various crash scenarios based on the accidents happening every day and improve the seat safety for their future models.

5.3 Predicting Occupant Behavior Using Machine Learning in RAMSIS

With the advancement of latest technologies like AI, Machine Learning, it has become an important tool for prediction. Machine Learning capabilities can be extended to RAMSIS software so that the software can learn and predict different behaviors of different types of occupants. It is impossible to incorporate different types of occupant behaviors based on age and gender. The behavior might also change depending on external factors like occupant comfort satisfaction levels inside the car, external weather, time etc. So, such multiple behaviors based on factors can be predicted using machine learning and those datapoints can be used for crash analysis and to do a seat safety analysis.

References

1. Van der Meulen, P., Seidl, A.: RAMSIS – the leading CAD tool for ergonomic analysis of vehicles. SAE Int. J. Passenger Cars Mech. Syst. 6(3), 883–890 (2013). https://doi.org/10.4271/2013-01-0457
2. Yang, J., Xu, B., Liu, M., Zhu, Y.: Safety Analysis of Seat Design using RAMSIS. Procedia Manuf. 47, 311–317 (2020). https://doi.org/10.1016/j.promfg.2020.04.057
3. Min, Y., Kim, H., Lee, J.: Analysis of center console reachability using RAMSIS software. Int. J. Automot. Technol. 22(1), 187–190 (2021)
4. Li, Y., Yan, L., Chen, T., Zhang, J., Fan, W.: Application of RAMSIS to occupant position and injury risk assessment in rear-end collisions. Int. J. Automot. Technol. 19(4), 691–699 (2018)

5. Sarode, V.V., Patil, Y.: Ergonomic analysis of seat design using RAMSIS software. Research-Gate (2019)
6. Kim, J., Chung, S.: Assessment of RAMSIS in predicting automotive seat comfort and safety design. Int. J. Autom. Eng. **4**(3), 283–290 (2013)
7. Bogerd, M., Linder, A., van Hoof, J., Wismans, J.: Optimization of car seat comfort and safety using RAMSIS. Int. J. Autom. Eng. **8**(2), 166–171 (2017)
8. Hassan, A., Rizvi, A.: Analysis of automotive seat safety using RAMSIS software. Int. J. Emerg. Technol. Adv. Eng. **4**(8), 736–743 (2014)
9. Chebbi, S., Zerhouni, N., Khalfallah, S., Gzara, L.: Evaluation of RAMSIS in predicting driver comfort and safety in automotive seating design. Int. J. Veh. Des. **80**(1/2/3), 81–97 (2019)

A Bibliometric Analysis of Cognitive Load Sensing Methodologies and Its Applications

Ryan Thomas Villarreal[1]([envelope]) [iD], Parker Andrew Nordstrom[2], and Vincent G. Duffy[1]

[1] School of Industrial Engineering, College of Engineering, Purdue University, West Lafayette, IN 47907, USA
{villar10,duffy}@purdue.edu

[2] Ray Ewry Sports Engineering Center, College of Engineering, Purdue University, West Lafayette, IN 47907, USA
pnordstr@purdue.edu

Abstract. Cognitive workload refers to the amount of mental resources a person expends while performing a task or processing information. Recent trends in the field have shown that cognitive load can be estimated through the use of physiological sensing techniques such as electroencephalograms (EEG), eye tracking, and electromyography (EMG). As these technologies are developed to be smaller, faster, smarter, and stronger, it has become more feasible to record physiological measurements in natural user environments and contexts, reducing challenges to generalizability and ecological validity. To gain a better understanding of the field and discuss where it is heading, our team completed a bibliometric analysis on the history, current state, and recent trends in the field of cognitive workload sensing and its applications. A literature review was conducted utilizing leading tables to analyze the most influential papers in the field. Further, an analysis of trends in the field is included to discuss the history of the field and its direction. It is shown that the field is still emerging, with a rapid growth of publications starting at the beginning of the 21st century.

Keywords: Cognitive Load · Ergonomics · Cognitive Load Applications

1 Introduction

Human error is one of the largest contributors to death in hospital settings, attacks on cyber infrastructure, and fratricide on the battlefield [1–3]. Cognitive load is one of the key contributors to human errors [4]. Finding methods to further understand how cognitive load is induced and how it is represented in humans could allow us to implement engineering controls to reduce cognitive workload and increase safety. The past twenty years have seen rapid development of compact, portable, and high-performance physiological sensing systems that can be relied upon. With these new technologies, it is no longer necessary to collect this data from within a constrained environment. Technologies such as mobile eye trackers allow researchers to gather data where the user is at, greatly increasing its validity in measuring context dependent behaviors [5, 6].

V. G. Duffy (Ed.): HCII 2024, LNCS 14709, pp. 113–134, 2024.
https://doi.org/10.1007/978-3-031-61060-8_9

This topic of physiologic sensing of cognitive load is a relatively recent development in the field. As physiological measurement technologies are developed to be smaller, faster, smarter, and stronger, it has become more feasible to record physiological measurements in natural user environments and contexts, reducing challenges to generalizability and ecological validity. Previously, cognitive load determination has primarily been evaluated through self-administered surveys such as the NASA-TLX [7]. Although these surveys have been validated and have high utility, they are suboptimal for real-time recording of cognitive workload, which is needed for real-time deployment of countermeasures to counteract high cognitive workload which may lead to errors. Real-time measurement of cognitive workload can be used to determine whether countermeasures should be put in place for safety critical systems [8, 9]. Domains such as automotive, aviation, and healthcare could benefit as these are domains in which cognitively intensive tasks are performed within safety critical contexts [10]. This paper conducts a bibliometric analysis aimed at exploring the current state of cognitive load sensing techniques, technologies, and applications in industry, while also presenting potential applications that this theory and methodology can be expand to.

1.1 Relevance to Applied Ergonomics at Large

Cognitive load sensing is the "measurement and assessment of the mental effort and resources that individuals expend when processing information or performing a task" [11]. This has been extensively studied as cognitive load theory, which emphasizes the interaction between information structures and cognitive architecture in instructional settings [12]. Cognitive load theory distinguishes between intrinsic cognitive which is determined by the number of information elements involved in the present learning, extraneous cognitive load which involves the learner using non-relevant cognitive processes, and germane cognitive load which describes the cognitive load required for connecting new materials with information from long term memory, each of which plays a significant role in learning and task performance [13]. The use of multiple psychometric instruments for each type of cognitive load has been suggested to provide a more precise measurement of cognitive load and enable researchers to differentiate between the different types more clearly [14].

Cognitive load is a fundamental theory in human factors and ergonomics. Therefore, there are multiple affiliated topics that are directly related to cognitive load sensing and application. One obvious and interchangeable topic is "mental workload" [10]. It is important to indicate that mental workload and cognitive workload are synonymous. This is an important statement as it expands the potential searches that can be conducted as part of a bibliometric analysis. Additionally, this topic further outlines and assesses the fundamental nature and characteristics of cognitive workload and how it has been defined. These definitions have largely come from decades of purely psychological research into how the brain reacts to stimuli and how attention plays a role in cognition. Theories explored within this topic, such as Resource Theory and Multiple Resource Theory, are introduced to grasp the intricacies between cognitive resources and task demands. As current applications of sensing mental workload aim to analyze the impact of various task and job demands, the findings from this field serves as a foundational guide, offering practical approaches to measure mental workload and understand the challenges posed by evolving technologies and automated systems in the contemporary work landscape.

Another related topic to cognitive load sensing is Neuroergonomics [15]. Neuroergonomics is an emerging new interdisciplinary field that aims to investigate how the human brain functions in its relation to everyday behavior in real-world contexts. This field is made possible in parallel to cognitive load sensing by the rapid development of physiological sensing techniques that are smaller, more powerful, and less intrusive. Neuroergonomics research aims to expand our understanding of human behavior by incorporating our understanding of the fundamental mechanisms underlying human cognitive, perceptual, and motor functioning with a focus on real-world contexts. This topic also presents various methodologies utilized in the field that are relevant to cognitive load sensing. Understanding the intricate dynamics of the human brain in real-world contexts, as emphasized in neuroergonomics, holds crucial implications for applications aimed at assessing effects on cognitive load. This knowledge becomes pivotal for designing systems, interfaces, and technologies that adapt to the cognitive demands of users in real time. The synthesis of neuroscience and human factors in neuroergonomics thus becomes a cornerstone for the development and refinement of applications focused on precisely measuring cognitive load, ultimately enhancing user experience and performance in complex, real-world scenarios.

Cognitive load sensing methods and applications are shown to be a very relevant topic in applied ergonomics at large. Through the use of physiological monitoring and neuroimaging, cognitive load can be modeled and understood. These models can then be applied to understand how differing tasks and contexts influence human performance in a generalized manner.

2 Methodology

2.1 Bibliometric Analysis

The systematic bibliometric analysis methodology applies quantitative techniques on bibliometric data [16]. To gain a deeper understanding of current literature on the topic, various tools were utilized to perform our bibliometric analysis. Articles for a literature review were obtained using multiple academic search databases. Articles to include in our leading tables were collected through Harzing's "Publish or Perish" tool [17]. For our leading tables, two leading metrics were considered for four different queries. Firstly, Harzing's "Publish or Perish" was used with Google Scholar to search for the keyword "neuroergonomics". Textbooks were not included in the search, as our goal was to find the top papers in the field as opposed to textbooks. The first 200 results were queried with no further filters applied. Secondly, the keywords "cognitive workload sensing" were queried in a similar manner. Further, the keywords "cognitive loading application" and "effects on cognitive loading" were searched in a similar manner, with focus on database relevance rank and number of citations for the first 100 results. From these results, leading tables were made from the top 10 papers by citations, and then the top 10 papers by citations per year. This provides the most influential papers of all time, while also allowing for more recent but impactful papers to appear as a leading paper. The Publish or Perish tool was used to query Google Scholar with the relevant keywords to find sources for use in the analysis. Table 1 provides an overview of search terms and results analyzed. This search was conducted on November 29, 2023. The search terms were chosen to give a broad view of current and influential cognitive load sensing methodologies and applications.

Table 1. Literature review methodology overview.

Tool Utilized	Search Terms	Database Queried	Num. of Results
Harzing's Publish or Perish	neuroergonomics	Google Scholar	200
Harzing's Publish or Perish	cognitive workload sensing	Google Scholar	200
Harzing's Publish or Perish	Cognitive Loading Application	Google Scholar	100
Harzing's Publish or Perish	effects on cognitive loading	Google Scholar	100

2.2 Visualization and Trend Analysis

To show relations between key topics in the field, visualizations were generated using a number of tools and techniques. Network visualization allows for a pragmatic approach to understanding the relationship and connectedness of keywords in a particular field of study [16]. To explore how keywords, connect in the Web of Science, VOS Viewer was used to build a web of keywords related to the topic of cognitive workload, as recommended in the bibliometric analysis methodology literature [16, 18]. A content analysis was performed using a word cloud created from the content of the top 10 articles by number of citations per year for "cognitive workload sensing" using maxQDA software [19, 20]. A trend analysis was completed to quantify keyword popularity changes and relevance through time using the frequency of publications in the field [21]. This analysis was completed utilizing various tools including Google's Ngram viewer [20, 22].

3 Results

3.1 Leading Tables

The results for the keyword "neuroergonomics" are shown below. The first leading table shows the top 10 articles by purely the number of citations in Table 2. Table 3 shows the top 10 articles by citations per year.

Table 2. Top 10 articles by number of citations for "neuroergonomics".

Cites	Authors	Title	Year
452	R Parasuraman	Neuroergonomics: research and practice	2003
323	H Ayaz, et al.	Continuous monitoring of brain dynamics with functional near Infrared spectroscopy as a tool for neuroergonomic research: empirical examples and a …	2013
302	RK Mehta, R Parasuraman	Neuroergonomics: a review of applications to physical and cognitive work	2013
289	R Parasuraman, GF Wilson	Putting the brain to work: Neuroergonomics past, present, and future	2008
188	R Parasuraman	Neuroergonomics: Brain, cognition, and performance at work	2011
153	F Dehais, et al.	A neuroergonomics approach to mental workload, engagement and human performance	2020
149	RK Mehta, et al.	Effects of mental fatigue on the development of physical fatigue: a neuroergonomic approach	2014
141	R McKendrick, et al.	Into the Wild: neuroergonomic differentiation of hand-held and augmented reality wearable displays during outdoor navigation with functional near infrared …	2016
111	M Causse, et al.	The effects of emotion on pilot decision-making: A neuroergonomic approach to aviation safety	2013
94	JS Warm, R Parasuraman	Cerebral hemodynamics and vigilance	2006

Table 3. Top 10 articles by number of citations per year for "neurergonomics".

Cites Per Year	Authors	Title	Year
51	F Dehais, et al.	A neuroergonomics approach to mental workload, engagement and human performance	2020
32.3	H Ayaz, et al.	Continuous monitoring of brain dynamics with functional near infrared spectroscopy as a tool for neuroergonomic research: empirical examples and a …	2013
30.2	RK Mehta, R Parasuraman	Neuroergonomics: a review of applications to physical and cognitive work	2013
22.6	R Parasuraman	Neuroergonomics: research and practice	2003
22.33	LE Ismail, W Karwowski	A graph theory-based modeling of functional brain connectivity based on eeg: A systematic review in the context of neuroergonomics	2020
21	E Wascher, et al.	Neuroergonomics on the go: An evaluation of the potential of mobile EEG for workplace assessment and design	2023
20.14	R McKendrick, et al.	Into the Wild: neuroergonomic differentiation of hand-held and augmented reality wearable displays during outdoor navigation with functional near infrared …	2016
19.27	R Parasuraman, GF Wilson	Putting the brain to work: Neuroergonomics past, present, and future	2008
17.67	F Dehais, et al.	Brain at work and in everyday life as the next frontier: grand field challenges for neuroergonomics	2020
17	A Curtin, H Ayaz	The age of neuroergonomics: towards ubiquitous and continuous measurement of brain function with fNIRS	2018

It can be seen in the tables above that multiple papers have made both lists. This can be interpreted as evidence that these papers are highly relevant to the field, and may play a part in defining the field itself. Articles that are included in both include primarily reviews of the topic and how they can be applied in industry.

It is also seen that by pure number of citations, most of the leading articles are more than a decade old. The two most recent articles to appear on that list were published in 2020 and 2014, respectively. This is controlled for in the second table showing citations per year. In this second table, those same papers plus more recent papers appear. This is evidence that the approach of reporting the leading papers by number of citations and number of citations per year is a potentially useful approach to viewing the most influential papers in the field at the current time.

The results for the keyword "cognitive workload sensing" are shown below. The first leading table, Table 4, shows the top 10 articles by purely the number of citations. The second table, Table 5, shows the top 10 articles by citations per year.

Table 4. Top 10 articles by number of citations for "cognitive workload sensing".

Cites	Authors	Title	Year
629	CJD Petten, et al.	Using mobile telephones: cognitive workload and attention resource allocation	2004
535	C Berka, et al.	Real-time analysis of EEG indexes of alertness, cognition, and memory acquired with a wireless EEG headset	2004
499	A Gevins, ME Smith	Neurophysiological measures of cognitive workload during human computer interaction	2003
475	B Mehler, et al.	Impact of incremental increases in cognitive workload on physiological arousal and performance in young adult drivers	2009
423	SP Marshall	The index of cognitive activity: Measuring cognitive workload	2002
298	K Izzetoglu, et al.	Functional optical brain imaging using near-infrared during cognitive tasks	2004
284	G Matthews, et al.	The psychometrics of mental workload: Multiple measures are sensitive but divergent	2015
279	N Nourbakhsh, et al.	Using galvanic skin response for cognitive load measurement in arithmetic and reading tasks	2012
225	B Reimer, B Mehler	The impact of cognitive workload on physiological arousal in young adult drivers; a field study and simulation validation	2011
214	ET Solovey, et al.	Classifying driver workload using physiological and driving performance data: two field studies	2014

Table 5. Top 10 articles by number of citations per year for "cognitive workload sensing".

Cites Per Year	Authors	Title	Year
35.5	G Matthews, et al.	The psychometrics of mental workload: Multiple measures are sensitive but divergent	2015
33.93	B Mehler, et al.	Impact of incremental increases in cognitive workload on physiological arousal and performance in young adult drivers	2009
33.11	CJD Petten, et al.	Using mobile telephones: cognitive workload and attention resource allocation	2004
31.4	RD Dias, et al.	Systematic review of measurement tools to assess surgeons' intraoperative cognitive workload	2018
30	F Dehais, et al.	Monitoring pilot's mental workload using ERPs and spectral power with a six-dry-electrode EEG system in real flight conditions	2019
30	T Kosch, et al.	A survey on measuring cognitive workload in human-computer interaction	2023
28.16	C Berka, et al.	Real-time analysis of EEG indexes of alertness, cognition, and memory acquired with a wireless EEG headset	2004
25.36	N Nourbakhsh, et al.	Using galvanic skin response for cognitive load measurement in arithmetic and reading tasks	2012
24.95	A Gevins, ME Smith	Neurophysiological measures of cognitive workload during human computer interaction	2003
24.71	B Pfleging, et al.	A model relating pupil diameter to mental workload and lighting conditions	2016

Similarly, for our search on neuroergonomics, the leading papers for overall citations are mostly papers that are older than 10 years, with the most recent paper published in 2015. In line with the previous search, there is also a significant overlap between the two leading tables. Articles that are included in both include primarily reviews of the topic and methodologies/techniques to collect more accurate and useful physiological data.

Interestingly, this search differs from the previous search in that the search for citations by year also mostly included older papers. There are more recent papers than in the overall citations table, but most papers are more than a decade old. This could be interpreted as evidence that this search term yielded results from a more established field. When the older papers are still receiving large amounts of citations, it can be implied that the fundamental findings from that paper are still largely relevant to ongoing work.

One interesting insight from these leading tables is that every paper is from the 21st century. This agrees with our trend analysis (discussed further below) which showed this field as being practically non-existent until the turn of the century. If a similar search was conducted simply for "cognitive workload" or "mental workload", the results could be expected to yield much older papers from the field of psychology when these ideas were first being analyzed from a purely fundamental psychology perspective.

Table 6. Top 10 articles by search engine rank for "Cognitive Loading Application".

Cites	Per Year	Rank	Authors	Title	Year
296	37.00	1	J Leppink, A van den Heuvel	The evolution of cognitive load theory and its application to medical education	2015
43	3.91	2	MS Kim, et al.	Development and effectiveness of a drug dosage calculation training program using cognitive loading theory based on smartphone application	2012
103	7.36	3	P Schmutz, et al.	Cognitive load in eCommerce applications—measurement and effects on user satisfaction	2009
49	1.69	4	A Kashihara, et al.	A cognitive load application in tutoring	1994
117	19.50	5	J Leppink	Cognitive load theory: Practical implications and an important challenge	2017
156	6.78	6	S Feinberg, M Murphy	Applying cognitive load theory to the design of web-based instruction	2000
67	33.50	7	HY Chang, et al.	The effects of virtual simulation-based, mobile technology application on nursing students' learning achievement and cognitive load: Random…	2021
132	7.33	8	GR Morrison, GJ Anglin	Research on cognitive load theory: Application to e-learning	2005
64	8.00	9	NH Jalani, LC Sern	The example-problem based learning model: applying cognitive load theory	2015
44	11.00	10	J Sentz, et al.	How do instructional designers manage learners' cognitive load? An examination of awareness and application of strategies	2019

Seeking out other sources that benefit the research on applications of measuring cognitive loading, and, therefore, the study of the effects on cognitive loading, results for searches for the keywords "Cognitive Loading Application" are shown in Table 6 and Table 7. Table 6 shows the top 10 papers by search engine rank related to this search. Further narrowing down these potential sources, we can find the top 10 papers by number of citations, which is shown below in Table 7. Utilizing these two different search techniques provides the top sources based on citations but then also based upon relevance to the search keywords. Evaluating results using these two methods allows for results that show articles that are both relevant and impactful.

Table 7. Top 10 articles by number of citations for "Cognitive Loading Application".

Cites	Per Year	Rank	Authors	Title	Year
5088	175.45	24	J Sweller	Cognitive load theory, learning difficulty, and instructional design	1994
4494	140.44	55	P Chandler, J Sweller	Cognitive load theory and the format of instruction	1991
3722	186.10	173	F Paas, et al.	Cognitive load theory and instructional design: Recent developments	2003
3219	459.86	60	F Paas, et al.	Cognitive load measurement as a means to advance cognitive load theory	2016
2798	155.44	52	JJG Van Merrienboer	Cognitive Load Theory and Complex Learning: Recent Developments and Future Directions	2005
2574	83.03	153	FGWC Paas	Training strategies for attaining transfer of problem-solving skill in statistics: a cognitive-load approach	1992
1543	128.58	67	RC Clark, et al.	Efficiency in learning: Evidence-based guidelines to manage cognitive load	2011
1538	102.53	191	JD Greene, et al.	Cognitive load selectively interferes with utilitarian moral judgment	2008

(continued)

Table 7. (*continued*)

Cites	Per Year	Rank	Authors	Title	Year
1524	117.23	28	T De Jong	Cognitive load theory, educational research, and instructional design: Some food for thought	2010
1431	110.08	46	JJG Van Merrienboer, J Sweller	Cognitive load theory in health professional education: design principles and strategies	2010

The results from the two top 10 lists in Tables 6 and 7 show an emphasis on design for consumer products and the education domain. Demonstrating the focus points in the application of cognitive load theory. Many of the most frequently used methodologies also rank within the top 100 most relevant sources, demonstrating that these articles have utility in the field and trusted to be used as sources.

As evidenced by the Google Ngram in Sect. 3.2, the application of cognitive load theory is a well-developed yet expanding field. This is supported by the search results above, as many of the top 10 ranked sources are from the year 2000 or later.

Expanding the search to the keywords "effects on cognitive loading" unveils even more sources that can show the application of the theory on real world cognitive stressors. Again, the top 10 ranked and top 10 used sources are shown below in Tables 8 and 9, respectively.

Table 8. Top 10 articles by search engine rank for "Effects on Cognitive Loading".

Cites	Per Year	Rank	Authors	Title	Year
52	13.00	1	CJ Burcal, et al.	The effects of cognitive loading on motor behavior in injured individuals: a systematic review	2019
224	37.33	2	J Engström, et al.	Effects of cognitive load on driving performance: The cognitive control hypothesis	2017
511	58.78	3	HH Choi, et al.	Effects of the physical environment on cognitive load and learning: Towards a new model of cognitive load	2014

(*continued*)

Table 8. (*continued*)

Cites	Per Year	Rank	Authors	Title	Year
233	12.26	4	A Drolet, M Frances Luce	The rationalizing effects of cognitive load on emotion-based trade-off avoidance	2004
172	10.75	5	YC Lee, et al.	Visual attention in driving: The effects of cognitive load and visual disruption	2007
471	22.43	6	JJG Van Merrienboer, et al.	Redirecting learners' attention during training: Effects on cognitive load, transfer test performance and training efficiency	2002
92	4.60	7	M Biernat, et al.	Stereotypes and shifting standards: Some paradoxical effects of cognitive load	2003
78	6.50	8	H Negahban, et al.	The effects of cognitive loading on balance control in patients with multiple sclerosis	2011
160	13.33	9	SL Mattys, L Wiget	Effects of cognitive load on speech recognition	2011
10266	293.31	10	J Sweller	Cognitive load during problem solving: Effects on learning	1988

Table 9. Top 10 articles by number of citations for "Effects on Cognitive Loading".

Cites	Per Year	Rank	Authors	Title	Year
10266	293.31	10	J Sweller	Cognitive load during problem solving: Effects on learning	1988
5088	175.45	177	J Sweller	Cognitive load theory, learning difficulty, and instructional design	1994
4494	140.44	161	P Chandler, J Sweller	Cognitive load theory and the format of instruction	1991
4474	372.83	175	J Sweller	Cognitive load theory	2011

(*continued*)

Table 9. (*continued*)

Cites	Per Year	Rank	Authors	Title	Year
3219	459.86	187	F Paas, et al.	Cognitive load measurement as a means to advance cognitive load theory	2016
2798	155.44	129	JJG Van Merrienboer	Cognitive load theory and complex learning: Recent developments and future directions	2005
2051	157.77	136	J Sweller	Element interactivity and intrinsic, extraneous, and germane cognitive load	2010
1760	62.86	198	SY Mousavi, et al.	Reducing cognitive load by mixing auditory and visual presentation modes	1995
1682	58.00	191	FGWC Paas, et al.	Variability of worked examples and transfer of geometrical problem-solving skills: A cognitive-load approach	1994
1629	85.74	182	F Paas, et al.	Cognitive load theory: Instructional implications of the interaction between information structures and cognitive architecture	2004

Again, the top 10 ranked sources by relevancy are also some of the most recent ones. This again shows that the application and study of cognitive loading on real world situations and stressors is an emerging area. Changing the keywords from the application of cognitive loading to the effects from cognitive loading yields the change from applying the theory to product design and evaluation to the fundamental research on cognitive loadings effects in various human factors relevant domains such as learning, healthcare, and problem solving.

One observation on the difference between the leading papers based on relevance and number of citations is that the most cited are also the oldest, with the oldest published in 1988. This shows the historical importance and development of the theory, in that the more recent applications are focused on product design and learning while the most cited research is focused on the fundamental psychological underpinnings of the concept. The more recent applications are made possible through the expanded use of advanced sensing-based techniques for measuring cognitive load, with an understanding of cognitive load being directly applicable to product design and learning.

3.2 Trend Analysis

Although cognitive load theory has been studied extensively and applied widely, the methodology and application of real-time cognitive load sensing is an emerging area. For real-time cognitive load sensing, it is important to note that most approaches for sensing cognitive states, including cognitive load, often involve obtrusive technologies, such as physiological sensors attached to users' bodies [23]. For this reason, the application of cognitive load sensing and measurement of it can be considered an emerging area. As smarter, smaller, and more powerful sensing technologies are developed, the ability and potential application of cognitive load sensing systems is rapidly growing. This trend is supported by the Google Ngram shown in Fig. 1 for the search "cognitive load measurement" between 1990 and 2019. It is shown that the actual objective measurement of cognitive load was hardly considered until its introduction at the start of the century. Since then, the idea has seen a rapid increase of interest in literature, with no signs of slowing down.

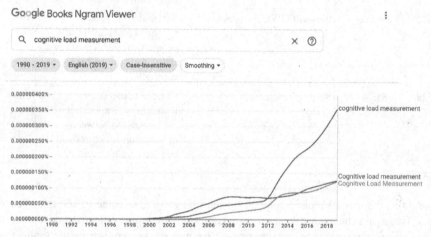

Fig. 1. Google Ngram Viewer for the search term "Cognitive Load Measurement".

Coupling cognitive load theory with advancements in sensing techniques and technologies has allowed for a more nuanced understanding of the impacts of diverse stressors on cognitive load [24]. Interest in the field of this evolving trend is evident as illustrated by the Google Ngram search in Fig. 2. In this search, the terms "effects on cognitive load", "cognitive loading", and "cognitive load effects" are shown from 1960 to 2019. Clearly, the advancement of sensing technologies since 2000 is shown to have influenced the study of effects on cognitive loading. The intersection of cognitive load theory and advanced technology is poised to refine our understanding of the dynamics of cognitive loading, marking a transformative phase in the measurement and application of cognitive loading.

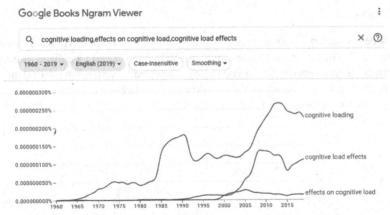

Fig. 2. Google Ngrams results for "effects on cognitive load", "cognitive loading", and "cognitive load effects".

This Ngram in Fig. 2 also shows how cognitive loading is not a new concept, and has been studied primarily in the field of psychology since the 1960's. The difference between the two Ngram trends is noted in that taking physiological approaches to measuring cognitive workload is a relatively recent trend that builds upon the foundations laid out it in the fundamental cognitive workload research. It is shown in the above Ngrams that the change in number of articles has grown rapidly in the past two decades. This clear increase that is still on the rise is evidence that this is an emerging field.

For further trend analysis, Scopus Analyze Result was used to visualize the search term "cognitive load sensing" from 1999–2023 in a second database. Figure 3 below further reinforces that the topic has seen rapid growth in recent years, agreeing with our Ngram results.

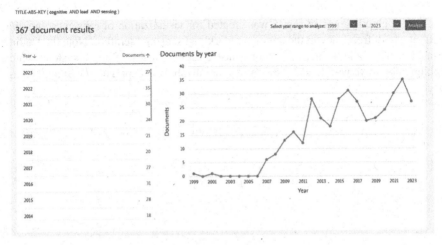

Fig. 3. Scopus Trend Diagram.

3.3 Visualization

Figure 4 below shows a Scopus export for the search "Cognitive AND workload AND measurement". The results were then input into VOS Viewer and visualized. It is shown that there are large connections between mental workload, eye tracking, EEG, memory, attention, and machine learning. Various domains applications are shown throughout including driving, aviation, and augmented reality.

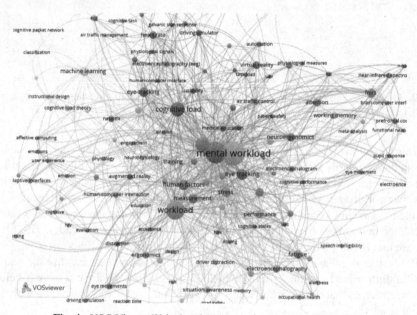

Fig. 4. VOS Viewer Web showing connections between keywords.

A word cloud shown in Fig. 5 was created for visualization of relevant terms that occur at a high frequency in the cognitive workload sensing literature. Note the leading terms shown in Table 10 such as "performance", "EEG", "measure", and "system" which highlight cognitive workload sensing as a generalizable concept with a vast application space.

Fig. 5. Word cloud based upon the content of the top 10 articles by number of citations per year for "cognitive workload sensing".

Table 10. Leading lexical search terms from word cloud.

Word	Frequency	Rank
workload	927	1
task	866	2
cognitive	764	3
use	553	4
measure	409	5
load	373	6
eeg	333	7
mental	257	8
performance	253	9
system	248	10

4 Discussion

We have shown how cognitive workload is relevant to and has high utility in human factors and applied ergonomics. As sensing based techniques for analyzing cognitive workload is an emerging area experiencing rapid growth, understanding the current landscape of relevant methodologies, applications, and domains is crucial to inspiring future research. Diving deeper and appraising the findings from our bibliometric analysis, we can investigate the current ideas of the field.

4.1 Use of Electroencephalogram (EEG) for Quantifying Cognitive Workload

The EEG is a widely used tool for quantifying cognitive workload. Advantages of EEG in cognitive workload sensing include the excellent temporal resolution and high sensitivity to human brain activity fluctuations that EEG allows [25]. This is particularly useful as it allows us to say with higher confidence which specific regions of the brain are correlated with different tasks and their contexts. Additionally, recent work has shown that this can be measured and processed in real time, allowing for real-time inferences of cognitive workload, alertness, and memory [8]. Various features of the EEG data stream can be fed into a classification machine learning model to better understand what cognitive workload state an individual is in [26]. This has the potential for applications across domains in which cognitively demanding tasks are required, such as aviation, automobiles, and healthcare.

4.2 Application of Cognitive Workload Sensing in Healthcare

As shown with EEGs, it is possible to infer cognitive workload with physiological sensors. However, using solely EEG is limited in that it only captures "above the neck" data. When combined with other physiological sensing techniques such as heart rate variability or muscle activation, the classification power can be increased [25, 27]. This powerful combination of tools has many applications, with recent works showing its usage in assisting in robot assisted surgery. When combined with a tool such as eye tracking, perceived cognitive workload could be predicted in a robotic assisted surgery task [5]. Applying this system, Barragan et al. found that once cognitive workload was detected to be elevated, countermeasures could be deployed to help reduce cognitive workload in surgeons [28].

4.3 Effect of Stressors on the Measurement of Cognitive Load

Understanding what external influences impact the physiological measurement of cognitive load is vital to ensuring the validity of sensing-based techniques. Conway et al. investigates this and highlights the intricate relationship between stressors and cognitive load, giving insights into how measurements themselves can be affected by external factors [24]. The experiment, utilizing galvanic skin response as the physiological measure, focuses on the impact of stress on cognitive load measurement. The findings show that average galvanic skin response values struggle to effectively measure cognitive load in the presence of fluctuating task stress levels. However, certain galvanic skin response features including peak frequency and peak duration showed promise in discerning cognitive load despite the influence of stress. The results demonstrate how physiological responses to cognitively demanding tasks and stress must be considered in cognitive workload research and applications in real-world scenarios. This study contributes to the development of more accurate and transferable applications of cognitive load sensing, particularly in contexts where stress is a confounding factor.

4.4 Impact of Cognitive Load on Language and Stimuli Processing

Further delving into the applications of the cognitive loading theory, effects on the processing of language and other stimuli have been widely studied. Models of speech perception have traditionally focused on sensory input and lexical representations, emphasizing sub-lexical cues and lexical-semantic knowledge [29]. While adverse listening conditions like signal degradation have been extensively explored, cognitive load resulting from concurrent tasks has received less attention. Under cognitive load, listeners tend to downplay acoustic details, relying more on lexical-semantic knowledge, leading to lexical drift [29]. Similarly, an experiment using the Stroop test demonstrated the impact of cognitive load on task performance, with increased cognitive load slowing down reaction times and increasing task completion times [30]. Utilizing subjective measures, task performance, and physiological measures, previous literature has shown how cognitive load impacts our ability to perform daily tasks including verbal communication and basic stimuli processing. These contributions give insight towards the design of systems which consider and evaluate cognitive load across domains and contexts.

5   Future Work

Applying the findings from work on cognitive load theory to emerging technologies is a clear avenue for future work on the topic. With an increased interest in artificial intelligence and human-computer interactions, funding and awards granted to cognitive load research has also increased. As evidenced by the award search section on the National Science Foundation (NSF) website, a wave of projects are being funded to investigate the workload level that interacting with emerging technologies elicits from users [31]. Searching NSF award databases for various keywords including "cognitive load application" and "cognitive load effects" gives further insight into the current funding trends in the field, and where future work is most fit. Potential opportunities for future work include studies on the effects of poor-quality lexicons among programming languages on the quality of the code itself and developer's mental workload [32].

The NSF currently accepts proposals to their Cyber-Physical Systems (CPS) group for funding research on CPS in which users must integrate with systems that are largely based on computational and physical components [31, 33]. Additionally, searching for "cognitive workload" on the NSF-funded projects search yields many ongoing projects directly utilizing cognitive workload sensing metrics and methodologies. One such funded project is "Electromyography (EMG)-Based Assistive Human-Machine Interface Design: Cognitive Workload and Motor Skill Learning Assessment" which seeks to use neuro-imaging techniques to understand fundamental motor skill training through EMG-based interaction with virtual reality [34].

Industrial engineering (IE) focuses on understanding processes and systems to create novel solutions that consider humans and the environments they operate in [35]. Understanding how humans experience cognitive workload in varying contexts is needed to develop novel solutions to address this issue. Currently, the IE realm is addressing the measurement and application of these measurements of cognitive load by implementing novel sensors and techniques aimed at measuring cognitive load. Furthering the field will require funding of cognitive load research as well as vast dissemination of findings on the subject. This will empower further breakthroughs in measurement and analyzation of cognitive load, giving industrial engineers and human factors specialists a powerful tool in their toolbox to address the shortcomings of current workload methodologies.

The results of our bibliometric analysis and insight into current funding trends show the utility and promising future of research on the emerging field of cognitive workload sensing. Through utilization and advanced development of physiological sensing techniques and technologies, cognitive workload can be modeled and understood across domains and contexts, allowing for designers and researchers to gain deeper insight into the systems they create.

Disclosure of Interests. The authors have no competing interests to declare that are relevant to the content of this article.

References

1. Institute of Medicine (US) Committee on Quality of Health Care in America, To Err is Human: Building a Safer Health System. Washington (DC): National Academies Press (US) (2000). http://www.ncbi.nlm.nih.gov/books/NBK225182/. Accessed 07 Dec 2023
2. Ncubukezit, T.: Human errors: a cybersecurity concern and the weakest link to small businesses. In: ICCWS, vol. 17, no. 1, Article no. 1 (2022). https://doi.org/10.34190/iccws.17.1.51
3. Wilson, K.A., Salas, E., Priest, H.A., Andrews, D.: Errors in the heat of battle: taking a closer look at shared cognition breakdowns through teamwork. Hum. Factors **49**(2), 243–256 (2007). https://doi.org/10.1518/001872007X312478
4. van Gog, T., Paas, F., Sweller, J.: Cognitive load theory: advances in research on worked examples, animations, and cognitive load measurement. Educ. Psychol. Rev. **22**(4), 375–378 (2010). https://doi.org/10.1007/s10648-010-9145-4
5. Wu, C., et al.: Eye-tracking metrics predict perceived workload in robotic surgical skills training. Hum. Factors **62**(8), 1365–1386 (2020). https://doi.org/10.1177/0018720819874544
6. Anton, N.E., et al.: Detailing experienced nurse decision making during acute patient care simulations. Appl. Ergon. **109**, 103988 (2023). https://doi.org/10.1016/j.apergo.2023.103988
7. Hart, S.G., Staveland, L.E.: Development of NASA-TLX (task load index): results of empirical and theoretical research. In: Hancock, P.A., Meshkati, N. (eds.) Advances in Psychology in Human Mental Workload, vol. 52, pp. 139–183. North-Holland (1988). https://doi.org/10.1016/S0166-4115(08)62386-9
8. Berka, C., et al.: Real-time analysis of EEG indexes of alertness, cognition, and memory acquired with a wireless EEG headset. Int. J. Hum.-Comput. Interact. **17**(2), 151–170 (2004). https://doi.org/10.1207/s15327590ijhc1702_3
9. Yang, J., Barragan, J.A., Farrow, J.M., Sundaram, C.P., Wachs, J.P., Yu, D.: An adaptive human-robotic interaction architecture for augmenting surgery performance using real-time workload sensing—demonstration of a semi-autonomous suction tool. Hum. Factors 00187208221129940 (2022). https://doi.org/10.1177/00187208221129940
10. Hancock, G.M., Longo, L., Young, M.S., Hancock, P.A.: Mental workload. In: Salvendy, G., Karwowski, W. (eds.) Handbook of Human Factors and Ergonomics, 5th edn., pp. 203–226. Wiley (2021)
11. Paas, F., Tuovinen, J.E., Tabbers, H., Van Gerven, P.W.M.: Cognitive load measurement as a means to advance cognitive load theory. Educ. Psychol. **38**(1), 63–71 (2003). https://doi.org/10.1207/S15326985EP3801_8

12. Paas, F., Renkl, A., Sweller, J.: Cognitive load theory: instructional implications of the interaction between information structures and cognitive architecture. Instr. Sci. **32**(1), 1–8 (2004). https://doi.org/10.1023/B:TRUC.0000021806.17516.d0
13. Sweller, J.: Element interactivity and intrinsic, extraneous, and germane cognitive load. Educ. Psychol. Rev. **22**(2), 123–138 (2010). https://doi.org/10.1007/s10648-010-9128-5
14. Leppink, J., Paas, F., van Gog, T., van der Vleuten, C.P.M., van Merriënboer, J.J.G.: Effects of pairs of problems and examples on task performance and different types of cognitive load. Learn. Instr. **30**, 32–42 (2014). https://doi.org/10.1016/j.learninstruc.2013.12.001
15. Ayaz, H., Dehais, F.: Neuroergonomics. In: Salvendy, G., Karwowski, W. (eds.) Handbook of Human Factors and Ergonomics, 5th edn., pp. 816–841. Wiley (2021)
16. Donthu, N., Kumar, S., Mukherjee, D., Pandey, N., Lim, W.M.: How to conduct a bibliometric analysis: an overview and guidelines. J. Bus. Res. **133**, 285–296 (2021). https://doi.org/10.1016/j.jbusres.2021.04.070
17. Harzing, A.-W.: "Publish or Perish," Harzing.com. https://harzing.com/resources/publish-or-perish. Accessed 15 Feb 2024
18. van Eck, N.J., Waltman, L.: Software survey: VOSviewer, a computer program for bibliometric mapping. Scientometrics **84**(2), 523–538 (2010). https://doi.org/10.1007/s11192-009-0146-3
19. "MAXQDA | All-In-One Qualitative & Mixed Methods Data Analysis Tool," MAXQDA. https://www.maxqda.com/. Accessed: Dec. 01, 2023
20. Obuseh, M., Duffy, V.G.: Surgical human-robot interaction: a bibliometric review. In: Kurosu, M., et al. (eds.) HCII 2022, pp. 293–312. Springer, Cham (2022). https://doi.org/10.1007/978-3-031-17618-0_22
21. Molotok, I.F.: Bibliometric and trend analysis of budget transparency. BEL **4**(2), 116–122 (2020). https://doi.org/10.21272/bel.4(2).116-122.2020
22. "Google Books Ngram Viewer." https://books.google.com/ngrams/. Accessed 01 Dec 2023
23. Abdelrahman, Y., Velloso, E., Dingler, T., Schmidt, A., Vetere, F.: Cognitive heat: exploring the usage of thermal imaging to unobtrusively estimate cognitive load. Proc. ACM Interact. Mob. Wearable Ubiquitous Technol. **1**(3), 33:1–33:20 (2017). https://doi.org/10.1145/3130898
24. Conway, D., Dick, I., Li, Z., Wang, Y., Chen, F.: The effect of stress on cognitive load measurement. In: Kotzé, P., Marsden, G., Lindgaard, G., Wesson, J., Winckler, M. (eds.) INTERACT 2013. LNCS, vol. 8120, pp. 659–666. Springer, Heidelberg (2013). https://doi.org/10.1007/978-3-642-40498-6_58
25. Ismail, L.E., Karwowski, W.: Applications of EEG indices for the quantification of human cognitive performance: a systematic review and bibliometric analysis. PLoS ONE **15**(12), e0242857 (2020). https://doi.org/10.1371/journal.pone.0242857
26. Yang, J., Liang, N., Pitts, B.J., Prakah-Asante, K., Curry, R., Yu, D.: An eye-fixation related electroencephalography technique for predicting situation awareness: implications for driver state monitoring systems. Hum. Factors 00187208231204570 (2023). https://doi.org/10.1177/00187208231204570
27. Yang, J., et al.: Multimodal sensing and computational intelligence for situation awareness classification in autonomous driving. IEEE Trans. Hum.-Mach. Syst. **53**(2), 270–281 (2023). https://doi.org/10.1109/THMS.2023.3234429
28. Barragan, J.A., Chanci, D., Yu, D., Wachs, J.P.: SACHETS: semi-autonomous cognitive hybrid emergency teleoperated suction. In: 2021 30th IEEE International Conference on Robot & Human Interactive Communication (RO-MAN), pp. 1243–1248 (2021). https://doi.org/10.1109/RO-MAN50785.2021.9515517
29. Mattys, S.L., Wiget, L.: Effects of cognitive load on speech recognition. J. Mem. Lang. **65**(2), 145–160 (2011). https://doi.org/10.1016/j.jml.2011.04.004

30. Zihisire Muke, P., Piwowarczyk, M., Telec, Z., Trawiński, B., Maharani, P.A., Bresso, P.: Impact of the Stroop effect on cognitive load using subjective and psychophysiological measures. In: Nguyen, N.T., Iliadis, L., Maglogiannis, I., Trawiński, B. (eds.) ICCCI 2021. LNCS (LNAI), vol. 12876, pp. 180–196. Springer, Cham (2021). https://doi.org/10.1007/978-3-030-88081-1_14

31. Mehta, R.: NSF Award Search: Award # 2343187 - CHS: Medium: Collaborative Research: Augmenting Human Cognition with Collaborative Robots. https://www.nsf.gov/awardsearch/showAward?AWD_ID=2343187. Accessed 01 Dec 2023

32. Arnaoudova, V.: NSF Award Search: Award # 1755995 - CRII: SHF: Quantifying the Impact of Poor Quality Lexicon on Developers' Cognitive Load. https://www.nsf.gov/awardsearch/showAward?AWD_ID=1755995. Accessed 01 Dec 2023

33. Cyber-Physical Systems (CPS) | NSF - National Science Foundation. https://new.nsf.gov/funding/opportunities/cyber-physical-systems-cps. Accessed 15 Feb 2024

34. Kaber, D.: NSF Award Search: Award # 1900044 - CHS: Medium: Collaborative Research: Electromyography (EMG)-Based Assistive Human-Machine Interface Design: Cognitive Workload and Motor Skill Learning Assessment. https://www.nsf.gov/awardsearch/showAward?AWD_ID=1900044. Accessed 01 Dec 2023

35. Salvendy, G., Karwowski, W.: Handbook of Human Factors and Ergonomics, 5th edn. Wiley, Hoboken (2021)

Analysis and Validation on Multi-dimensional Assessment for Comfort of In-Ear Headphones

Tingting Wang[1], Yewei Wang[2], Guangzheng Yu[1,2]([✉]), Zihan Chen[1], and Zhelin Li[1]

[1] School of Design, South China University of Technology, Guangzhou 510641,
People's Republic of China
scgzyu@scut.edu.cn

[2] School of Physics and Optoelectronics, South China University of Technology,
Guangzhou 510641, People's Republic of China

Abstract. The comfort of in-ear headphones is becoming more and more important nowadays as people use them more frequently and for longer periods of time. Past studies related to headphones have differed in their definitions of comfort, have not been uniform in their assessment methods, and have rarely considered sound related attributes and human psychological states. In this study, an attempt was made to create an in-ear headphone comfort assessment questionnaire containing four dimensions: physical, functional, acoustic and psychological, comprising 17 entries scored on a 7-point Likert scale format. A total of 20 participants (10 male and 10 female) participated in the experiment, each of whom took turns wearing five test headphones with different in-ear angles, and scored the test headphones one by one using the established multidimensional assessment questionnaire. The collected data were analyzed to further modify the structure of the questionnaire and to test its validity and reliability. The results showed that the amended questionnaire had good reliability and acceptable validity, but further refinement is still needed. This study provides a reference for a multidimensional approach to assessing the comfort of in-ear headphones.

Keywords: In-ear Headphones · Comfort · Multidimensional Assessment · Questionnaire

1 Introduction

Headphone has become one of the indispensable products in modern people's daily life, and also subconsciously influence people's life and work style. With the accelerated pace of life, increasingly busy work, mixed office demand continues to grow, people need to make voice or video calls in different environments, in order not to interfere with each other people often rely on headphones for sound playback. Compared to over-ear headphones, in-ear headphones have the advantages of small size and good sound insulation, making them the most popular type of headphones, and people are wearing in-ear headphones for longer and longer periods of time.

For the first time, comfort in the ear while wearing is the biggest driver of consumer purchases, according to Qualcomm State of Sound 2023 Report [1]. In-ear headphones

V. G. Duffy (Ed.): HCII 2024, LNCS 14709, pp. 135–149, 2024.
https://doi.org/10.1007/978-3-031-61060-8_10

fit snugly in the human ear, and if they are not properly sized and shaped, it will be difficult for people to get a consistent fit and comfort when wearing them, and they can be prone to pain with prolonged use. In addition, because in-ear headphones close off the outer ear canal, they are prone to a stuffy, blocked feeling (also known as the occlusion effect). All these factors are critical to reduced comfort.

Currently the ergonomic design of headphones cannot adapt to the shape of different people's ears is still a technical pain point, but there is no international standard or authoritative specification of the size of the headphone, for example, the angle of in-ear (it can be interpreted as the angle of the earbuds out of the ear with the in-ear headphone against the inner side of the ear cavity, there has not yet been a unified definition), this is the size of in-ear headphones as compared to the other types of headphone specific parameters, the angle of the different brands of in-ear headphones into the ear is a big difference, but are claimed to be in line with the ergonomics of the angle of the in-ear [2].

Over the years, many scholars have conducted experiments using different methods dedicated to optimizing the ergonomic design of headphones. The main research methods can be summarized as follows: obtaining ear anthropometric data, making headphone models with different sizes, conducting wearing experiments, and analyzing the relationship between headphone size and ear size and wearing comfort. For example, Lee et al. [3] produced nine prototypes with different size of earphone-heads to study the correlation between earphone size and its ear size. Park et al. [4] produced 20 prototypes with different lengths, widths, and thicknesses of earphones to study the main factors affecting the wearing sensation and the range of suitable headphone parameters. Wang et al. [5] created 30 prototypes with different angles to simulate different auricular expansion angles (the extent to which the cartilage of the auricular screen expands outward) of the ear when wearing an in-ear wearable device, and investigated the effect of changes in the auricular expansion angle on the comfort of various parts of the auricle. Methodologically for prototype assessment, these studies typically have participants choose the model that they are most satisfied with or begin to feel pain with, or fill out a comfort assessment questionnaire to compare comfort differences between models.

However, comfort is a complex concept that is related to a variety of factors such as a person's physiological attributes, psychological state, product usability, and the environment in which they are located [6], and multiple more specific and detailed metrics and questions are needed to characterize comfort. Most current assessments of headphone comfort have focused on pain-related comfort and fit. The questionnaires used in different studies vary and there is no standardized questionnaire. Therefore, this paper attempts to propose and pre-test a multidimensional questionnaire for comfort assessment of in-ear headphones. The reliability and validity of the questionnaire in comfort assessment is tested through a series of analyses.

2 In-Ear Headphone Comfort Assessment Questionnaire

2.1 Multidimensional Structure of the Questionnaire

Doutres and Terroir et al. [6–9] did an in-depth study on the comfort of hearing protection devices (HPDs) and proposed a multidimensional structure of HPD comfort, including physical dimensions related to biomechanical and thermal interactions; functional dimensions related to HPD usability, efficiency, and usefulness; internal and external sound perception-related acoustic dimensions; and psychological dimensions related to the user's well-being. Further, they designed the COPROD (COmfort of Hearing PROtection Devices) questionnaire and tested the reliability of the questionnaire structure. In-ear headphones and hearing protection earplugs are both wearable products for the ear and have similarities in the way they are used, both need to be inserted into the ear canal. Therefore the comfort assessment questionnaire for in-ear headphones uses the multidimensional structure of COPROD, which is also divided into four dimensions: physical, functional, acoustic, and psychological.

2.2 Questionnaire Design

In past studies on earphone wearing perception, researchers have proposed different questionnaires and items. Chiu et al. [10] evaluated the overall and specific comfort of earphones using six items, which were overall comfort perception, overall fit perception, load perception, and wearing convenience perception (ease of putting on and ease of taking off). Song et al. [11] designed a Evaluation questionnaires for wearing comfort, including wearing comfort, pain (during wearing, operation, and after use), pressure, fixation, and satisfaction; Liu et al. [12] established an evaluation index system for true wireless earphone fit, which was categorized into padding sense, stability sense, and pressure sense. In summary, the evaluation questionnaires and entries focus on the concepts of comfort, pain, fit or suitability, pressure or compression, and stability or fixation. The design of the questions usually distinguishes between the auricular nail cavity and the ear canal area, static and dynamic.

In summary, with reference to the COPROD questionnaire and the assessment content related to the wearing sensation of earphones, the final in-ear headphones comfort assessment questionnaire was designed with 17 items. In order to more accurately quantify the subjective feelings and improve the differentiation of inter-model evaluation, the questions were scored using a Likert 7-point scale format (1 = fully non-compliant, 7 = full compliant).

Physical Comfort. Physical comfort is related to the physical sensations generated by the contact of the in-ear headphones on the skin of the ear, including pain caused by static mechanical pressure, compression, and a sense of fit that reflects the degree of fit of the headphones with the shape of the ear, there are five entries: PH1 - No pain in the region of the ear nail cavity, PH2 - No pain in the region of the ear canal, PH3 - No compression in the region of the ear nail cavity, PH4 - No compression in the region of the ear canal, PH5 - In-ear headphones is very well suited to the ear (the shape of the in-ear headphones fits the shape of the ear perfectly is considered to be a perfect fit).

Functional Comfort. Functional comfort is related to the usability of the in-ear headphones. The main concerned with the in-ear headphones as a wearable product wearing, in-wearing, and removing the three processes, including the difficulty of finding the position to wear, wearing comfort and wearing stability. There are five entries: F1 - Easy to find the correct wearing position of the in-ear headphones, F2 - Comfortable in the process of putting in the in-ear headphones, F3 - Comfortable in the process of removing the in-ear headphones, F4 - Able to keep the in-ear headphones in the wearing position after wearing it under static conditions, F5 - Able to keep the in-ear headphones in the wearing position after wearing it under dynamic conditions.

Acoustic Comfort. Acoustic comfort is related to the acoustic properties of the in-ear headphones. The main concern of the earplugs plugged into the ear canal produced by the occlusion effect of the ear, including the degree of influence by the sound in the human body on the outside world of sound and the direction of the source of the perception of the degree of the sound source, there are three entries: A1 - You will not be affected by their own speech, chewing sound or other sounds from the body (heartbeat, breathing), A2 - You can perceive the sound of other people talking to you, A3 - You can perceive the direction from which the sound is coming from.

Psychological Comfort. Psychological comfort reflects the psychological state when wearing the in-ear headphones and has four items: PS1 - You feel isolated from the outside world, PS2 - You feel free when using the in-ear headphones, PS3 - You feel relaxed when using the in-ear headphones, and PS4 - You feel satisfied with the pair of in-ear headphones.

3   Method

3.1   Experiment Design and Procedure

Participants. Twenty Chinese adults (10 males and 10 females) between the ages of 19 and 30, all of whom were college students, were recruited for this study. Before the start of the experiment, the participants filled out the user profile questionnaire, which was used to collect their basic information and headphones usage habits, and about half of the participants had used in-ear headphones, and most of them used headphones with a high frequency and wore them every day. The related statistical results are shown in Table 1 and Table 2.

Table 1. Basic information on the participants.

		Age	Height/cm	Weight/kg	BMI
Male (N = 10)	Mean	24.10	173.90	68.50	22.52
	SD	2.92	0.06	12.74	3.01
Female (N = 10)	Mean	24.20	162.90	53.60	20.20
	SD	1.03	0.04	5.46	1.90

Table 2. Headphones usage habits on the participants.

Characteristics	Conditions	N = 20	Frequency (%)
Types of headphones often used (multiple answers possible)	Headband headphones	12	60
	In-ear headphones	11	55
	Semi-in-ear headphones	8	40
	Open headphones	1	5
Frequency of headphones use	Basically not used	0	0
	Used 1 or 2 times per month	1	5
	Used 1 or 2 times per week	0	0
	Multiple times per week	3	20
	Used every day	16	80
Average duration of each continuous wearing of the headphones	Less than half an hour	1	5
	0.5–1 h	2	10
	1–2 h	6	30
	2–3 h	4	50
	More than 3 h	7	35

Test In-Ear Headphones. Based on the common shapes of in-ear headphones in the market, in the 3D modeling software, 5 pairs of curved surface models were independently designed with the in-ear angles at 15° intervals. Each pair contains 2 symmetrical models, and their in-ear angles are 90°, 75°, 60°, 45° and 30°, as shown in Fig. 1. (A) In-ear angle. (B) 3D printed prototype. (C) Schematic of test in-ear headphones assembly. (a). The in-ear headphones prototypes (referred to as prototypes) were 3D printed using white ABS resin material. The five pairs of prototypes were named A_1 (90°), A_2 (75°), A_3 (60°), A_4 (45°), and A_5 (30°) in order of the in-ear angle from the largest to the smallest as shown in Fig. 1. (B). At the center of each prototype, a hollow cylindrical hole is reserved in the model according to the size of Etymotic's ER-2 TUBEPHONE Tubal Insert Earphones (referred to as ER2 Earphones), as shown in Fig. 1. (c). In order to simulate the actual use of headphones, the earplug part of the ER2 Earphone was placed in the space reserved in advance by the prototype, allowing the prototype to achieve sound reproduction. The experimental environment for sound reproduction is a sound-insulated listening room. In addition, soft silicone earplugs of different sizes are prepared and can be fitted to the prototype. The prototype, earplugs, and ER-2 TUBE-PHONE were assembled to form a complete test in-ear headphones, which was worn multiple times by the same subject by replacing parts of the prototype.

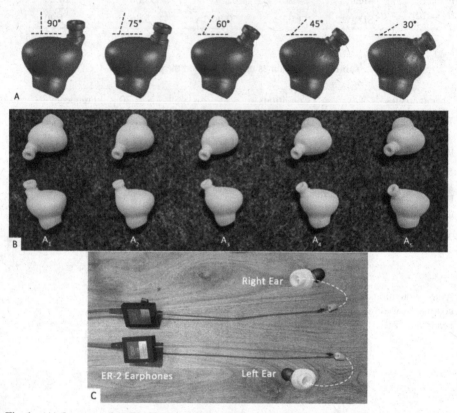

Fig. 1. (A) In-ear angle. (B) 3D printed prototype. (C) Schematic of test in-ear headphones assembly.

Experimental Procedure. The experiment was conducted in a room with noise not exceeding 30 dB, simulating a daily study and work environment, and the experimental procedure is organized in Fig. 2. Before the start of the experiment, the researcher introduced the experimental procedure and important concepts to the participants, and the relevant information was printed out in paper for reading to help the participants understand the purpose and key points of the experiment quickly and accurately. Each subject was assigned a number from 1 to 20 in the order of the experiment, with odd-numbered participants wearing the prototypes in the order of largest to smallest in-ear angle and even-numbered participants wearing the prototypes in the opposite order. The test headphones were prepared by the researcher and given to the participants to wear, without the participants knowing the exact in-ear angle. Each test in-ear headphones was worn for 8 min, and the computer simultaneously played pure music, with the same music played for all experiments. Two wearing interval of 2 min, if wearing discomfort still exists then extend the rest time, each person for a total of five wearing (Fig. 3).

1.Fill in the user profile questionnaire

2.Familiarize yourself with the experimental process and the content of the in-ear headphone comfort assessment questionnaire

3. Try on the prototype and determine the size of the earbuds

Wear the test in-ear headphone and adjust it to the proper position

Completion of the first part of the questionnaire (F1, F2)

Complete the following tasks while wearing the device:

1. feel the sound of other people talking in different locations in the room

2. chewing (researcher provides food)

3. Perform movements such as bobbing the head, standing up, and jumping in place (dynamic condition)

Completion of the second part of the questionnaire (physical, acoustic, psychological comfort and F4, F5)

Take off test in-ear headphones

Completion of the third part of the questionnaire (F3)

Rest for about 2 minutes until the discomfort in the ear disappears and wear the next test device

Fig. 2. Experimental procedure.

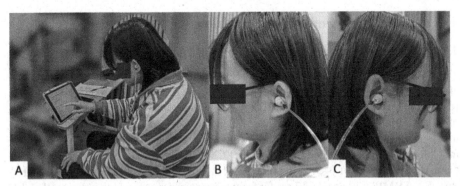

Fig. 3. (A) Photographs of the experimental procedure. (B) Wearing state of the left ear. (C) Wearing state of the right ear.

3.2   Questionnaire Examination

The data were summarized and analyzed for reliability and validity to test the reasonableness and quality of the designed questionnaire for assessing the comfort level of in-ear headphones. Reliability refers to the consistency of the measurements, reflecting the stability and reliability of the data, and the internal consistency of the questionnaire was tested using the Cronbach's alpha coefficient ($\alpha > 0.8$: high) [13]. Validity is the degree of closeness between the measurement results and the objectives attempted to be achieved, reflecting the validity of the questionnaire, the structural validity of the questionnaire was examined by confirmatory factor analysis (CFA) in structural equation modeling (SEM), CFA The assessment includes the overall goodness of fit, convergent validity, and discriminant validity of the model. The goodness of fit (GOF) of the CFA was comprehensively assessed using a number of indicators index: (1) the relative chi-square of degrees of freedom ratio, which was shown in the results as CMIN/DF (Minimum Discrepancy Function by Degrees of Freedom divided). (2) Root Mean Square Error of Approximation (RMSEA). (3) Standardized Root Mean Squared Residual (SRMR). In addition, Goodness of Fit Index (GFI), Adjusted Goodness of Fit IndexI (AGF), Comparative Fit Index (CFI), and Incremental Fit Index (IFI) were also selected, which all need to be greater than 0.9 [14], and some scholars believe that results greater than 0.85 or 0.80 are also acceptable [15–17]. The evaluation criteria for each indicator [18–20] are summarized in Table 3.

The goodness-of-fit of the model was good, then tested for convergent validity, Composite Reliability (CR) and discriminant validity in the next step. Convergent validity was assessed by calculating the Average Variance Extracted (AVE) and CR together, with AVE reaching 0.5 and CR reaching 0.7, and discriminant validity was assessed by comparing the square root of AVE with the correlation results, with the square root of ACE being greater than the "maximum value of correlation coefficient between this factor and other factors", indicating that the discriminant validity was good.

4   Questionnaire Analysis and Revision

4.1   Initial Questionnaire Confirmatory Factor Analysis

In this experiment, 100 questionnaires were returned (20 people * 5 tests). Based on the aforementioned multidimensional in-ear headphones comfort assessment questionnaire (called the initial questionnaire), a CFA model was established with each items as an observed variable and the corresponding dimension as a latent variable (factor), and the measurement model was estimated after importing the data. According to the results in Table 3, it can be obtained that the model CMIN/DF ratio is 3.836, which is within the acceptable range of 3–5. However, the other fitting metrics are not up to standard, RMSEA, SRMR, GFI and AGFI are far from the required range, which indicates that the model's goodness of fit is poor and the model structure needs to be adjusted. Figure 4 illustrates the standardized path coefficients from each entry to the factor to which it belongs (the factor points to the number above the straight line of the entry), with greater than 0.5 indicating a strong correlation [8]. The coefficients of the entries range from 0.57 to 0.89, except for entries 9 and 12, which have values below 0.5, indicating that most of the entries of the questionnaire are set more reasonably.

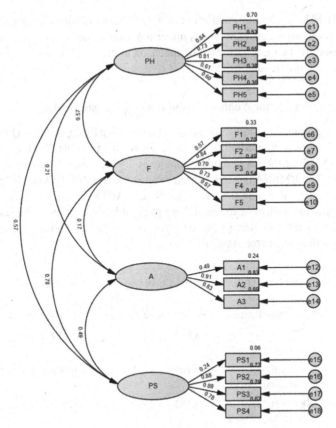

Fig. 4. Initial questionnaire CFA model diagram.

4.2 Questionnaire Revision

There are usually three ways to deal with the problem of substandard model fitting indicators: (1) Adjust the structure and correct the correspondence between factors and measurement items; (2) Delete unreasonable measurement items; (3) Modification Indices (MI) index correction, based on the MI index Values (larger values are significantly greater than other groups) establish the correlation between measurement items. The relationship between A1 ($\lambda = 0.49$) and PS1 ($\lambda = 0.24$) and their respective factors is weak, so we first try to adjust the two items. At the same time, the relevance of the meaning of the item is taken into account and the MI indicator is used for correction.

Finally, the questionnaire and CFA model were modified: (1) Delete A1, which has a weak relationship with each factor. (2) Adjust PS1 "You feel isolated from the outside world" to the acoustic comfort dimension (renamed A1). (3) Adjust PH5 "In-ear headphones is very well suited to the ear" to the dimension of psychological comfort (renamed PS1). When filling in this question, participants subjectively felt whether the headphones fit their ears well, rather than observing the actual wearing status of the headphones, and the analysis results showed that this question was more closely related to psychological comfort. (4) Based on the MI index correction, establish the correlation between PH1-PH4, F4 and F5, and PS2 and PS3. These questions are all descriptions of different positions or different states under the same concept, or states at the same position caused by the same factor (static mechanical pressure causes compression and pain), so a correlation is established.

4.3 Confirmatory Factor Analysis of the Revised Questionnaire

The revised questionnaire establishment model is shown in Fig. 5. Revised Questionnaire CFA Model Diagram. According to the indicator results in Table 3, it can be obtained that the CMIN/DF of the revised questionnaire is 1.977, which is less than 3, and the result is good. The RMSEA is 0.099, which is barely acceptable. CFI and IFI are greater than 0.9, GFI is greater than 0.8, and SRMR and AGFI do not meet the standards. Overall, the goodness of fit of the model is not good but acceptable. The standardized path coefficients from each item to the corresponding factors are above 0.5, ranging from 0.55 to 0.95, which meets the standard.

Table 3. Overall fitting results of two models for CFA.

Indexes	Acceptable Range	Initial Questionnaire	Revised Questionnaire
CMIN/DF	Good 1–3, acceptable3–5	3.836	1.977
RMSEA	Good < 0.08, acceptable0.08–0.1	0.169	0.099
SRMR	Good < 0.05, acceptable0.05–0.8	0.152	0.092
GFI	>0.9	0.667	0.817
AGFI	>0.9	0.550	0.727
CFI	>0.9	0.700	0.914
IFI	>0.9	0.706	0.916

4.4 Convergent Validity and Discriminant Validity

Under the condition that the revised questionnaire has acceptable goodness of fit, the convergent validity and discriminant validity of each dimension will be further tested. AVE and CR are calculated based on the standardized path coefficient values of each item. According to the analysis results in Table 4, it can be seen that the AVE of the two dimensions of physical comfort and functional comfort does not meet the requirement of greater than 0.5. In the range of 0.46–0.48, the AVE of the two dimensions of acoustic comfort and psychological comfort is greater than 0.5, reaching about 0.66, and CR in the four dimensions are all greater than 0.7. Some scholars believe that if AVE is less than 0.5 but CR is greater than 0.6, then the convergent validity of the model is still sufficient [21].

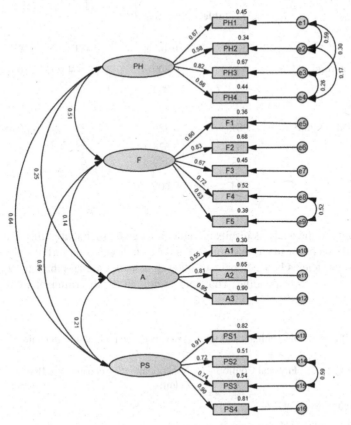

Fig. 5. Revised Questionnaire CFA Model Diagram.

Table 4. Convergent validity and combined reliability testing of the revised model.

Factors	Items	Estimate	AVE	CR
Physical Comfort	PH1	0.669	0.474	0.780
	PH2	0.581		
	PH3	0.819		
	PH4	0.663		
Functional Comfort	F1	0.598	0.462	0.808
	F2	0.827		
	F3	0.668		
	F4	0.724		
	F5	0.547		

(*continued*)

Table 4. (*continued*)

Factors	Items	Estimate	AVE	CR
Acoustic Comfort	A1	0.809	0.664	0.854
	A2	0.907		
	A3	0.717		
Psychological Comfort	PS1	0.736	0.660	0.884
	PS2	0.628		
	PS3	0.947		
	PS4	0.900		

According to the analysis results in Table 5, it can be seen that in this discriminant validity test, except for functional comfort and psychological comfort, the standardized correlation coefficients between pairs of other dimensions are less than the square root of the AVE value corresponding. Thus indicating that the discriminant validity of the revised model is better.

Table 5. Discriminant validity test results of the revised questionnaire.

	Physical Comfort	Functional Comfort	Acoustic Comfort	Psychological Comfort
Physical Comfort	0.474			
Functional Comfort	0.509*	0.462		
Acoustic Comfort	0.253	0.143	0.664	
Psychological Comfort	0.640**	0.958**	0.209	0.660
The Square Root of the AVE	0.688	0.680	0.815	0.812

*. $p < 0.05$. **. $p < 0.01$. The diagonal number is the AVE value of the factor.

4.5 Internal Consistency Reliability

The reliability analysis of the revised in-ear headphones comfort assessment questionnaire showed that the Cronbach's alpha coefficient of each dimension ranged from 0.801 to 0.907, and the Cronbach's alpha coefficient of the entire questionnaire was 0.879, both greater than 0.8. This shows that the questionnaire has good reliability.

5 Discussion and Conclusion

During the above analysis process, the confirmatory factor analysis results of the initial questionnaire were not ideal. Except for CMIN/DF, the other model fitting indicators did not meet the standards, so the questionnaire structure was adjusted. The revised questionnaire has good reliability, but some indicators of validity analysis are not good. The RMSEA value is 0.099, which is close to 1. SRMR and AGFI did not meet the standards. The AVE of the two dimensions of physical and functional comfort is less than 0.5. The standardized correlation coefficient between functional comfort and psychological comfort is higher than the square root of the AVE value corresponding to the dimension. MI index correction is used in the confirmatory factor analysis model. Although this method is often used to improve the goodness of model fitting, it is not a recommended method [22].

Combining the analysis results and the interview content of the participants, we try to analyze the possible reasons for the poor validity of the questionnaire: (1) The item content is deviated from the concept of comfort. The standardized correlation coefficients between acoustic comfort and other dimensions are all low (Table 5), indicating that the higher the score for each item under acoustic comfort, the better the comfort. Some participants said that it is more comfortable to achieve a balance between external sound and the sound isolation effect of the headphones, that is, they can perceive a certain amount of external sounds while immersing themselves in enjoying the sound in the headphones. (2) Some problems may cause errors in the comfort evaluation of multiple similar headphones that only change some size parameters. For example, F1 "Easy to find the correct wearing position of the in-ear headphones". Since the models used are similar in shape and only a certain size parameter is changed, the participants will gradually become familiar with the wearing method after repeated wearing, resulting in higher scores for subsequent wearing of earphones, which will cause errors in the results. (3) There are differences understanding of the words in the questions in participants. Taking the F2 "Comfortable in the process of putting in the in-ear headphones" as an example, some participants thought it was very comfortable if there was no special feeling, while some subjects thought it was generally comfortable.

The item "You are not affected by the sound of yourself talking, chewing, or other sounds from the body (heartbeat, breathing)" was deleted from the questionnaire. Participants believed that chewing sounds have a greater impact than sounds from the body, which would affect their choice of this question. It may be that for this reason this item cannot effectively express acoustic comfort. Chewing is not a frequent action, but heartbeat and breathing are always present. Although this item was deleted in the analysis of this article, it is still recommended to evaluate speech sounds and sounds from the body separately in subsequent studies. The sample size of this study is relatively small, only 100, which can be used as a pre-test to provide reference opinions for modifying the questionnaire. If the questionnaire test results are to be more powerful, further research requires a sample size of more than 200.

This study constructed an in-ear headphones comfort assessment questionnaire including four dimensions: physical, functional, acoustic, and psychological. The questionnaire was used to evaluate the comfort of the five test pairs of in-ear headphones, in order to verify the reliability and validity of the questionnaire for assessing in-ear head-phones comfort through pretesting. In general, the reliability and validity test results of the revised in-ear headphones comfort multi-dimensional assessment questionnaire are acceptable, but the quality of the questionnaire is not good. It is necessary to further optimize based on the issues raised above.

Acknowledgments. This work was supported by the National Natural Science Foundation of China (grant number 12074129), the Fundamental Research Funds for the Central Universities (grant number 2022ZYGXZR104) and the National Key Research and Development Program of China (grant number 2022YFF0607000): Research and Application of Ergonomics Key Technical Standards for Elderly-oriented Community.

References

1. The State of Sound 2023 Report – Qualcomm. https://assets.qualcomm.com/State_of_Sound_2023_asset_reg.html. Accessed 31 Aug 2022
2. Liu, C.: Anthropometric Measurements of Chinese Ear Using 3D In-Ear Scanning (Master thesis) Hunan University, Changsha, Hunan, China (2021)
3. Lee, W., et al.: Measurement and application of 3D ear images for earphone design. Proc. Hum. Factors Ergon. Soc. Ann. Meeting **60**, 1053–1057 (2016). https://doi.org/10.1177/1541931213601244
4. Park, K.Y., Ban, K.M., Woo, L.H., Seung, J.E.: Ergonomic analysis of ear anthropometry for the design specifications of open-type wireless earbuds. J. Ergon. Soc. Korea **40**, 389–400 (2021)
5. Wang, M., et al.: Effects of variations in the tragus expansion angle on physical comfort for in-ear wearables. Ergonomics 1–21 (2022). https://doi.org/10.1080/00140139.2022.2032377
6. Terroir, J., Doutres, O., Sgard, F.: Towards a "global" definition of the comfort of earplugs (2017)
7. Doutres, O., et al.: A critical review of the literature on comfort of hearing protection devices: definition of comfort and identification of its main attributes for earplug types. Int. J. Audiol. **58**, 824–833 (2019). https://doi.org/10.1080/14992027.2019.1646930
8. Terroir, J., Perrin, N.: Earplugs comfort: development of a laboratory evaluation protocol, p. 5 (2020). https://doi.org/10.48465/FA.2020.0014
9. Terroir, J., et al.: Assessing the comfort of earplugs: development and validation of the French version of the COPROD questionnaire. Ergonomics **64**, 912–925 (2021). https://doi.org/10.1080/00140139.2021.1880027
10. Chiu, H.-P., Chiang, H.-Y., Liu, C.-H., Wang, M.-H., Chiou, W.-K.: Surveying the comfort perception of the ergonomic design of Bluetooth earphones. Work **49**, 235–243 (2014). https://doi.org/10.3233/WOR-131723
11. Song, H., Shin, G.W., Yoon, Y., Bahn, S.: The effects of ear dimensions and product attributes on the wearing comfort of wireless earphones. Appl. Sci. **10**, 8890 (2020). https://doi.org/10.3390/app10248890
12. Liu, Y., Yan, Y., Wang, H.: True wireless stereo earphone fit design based on analytic hierarchy process and grey relational analysis. Packaging Eng. **42**, 153–160 (2021). https://doi.org/10.19554/j.cnki.1001-3563.2021.24.017
13. Moret, L., Mesbah, M., Chwalow, J., Lellouch, J.: Validation interne d'une échelle de mesure: relation entre analyse en composantes principales, coefficient α de Cronbach et coefficient de corrélation intra-classe. Rev. épidémiol. santé publique. **41**, 179–186 (1993)

14. How To Interpret Model Fit Results In AMOS – Uedufy. https://uedufy.com/how-to-inter-pret-model-fit-results-in-amos/. Accessed 11 Feb 2024

15. Doll, W.J., Xia, W., Torkzadeh, G.: A confirmatory factor analysis of the end-user computing satisfaction instrument. MIS Q. **18**, 453–461 (1994). https://doi.org/10.2307/249524

16. Byrne, B.M., Campbell, T.L.: Cross-cultural comparisons and the presumption of equivalent measurement and theoretical structure: a look beneath the surface. J. Cross Cult. Psychol. **30**(5), 555–574 (1999). https://doi.org/10.1177/0022022199030005001

17. Akkuş, A.: Developing a scale to measure students' attitudes toward science. Int. J. Assess. Tools Educ. **6**(4), 706–720 (2020). https://doi.org/10.21449/ijate.548516

18. Wheaton, B., Muthén, B., Alwin, D.F., Summers, G.F.: Assessing reliability and stability in panel models. Sociol. Methodol. **8**, 84–136 (1977). https://doi.org/10.2307/270754

19. Nikkhah, M., Heravi-Karimooi, M., Montazeri, A., Rejeh, N., Sharif Nia, H.: Psychometric properties the Iranian version of older people's quality of life questionnaire (OPQOL). Health Qual. Life Outcomes **16**, 174 (2018). https://doi.org/10.1186/s12955-018-1002-z

20. Cheng, S.-I.: Comparisons of competing models between attitudinal loyalty and behavioral loyalty. Int. J. Bus. Soc. Sci. **2**(10), 149–166 (2011)

21. Lam, L.W.: Impact of competitiveness on salespeople's commitment and performance. J. Bus. Res. **65**, 1328–1334 (2012). https://doi.org/10.1016/j.jbusres.2011.10.026

22. Hu, P., Lu, H., Ma, Z.: Feasibility and condition of allowable error correlation in confirmatory factor analysis. Stat. Decis. **34**(19), 37–41 (2018)

User Experience and Assistive Technologies

StairMate: Design and Evaluation of a Walking Assistive Device Along the Handrail for Older Adults

Hanyang Hu[1], Jie Liu[2], and Weiguo Xu[1,3]

[1] School of Architecture, Tsinghua University, Beijing, China
hy-hu22@mails.tsinghua.edu.cn, xwg@mail.tsinghua.edu.cn
[2] School of Digital Media and Design Arts, Beijing University of Posts and Telecommunications, Beijing, China
jie.liu@bupt.edu.cn
[3] Institute of Future Human Habitat, Shenzhen International Graduate School, Tsinghua University, Shenzhen, China

Abstract. Enhancing accessibility for older adults, particularly addressing challenges related to seniors navigating stairs, constitutes a significant theme in current human-computer interaction research. This paper details the design and development of an economical, small-scale walking assistive device, StairMate, to substantially increase the balance in older adults during stair use. The device can facilitate the convenient carriage of daily necessities for older adults and support ascending and descending stairs through its front handle. The preliminary verification of StairMate's effectiveness in assisting elderly individuals in navigating stairs is conducted by measuring surface electromyography activity in muscles. The results demonstrate over 65% increased lower limb stability for elderly individuals ascending stairs and over 55% during descent. The device offers a practical approach to accessible design, bringing great convenience to daily life and enhancing the living environment for older adults.

Keywords: Accessibility in Older Adults · Stair navigation · Walking assistive device

1 Introduction

Enhancing mobility in walk-up apartments, apartments that lack lifts in multi-storey structures, is essential for supporting aging in place [19,29]. The challenge of stair navigating in such apartments may increase fall risks in older adults [8], which leads to severe consequences such as fractures, soft tissue damage, and even death [25], potentially restricting their ability to live independently, decreasing their willingness to go out [30], and may even lead to psychological issues [4]. Therefore, smart technology for such issue of aging in place has become a prominent focus in human-computer interaction [7,23]. Deficiencies in lower

V. G. Duffy (Ed.): HCII 2024, LNCS 14709, pp. 153–169, 2024.
https://doi.org/10.1007/978-3-031-61060-8_11

limb muscle strength and balance contribute to the high occurrence of falls in older adults [13], especially during weight-bearing walking and stair navigation [27] (see Fig. 1).

Fig. 1. Weight bearing in older adults' daily routine (Image courtesy of authors)

Therefore, improving body balance and reducing the load on lower limb muscles while navigating stairs can enhance the mobility and safety of older adults. This study aims to prototype and evaluate a walking assistive device for older adults to carry objects and support them during stair navigation, thereby increasing their balance.

2   Related Work

Most factors related to falls in older adults during stair navigation can be divided into the built environment and physiological condition [11]. Regarding the built environment, the steps' size, the staircase's lighting, and other physical conditions in staircases may contribute to falls among older adults. Physiological conditions, such as decreased muscle mass, strength, bone density, and balance, can also lead to falls in older adults [5,11,22]. The related work in this paper mainly classifies devices assisting older adults in navigating stairs (Table 1).

– Built environment. Devices related to built environment issues, such as lifts (see Fig. 2(a)) and stair lifts(see Fig. 2(b)(c)) [2,6], fundamentally change how people move between floors. Lifts, while efficient, require significant modifications to the existing structure of apartment buildings and are costly to install. As a cost-effective alternative to lifts, stair lifts are relatively easy to install, but stairlifts' main body and track occupy space within the staircase [24], which impede evacuation routes and potentially pose a security hazard. Therefore, there is a clear need for this research to focus on designing a device that is both smaller in scale and lower in cost, effectively addressing these limitations.
– **Physiological condition.** Devices designed to address the weakened physiological conditions of older adults encompass sliding auxiliary bars, exoskeletons, walkers, and stair-climbing wheelchairs (see Fig. 2(d)(e)(f)(g)) [3,10, 16,17]. The sliding auxiliary bar [1,26], exoskeletons, and walkers could be independently used by older adults, while stair-climbing wheelchairs require professional assistance. None of these devices consider scenarios where older

Table 1. Devices helping elderly people ascending and descending stairs

Category	Item	Usage	Load-bearing	Elderly's Activities	Elderly's Use Independence	Price (US$)	Defects
Built Environment	Lift	Stand in the elevator and follow it up and down the stairs	✓	✗	✓	40,000–70,000 /6 storeys	·High cost ·Long construction period/1 month ·Large changes to the original building structure ·No chance to walk
	Stair Lift	Stand on the pedal that runs up and down an additional track on the side of the stairway	✓	✗	✓	1,000–5,000 /half storey	·High cost ·Long construction period/1 week ·Large changes to the original architectural space ·No chance to walk
		Sit in seats that run up and down an additional track on the side of the stairway	✓	✗	✓	2,500–10,000 /half storey	·High cost ·Long construction period/1 week ·Large changes to the original architectural space ·No chance to walk
Physiological Condition	Sliding Auxiliary Bar	Control the movement according to an auxiliary bar	✗	✓	✓	about 1000 /half storey	·Large changes to the original architectural space ·No load-bearing functions
	Exoskeleton	Wearing the exoskeleton with mechanical support while using the stairs	✗	✓	✓	50-1,000	·Need to carry along ·No load-bearing functions
	Walker	Move the folding walker to increase body stability while using the stairs	✗	✓	✓	<500	·Need to carry along ·No load-bearing functions
	Stair Climbing Wheelchair	Sit in wheelchairs and need professional assistance	✓	✗	✓	100-15,000	·Need professional assistance

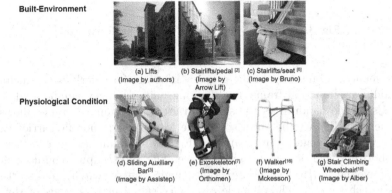

Built-Environment

(a) Lifts (Image by authors)

(b) Stairlifts/pedal [2] (Image by Arrow Lift)

(c) Stairlifts/seat [6] (Image by Bruno)

Physiological Condition

(d) Sliding Auxiliary Bar[3] (Image by Assistep)

(e) Exoskeleton[7] (Image by Orthomen)

(f) Walker[16] (Image by Mckesson)

(g) Stair Climbing Wheelchair[10] (Image by Alber)

Fig. 2. Images of devices in Table 1

people use stairs by themselves with belongings, which is a frequent and practical aspect of their daily lives. Furthermore, there are the health benefits of stair usage under safe conditions, including enhancement of limb muscle strength [18], the cardio-pulmonary function [20], and reduction in metabolic syndrome risks [28].

Consequently, the walking assistive device in this study should have the following characteristics:

a. cost-effective and small-scale;
b. load-bearing;
c. stable support during stair navigation.

3   Prototype of StairMate

The comprehensive system of the walking assistive device, namely StairMate, comprises three subsystems (see Fig. 3): main section, power section, and balance section.

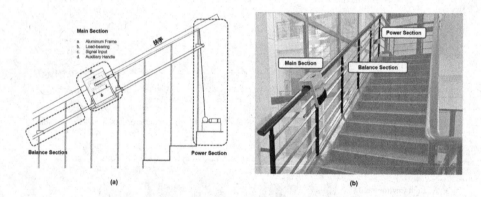

Fig. 3. Design of StairMate (a) and its prototype(b)

The main section serves as the primary interface for elderly users, including four modules: aluminum frame, load-bearing unit, auxiliary handle, and signal input. Using the handrail as the sliding track, the aluminum frame allows for adjustment to different handrail sizes. The load-bearing module carries items, and the auxiliary handle, integrated with the aluminum frame, provides stable support and can be folded to save space. The Signal input module includes obstacle avoidance (IR sensor), direction (single control switch), and start-stop signals (crash sensor). The obstacle avoidance signal at both ends of the aluminum frame halts movement if an obstacle is detected. The direction signal corresponds to the two gears of the single control switch, and the start-stop signal is controlled by a crash sensor built into the auxiliary handle.

In Fig. 4, we utilize a pair of BLE NANO boards integrated with Bluetooth 4.2 to facilitate signal transmission between the main and power sections. The

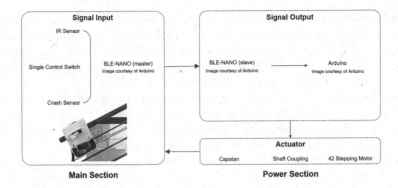

Fig. 4. Signal transmission of the main section and power section

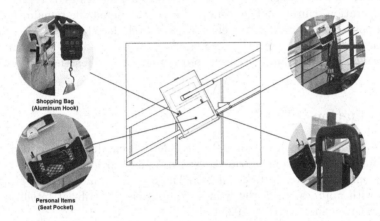

Fig. 5. The load-bearing module

Fig. 6. (a)Two states of the handle; (b)Usage of the handle

BLE-NANO (master) is positioned in the main section, while the BLE-NANO (slave) is in the power section. The power section receives directional and start-stop signals from the main section and propels the main section to move vertically through the actuator. Enhancing StairMate's stability, the balance section is situated under the handrail.

StairMate implements the following three features:

- **Cost and Scale:** To achieve the purpose of cost-effectiveness and small scale, StairMate is elaborately designed and implemented by three subsystems. The cost primarily involves expenses and modifications to existing staircases, which are limited to 120 US dollars. To cover a 10-centimeter-wide handrail, the size of the main section is adjusted to 20*26*37 cm.
- **Load-bearing:** To accommodate three common categories of items carried by older adults while navigating stairs: small personal belongings, shopping bags, and shopping carts, the inner side of the main section features mesh pockets, hooks, and L-shaped aluminum rods designed (see Fig. 5).
- **Stable Support:** To provide support for users' upper limbs, we integrated a handle, which is ergonomically designed and facilitates an easy single-handed grip for elderly individuals, on the stairway side of the main section. It folds to a width of 5cm when not in use (see Fig. 6(a)) and extends to 25cm during operation. During both ascent and descent, the handle remains horizontally positioned in front of the elderly user's body (see Fig. 6(b)). It provides upward force during ascent, reducing effort for older adults' lower limbs. It is a safety measure during descent, preventing forward-leaning and potential falls.

4 Evaluation

To assess StairMate's efficacy in assisting elderly users during stair navigation, we conducted an experiment analyzing users' physical fatigue and lower limb load. The prototype was installed at Tsinghua Shenzhen International Graduate School, with approval from the Ethics Committee of Artificial Intelligence at Tsinghua University (THU-03-2023-0012).

4.1 Participants and Experiment Setup

According to previous research [1,12], 12 elderly participants (7 females, 5 males, mean age = 64.67 ± 3.03 years old, height = 1.63 ± 0.07 m, weight = 105.00 ± 23.11 g) were recruited. All participants had basic literacy skills and experience with smart devices. During recruitment and the experiment, they reported being in good physical condition without injuries affecting walking or navigating stairs.

4.2 Procedure and Experimental Design

The whole experiment is divided into three steps (see Fig. 7):

- **Step A: Pre-Experiment.** Before the experiment, each participant was briefed on the procedure by the researcher, signed a consent form, and completed a basic information survey. Participants were instructed to complete tasks at an appropriate pace, with the option to withdraw if they felt uncomfortable.
- **Step B: Experiment.** The experiment comprised three rounds of tasks (see Fig. 8) to evaluate participants' physical fatigue and lower limb load.

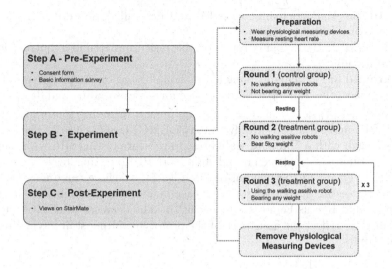

Fig. 7. The procedure of the experiment

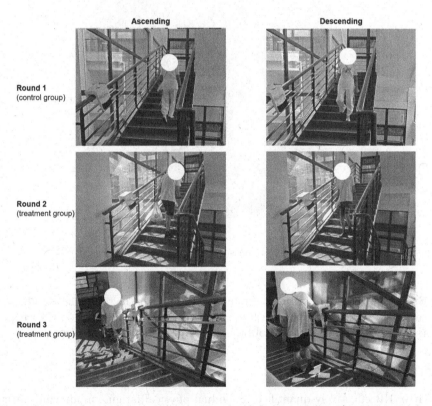

Fig. 8. Images of participants in three rounds of the experiment (participants' faces obscured to protect their privacy)

- **Round 1:** Participants ascended and descended 10 steps without any assistive device or load.
- **Round 2:** Participants repeated the task from Round 1 but carried a 5kg load.
- **Round 3:** Participants hung a 5kg shopping bag on the prototype's hook and used the walking assistive device for stair ascending and descending.

We adopted physiological measuring equipment, including sensors for heart rate (HR) and surface electromyography (sEMG) (see Fig. 9(a)). The experiment began with a 5-minute seated rest to measure resting HR, with a minimum 5-minute rest between rounds to restore HR to resting levels. According to Geiger et al. 's experimental research [9, 15], we chose three muscles contributing to stair navigation for the measurement: Anterior Tibialis, Gastrocnemius, and Rectus Femoris (see Fig. 9(b)). The decrease in sEMG activity will directly reflect the assistance of the prototype during stair navigation for older adults.

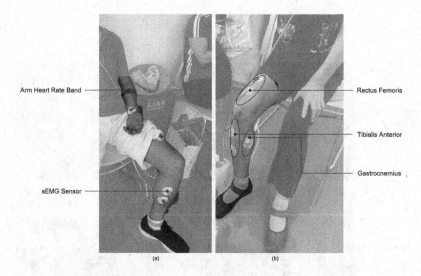

Fig. 9. Sensors' placements (a) and measured muscles (b)

- **Step C: Post-Experiment.** After the experiment, the researcher conducted semi-structured interviews with participants to gather insights on their experiences using StairMate and obtain suggestions for future development.

4.3   Data Analysis Method

Relative HR effectively quantified individual physical fatigue, minimizing variations between individuals [12]. Lower relative HR indicated lower exercise intensity and reduced fatigue. We adopted equation (1) for calculating relative HR

(HR_r), where HR_a (bmp) represents real-time HR, and HR_c (bmp) represents the participant's resting HR:

$$HR_r = \frac{HR_a}{HR_c} \qquad (1)$$

sEMG activity directly reflects the effectiveness of StairMate in assisting stair navigation. The prototype enhances the balance by lightening the load on lower limbs during ascent and descent. Visual charts and statistical methods were used for analysis, including the Kruskal-Wallis H Test [14] and Spearman's rank correlation coefficient [21].

5 Results and Discussion

5.1 Results of Main Experiment

Relative HR's Changes. In three rounds, Fig. 10 compares relative HR during ascending and descending progress.

- In Rounds 1 and 2 (without assistance), relative HR increases with the progress, indicating participants' fatigue increases when ascending and descending stairs.
- In Round 2 (bearing load), both the magnitude and value of relative HR exceed those in Round 1, indicating more significant exercise intensity and fatigue.
- In Round 3 (with assistance), participants experience a rapid increase in relative HR midway through the process, exceeding the level in Round 2. However, the relative HR subsequently slows down and stabilizes, revealing a distinctive pattern.

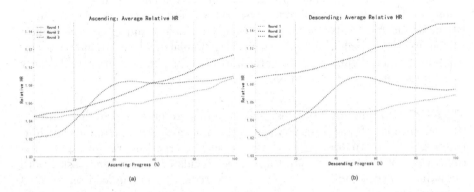

Fig. 10. Changes in Average relative HR during (a) ascending progress and (b) descending progress

Relative HR's Kruskal-Wallis H Tests. To discern distinct trends in relative HR across three experimental rounds, the ascending and descending process was divided into five stages: Stage 1 (0–20%), Stage 2 (20%–40%), Stage 3 (40%–60%), Stage 4 (60%-80%), and Stage 5 (80%–100%). The Kruskal-Wallis H test revealed significant variations in relative HR across all stages of stair ascent and descent for elderly participants in three experimental rounds (Ascending Progress: $2170.54 < H < 5238.95$, $p < 0.001$; Descending Progress: $2205.26 < H < 5332.44$, $p < 0.001$). These differences primarily stem from distinctions in each experimental task, surpassing individual participant variances.

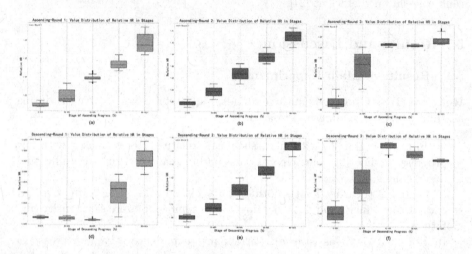

Fig. 11. Average relative HR in different stages during (a)(b)(c) ascending progress and (d)(e)(f) descending progress

Boxplots further highlight noticeable differences in participants' relative HR among the three experimental rounds across the five stages (see Fig. 11). Relative HR in Round 3 exhibits the largest variance in Stage 1 and 2, and the highest median in Stage 2 and 3. However, since Stage 3, relative HR in Round 3 remains stable or declines slightly, indicating the impact of StairMate on the HR of elderly individuals during stair navigation.

sEMG' S Changes of Muscles. sEMG data were processed to illustrate the smooth envelope of sEMG activity across the three experimental rounds for three muscles: Tibialis Anterior, Gastrocnemius, and Rectus Femoris. In Fig. 12, the comparison of sEMG activity during three rounds of stair-related tasks, both ascending and descending, reveals a notable reduction in the load on selected muscles in Round 3 compared to Round 1.

- During ascending progress in Round 3, the reduction of activity level: $75.99 \pm 11.63\%$ for tibialis anterior, $74.90 \pm 9.77\%$ for gastrocnemius, and $63.49 \pm 15.06\%$ for rectus femoris.

– During descending progress in Round 3, the reduction of activity level: 75.22 ± 11.72% for tibialis anterior, 67.48 ± 9.76% for gastrocnemius, and 59.61 ± 11.45% for rectus femoris.

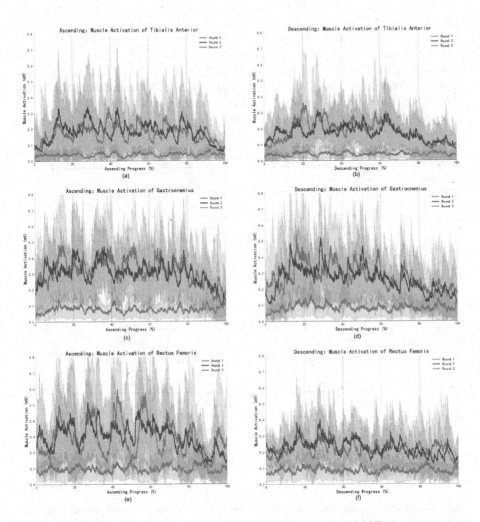

Fig. 12. Changes in sEMG activity of (a)(b) Tibialis Anterior, (c)(d) Gastrocnemius, and (e)(f) Rectus Femoris during stair ascent and descent. Shaded areas represent 95% confidence intervals

The reduction indicates a significant increase in balance during stair navigation when using StairMate, a sentiment widely acknowledged by participants.

Relationship Between Relative HR and sEMG. This study employs Spearman's correlation coefficient for analysis (see Fig. 13) to validate the impact of increased relative HR on sEMG activity and explore potential reasons.

- According to Fig. 13(a)(b)(c)(d), sEMG activity of each muscle shows a significant correlation with relative HR during the ascending and descending progress in Round 1 and Round 2 (without assistance), with values of Spearman correlation coefficients exceeding 0.05 ($p < 0.001$).
- According to Fig. 13(e)(f), in Round 3, Spearman correlation coefficients between each muscle's sEMG activity and relative HR are substantially lower compared to Rounds 1 and 2. This shows that using StairMate significantly weakens the association between HR and sEMG.

Muscle Activation (mV)		Relative HR
Tibialis Anterior	Spearman Correlation	-0.33956
	P-Value	< 0.001
Gastrocnemius	Spearman Correlation	-0.341747
	P-Value	< 0.001
Rectus Femoris	Spearman Correlation	-0.124713
	P-Value	< 0.001

(a) Round 1 - Ascending: Correlation between Relative HR and Muscle Activation

Muscle Activation (mV)		Relative HR
Tibialis Anterior	Spearman Correlation	-0.5506
	P-Value	< 0.001
Gastrocnemius	Spearman Correlation	-0.531906
	P-Value	< 0.001
Rectus Femoris	Spearman Correlation	-0.209364
	P-Value	< 0.001

(b) Round 1 - Descending: Correlation between Relative HR and Muscle Activation

Muscle Activation (mV)		Relative HR
Tibialis Anterior	Spearman Correlation	-0.164807
	P-Value	< 0.001
Gastrocnemius	Spearman Correlation	-0.383792
	P-Value	< 0.001
Rectus Femoris	Spearman Correlation	-0.4204
	P-Value	< 0.001

(c) Round 2 - Ascending: Correlation between Relative HR and Muscle Activation

Muscle Activation (mV)		Relative HR
Tibialis Anterior	Spearman Correlation	-0.422332
	P-Value	< 0.001
Gastrocnemius	Spearman Correlation	-0.512477
	P-Value	< 0.001
Rectus Femoris	Spearman Correlation	-0.462381
	P-Value	< 0.001

(d) Round 2 - Descending: Correlation between Relative HR and Muscle Activation

Muscle Activation (mV)		Relative HR
Tibialis Anterior	Spearman Correlation	0.056785
	P-Value	< 0.001
Gastrocnemius	Spearman Correlation	0.030155
	P-Value	< 0.001
Rectus Femoris	Spearman Correlation	0.073367
	P-Value	< 0.001

(e) Round 3 - Ascending: Correlation between Relative HR and Muscle Activation

Muscle Activation (mV)		Relative HR
Tibialis Anterior	Spearman Correlation	0.049701
	P-Value	< 0.001
Gastrocnemius	Spearman Correlation	-0.071759
	P-Value	< 0.001
Rectus Femoris	Spearman Correlation	-0.095481
	P-Value	< 0.001

(f) Round 3 - Descending: Correlation between Relative HR and Muscle Activation

Fig. 13. Spearman correlation coefficient between relative HR and average sEMG activity in three experimental rounds: (a) Round 1-Ascending, (b) Round 1-Descending, (c) Round 2-Ascending, (d) Round 2-Descending, (e) Round 3-Ascending, and (f) Round 3-Descending

5.2　Discussion

- **Novel Device's Impact on Older Adults' HR Changes.** The experimental results indicated an initial significant rise in relative heart rate (HR), followed by a stabilization phase. Using the newly developed walking assistive device might impose a psychological burden on the elderly, increasing their

nervousness and concentration compared to regular tasks in Rounds 1 and 2. As the duration of use extends, participants gradually adapt, and their relative HR stabilizes.
- **Data Collection of Older Adults' Movement.** In this study, we measured muscles' sEMG activity by sEMG sensors. However, some participants felt wearing unusual sensors discomforting, affecting their natural stair movements. Employing discreet methods such as the Vicon motion capture system could minimize interference, ensuring better user comfort and data accuracy.

6 Limitations and Prospects

Regarding the prototype of StairMate in the experiment, we conducted semi-structured interviews between researchers and participants to gain more scientific insights of the limitations and prospects of this research (Table 2).

Target User. 25% of the participants in the experiment deemed the walking assistive device suitable for individuals aged 75 and above.

Capability.

Speed and Auxiliary Handle. Among the participants, 83% found the Stair-Mate's movement speed to be slow and recommended the inclusion of a speed adjustment feature. Conversely, the remaining participants favored the slower speed, citing its role in reducing anxiety. Furthermore, 16% of the participants expressed a wish for a longer handle that could be held with both hands, and all participants voiced a desire to integrate voice control functionality into the device.

Multi-modal Interactions. All participants preferred adding the voice control function while maintaining the current physical buttons because this will both simplify the interaction process and ensure the security of use.

Cognitive Load. All participants agreed that the functionality and interface of the StairMate were clear and easily comprehensible.

Social Attributes

Publicity. 83% of the participants believed it could be permanently installed in residential staircases, while the rest of the participants suggested it could be further developed as a personal product.

Security. Only one participant expressed concerns about potential risks, especially if children mistake it for a toy.

Cost. All participants highlighted the significant cost advantage and a shared desire to minimize its impact on the living environment.

Table 2. Results of semi-structured interviews

CATEGORY	SUBCA-TEGORY	DETAILS		DESIGN SUGGESTIONS
Target User	*Age*	people aged 75 a-nd above	All participants (U7) "*When using the handle to ascend the stairs, I feel the effect of effort saving, but it was not obvious when descending the stairs.*" (U12) "*With the improvement of living conditions, our generation of elderly people are in better physical condition than in the past.*"	*01 Participants' Recruitment*
Capability	*Speed*	too slow	U1, 2, 3, 4, 5, 6, 9, 10, 11, 12	*02 Adjustable Speed*
		appropriate	U7, 8 (U8) "*Unlike young people rushing to work, we have ample time, and moving slowly with the device makes me feel at ease.*"	
	Auxiliary Handle	lengthen	U11, 12 (U12) "*If the handle could be grasped with both hands, it would significantly reduce physical exertion, especially when fatigued.*"	*03 Adjustable Handle*
	Multi-modal Interactions	reliable physical buttons	All participants (U11) "*I think current physical buttons are better than touch screens because I think touch screens are easily touched by mistake while physical buttons ensure stable control. Pressing them means starting without worrying about malfunction.*"	*04 Adding Voice Control Function*
		adding voice control function re-taining physical buttons	All participants (U3) "*Even with voice control, physical buttons should be retained as a standby choice.*" (U11) "*I will still use buttons because I speak with an accent, and the voice control system may not recognize accurately.*"	
	Cognitive Load	clear functions simple interface	All participants (U4) "*The functions are intuitive. Hanging items, controlling direction, and controlling start-stop, are straightforward operations for me.*"	
Social Attributes	*Publicity*	public use	U1, 2, 3, 4, 5, 6, 9, 10, 11, 12	*05 Prepare Using Instructions*
		private use	U7, 8 (U8) "*In the future, it could be smaller and lighter, so that each family could purchase one. We could carry it with us and use it when needed.*"	
	Security	potential risks f-or children	U2 (U2) "*Children might mistake it for a toy, leading to improper operation, potential damage, or even injury.*"	
	Cost	low expenses	All participants	
		small modificati-ons to staircases	All participants (U3) "*I was initially concerned about altering my living space with it, but the walking assistant device doesn't occupy stair space, and the installation is swift, which satisfies me.*"	

7   Conclusion

As preliminary research, this work effectively explores the feasibility and effectiveness of StairMate in assisting elderly individuals to navigate stairs. StairMate, featuring an innovative support mechanism and actuating system, tackles the issues related to cost and size, and it also addresses the need to carry objects while enhancing the balance of older adults.

The prototype of StairMate underwent a small-scale user experiment with elderly participants on a real staircase. Findings revealed an initial increase in participants' heart rate (HR) when using StairMate, followed by stabilization or even a decrease in HR ($p < 0.001$). This contrasts with the upward trend observed in the HR of elderly individuals during stair navigation without the assistive device. Measurement of surface electromyography (sEMG) on participants' lower limbs demonstrated a reduction of over 65% in lower limb muscle activity during stair ascent and 55% during descent with StairMate ($p < 0.001$). Additionally, StairMate attenuated the potential impact of HR changes on lower limb muscle activity during stair navigation. Based on semi-structured interviews, we gained suggestions for future improvements, including participants' age, adjustable speed, handle length and height, integration of voice control features, and additional user instructions. The outcomes of this research significantly contribute to improving the balance of older adults during stair navigation, thereby enhancing accessibility in walk-up apartments.

Acknowledgements. This work was supported by Shenzhen Science and Technology Innovation Committee (Grant No. WDZC20200822215113001).

References

1. Afsar, R., Haque, R., Dooley, M., Shen, X.: Railbot: a novel assistive device for stair climbing. J. Med. Devices-Trans. Asme **15** (2021). https://api.semanticscholar.org/CorpusID:233783804
2. ArrowLift: Stair lifts and home elevators | mobility solutions. https://arrowlift.com/
3. Assistep: Stay safe and active with the assistep stair walker (2018). https://assistep.com/
4. Baker, E., Clark, L.L.: Biopsychopharmacosocial approach to assess impact of social distancing and isolation on mental health in older adults. Br. J. Community Nurs. **25**(5), 231–238 (2020)
5. Bean, J.F., Kiely, D.K., LaRose, S.I., Alian, J., Frontera, W.R.: Is stair climb power a clinically relevant measure of leg power impairments in at-risk older adults? Arch. Phys. Med. Rehab. **88 5**, 604–9 (2007). https://api.semanticscholar.org/CorpusID:23924155
6. Bruno: Stair lifts | made in usa | bruno®. https://www.bruno.com/stair-lifts
7. Fournier, H., Kondratova, I., Katsuragawa, K.: Smart technologies and internet of things designed for aging in place. In: Interacción (2021). https://api.semanticscholar.org/CorpusID:236150043

8. Ganz, D.A., Latham, N.K.: Prevention of falls in community-dwelling older adults. New England J. Med. **382** 8, 734–743 (2020). https://api.semanticscholar.org/CorpusID:211213832

9. Geiger, D.E., Behrendt, F., Schuster-Amft, C.: Emg muscle activation pattern of four lower extremity muscles during stair climbing, motor imagery, and robot-assisted stepping: a cross-sectional study in healthy individuals. BioMed Res. Int. **2019** (2019). https://api.semanticscholar.org/CorpusID:108368834

10. GmbH, A.: scalamobil. https://www.alber-usa.com/us/products/stairclimbing-aids/scalamobil/#app

11. Jacobs, J.V.: A review of stairway falls and stair negotiation: lessons learned and future needs to reduce injury. Gait and posture **49**, 159–167 (2016). https://api.semanticscholar.org/CorpusID:8077060

12. Jiang, R., Wang, Y.Y., Xie, R., Zhou, T., Wang, D.: Effect of stairway handrails on pedestrian fatigue and speed during ascending evacuation. ASCE-ASME J. Risk Uncertainty Eng. Syst., Part A: Civil Eng. (2022). https://api.semanticscholar.org/CorpusID:251177320

13. Kováčiková, Z., Sarvestan, J., Neumannova, K., Linduška, P., Gonosova, Z., Pecho, J.: Balance control during stair descent on compliant surface is associated with knee flexor and ankle plantar flexor strength in older adults. J. Biomech. **111**, 110013 (2020). https://api.semanticscholar.org/CorpusID:221572315

14. MacFarland, T.W., Yates, J.M., MacFarland, T.W., Yates, J.M.: Kruskal–wallis h-test for oneway analysis of variance (anova) by ranks. Introduction to nonparametric statistics for the biological sciences using R, pp. 177–211 (2016)

15. Masuda, K., Kim, J., Kinugasa, R., Tanabe, K., Kuno, S.: Determinants for stair climbing by elderly from muscle morphology. Perceptual and Motor Skills **94**, 814 – 816 (2002). https://api.semanticscholar.org/CorpusID:22397722

16. McKesson: Mckesson | medical supplies, pharmaceuticals & healthcare solutions (2019). https://www.mckesson.com/

17. Orthomen: Knee brace. https://www.orthomen.com/collections/knee-braces

18. Ozaki, H., et al.: Effects of progressive walking and stair-climbing training program on muscle size and strength of the lower body in untrained older adults. J. Sports Sci. Med. **18** 4, 722–728 (2019). https://api.semanticscholar.org/CorpusID:207970191

19. Podbielski, T.: Finding the suburban "missing middle" : case study analysis of housing supply trends and needs in buda, kyle and san marcos, texas (2021). https://api.semanticscholar.org/CorpusID:245746403

20. Regnersgaard, S., et al.:Down stair walking: A simple method to increase muscle mass and performance in 65+ year healthy people. Europ. J. Sport Sci. **22**, 279 – 288 (2020). https://api.semanticscholar.org/CorpusID:227175565

21. Song, H.Y., Park, S.: An analysis of correlation between personality and visiting place using spearman's rank correlation coefficient. KSII Trans. Internet Inform. Syst. (TIIS) **14**(5), 1951–1966 (2020)

22. Startzell, J.K., Owens, D.A., Mulfinger, L.M., Cavanagh, P.R.: Stair negotiation in older people: A review. J. American Geriatrics Society **48** (2000). https://api.semanticscholar.org/CorpusID:12359772

23. Street, J.M., et al.: Older adults' perspectives of smart technologies to support aging at home: Insights from five world café forums. Int. J. Environ. Res. Public Health **19** (2022).https://api.semanticscholar.org/CorpusID:250080417

24. Sulistiyo, W., Sumarsono, D.A.: Optimization of a stair lift design to realize a safe transportation system for the elderly and the disabled when using stairs (2020). https://api.semanticscholar.org/CorpusID:218941957

25. Tornero-Quiñones, I., Sáez-Padilla, J., Díaz, A.E., Robles, M.T.A., Robles, Á.S.: Functional ability, frailty and risk of falls in the elderly: Relations with autonomy in daily living. Int. J. Environ. Res. Public Health **17** (2020). https://api. semanticscholar.org/CorpusID:211064049

26. Tural, E., Lu, D., Cole, D.A.: Factors predicting older adults' attitudes toward and intentions to use stair mobility assistive designs at home. Preventive Med. Reports **18** (2020). https://api.semanticscholar.org/CorpusID:214855466

27. Wang, J., Gillette, J.C.: Mediolateral postural stability when carrying asymmetric loads during stair negotiation. Appl. Ergonom. **85**, 103057 (2020). https://api. semanticscholar.org/CorpusID:212731344

28. Whittaker, A.C., et al.: Daily stair climbing is associated with decreased risk for the metabolic syndrome. BMC Public Health **21** (2021). https://api.semanticscholar. org/CorpusID:234498991

29. Xu, J.: The impact of epidemics on future residential buildings in china (2019). https://api.semanticscholar.org/CorpusID:228528125

30. Yu, Y., Chen, Z., Bu, J., Zhang, Q.: Do stairs inhibit seniors who live on upper floors from going out? HERD: Health Environ. Res. Design J. **13**, 128–143 (2020). https://api.semanticscholar.org/CorpusID:220528827

Effects of Passive Arm Support Exoskeleton on Static Postural Balance

Erik Jonathan and Shuping Xiong(✉)

Department of Industrial and Systems Engineering , Korea Advanced Institute of Science and Technology (KAIST), Daejeon 34141, Republic of Korea
{erikjonath,shupingx}@kaist.ac.kr

Abstract. Work-related musculoskeletal disorders (WMSDs) pose a significant health risk in industries, particularly those involving overhead work. Passive Arm-support Exoskeletons (ASEs) have emerged as potential interventions to mitigate WMSDs, but their impact on postural balance and fall risks remains uncertain. This study aimed to investigate how a passive ASE influences static postural balance under varying weight conditions and load locations. A preliminary experiment involving six healthy young males was conducted, employing a $3 \times 3 \times 3$ within-subjects design with Intervention (without exoskeleton, exoskeleton without supportive force, and exoskeleton with supportive force), Weight (2.5 kg, 5 kg, and 7.5 kg), and Load location (Low, Mid, High) as independent variables. The experiment utilized a Wii balance board to measure participants' body sway by calculating the normalized mean velocity of center of pressure (COP) during static holding tasks. Results indicated that wearing ASE with the supportive force turned on significantly reduced postural sway by 23.2% and 21.7% across all task conditions compared to when the exoskeleton was not worn and when the supportive force was turned off, respectively. Specifically, the magnitude of this decrease was contingent on both the weight being carried and the specific location of the load. In conclusion, this pilot study suggests that the supportive force provided by the ASE has the potential to enhance static postural balance, with effectiveness influenced by factors such as weight condition and load location. Future work should involve larger sample sizes and better control over gripping posture, incorporating alternative load representations and considering the ASE's torque profile.

Keywords: Exoskeleton · Postural Balance · Fall Risk · Center of Pressure

1 Introduction

Shoulder work-related musculoskeletal disorders (WMSDs) persist as a serious health problem in the industry. In the United States, shoulder WMSD cases comprised about 5.4% of the total 2,246,900 occupational injuries in 2020, resulting in a median of 28 workdays lost [17]. One important risk factor for shoulder WMSDs is overhead work [15], or work performed at or beyond the shoulder level [2]. In recent years, passive Arm-support Exoskeletons (ASEs) have been developed to alleviate the severity of WMSDs associated with overhead work. Several studies have investigated various passive ASEs

V. G. Duffy (Ed.): HCII 2024, LNCS 14709, pp. 170–180, 2024.
https://doi.org/10.1007/978-3-031-61060-8_12

across different overhead tasks and found that ASEs helped reduce shoulder muscle activity, perceived exertion and fatigue [1, 7, 10]. However, despite the potential benefits of using passive ASEs as an intervention to reduce the risks of WMSDs during overhead work, ASEs use may also introduce some unexpected or unintended challenges [11]. These drawbacks may introduce undesired health and safety challenges to the workers, thereby limiting the interest in and adoption of ASEs in the industry.

One major issue concerning the use of ASEs is the potential impacts it may have on postural balance, as the extra weight of the exoskeleton and the exoskeleton's supportive force might hinder the user's balance control and induce potential risk of falling. Previous work demonstrated that carrying extra load on the body, similar to wearing ASEs, can negatively affect postural balance [14]. In addition, prior research indicated that depending on the design of the ASEs and the load condition, wearing ASEs may have moderate consequences for balance regulation [6]. Considering the real conditions of occupational settings, ASEs have been utilized in various working scenarios, such as lifting loads to a certain height, of which may impose further risk of falling.

Understanding the effects of ASE on postural balance is crucial for preventing fall-related injuries among workers in the workplace. However, there is currently limited empirical evidence on the potential influence of ASE on postural balance, especially with regard to its supportive force. Therefore, the objective of this study is to investigate how a passive ASE affects static postural balance under different weight conditions and load locations.

2 Methods

2.1 Participants

We conducted a preliminary experiment on 6 healthy young male volunteers, who were university students from KAIST in South Korea. Respective means (SD) of age, body mass, and stature, and body mass index were 26.7 (2.3) years, 75.2 (10.0) kg, 172.9 (4.0) cm, and 25.2 (3.7) kg/m^2. All reported no current or recent (past 12 months) musculoskeletal disorders or injuries. The experiment protocol was approved by the KAIST Institutional Review Board (KH2023-196).

2.2 Exoskeleton

Among commercially-available passive arm-support exoskeleton devices, the CDYS shoulder exoskeleton (Crimson Dynamics Technology Co. Ltd., Dalian, China, www.c-dyn.com) as shown in Fig. 1 was investigated. In our study, passive devices were chosen over their active or powered counterparts because currently they are more relevant for occupational use due to their cost-effectiveness, established design, and ease of implementation [5]. The mass of the exoskeleton was 2.6 kg, and it featured seven adjustable assistive levels. The exoskeleton started to generate assistive torque when arms are lifted at a certain location. In this study, the assistive level was set to its maximum to represent the application of supportive torque, while the absence of the assistive torque signifies the supportive torque being turned off. In total, three Exo conditions were included in this study: NoExo (no exoskeleton), ExoForceOff (supportive torque off), and ExoForceOn (supportive torque on).

Fig. 1. CDYS shoulder exoskeleton (Crimson Dynamics Technology Co. Ltd., Dalian, China)

2.3 Experimental Design

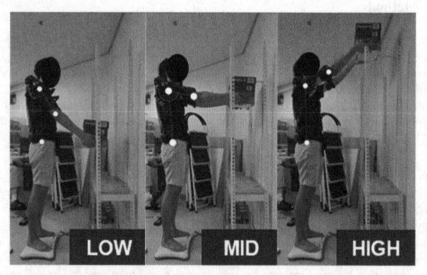

Fig. 2. Experimental task performed with a shoulder exoskeleton under three different *Load Locations* (Low, Mid, High)

This study used a $3 \times 3 \times 3$ within-subjects design with *Intervention* (NoExo: without exoskeleton, ExoForceOff: exoskeleton without supportive force, and ExoForceOn: exoskeleton with supportive force), *Weight Condition* (2.5 kg, 5 kg, and 7.5 kg), and

Load Location (Low, Mid, High) as the three independent variables. The three weight conditions were represented by a box measuring 300 mm × 210 mm × 210 mm, containing 1 pack of A4 papers (2.5 kg), 2 packs of A4 papers (5 kg), and 3 packs of A4 papers (7.5 kg), respectively. These weights were chosen with consideration of participants' safety in the experiment [9]. Four feet, each approximately 20 mm in height, were affixed to the four bottom corners of the box [8], allowing participants to easily place their fingers underneath during the lifting and carrying task (see Fig. 2). The three different load locations were designed according to the participant shoulder flexion angle of 30°, 80°, and 130° respectively, considering the ASE assistive torque profile (see Fig. 2). The presentation order of *Intervention* levels, *Weight Condition*, and *Load Location* were counterbalanced across participants using 3 × 3 balanced Latin Squares.

2.4   Experimental Setup and Procedures

Figure 3 shows the experimental setup for simulating the holding or carrying tasks in the industry. A custom-made storage shelf was placed in front of each participant with an adjustable height marker attached on the wall as the reference for different *Load Location* conditions. A box containing 3 packs of A4 papers was placed on the shelf adjusted to 60 cm height above ground level to facilitate load lifting. The horizontal separation distance from the center of the balance board to the wall was defined as each participant's arm length. This measure assists participants in maintaining a safe distance to prevent any contact between the box and the wall.

Prior to the experimental conditions, participants were given verbal explanations of the entire testing procedure and introduced to the passive arm-support exoskeleton. During this training session, participants were guided to try on the device and were provided with a familiarization period. They were asked to perform the experiment task in different conditions. Participants were also instructed to perform optimum standing balance in both with exoskeleton and without wearing exoskeleton, by standing as still as possible barefoot on the balance board for 30s repeated for two times, with both arms at their sides, and looking straight to the reference marker in front of them that has been adjusted to their eye level.

The foot position was set on the balance board using a marker, with a stance width and angle of 0.17 m and 14°, respectively, based on a previous study [12]. In addition, the placement of the heels was fixed in the same location for all the experimental conditions. This was done to maintain consistent placement across all conditions as shown in Fig. 4.

In the main experiment session, all subjects were instructed to stand straight on the balance board barefoot and perform an experimental static holding or carrying task with both hands at a specified height for 10 s without bending their elbows. The task was repeated 3 times for each condition, with a total of 27 conditions (3 *Interventions* x 3 *Weight Conditions* × 3 *Load Locations*). In between each cycle or after every 3 trials, a minimum of 1-min rest was provided to help reduce any influences from fatigue, and a minimum of 5-min rest after each *Intervention*.

Fig. 3. Experiment setup to simulate the holding tasks in industry: Wii balance board placed in front of the custom-made storage shelf

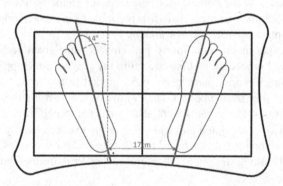

Fig. 4. Foot Position on Wii balance board

2.5 Data Collection and Processing

In each experimental condition, the subject's center of pressure (COP) was recorded using a Wii balance board (Nintendo, Kyoto, Japan), due to its portability, availability, and lower cost compared to a force plate [3]. These signals were sampled at 40 Hz and then low-pass filtered (8th order, Butterworth, 12 Hz cut-off frequency) [3]. In addition, subjects' optimal standing balance COP with and without exoskeleton was also collected for normalization. To examine postural sway and static postural balance, the normalized mean velocity of COP (Norm. MVELO) was calculated by taking the ratio of the mean velocity [13] of each experimental task to that of the optimal standing balance. Mean velocity was chosen as the outcome measure used in this study because of its common usage as a reliable and valid Center of Pressure (COP) parameter [16].

2.6 Statistical Analysis

A three-way repeated measures analysis of variance (ANOVA) was used to assess the effects of *Intervention, Weight Condition*, and *Load Location* on the outcome measure. The subject was included as a blocking effect. Statistical significance was concluded when p < 0.05 and significant main and interaction effects were followed by post-hoc pairwise comparisons via Tukey's test. Simple-effects analysis was used to further investigate significant interaction effects. Effect sizes for significant main/interaction effects and pairwise differences were measured using partial eta-squared (η_p^2) and Cohen's d [4], respectively. All statistical analyses were performed using Minitab® (Version 19). Given the objectives of the study, only the main and the interactive effects of *Intervention* are highlighted in the results presentation that follows.

3 Results and Discussion

Table 1 summarizes the results from normalized mean velocity of CoP between *Intervention, Weight Condition, Load Location* conditions and the associated statistical results.

Table 1. Summary of ANOVA results regarding the main and interaction effects of *Intervention, Weight Condition*, and *Load Location* on normalized mean velocity of CoP. Entries are F statistic (*p* value, η_p^2), and significant effects are highlighted in bold font.

Factor Effect	F statistic (p value, η_p^2)
Intervention (I)	**$F_{2,454} = 328.9$ (<0.001, 0.113)**
Weight Condition (W)	**$F_{2,454} = 358.9$ (<0.001, 0.613)**
Load Location (L)	**$F_{2,454} = 177.7$ (<0.001, 0.439)**
I × W	**$F_{4,454} = 2.8$ (0.027, 0.024)**
I × L	**$F_{4,454} = 6.0$ (<0.001, 0.050)**
W × L	**$F_{4,454} = 23.3$ (<0.001, 0.170)**
I × W × L	$F_{8,454} = 1.3$ (0.237, 0.023)

3.1 Intervention

Intervention had a significant main effect on Norm. MVELO (Fig. 5). ExoForceOn significantly reduced the value of Norm. MVELO by 23.18% and 21.65% respectively compared to NoExo ($p < 0.001$, d = 0.38) and ExoForceOff ($p < 0.001$, d = 0.34). Conversely, no significant difference was observed between the NoExo and ExoForceOff conditions ($p = 0.896$, d = 0.02).

Experimental results showed that wearing ASE with the supportive force turned on significantly reduced postural sway compared to conditions where the supportive

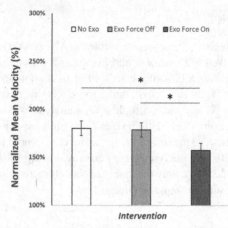

Fig. 5. *Intervention* main effects on Norm. MVELO. Note that symbol * here indicates a significant difference (p < 0.05) between different levels of *Intervention*. Error bars indicate 95% confidence intervals.

force was turned off or when the exoskeleton was not worn. Conversely, no significant differences were found when the exoskeleton was worn without supportive force. These findings corroborate a prior study that highlighted the impact of using a passive ASE (EksoVest™) on the velocity of postural sway [11]. Additionally, the utilization of ASE with supportive force was shown to reduce the total length of COP, analogous to a measure of mean velocity [6]. The present results demonstrated that the supportive force of the ASE improves balance performance. Simultaneously, the wearing effect of the exoskeleton itself (e.g., exoskeleton weight, rigidity, etc.) has no statistically significant adverse effect on static postural balance.

3.2 Intervention × Weight Condition

Norm. MVELO was significantly affected by the *Intervention* × *Weight Condition* interaction effects (Fig. 6). Using the ASE with supportive force led to significant reductions in Norm. MVELO for 5 kg and 7.5 kg *Weight Condition*, compared to NoExo ($p < 0.001$ and d = 0.63, $p < 0.001$ and d = 0.46, respectively) and ExoForceOff ($p < 0.001$ and d = 0.55, $p < 0.001$ and d = 0.42, respectively). However, no significant paired differences were found across *Intervention* for 2.5 kg *Weight Condition*. This finding can be attributed to the comparable weights between the ASE and the 2.5 kg load, resulting in a counterbalancing effect. Moreover, it aligns with a prior study investigating two distinct arm support exoskeletons, confirming that variations in carried load and the exoskeleton's assistive torque can impact balance regulation [6].

3.3 *Intervention × Load Location*

Norm. MVELO was significantly affected by the *Intervention* × *Load Location* interaction effects (Fig. 7). In both mid and high *Load Location*, Norm. MVELO was significantly decreased in the ExoForceOn condition when compared to either the NoExo

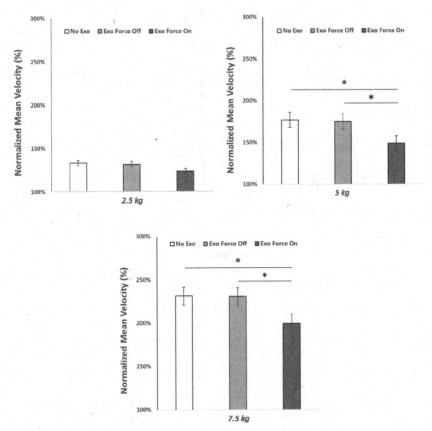

Fig. 6. Intervention × *Weight Condition* interaction effects on Norm. MVELO. Note that symbol * here indicates a significant difference ($p < 0.05$) between different levels of *Intervention* at a given *Weight Condition*. Error bars indicate 95% confidence intervals.

($p < 0.001$ and d = 0.35, $p < 0.001$, d = 0.43, respectively) or the ExoForceOff ($p = 0.002$ and d = 0.32, $p < 0.001$ and d = 0.66, respectively) condition. In contrast, in the low *Load Location*, no significant differences were observed across *Intervention*.

The results indicated that wearing ASE with supportive force when performing the task in both high and mid *Load Location* significantly decreased postural sway, while no significant differences were observed in low *Load Location*. Comparing ExoForceOn to ExoForceOff under mid and high Load Location conditions reveals a significant decrease in normalized mean velocity when the ASE was worn with the supportive force activated. In the mid Load Location, the reduction amounted to 23.54%, while in the high Load Location, it was higher at 40.06%. This disparity can be attributed to the greater supportive force exerted by the ASE in the high load location compared to the mid location. In contrast, in the low load location, where there was even less supportive force, no statistically significant differences were observed across *Intervention*.

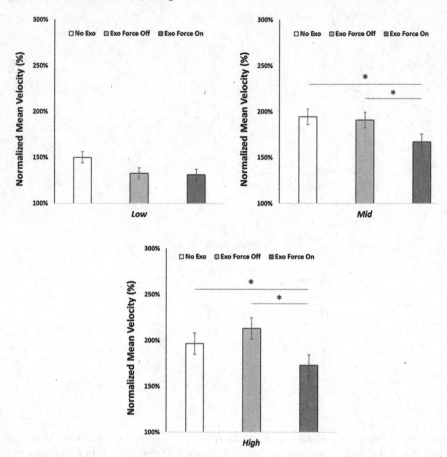

Fig. 7. Intervention × *Load Location* interaction effects on Norm. MVELO. Note that symbol * here indicates a significant difference ($p < 0.05$) between different levels of *Intervention* at a given *Load Location*. Error bars indicate 95% confidence intervals.

3.4 Limitations and Future Work

This preliminary study has several major limitations. Firstly, the participant pool was limited and only consisted of young males. Secondly, while the gripping area for holding the load was defined, the study couldn't entirely control gripping posture, especially in the high load location, as participants adopted their own strategies to facilitate easier holding tasks. Future research may explore alternatives to using a box as a representative load. Thirdly, the current study did not collect subjective perceptions regarding balance from the participants, which could have added depth to the experimental results and facilitated a comparison between objective and subjective assessments. Additionally, important shoulder angle data and the torque profile of exoskeleton should be further recorded, which may offer valuable insights for the obtained experimental results. Addressing these limitations could contribute to a more comprehensive understanding of the implications of the study's findings.

4 Conclusions

In conclusion, the findings from this pilot study suggest that the supportive force provided by the ASE has the potential to enhance static postural balance. The effectiveness of the balance improvement appears to depend on a certain weight and specific location of the load. Future research and larger-scale studies are necessary to validate and extend these initial findings, contributing to a more comprehensive understanding of the factors influencing the effectiveness of the ASE in improving static postural balance.

Acknowledgments. This work was supported by the National Research Foundation of Korea (NRF) funded by the Ministry of Science and ICT (NRF-2022R1F1A1061045, NRF-2022M3J6A1063021).

Disclosure of Interests. The authors have no competing interests to declare that are relevant to the content of this article.

References

1. Alabdulkarim, S., Nussbaum, M.A.: Influences of different exoskeleton de-signs and tool mass on physical demands and performance in a simulated over-head drilling task. Appl. Ergon. **74**, 55–66 (2019). https://doi.org/10.1016/j.apergo.2018.08.004
2. Bjelle, A., Hagberg, M., Michaelsson, G.: Clinical and ergonomic factors in prolonged shoulder pain among industrial workers. Scand. J. Work, Environ. Health, 205–210 (1979)
3. Clark, R.A., Bryant, A.L., Pua, Y., McCrory, P., Bennell, K., Hunt, M.: Validity and reliability of the Nintendo Wii balance board for assessment of standing balance. Gait Posture **31**(3), 307–310 (2010). https://doi.org/10.1016/j.gaitpost.2009.11.012
4. Cohen, J.: Statistical Power Analysis for the Behavioral Sciences. Academic press, Cambridge (2013)
5. De Looze, M.P., Bosch, T., Krause, F., Stadler, K.S., O'sullivan, L.W.: Exoskeletons for industrial application and their potential effects on physical work load. Ergonomics **59**(5), 671–681 (2016). https://doi.org/10.1080/00140139.2015.1081988
6. Desbrosses, K., Schwartz, M., Theurel, J.: Evaluation of two upper-limb exoskeletons during overhead work: influence of exoskeleton design and load on muscular adaptations and balance regulation. Eur. J. Appl. Physiol. **121**(10), 2811–2823 (2021). https://doi.org/10.1007/s00421-021-04747-9
7. Gillette, J.C., Saadat, S., Butler, T.: Electromyography-based fatigue assessment of an upper body exoskeleton during automotive assembly. Wearable Technol. **3**, e23 (2022). https://doi.org/10.1017/wtc.2022.20
8. Guo, L., Xiong, S.: Effects of working posture, lifting load, and standing surface on postural instability during simulated lifting tasks in construction. Ergonomics **63**(12), 1571–1583 (2020). https://doi.org/10.1080/00140139.2020.1807614
9. HSE: Manual handling – Manual Handling Operations Regulations 1992 - Guidance on Regulations, 4th edn. The Health and Safety Executive, London (2016)
10. Kim, S., Nussbaum, M.A., Esfahani, M.I.M., Alemi, M.M., Alabdulkarim, S., Rashedi, E.: Assessing the influence of a passive, upper extremity exoskeletal vest for tasks requiring arm elevation: Part I– "expected" effects on discomfort, shoulder muscle activity, and work task performance. Appl. Ergon. **70**, 315–322 (2018). https://doi.org/10.1016/j.apergo.2018.02.025

11. Kim, S., Nussbaum, M.A., Esfahani, M.I.M., Alemi, M.M., Jia, B., Rashedi, E.: Assessing the influence of a passive, upper extremity exoskeletal vest for tasks requiring arm elevation: part II– "unexpected" effects on shoulder motion, balance, and spine loading. Appl. Ergon. **70**, 323–330 (2018). https://doi.org/10.1016/j.apergo.2018.02.024

12. McIlroy, W.E., Maki, B.E.: Preferred placement of the feet during quiet stance: development of a standardized foot placement for balance testing. Clin. Bio-mech. **12**(1), 66–70 (1997). https://doi.org/10.1016/s0268-0033(96)00040-x

13. Qiu, H., Xiong, S.: Center-of-pressure based postural sway measures: reliability and ability to distinguish between age, fear of falling and fall history. Int. J. Ind. Ergon. **47**, 37–44 (2015). https://doi.org/10.1016/j.ergon.2015.02.004

14. Qu, X., Nussbaum, M.A.: Effects of external loads on balance control during upright stance: experimental results and model-based predictions. Gait Posture **29**(1), 23–30 (2009). https://doi.org/10.1016/j.gaitpost.2008.05.014

15. Roquelaure, Y., Ha, C., Rouillon, C., Fouquet, N., Leclerc, A., Descatha, A., Members of Occupational Health Services of the Pays de la Loire Region: Risk factors for upper-extremity musculoskeletal disorders in the working population. Arthritis Care Res. **61**(10), 1425–1434 (2009)https://doi.org/10.1002/art.24740

16. Ruhe, A., Fejer, R., Walker, B.: The test–retest reliability of centre of pressure measures in bipedal static task conditions–a systematic review of the literature. Gait Posture **32**(4), 436–445 (2010). https://doi.org/10.1016/j.gaitpost.2010.09.012

17. U.S. Bureau of Labor Statistics, 2021. Nonfatal Occupational Injuries and Illnesses Re-quiring Days Away from Work. bls.gov, Washington, DC

Usability Evaluation and Age-Appropriate Design of Wearable Fall Protection Devices

Haoran Li and Siu Shing Man[⊠]

School of Design, South China University of Technology, Guangzhou, China
ssman6@cityu.edu.hk

Abstract. Falls among the elderly have become a significant contributor to the growing burden of late-life medical care, resulting in a decline in quality of life and premature death. Various measures have been implemented to reduce the risk of falls and minimize related injuries. Wearable fall protection device (WFPD) is one of these solutions. The paper, based on usability assessments and AHP, summarized the principles of designing fall protection devices for the elderly and, in the practical stage, designs wearable fall protection products that better align with the physiological and psychological characteristics and needs of the elderly. The outcomes of this paper can assist businesses in designing and developing elderly fall protection products by considering the user characteristics of the elderly through various approaches to improve product design and user experience, further increasing the acceptance and prevalence of WFPDs among the elderly.

Keywords: AHP · Age-appropriate design · Usability evaluation · Wearable fall protection device

1 Introduction

China is facing a significant challenge of population aging. In 2021, the total population aged 60 and above was 267 million, accounting for 18.9% of the national population. By 2035, this figure is projected to reach 400 million, constituting 30% of the population [1]. Falls are a major cause of premature death and decreased quality of life in the elderly. Between 1990 and 2019, the Disability-Adjusted Life Years (DALYs) due to falls among Chinese elderly increased by 220.7% [2]. According to the World Health Organization, approximately 30% of people aged 65 and above globally have experienced a fall, with 15% experiencing multiple falls. Reducing the risk and severity of falls in the elderly has become a hot topic. Various measures have been implemented to address this issue, which can be categorized into proactive prevention measures and passive protection measures. Proactive prevention measures include the use of walking aids such as canes, mobility scooters for the elderly, and the installation of handrails and non-slip pads. Passive protection measures include the installation of impact-absorbing foam cushions indoors and the use of wearable fall protection products. Wearable fall protection products are the focus of this study. Smart protective vests have been selected as the research subject to evaluate their usability and obtain weight data for design elements using the Analytic Hierarchy Process as the basis for design improvements.

© The Author(s), under exclusive license to Springer Nature Switzerland AG 2024
V. G. Duffy (Ed.): HCII 2024, LNCS 14709, pp. 181–191, 2024.
https://doi.org/10.1007/978-3-031-61060-8_13

2 Methodology

This study initially obtained four indicators and sub-dimensions for evaluating wearable fall protection devices through offline interviews. A judgment matrix based on the Analytic Hierarchy Process was constructed to calculate the weights assigned to each element, which serve as important reference indicators for improving such products. Subsequently, a usability assessment model for these products was developed based on existing usability research and features tailored to the elderly, who are the target users of wearable fall protection devices. This model aimed to predict and analyze the difficulties and challenges that the elderly may encounter when completing tasks. Finally, by integrating the weights of various indicators with the results of usability assessments, improvement and redesign schemes were proposed for smart protective vests. The research methodology is illustrated in Fig. 1.

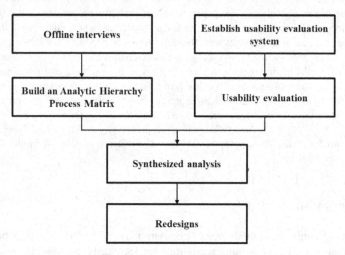

Fig. 1. Research methodology

2.1 Usability

The definition of usability has been proposed by multiple scholars, with various connotations and applications. Nielsen defined usability as the functionality of a system that can be used easily, with five evaluation dimensions set as ease of learning, memorability, simplicity of operation, effectiveness, and user satisfaction [3]. Subsequently, in 1994, Preece proposed adding efficiency and safety to the dimensions of usability evaluation [4]. In 2003, Iwarsson suggested that the usability of systems, products, and services should be evaluated based on whether users can effectively and efficiently complete tasks in specific contexts [5]. In 2010, the international standard ISO 9214 defined usability as the effectiveness, efficiency, and user satisfaction of the interaction process when users use products to complete specific tasks in particular situations [6].

Eason's usability evaluation model proposed in 1984 includes the evaluation of user characteristics, product interaction interfaces, and various tasks during product use [7]. (Fig. 2) From the analysis results of the Analytic Hierarchy Process model, this classic usability model aligns with the requirements of analyzing fall protection vests for the elderly in this study.

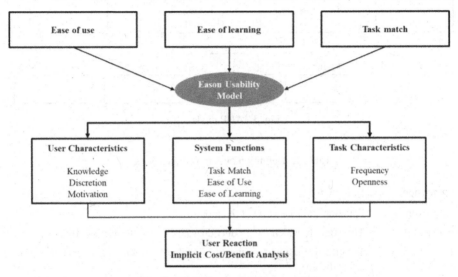

Fig. 2. Usability model (Eason .1984)

2.2 Analytic Hierarchy Process

Analytic Hierarchy Process (AHP) was first proposed by the American scholar Alsaaty in 1971 in the 1970s, which divides goals into multiple levels of elements related to the goals and analyzes the elements between the levels both quantitatively and qualitatively, and finally calculates the weights of each element through a judgment matrix.

Explaining and ensuring elderly individuals fully and accurately understand the dimensions of usability assessment poses a challenge. Therefore, this study did not directly measure and compare the various elements of usability. Instead, interviews were conducted with 40 elderly individuals to gather their evaluations of such products. The specific procedure was as follows.

1. After organizing the keywords and word frequencies mentioned in the interviews, the following model was derived (Fig. 3).

    The dimensions of the diagram are defined in the following table.

2. The elements were pairwise compared to determine their importance. Relative importance of the evaluation factors was indicated using a scale of 1 to 5 and their reciprocals, as shown in Table 3. Based on consultation with relevant experts, the final comparison results are presented in judgment matrix Table 4.

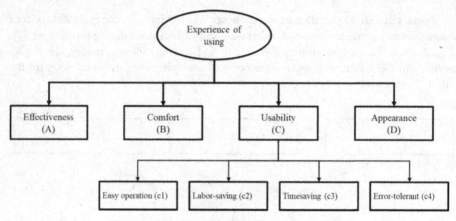

Fig. 3. AHP model.

Table 1. Definition of A to D dimensions

Dimension	Definition
Effectiveness (A)	Function and protection of the product
Comfort (B)	The extent to which the product does not burden the user's body
Ease of use (C)	The effectiveness and efficiency with which a user uses a product to achieve a specific goal
Appearance (D)	The shape, color, and material of the product

Table 2. Definition of c1 to c4 dimensions

Dimension	Definition
Easy operation (c1)	Operate without learning as much as possible
Labor-saving (c2)	Operate with as little effort as possible
Timesaving (c3)	The process takes as little time as possible
Error-tolerant (c4)	The system automatically correct errors when the user operates incorrectly

3. Calculate the weight vector of the judgment matrix by geometric mean method. The weight values are normalized and check consistency. The results are shown in Tables 4, 5, 6, 7 and 8.

This study considers that the respondents' description of "Easy operation (c1)" is equivalent to "Ease of use" in usability assessment. "Error-tolerant (c4)" is equivalent to "Ease of Learning". "Labor-saving (c2)" and "Timesaving (c3)" collectively match with "Task Match". Referring to the data in Tables 6 and 7, the corresponding weights

Table 3. Comparison scale description

Importance scale	Importance description
1	"i" and "j" are equally important
2	Weaker importance of "i" versus "j"
3	"i" is much more important than "j"
4	Demonstrated importance of "i" over "j"
5	Absolute importance of "i" over

Table 4. Judgment matrix of A to D.

	A	B	C	D
A	1	2	3	5
B	1/2	1	1	2
C	1/3	1	1	2
D	1/5	1/2	1/2	1

Table 5. Judgment matrix of c1 to D c4.

	c1	c2	c3	c4
c1	1	3	2	1
c2	1/3	1	1/2	1/2
c3	1/2	2	1	1/4
c4	1	2	4	1

Table 6. Calculation results of A to D.

Items	Feature vector	Weights	Maximum eigenvalue
A	1.985	49.625%	4.016
B	0.849	21.234%	
C	0.766	19.140%	
D	0.400	10.001%	

for "Ease of Learning", "Ease of use", and "Task Match" are 37.496%, 33.963%, and 28.541%, respectively. The differences between them are relatively small, collectively constituting 19.140% of the user experience.

Table 7. Calculation results of c1 to D c4.

Items	Feature vector	Weights	Maximum eigenvalue
c1	1.359	33.963%	4.171
c2	0.491	12.275%	
c3	0.651	16.266%	
c4	1.5	37.496%	

Table 8. Consistency test

Table	CI	RI	CR
6	0.005	0.890	0.006
7	0.057	0.890	0.064

Typically, a smaller Consistency Ratio (CR) indicates better consistency in the judgment matrix. In general, if the CR is less than 0.1, the judgment matrix is considered consistent. If the CR exceeds 0.1, it indicates inconsistency, and appropriate adjustments should be made to the judgment matrix before further analysis. In this study, all CR values calculated for the 4th-order judgment matrices are less than 0.1. Referring to the international average random consistency index table, when the matrix dimension is 4, the RI (Random Index) equals 0.890. This implies that the judgment matrices in this study satisfy the consistency test, and the calculated weights demonstrate consistency.

2.3 Usability Evaluation

The investigation and evaluation process of this study are as follows: Participants were asked to attempt using experimental samples and complete tasks without prior knowledge of WFPE. During usage, observations were made, and records kept of the time taken to complete tasks, the number of attempts made, and the instances of seeking assistance. After task completion, participants were invited for interviews, encouraging them to express any obstacles encountered during usage, provide feedback on product defects, and suggest improvements.

Tasks in detail are demonstrated in Table 9. The time taken to complete specific tasks, the number of attempts made, and the instances of requesting assistance have been recorded in Tables 10 and 11.

Table 9. Task sheet

Tasks	Content
Task 1: Put on WFPD	1-1. Adjust the devices
	1-2. Put on the devices
	1-3. Fasten WFPD
Task 2: Keep wearing WFPD	2-1. Put on the WFPD walk for 3 min
Task 3: Take off WFPD	3-1. Release the belt, buttons, etc
	3-2. Take off WFPD

Table 10. Record of task1

No.	1-1 Time	1-1 Attempt	1-1 Assistance	1-2 Time	1-2 Attempt	1-2 Assistance	1-3 Time	1-3 Attempt	1-3 Assistance
1	12	1	0	2	1	0	30	2	0
2	9	1	0	2	1	0	37	2	1
3	7	1	0	2	1	0	39	2	1
4	13	2	0	4	1	1	64	3	2
Sum	41	5	0	10	4	1	170	9	4
Average	10.25	1.25	0	2.5	1	0.25	42.5	2.25	1

Table 11. Record of task 2 and task 3

Participants	2-1 Time	2-1 Attempt	2-1 Assistance	3-1 Time	3-1 Attempt	3-1 Assistance	3-2 Time	3-2 Attempt	3-2 Assistance
1	183	1	0	10	1	0	2	1	0
2	169	1	0	13	3	0	3	1	0
3	177	1	0	12	2	1	3	1	0
4	182	1	0	18	2	0	2	1	0
Sum	711	4	0	53	8	1	10	4	0
Average	177.75	1	0	13.25	2	0.25	2.5	1	0

3 Result

3.1 Task Performance

Except for Task2-1, which has a predetermined time, the top three tasks where users spend the most time in donning and doffing the WFPD are "Fasten WFPD", "Adjust the devices", and "Release the belt, buttons, etc." Users frequently interact with the product during these three tasks, as evidenced by the concentrated number of attempts.

The instances of requesting assistance to complete tasks are relatively low but are also primarily concentrated in these three tasks. Refer to Tables 10 and 11.

Users are trapped in the process of interacting with the product. Due to the decline in motor function among the elderly, accurately controlling limb movements becomes difficult, and aging sensory functions also pose more human-machine interaction barriers for the elderly. Refer to Table 12.

Table 12. Quotation and possible causes

Quotation	Possible causes
It is a little hard to aim and lock the Quick Release Buckle	Participants had poor vision and made several attempts to align the socket while using the WFPD
I spend some time on the zippers. My hands are a little weak when it comes to handling these little things	The participants had muscle atrophy in their hands, making it difficult for them to control hand movements precisely
I can't read the words very well, so if someone can teach me once I should be able to learn	The participants had a low level of education and struggled to understand the meanings of text and symbols
These snap buttons don't seem very friendly to us	The participants found using the Snap Button to be repetitive and laborious
Zippers were a great design when I was young	Using a small zipper is laborious for the elderly

3.2   The Interaction Characteristics Between the Elderly and WFPD

By observing the elderly using WFPD, combined with data recording and human factors analysis, the following aspects need to be considered when elderly individuals use WFPD:

1. Error-tolerant: The product should be forgiving, meaning that even if elderly individuals make mistakes during operation, it should not cause issues. Additionally, the product should be able to self-correct errors during use, assisting elderly users in using it correctly.
2. Interaction methods aligned with elderly habits: Existing conceptual models should be used to reduce the difficulty of learning for the elderly.
3. Intuitive information exchange: Given the generally lower educational levels and declining vision among the elderly in China, the use of text instructions should be minimized, and information exchange should be intuitive.

4   Redesign

4.1   Pain Points and Redesign

Based on participant feedback, evaluation criteria weights, and task data analysis, the design of WFPD is optimized in the following aspects (Table 13).

Table 13. Pain points and redesign.

Product	Pain points	Redesign
	1.Quick release buckles 	Magnetic buckle
	2. Adjustable buckle 	Spring-loaded rope buckle
	3.Snap button and zipper. 	Fabric fastener tape

4.2 Design Instructions

The quick buckle has been replaced with a magnetic buckle. The feature of the magnetic snap buckle lies in its inclined surface contact and magnetic constraint, which can easily assist elderly individuals in positioning the buckle, greatly reducing the requirement for precise operation by the elderly.

The adjustable buckle has been replaced with a spring rope buckle, which can be adjusted simply by pressing, saving time and effort.

Buckles and zippers have been supplemented with nylon fastener options. The precision operation requirements for buckles and zippers are higher than for nylon fasteners, and the use of nylon fasteners requires almost no learning, greatly facilitating the mobility-impaired elderly population.

5 Discussion and Conclusion

This study explored the issue of falls among elderly individuals in the context of rapid aging in China and analyzed the current usability status of WFPD among the elderly based on previous research. Experimental results indicate that there is room for improvement in usability design for such products. The following is a summary of the age-friendly design for WFPD:

1. According to Analytic Hierarchy Process data, usability accounts for approximately 20% of the elderly population's experience in using WFPD. The determinants of usability consist of fault tolerance, ease of learning, and ease of use, with fault tolerance having the highest weight.
2. One of the characteristics of the elderly population in China is generally low education levels. Therefore, products should adopt simple and effective operation methods as much as possible.
3. The elderly population generally experiences decline in sensory and motor functions. Therefore, product grips should be ergonomic and consider lightweight wearable device designs.

The usability evaluation and age-appropriate redesign discussed in this paper have a certain reference significance for optimizing WFPD. However, they are limited by the relatively small number of participants in the experiments. It is hoped that future research can incorporate more instances for a comprehensive analysis.

References

1. A research agenda for aging in China in the 21st century. Ageing Res. Rev. **24**, 197–205 (2015). https://doi.org/10.1016/j.arr.2015.08.003
2. Hu, Y., Guo, R., Min, S., Li, B.: Disease burden on falls among older adults in China, 1990–2019. Mod. Preventive Med. (2021). (in Chinese)
3. Nielsen, J.: Usability Engineering. Academic Press, Boston (1993)
4. Preece, J., Rogers, Y., Sharp, H., Benyon, D., Holland, S., Carey, T.: Human-computer Interaction, pp. 17–18. Addison-Wesley, Harlow (1994)

5. Iwarsson, S., Ståhl, A.: Accessibility, usability and universal design–positioning and definition of concepts describing person-environment relationships. Disabil. Rehabil. **25**, 57–66 (2003)
6. Jeng, J.: What is usability in the context of the digital library and how can it be measured? Inf. Technol. Librar. **24**, 5 (2013)
7. Eason, K.D.: Towards the experimental study of usability. Behav. Inf. Technol. **3**(2), 133–143 (1984). https://doi.org/10.1080/01449298408901744

Acquiring Emotional Needs for Power Wheelchair Styling Oriented to Elderly Users

Ang Li, Weilin Liu(✉) [ID], and Peng Wan

School of Management Engineering, Qingdao University of Technology, Qingdao 266520, People's Republic of China
lwl0446@163.com

Abstract. With the intensification of population aging in society, electric wheelchairs have become an important means of transportation for many elderly users. While electric wheelchair products are becoming more similar in function, their styling designs are showing differentiation. Whether the styling design matches the actual emotional needs of elderly users will directly affect the usage experience of electric wheelchairs by the elderly. Therefore, this study aims to adhere to the concept of "user-centricity" and obtain the real emotional needs of elderly users for the styling of electric wheelchairs. Firstly, this paper analyzes the real needs of users for electric wheelchairs and the functional characteristics of electric wheelchairs from the three levels of user experience: instinct, behavior, and reflection. Based on that, an initial comprehensive list of emotional needs of users for electric wheelchairs is established. Next, through questionnaires, elderly users are invited to score the importance of the initially identified user needs. Finally, factor analysis is performed on the scoring data to determine the final emotional needs factors and important emotional needs. The research results help reveal the real emotional needs of elderly users for electric wheelchairs, and can provide important references for the subsequent styling optimization and design of electric wheelchairs.

Keywords: Electric wheelchair styling · emotional needs · factor analysis

1 Introduction

Against the deepening trend of population aging, more and more elderly people are experiencing gradual decline in various bodily functions, which has brought many inconveniences to their daily lives, especially in terms of mobility. Therefore, helping the elderly solve the inconvenience of traveling has become a very important matter [1]. Wheelchairs have thus become an important tool to address this problem. From the more common old-style wheelchairs in the past, electric wheelchairs with motorized brakes and various additional functions have emerged, thus satisfying the mobility needs of more and more elderly users. As a necessary product under population aging, electric wheelchairs need not only to meet users' basic needs, but also cater to the personalized demands of the elderly. While functions remain consistent across models, there is currently little

© The Author(s), under exclusive license to Springer Nature Switzerland AG 2024
V. G. Duffy (Ed.): HCII 2024, LNCS 14709, pp. 192–203, 2024.
https://doi.org/10.1007/978-3-031-61060-8_14

research on electric wheelchair design aiming to provide elderly users with better experience. Research on electric wheelchair design based on user experience can better meet users' personalized needs and provide references for future human-machine interaction design to serve users better. Emotional design focuses on users' emotional experience on top of meeting their functional needs, creating products that can elicit positive emotions. Emotional design cares not only about products' practicality, but also users' inner feelings [2]. In his seminal book Emotional Design, Norman proposed the three levels theory of emotional design, stating that design should pursue not only functionality and practicality, but also users' emotional experience [3].

Currently, user experience and emotional design theories have gained widespread attention and are actively applied in product design. For example, Du et al. used eye tracking technology to compare the effects of different background colors and font sizes on elderly users' experience to optimize interfaces for the elderly [4]. Huang et al. employed the three levels cultural hierarchy theory to extract and categorize cultural characteristics of museum cultural and creative products, analyzing consumers' cognition of these characteristics [5]. Liu et al. built an AR interactive picture book image emotion analysis platform based on a sample image database using interactive picture book AR virtual implantation technology based on deep learning and affective computing [6]. Through experimental research, Pengnate et al. examined how emotional design features of websites such as visual appeal and ease of use affect users' trust in unfamiliar websites, finding visual appeal plays a bigger role in establishing user trust [7]. Fang et al. compared users' satisfaction, positive/negative emotions, and social interaction between digital and traditional versions of a board game using the three levels emotional design theoretical framework, showing the traditional game elicits stronger emotional reactions and higher preference from users, also improving interpersonal relationships [8]. Employing emotional design and the KANO model, Yang constructed an emotional need model of postpartum women for body shaping products, effectively addressing postpartum women's psychological health issues [9]. Fu et al. used analytic hierarchy process to construct an emotional design model for campus souvenirs, calculating the weights of various emotional factors to transform users' emotional needs into product design to enhance campus cultural connotations [10]. Through situational research analyzing elderly people's intergenerational narrative emotional needs, Zhang et al. built a three levels product design requirements framework to decode seniors' emotions and enable them to obtain positive emotional experiences when using the products [11].

There has been little research on emotional design of electric wheelchairs targeting Chinese seniors. There is still much room for improvement regarding emotional experience of electric wheelchairs. Therefore, this paper first analyzes user needs and product characteristics from the three levels of emotional design theory to establish a preliminary requirements list. Questionnaire surveys are then conducted to acquire users' ratings of the preliminary requirements. Finally, factor analysis methods are used to determine the most important user emotional needs. The research identifies Chinese seniors' emotional needs regarding electric wheelchair styling, which can inform subsequent senior-friendly optimization of electric wheelchair designs.

2 Emotional Needs Elicitation of Electric Wheelchairs

2.1 Instinctual Level Needs Elicitation

When users first come into contact with a product, their instinctual emotional reactions stem from spontaneous feelings towards the product's appearance. Therefore, the core of design at the instinctual level lies in catering to consumers' sensory experience, such as visual effects, sound effects, olfactory effects and tactile feelings, thereby eliciting sensory experience and emotional interaction [12].

As the target users of electric wheelchairs, 12 elderly users were invited to participate in the emotional needs elicitation process. The users met the following requirements: aged between 60–70 years old; having mobility impairments; having no prior experience using electric wheelchairs; having the intention to purchase an electric wheelchair to assist with mobility; having no mental illnesses and sound cognitive abilities; gender ratio of 1:1.

Fig. 1. Electric wheelchairs used in interviews.

With the development of e-commerce platforms, online shopping has gradually become prevalent. Therefore, this study chose the JD e-commerce platform and searched for the keyword "electric wheelchairs for the elderly". Videos of the top three best-selling products were selected for viewing, which were: Mateside electric wheelchair, LONNGWAY electric wheelchair and Yuyue electric wheelchair (as shown in Fig. 1). Ten elderly people with no prior electric wheelchair experience were shown the above electric wheelchair product videos. After viewing, open interviews were conducted for them to express and describe their intuitive feelings and impressions during observation. Their verbatim descriptions were recorded and sorted. The elderly's actual needs towards electric wheelchairs were further summarized as shown in Table 1.

Table 1. Elderly's Intuitive Feelings and Needs Descriptions

NO	Intuitive Feelings	Needs Descriptions
1	The electric wheelchair designs are innovative	Providing diversified appearance options to meet personal aesthetic needs
2	The colors make people feel comfortable	Optimize styling and color schemes to make elderly users feel cared for
3	The armrests have anti-slip textures	Optimize armrest materials to improve fit and comfort for elderly users' palms
4	Looks high-end	Simplify the overall structure while ensuring basic functions
5	The metal frame is sturdy	Ensure structural sturdiness and stability to prolong service life
6	The wheelchair structure is complex	Optimize structural design to retain core functions and simplify operation

2.2 Behavioral Level Needs Elicitation

The behavioral level emphasizes the practicality and refinement of products, allowing users to feel comfortable and easy to use during actual use. This stems from users' needs for products' practical functions. The behavioral level focuses most on users' actual experience. After receiving sensory stimuli, users further interact with the product to check whether it can truly achieve expected purposes and meet needs [12].

The interviewees for behavioral level needs elicitation were mainly 8 elderly electric wheelchair users meeting the following criteria: aged between 60–75 years old; including proficient expert users with over 3 years of experience and novice users; no mental illnesses and sound cognitive abilities; different extents of age-related physical deterioration; gender ratio of 1:1.

Open interviews were conducted for the elderly users to express and describe their real feelings and experiences during electric wheelchair use. Their verbatim descriptions were recorded and sorted, analyzing and eliciting user needs as shown in Table 2.

2.3 Reflective Level Needs Elicitation

Reflective level design is the focus of emotional design. It is based on users' deeper thoughts and mental reactions. When recalling the process of using the product, users conduct comprehensive contemplation and judgment on various dimensions such as appearance and usage experience. After integrating different factors, users' emotional connection with the product becomes more multidimensional and thorough. Such in-depth reflection best showcases the emotional design effects [13].

The emotional feedback from the above 8 elderly users after using electric wheelchairs were recorded and summarized via interviews, analyzing and eliciting their emotional needs as shown in Table 3.

Table 2. Elderly's Actual Use Experiences and Needs Analysis.

NO	Use Experiences	Needs Analysis
1	The backrest feels comfortable during use	Adopt ergonomic design and pressure relief cushioning materials to maintain backrest comfort
2	Convenient for short distance mobility	Optimize control system sensitivity to ensure simple and efficient completion of needs for elderly users
3	The electric wheelchair itself is too heavy	Use lightweight materials for the frame and optimize the structure to reduce weight
4	Abnormal noises occur during traveling	Regularly inspect components to minimize friction noise from motions
5	Able to control the electric wheelchair independently without needing assistance from others	Should meet users' daily needs
6	There are usage environment limitations	More open environments are needed to meet basic needs
7	The seat height provides a good view	Maintain seat height design to avoid limiting vision and provide open views
8	The dimensions are appropriate	More suitable dimensions facilitate maneuvering and turning in different occasions
9	The seat cushion provides shock absorption	Ensure shock absorption while increasing comfort and fit

Table 3. Elderly's Emotional Feedback and Emotional Needs.

NO	Emotional Feedback	Emotional Needs
1	Whether it feels safe to manipulate the electric wheelchair and travel	Safe
2	Whether the structural materials are sturdy for long-term use	Durable
3	How's the cost over the full life span of use	Affordable
4	Whether it's convenient to repair malfunctions of the electric wheelchair	Convenient
5	Whether battery life permits sufficient travel range	Continuous
6	Whether the electric wheelchair fulfills humanized details	Humanized
7	Whether the electric wheelchair has high visibility for timely status checks	Visible

2.4 Establishing a Comprehensive Emotional Needs List

By analyzing the instinctual, behavioral and reflective level needs of the above elderly users, the elicited needs are sorted and analyzed to obtain an emotional needs list of elderly users towards electric wheelchairs, as shown in Table 4.

Table 4. Emotional Needs List of Users.

Variable	Emotional Needs	Variable	Emotional Needs
X1	Technological	X9	Daily
X2	Convenient	X10	Efficient
X3	Safe	X11	Lightweight
X4	Durable	X12	Quiet
X5	Minimalist	X13	Independent
X6	Warm	X14	Spacious
X7	Affordable	X15	Simple
X8	Comfortable	X16	Sturdy

3 Determining Importance of Elderly Users' Emotional Needs for Electric Wheelchairs

The above data analysis elicited elderly users' emotional needs towards electric wheelchairs. To more effectively reflect these needs in product design, dimension reduction methods are used to simplify and grasp elderly users' core needs, informing subsequent optimization of electric wheelchair styling design.

Factor analysis uses dimension reduction techniques to derive a few common factors that retain as much information from the original variables as possible. The influence and importance of each factor is then determined based on their variance contribution rates [14].

Surveys on importance ratings of electric wheelchair needs were administered among senior users requiring electric wheelchairs for mobility impairment. The survey consisted of two parts. Part one collects user information; part two asks respondents to rate the importance of 16 electric wheelchair emotional needs using a five-point scale (scores range from 1 to 5; 1 being very unimportant, 5 being very important). Considering the questionnaires comprehension abilities of elderly users, the five-point scale was used to obtain ratings of electric wheelchair needs. A total of 170 survey questionnaires were administered and 150 valid responses were returned at a response rate of 88%.

	Options	Frequency	Percentage (%)
gender	male	82	54.67
	female	68	45.33
Age	60–65	44	29.33
	65–70	49	32.67
	70–75	31	20.67
	> 75	26	17.33

3.1 Factor Analysis

First, SPSS software is used to perform KMO test and Bartlett's test of sphericity on the sample data. The KMO value is greater than 0.8 and the significance of Bartlett's test is less than 0.001 (Table 5), indicating the questionnaire results are suitable for factor analysis [15].

Table 5. Shows the KMO and Bartlett's test results.

KMO and Bartlett's Test		
Kaiser-Meyer-Olkin Measure of Sampling Adequacy		0.875
Bartlett's Test of Sphericity	Approx. Chi-Square	1258.301
	df	120
	Sig	0.000

Factor analysis and orthogonal rotation are performed on the 16 original variables in SPSS. Based on factor extraction results in factor analysis, the number of public factors is deter-mined by having eigenvalues greater than 1 [16]. (Table 6) Four public factors are extracted.

Table 6. Factor Total Variance Explained

Component	Initial Eigenvalues			Extraction Sums of Squared Loadings			Rotation Sums of Squared Loadings		
	Total	%of Variance	Cumulative %	Total	%of Variance	Cumulative %	Total	%of Variance	Cumulative %
1	6.205	38.78	38.78	6.205	38.78	38.78	3.746	23.412	23.412
2	2.272	14.203	52.983	2.272	14.203	52.983	2.711	16.941	40.353
3	1.751	10.941	63.924	1.751	10.941	63.924	2.667	16.667	57.02
4	1.139	7.118	71.041	1.139	7.118	71.041	2.243	14.021	71.041

(continued)

Table 6. (*continued*)

Component	Initial Eigenvalues			Extraction Sums of Squared Loadings			Rotation Sums of Squared Loadings		
	Total	%of Variance	Cumulative %	Total	%of Variance	Cumulative %	Total	%of Variance	Cumulative %
5	0.605	3.784	74.825						
6	0.564	3.524	78.349						
7	0.516	3.224	81.573						
8	0.501	3.131	84.704						
9	0.4	2.503	87.207						
10	0.379	2.369	89.576						
11	0.36	2.247	91.823						
12	0.338	2.111	93.935						
13	0.291	1.819	95.754						
14	0.272	1.703	97.456						
15	0.218	1.365	98.821						
16	0.189	1.179	100						

Factor analysis results show that the cumulative variance contribution rate of the first four public factors reaches 71.041%. Considering characteristics of social science research, the first four public factors contain most information of the original variables. Therefore, the 16 emotional needs can be categorized into four factors for analysis. The greater the factor loading of an emotional need variable, the higher its correlation with that factor. According to the loadings of each emotional need across factors, the four factors are defined as Interaction, Design, Performance and Characteristics. The factor loadings are shown in Table 7.

Table 7. Factor Loadings.

Emotional needs	Interaction factor	Design factor	Performance factor	Characteristics factor
X2	0.828			
X8	0.809			
X13	0.857			
X14	0.811			
X15	0.864			

(*continued*)

Table 7. (*continued*)

Emotional needs	Interaction factor	Design factor	Performance factor	Characteristics factor
X1		0.773		
X4		0.741		
X6		0.73		
X9		0.785		
X3			0.814	
X5			0.686	
X10			0.811	
X12			0.754	
X7				0.857
X11				0.803
X16				0.827

3.2 Ranking Emotional Needs Importance

Based on factor analysis of the user needs items, weights are calculated for the main factors and emotional needs to determine their influence on importance of elderly users' emotional needs for electric wheelchairs [17].

The weights for each main factor are denoted as T_i and the calculation formula is:

$$T_i = \frac{\lambda_i}{\sum\limits_{i=1}^{k} \lambda_i} \tag{1}$$

where λ_i represents the contribution rate of main factor, and $\sum\limits_{i=1}^{k} \lambda_i$ represents the cumulative contribution rate of the k main factors.

The weights for each emotional need is denoted as ω_j and the calculation formula is:

$$C_{ij} = \frac{\alpha_{ij}}{\sum \alpha_{ij}} \tag{2}$$

$$\omega_j = \sum\limits_{i=1} C_{ij} \times T_i \tag{3}$$

where α_{ij} represents the rotated loading coefficient, and $\sum \alpha_{ij}$ represents the cumulative squared loading of the emotional need. The analysis results are shown in Table 8 below:

Table 8. Weights of Main Factors and Emotional Needs.

Main Factors	Weights of Main Factors	Emotional Needs	Weights of Emotional Needs
Interaction factor	0.330	Spacious	0.060
		Convenient	0.072
		Comfortable	0.057
		Simple	0.065
		Independent	0.058
Design factor	0.248	Technological	0.062
		Minimalist	0.065
		Warm	0.067
		Daily	0.068
Performance factor	0.235	Safe	0.057
		Durable	0.055
		Efficient	0.061
		Quiet	0.067
Characteristics factor	0.197	Affordable	0.060
		Sturdy	0.065
		Lightweight	0.061

According to the table, the order of importance for electric wheelchair emotional needs main factors from high to low is: Interaction, Design, Performance, and Characteristics. The Interaction factor is the most important, with a weight of 0.330 and a variance contribution rate of 38.78%, indicating its high significance. The Interaction factor is the most influential factor on importance of elderly users' electric wheelchair emotional needs. Based on emotional needs weights, the need "Convenient" has the highest weight ratio of 0.072. Considering impact of needs weights synthetically, the six emotional needs with highest weights, in order, are: Convenient, Daily, Warm, Quiet, Simple, Sturdy. In subsequent electric wheelchair styling design, the semantics conveyed by the above emotional imagery words should be highly emphasized.

4 Conclusion

This study conducts preliminary exploration on emotionalized design of electric wheelchair styling through questionnaire surveys, user interviews, and factor analysis based on emotional design theory. Certain achievements have been made in eliciting emotional needs for electric wheelchair styling targeting the elderly.

1. 16 potential user needs for electric wheelchairs are analyzed from the instinctual, behavioral, and reflective levels.

2. Four main factors of elderly users' emotional needs for electric wheelchair styling design are obtained, namely Interaction, Design, Performance, and Characteristics.
3. The four main factors are ranked by their influence degree on electric wheelchair emotional needs from high to low as follows: Interaction, Design, Performance, Characteristics. For the Interaction factor, the emotional need "Convenient" is of higher concern among elderly users. For the Design factor, users pay more attention to "Daily". For the Performance factor, users care more about "Quiet". For the Characteristics factor, users focus more on the emotional need "Sturdy".

The systematic, hierarchical and comprehensive emotional needs framework obtained by this study can provide theoretical support and practical guidance for subsequent optimization of electric wheelchair styling design. The semantics conveyed by emotional imagery words related to electric wheelchairs should be highly valued in follow-up styling design, serving as important references for optimization of electric wheelchair styling.

Acknowledgments. This study was funded by Undergraduate Teaching Reform and Research Project at Qingdao University of Technology (grant number F2023-025).

Disclosure of Interests. The authors have no competing interests to declare that are relevant to the content of this article.

References

1. Sun, Y.J., Chen, Y.H.: Marketization of elderly care services and transformation of filial piety culture against the backdrop of population aging. Jiangsu Soc. Sci. **05**, 134–143 (2023)
2. Ding, J.W., Yang, D.T., Cao, Y.D., Wang, L.: Major theories, methods and development trends of emotional design. J. Eng. Des. **17**(1), 12–18 (2010)
3. Norman, D.: Emotion. design: attractive things work better. Interactions **9**(4), 36–42 (2002)
4. Du, H., Liu, W., Wang, P., Sun, X., Zhang, W.: The influence of background color and font size of mobile payment app interface on elderly user experience. In: Duffy, V.G. (ed.) HCII 2023. LNCS, vol. 14029, pp. 392–401. Springer, Cham (2023). https://doi.org/10.1007/978-3-031-35748-0_29
5. Huang, H., Chen, H., Zhan, Y.: A study on consumers' perceptions of museum cultural and creative products through online textual reviews: an example from palace museum's cultural and creative flagship store. Behav. Sci. **13**(4), 318 (2023)
6. Liu, S,D., Peng, P., Cao, L.: Application of AR virtual implantation technology based on deep learning and emotional technology in the creation of interactive picture books. 3 c TIC: cuadernos de desarrollo aplicados a las TIC. **12**(1), 176–198 (2023)
7. Pengnate, S,F., Sarathy, R.: An experimental investigation of the influence of website emotional design features on trust in unfamiliar online vendors. Comput. Human Behavior. **67**, 49–60 (2017)
8. Fang, Y,M., Chen, K,M., Huang, Y,J.: Emotional reactions of different interface formats: Comparing digital and traditional board games. Adv. Mech. Eng. **8**(3) (2016)
9. Yang, M.: Research on emotional design of postpartum body shaping products based on KANO model. Packag. Eng. **44**(12), 165–171 (2023)
10. Fu, R.Y., Chen, G.H.: Research on emotional design of campus souvenirs based on analytic hierarchy process. Ind. Des. **07**, 148–151 (2023)

11. Zhang, Y.Y., Zhou, C.Y.: Elderly emotionalized product design research for intergenerational narratives. Packag. Eng. **44**(10), 108–115 (2023)
12. Gu, L.: Research on user experience of news and information app. Insight-Inf. 2(1) (2020)
13. Chen, Y., Chen, R.: Design thinking based on reflective level in emotional design. In: E3S Web of Conferences, vol. 179, p. 02082. E3S Web of Conferences (2020)
14. Liu, Z.D., Zhan, Q.Z., Tian, G.L.: Review of comprehensive evaluation research based on factor analysis. Stat. Decision. **35**(19), 68–73 (2019)
15. Fu, D.Y.: An investigation of statistical test framework for factor analysis. Stat. Res. 06, 86–90 (2007)
16. You, J.X.: How to properly apply factor analysis for comprehensive evaluation. Statis-tical Educ. **5**(10), 10–11 (2003)
17. Yan, C.L.: Several issues on conducting comprehensive evaluations using principal component analysis. Math. Statistics Manage. **02**, 23–26 (1998)

Sensor-Based Assistive Technology as a Support to Reduce Intra-hospital Infection and Mortality Due to Epidemic Respiratory Diseases: A Proposal

Javier Lizarazo-Gutiérrez[1], Miguel Ortiz-Barrios[2,3(✉)], Helder Celani de Souza[4], Genett Isabel Jiménez-Delgado[5], Andrés Ariza-Ortiz[5], Zaury Estela Fernández-Mendoza[5], and Natali Johanna Alfaro-Parada[6]

[1] Department of Computer Science and Electronics, Universidad de la Costa CUC, 080002 Barranquilla, Colombia
jlizaraz3@cuc.edu.co

[2] Centro de Investigación en Gestión e Ingeniería de Producción, (CIGIP), Universitat Politecnica de Valencia, Camino de Vera, s/n, 46022 Valencia, Valencia, Spain
miorbar@upv.es, mortiz1@cuc.edu.co

[3] Department of Productivity and Innovation, Universidad de la Costa CUC, 080002 Barranquilla, Colombia

[4] Departament of Production Engineering, Universidade Estadual Paulista, Guaratinguetá, São Paulo, Brazil
hjcelani@lidproj.com.br

[5] Departament of Industrial Engineering, Institución Universitaria de Barranquilla IUB, Barranquilla, Colombia
{gjimenez,arariza,zefernandez}@unibarranquilla.edu.co

[6] Universidad del Magdalena, Santa Marta, Colombia
nalfaro@unimagdalena.edu.co

Abstract. The rapid spread of Seasonal Respiratory Diseases (SRDs) has put hospitals in need of improving their preventive measures. Contact and proximity are two events that cause the transmission of most respiratory infections. For this reason, the infected patients are generally placed in isolation. Still, even so, they must receive care in hospitals where contact and proximity are almost inevitable i) between patients, ii) between health professionals and patients, and iii) between health professionals, causing intra-hospital transmission of SRDs. This paper presents the design of a sensor-based Assistive Technology (AT) as a support to reduce intra-hospital infection and mortality due to epidemic respiratory diseases. Initially, we characterized the main SRDs. Second, we defined the leading clinical indicators to be monitored in patients with an SRD. Then, we designed the healthcare protocols responding to health deviations in patients with SRD. Fourth, we characterized the targeted population in terms of sociodemographic indicators that may affect the operationalization of the AT in the wild. Finally, we laid the groundwork for the sensor-based AT design. This proposal is an effort to ensure the continuing care of patients with SRD, reducing overcrowding and waiting times in healthcare systems during these periods and consequently tackling high mortality rates.

© The Author(s), under exclusive license to Springer Nature Switzerland AG 2024
V. G. Duffy (Ed.): HCII 2024, LNCS 14709, pp. 204–218, 2024.
https://doi.org/10.1007/978-3-031-61060-8_15

Keywords: Sensor-based Systems · Seasonal Respiratory Diseases (SRDs) · Intra-hospital Infection · Assistive Technologies (ATs) · Healthcare

1 Introduction

The rapid increase in Seasonal Respiratory Diseases (RSDs) has demanded the immediate implementation of actions to strengthen preventive strategies in hospital institutions. According to Jefferson et al. [1], one of the significant sources of contagion in these spaces lies in contact and proximity; although measures such as isolation of infected individuals are applied, the spread of respiratory epidemics affects patients and healthcare professionals across the board [2]. Additionally, controls such as medical/surgical masks, N95/P2 respirators, and hand hygiene relatively decrease the risk of spread [3, 4]. However, they still need to be more effective and much less definitive measures for their eradication.

To address this critical issue, this research proposes a five-step methodology. In the first step, we clearly described the symptoms of the principal RSDs addressed by medical centers. Then, an exhaustive identification of relevant clinical indicators is conducted to ensure continuous and personalized care according to each patient's profile. This phase is carried out through a bibliographic review that examines the relationship between each symptom or indicator and the patient's condition due to the disease. In the third step, precise protocols are defined in case of overpassing the thresholds established for each clinical indicator. These thresholds enable the implementation of an alert system that notifies the hospital of any deviation in the patient's health. As a fourth step, we set sociodemographic indicators that must be considered in profiling the target population as they may affect the operability of the sensor-based technology in the real context. Finally, a sensor-based technological proposal is presented to reduce intrahospital infections and mortality associated with epidemic respiratory diseases.

The results have highlighted that temperature, respiratory rate, heart rate, and blood oxygen saturation are features that can evidence the progress of SRDs. Similarly, symptoms such as sore throat, muscle aches, vomiting, and diarrhea can be remotely monitored through scheduled surveys incorporated into assistive technology, complemented by virtual appointments with healthcare professionals. However, technologies like these require a prior feasibility process to determine if a particular patient may be a suitable adopter of the technology based on their clinical profile and medical requests. With this comprehensive approach, we hope to significantly contribute to improving the prevention and management of epidemic respiratory diseases in hospital settings. The remainder of this paper is as follows: Sect. 2 depicts a literature review on the application of sensor-based technologies for coping with SRDs. Section 3 illustrates the proposed methodology. Finally, Sect. 4 presents the results, and Sect. 5 elucidates the conclusions.

2 Literature Review

Sensor-based assistive technologies have the potential to play a significant role in infection control and mortality reduction in various settings, including healthcare facilities, nursing homes, and even home care environments. Table 1 shows some applications.

Table 1. List of main Sensor-based assistive technologies contributions

Application	Description	Reference
Remote Patient Monitoring (RPM)	It enables remote monitoring of vital signs such as temperature, heart rate, blood pressure, and oxygen saturation levels. This allows healthcare providers to track patients' health status without direct physical contact, reducing the risk of infection transmission. Early detection of abnormal vital signs can also prompt timely interventions, potentially preventing adverse health events and reducing mortality rates	Mecklai et al. [5]
Fall Detection Systems	Falls are a significant cause of injury and mortality, especially among the elderly population. They detect falls and alert caregivers or emergency responders, enabling prompt assistance. By reducing response times to fall incidents, these technologies can help prevent complications	Singh et al. [6]
Healthcare Environmental Monitoring	Sensors can be deployed to monitor environmental conditions such as air quality, temperature, humidity, and surface contamination levels in healthcare facilities. Timely detection of airborne pathogens, pollutants, or microbial contamination can facilitate proactive infection control measures, including ventilation adjustments, surface disinfection, and isolation protocols, thus minimizing the risk of Healthcare-Associated Infections (HAIs) and mortality rates	Hina et al. [7]
Hand Hygiene Compliance Monitoring	Hand hygiene is a critical component of infection control in healthcare settings. Sensor-based systems can monitor healthcare workers' hand hygiene compliance by tracking their movements and interactions with patients and hand hygiene stations. Real-time feedback and reminders can encourage adherence to hand hygiene protocols, reducing the transmission of infectious agents and preventing healthcare-associated infections that contribute to mortality	Karimpour et al. [8]

(continued)

Table 1. (*continued*)

Application	Description	Reference
Wearable Devices for Contact Tracing	During infectious disease outbreaks, wearable devices with proximity sensors and Bluetooth technology can facilitate contact tracing efforts. By identifying individuals who have been near confirmed cases, these devices enable timely notification, testing, and quarantine of potentially exposed individuals, thus helping to contain the spread of infections and reduce mortality rates within communities	Khaliq et al. [9]
Smart Assistive Devices	Sensor-equipped assistive devices such as smart beds, smart wheelchairs, and motion-sensing alarms can enhance patient safety and reduce the risk of adverse events. These devices can detect changes in patient movement, position, or behavior, alerting caregivers to potential issues such as pressure ulcers, respiratory distress, or medication non-adherence. Smart assistive devices can help prevent complications and improve patient outcomes by providing early warning signs and enabling timely interventions	Krishnan and Pugazhenthi [10]

Sensor-based assistive technologies offer promising infection control and mortality reduction solutions in hospital settings, particularly amidst epidemic respiratory diseases like influenza, COVID-19, and SARS. These technologies enable remote monitoring, early symptom detection, and proactive intervention, enhancing patient safety and optimized resource utilization. By tracking patient movements, monitoring hand hygiene compliance, and conducting real-time environmental surveillance, sensor-based systems help mitigate nosocomial transmission and improve outbreak management. Despite their potential benefits, challenges such as privacy concerns, integration issues, and cost-effectiveness must be addressed. Empirical evidence suggests that sensor-based technologies facilitate the timely identification of infected patients, support data-driven decision-making, and improve healthcare delivery. Future directions include advancing sensor technology, fostering collaborative partnerships, and addressing user acceptance and training needs. In summary, sensor-based assistive technologies present innovative solutions for enhancing infection control and reducing mortality rates. These technologies enable remote monitoring, early detection of health risks, proactive intervention, and improved compliance with infection control protocols across diverse healthcare settings [11, 12]. By effectively harnessing these advancements, healthcare providers can elevate patient safety, optimize resource allocation, and attenuate the impact of infectious diseases on public health outcomes [13].

3 Proposed Methodology

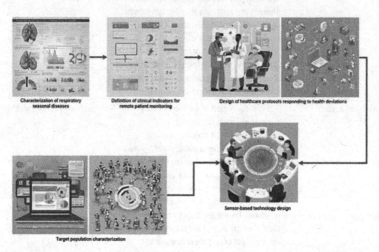

Fig. 1. Proposed methodology for the implementation of sensor-based assistive technologies during SRDs

A five-step approach (Fig. 1) is suggested for the effective use of sensor-based assistive technologies as a support to reduce intra-hospital infection during SRDs:

Step 1. *Characterization of Seasonal Respiratory Diseases (SRDs).* List the principal SRDs by identifying their symptoms and describing their main characteristics considering the reported literature review.

Step 2. *Definition of clinical indicators for remote monitoring.* Establish clinical indicators to monitor the candidate patients remotely considering the disease symptoms.

Step 3. *Design of healthcare protocols responding to health deviations.* Specify threshold values for clinical indicators to design protocols for health deviations. The objective is to deploy an alert system that notifies the hospital about a special variation observed in these indicators. The hospital is called to provide a diagnosis and treatment in time consistent with the patient's needs.

Step 4. *Target population characterization.* Define the characteristics of the target population that will have access to the technology based on various sociodemographic aspects that may affect its deployment in the wild.

Step 5. *Sensor-based technology design.* Design the sensor-based technology taking into account the clinical indicators, symptoms to monitor, and the healthcare protocols to be deployed in case of deviation.

4 Results

4.1 Characterization of Seasonal Respiratory Diseases (SRDs)

Table 2 shows the respiratory viruses that have widely been identified as highly pathogenic and highly transmissible together with their symptoms.

Table 2. Description of the main SRDs

Respiratory virus	Description and symptoms	Reference
SARS-CoV-2	SARS-CoV-2 is a kind of coronavirus that leads to COVID-19 infection. Patients had clinical manifestations of fever, cough, shortness of breath, and muscle aches. And in some cases, confusion, headache, sore throat, nausea, and vomiting	Chen et al. [14]; Rodriguez-Morales et al. [15]
H7N9 Influenza A virus	In the spring of 2013, a new type of bird flu virus, avian-origin influenza A (H7N9), emerged. The patients infected with H7N9 usually experience fever, cough, expectoration, fatigue, poor appetite, dry mouth, thirst, difficulty breathing, chest discomfort, and a bitter mouth taste	Chen et al. [16]
H1N1 Influenza A virus	Also known as swine flu, it is a type of influenza A virus; hospitalized patients typically present with fever, cough, shortness of breath, fatigue, runny nose, sore throat, headache, and myalgia. A proportion of affected patients have presented with gastrointestinal symptoms such as diarrhea and vomiting	Da Costa et al. [17]
H5N1 Influenza A virus	Fever, cough, and difficulty breathing are common symptoms in people infected with avian H5N1 Influenza A. Some people may also have diarrhea and bleeding from the mucous membranes	Jiang et al. [18]

(continued)

Table 2. (*continued*)

Respiratory virus	Description and symptoms	Reference
HCoVs	Seasonal viruses represent the four CoVs that cause the common cold, HCoV229E, HCoV-OC43, HCoV-NL63, and HCoV-HKU1. Patients often present cough, nasal congestion, and rhinorrhea	Jiang et al. [18]
H3N2 Influenza A Virus	Frequent flu outbreaks yearly are caused by H3N2 influenza viruses that have undergone extensive evolution in their genes and antigens. The symptoms are fever, sore throat, coughing, nasal discharge, headache, and myalgia. More severe cases can also lead to the development of conditions such as bronchitis or pneumonia	Allen & Ross [19]

4.2 Definition of Clinical Indicators for Remote Monitoring

Clinical indicators are used to monitor the symptomatology and disease progress over time. Table 3 relates each metric with its respective symptoms and SRDs. Thereby, it is possible to have a complete overview of the patient's health status and define if some interventions are necessary.

Table 3. Symptoms and SRDs associated with each clinical indicator.

Clinical Indicator	Symptom	Respiratory Disease	Reference
Temperature	Fever	COVID-19 (SARS-CoV-2), Influenza A (H7N9, H1N1, H5N1, H3N2)	Chughtai et al. [21]
Cough frequency	Cough	COVID-19 (SARS-CoV-2), Influenza A (H7N9, H1N1, H5N1, H3N2), common cold (HCoVs)	Spinou & Birring [22]
Chest pain, weariness	Sore throat, myalgia, headache, fatigue	COVID-19 (SARS-CoV-2), Influenza A (H7N9, H1N1, H5N1, H3N2), common cold (HCoVs)	Chan [23]

(*continued*)

Table 3. (*continued*)

Clinical Indicator	Symptom	Respiratory Disease	Reference
Respiratory rate	Shortness of breath,	COVID-19 (SARS-CoV-2), Influenza A (H7N9, H1N1, H5N1), common cold (HCoVs)	O'Driscoll et al. [24]
Oxygen saturation	Shortness of breath	COVID-19 (SARS-CoV-2), Influenza A (H7N9, H1N1, H5N1), common cold (HCoVs)	Mejía et al. [18]; Qadir et al. [25]
Heart rate	Shortness of breath, chest discomfort	COVID-19 (SARS-CoV-2), Influenza A (H7N9, H1N1, H5N1), common cold (HCoVs)	Davidson & Warren-Gash [26]

4.3 Design of Healthcare Protocols Responding to Health Deviations

Table 4 shows the protocols that should be followed by the healthcare systems in case the sensor-based technologies report that the threshold values of any clinical indicator have been exceeded in the remotely monitored patients. Figure 2 rapidly summarizes how these protocols would be deployed in the actual scenario.

4.4 Target Population Characterization

We then determined the sociodemographic features that should be measured in the target population for translation into specific operational characteristics of the sensor-based technology (Table 5).

Table 4. Threshold values of clinical indicators and healthcare protocols

Temperature	Threshold values	Reference
The system will indicate a "Fever" alert highlighted in red color and send a sound notification to the hospital when overpassing the threshold. The allocated nursing team will have to provide medical instructions via phone call according to this symptom and the patient's clinical profile In case of severe and extreme body temperature (hyperpyrexia), the patient will be contacted by the medical staff to ensure immediate admission to the emergency department	*Normal* 36.5–37.5 °C *Fever* > 37.5 °C *Severe* (hyperpyrexia) ≥ 40 °C Extreme (hyperpyrexia) ≥ 42 °C	Tharakan et al. [27]
Oxygen saturation/Respiratory rate		
The high respiratory rate is a consequence of the SRDs and may be due to oxygen reduction or airway obstruction. Therefore, when the sensor-based technology detects a deviation in oxygen saturation, an alarm sign will be sent to the doctor and the current patient's geographical location. The medical system will have to assign an ambulance to deliver oxygen to the patient continuously. In case of no-good evolution, the patient will be transferred to the hospital, where orotracheal intubation will be performed to begin mechanical ventilation support	Hypoxemia SpO_2 < 95% Abnormal > 14 breaths/minute Critical > 24 breaths/minute	Mejía et al. [24]; Sharma et al. [28]
Heart rate (HR)		
The dispositive will send an alarm to the doctor with a message indicating the abnormality according to the threshold values. Then, the doctor will track the patient's current location of the patient to go and attend to the patient or send an ambulance to transfer the patient to the hospital if necessary	Resting HR 50 – 90 bpm Bradycardia HR < 50 bpm Tachycardia HR > 90 bpm	Nanchen [29]

(continued)

Table 4. (*continued*)

Temperature	Threshold values	Reference
Cough frequency		
The sensor-based technology will detect elevated cough intensity and frequency, followed by warning the doctors to prevent choking due to i) low oxygen saturation and ii) airway obstruction The doctor will track the patient's current location of the patient to go and attend to the patient or send an ambulance to transfer the patient to the hospital if necessary	***Maximum number of cough sounds:*** *Male: 4.6 coughs/hour* *Female: 1.9 coughs/hour*	Turner et al. [30]; Schelfhout et al. [31]; Holt & Smith [32]
Chest pain, weariness		
Pain and weariness symptoms, such as fatigue, myalgia, headache, and sore throat, can be remotely monitored through meeting appointments and virtual surveys	Not applicable as the patient or his/her carer will report this through the system (or video calls) if present	Weng et al. [33]

Fig. 2. Deployment of healthcare protocols in case of health deviations reported by sensors.

Table 5. Sociodemographic features of the target population and their influence on the technology deployment

Feature	Description	Relation to sensor-assisted technology
Age	The number of years a person has been alive since their birth	This information is necessary for properly configuring the threshold values of heart rate and respiratory rate indicators because they differ according to age
Sex	Biological classification of individuals as male and female	It is related to the configuration of some threshold values that differ due to sex such as cough and heart rate
Education	Maximum academic degree of a patient (bachelor, technician, technologist, professional, specialist, master, doctor)	The correct use of the sensor and interpretation of error messages can be influenced by the education level of patients and their carers, thereby defining the implementation of measures to prevent early damage or deterioration
Residential address	The patient's current and intended long-term residence	Patient location is required for effective physician response to health deviations. Also, it is for validation of coverage and connectivity of sensors
Type of dwelling	Description of patient's place of residence (townhouse, apartment, size)	It is needed for verifying sensor system installation requirements compliance
Civil status	The legal status of a patient possibly affected by whether he/she has a partner	It is important to determine if the patient lives alone and can be assisted by a family member
Health Insurance Company	The healthcare provider that the patient is affiliated with	It affects the cost of the technology service

4.5 Design of the Remote Sensor-Based Assistive Technology

The system is composed of two main parts (Fig. 3). First, the sensors will track the patient's condition remotely in real-time through the detection of symptoms that are mainly related to SRDs: fever, cough, sore throat, myalgia, headache, fatigue, shortness of breath, and chest discomfort. The clinical indicators (Table 2) help monitor these symptoms' development as the disease progresses. The sensors will capture any health deviation considering the predefined threshold values (Table 3). The sensors collect real-time information from the patient and send it to the hospital. This helps healthcare

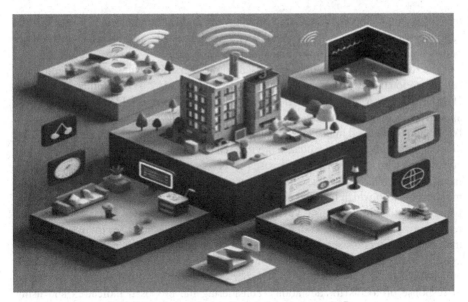

Fig. 3. Proposed Sensor-based assistive technology.

professionals monitor the patient's condition accurately and remotely. This approach eliminates the need for direct contact between the patient with respiratory disease and healthcare professionals, which can help prevent intra-hospital infections. As soon as the sensors detect values outside the thresholds, they will send alerts, alarms, and messages describing the patient's condition along with their geographical location. Healthcare professionals and administrative staff can then respond by sending a medical team to the patient's location or dispatching an ambulance to transfer the patient to the hospital for appropriate treatment according to the protocols (Table 3). Lastly, all the information about the patient, including health deviations, treatments, and monitoring plans, will be stored in the system linked to their medical history.

5   Conclusions

This study presents a methodological approach for designing sensor-based assistance technology to reduce in-hospital infection and mortality associated with epidemic respiratory diseases, motivated by the rapid increase in the spread, diversity, and characteristics of this type of disease, measures, and opportunities for improvement in in-hospital management to reduce infections through adequate diagnosis, monitoring, and referral of cases, with better use of available resources and hospital installed capacity. Furthermore, patient safety is a global challenge that demands preventive strategies from countries and institutions in the health sector to improve patient safety and the management of infections related to hospital care, classified among the leading causes of death and increase in morbidity in hospitalized patients. The proposal is based on a combined approach that integrates clinical, technological, and process aspects for designing healthcare technology that supports diagnosing, monitoring, and developing medical and health-care interventions for managing patients with respiratory diseases and reducing contact between patients, patient-doctor, and health professionals.

The results of this study allowed, based on the literature review, to first identify the central stationary respiratory diseases, such as SARS-CoV-2, H7N9 Influenza A virus, H1N1 Influenza A virus, H5N1 Influenza A virus, HCoVs, H3N2 Influenza A Virus, as well as its characteristic symptoms, with which elements of health technology can be adapted (scheduled interviews, virtual appointments) to manage the symptoms. This identification constituted a valuable input when designing the technology since it must correspond with the respiratory diseases to be controlled. The second key aspect to incorporate into the sensor-based assistive technology is the set of indicators for remote monitoring, with which hospital or home management can be determined based on the patient's profile. In this sense, key indicators such as temperature, oxygen saturation, respiratory rate, heart rate, cough intensity, pain, and weariness are the most relevant metrics for the diagnosis, monitoring, and management of seasonal respiratory diseases, as well as the decision of the adoption of technology by the patient based on these indicators and the patient's profile. Another essential input of the study is the design of response protocols for deviations, considering the proposed indicators and using threshold values for each indicator, with which the sensor-based assistive technology can generate early alerts and notifications to the hospital, doctors, patients, and caregivers for a timely and specific diagnosis and management of the respiratory disease, reducing contacts and infections.

Furthermore, the study made it possible to determine the main characteristics of the target population for the use of the technology based on their demographic character-istics, to achieve greater adherence to the technology through the adapt-ability of the patient to the system, the accessibility in the use, security and proper handling of technol-ogy, among others. Finally, the sensor-based assistive technology design integrates the clinical indicators and symptoms previously identified and the threshold values, through which deviations in the critical monitoring parameters of the respiratory disease can be detected and alerts directed to the hospital can be generated. Medical and health-care personnel activate management protocols, both at the intra-hospital level and home management, in cases of patient referral. Therefore, this study offers relevant and sig-nificant information for the development of health technology to reduce infections and in-hospital mortality in the face of epidemic respiratory diseases, considering not only medical aspects but also administrative aspects and the demographic characterization of the patient, providing a vision design focused on the safety of the patient and medical staff, with benefits for patients, their families, the medical and care team and health decision-makers, who will be able to make efficient use of the available resources.

In future work, the implementation of technology in the actual context of the health sector is proposed, as well as extending this proposal to the management of other types of contagious and epidemic diseases, with which health systems will be able to establish strategic plans oriented to the prevention of mortality and morbidity in the management of highly infectious diseases and to continually prepare its available resources, guaranteeing continuity in the provision of health services, and increasing the safety of the patient and collaborators.

Acknowledgments. The authors acknowledge the support of Sebastian Arias Fonseca during this research. This work was supported by the European Union Next Generation EU under the Margarita Salas grant launched by Universitat Politècnica de Valencia (Recovery, Transformation, and Resilience Plan) and Ministerio de Ciencia, Innovación y Universidades (Program for Retraining of the Spanish University System).

Disclosure of Interests. The authors declare no conflict of interest regarding this manuscript.

References

1. Jefferson, T., et al.: Physical interventions to interrupt or reduce the spread of respiratory viruses. Cochrane Database of Systematic Reviews (2023). Issue 1. Art. No.: CD006207. DOI: https://doi.org/10.1002/14651858.CD006207.pub6. Accessed 29 Feb 2024
2. Navarro-Romero, E. D. C., Gelves-Alarcón, Ó. M., & García-Corrales, N. (2021). Análisis correlacional entre la economía, los índices sociodemográficos y las estadísticas de contagio por Covid-19, aplicando la metodología de Clustering en países de América. *INGE CUC, 17*(1)
3. Ortíz-Barrios, M., Jaramillo-Rueda, N., Gul, M., Yucesan, M., Jiménez-Delgado, G., Alfaro-Saíz, J.J.: A Fuzzy Hybrid MCDM approach for assessing the emergency department performance during the COVID-19 Outbreak. Int. J. Environ. Res. Public Health **20**(5), 4591 (2023)
4. Ortíz-Barrios, M.A., Coba-Blanco, D.M., Alfaro-Saíz, J.J., Stand-González, D.: Process improvement approaches for increasing the response of emergency departments against the COVID-19 pandemic: a systematic review. Int. J. Environ. Res. Public Health **18**(16), 8814 (2021)
5. Mecklai, K., Nicholas, S., Ariel, D.S., Daniel, B.K.: Remote patient monitoring – overdue or overused? New Engl. J. Med. **384**(15), 1384–1386 (2021)
6. Singh, A., Rehman, S.U., Yongchareon, S., Chong, P.H.J.: Sensor technologies for fall detection systems: a review. IEEE Sens. J. **20**(13), 6889–6919 (2020). https://doi.org/10.1109/JSEN.2020.2976554,(2020)
7. Hina, S., et al.: An intelligent and smart environment monitoring system for healthcare. MDPI Appl. Sci. **9**(19), 4172 (2019). https://doi.org/10.3390/app9194172
8. Karimpour, N., Karaduman, B., Ural, A., Challenger, M., Dagdeviren, O.: IoT based hand hygiene compliance monitoring. In 2019 International Symposium on Networks, Computers and Communications (ISNCC), pp. 1–6. IEEE (2019)
9. Khaliq, K.A., Noakes, C., Kemp, A.H., Thompson, C., CONTACT Trial Team.: Evaluating the performance of wearable devices for contact tracing in care home environments. J. Occup. Environ. Hyg. **20**(10), 468–479 (2023)
10. Krishnan, R.H., Pugazhenthi, S.: Mobility assistive devices and self-transfer robotic systems for elderly, a review. Intel. Serv. Robot. **7**, 37–49 (2014)
11. Ortiz-Barrios, M.A., Cleland, I., Nugent, C., Pancardo, P., Järpe, E., Synnott, J.: Simulated data to estimate real sensor events—a poisson-regression-based modelling. Remote Sens. **12**(5), 771 (2020)
12. Ortiz-Barrios, M., et al.: Predicting activity duration in smart sensing environments using synthetic data and partial least squares regression: the case of dementia patients. Sensors **22**(14), 5410 (2022)
13. Pramanik, P.K.D., Pareek, G., Nayyar, A.: Security and privacy in remote healthcare: issues, solutions, and standards. In: Telemedicine Technologies, pp. 201–225. Academic Press (2019)

14. Chen, N., et al.: Epidemiological and clinical characteristics of 99 cases of 2019 novel coronavirus pneumonia in Wuhan, China: a descriptive study. The Lancet **395**(10223), 507–513 (2020). https://doi.org/10.1016/S0140-6736(20)30211-7

15. Rodriguez-Morales, A.J., et al.: Clinical, laboratory and imaging features of COVID-19: A systematic review and meta-analysis. Travel Med. Infect. Dis. **34**, 101623 (2020). https://doi.org/10.1016/J.TMAID.2020.101623

16. Chen, X., Yang, Z., Lu, Y., Xu, Q., Wang, Q., Chen, L.: Clinical features and factors associated with outcomes of patients infected with a novel influenza a (H7N9) virus: a preliminary study. PLoS ONE **8**(9), e73362 (2013). https://doi.org/10.1371/JOURNAL.PONE.0073362

17. Da Costa, V.G., Saivish, M.V., Santos, D.E.R., de Lima Silva, R.F., Moreli, M.L.: Comparative epidemiology between the 2009 H1N1 influenza and COVID-19 pandemics. J. Infect. Public Health **13**(12), 1797–1804 (2020)

18. Jiang, C., et al.: Comparative review of respiratory diseases caused by coronaviruses and influenza A viruses during epidemic season. Microbes Infect. **22**(6–7), 236–244 (2020). https://doi.org/10.1016/J.MICINF.2020.05.005

19. Allen, J.D., Ross, T.M.: H3N2 influenza viruses in humans: viral mechanisms, evolution, and evaluation. Hum. Vaccin. Immunother. **14**(8), 1840–1847 (2018). https://doi.org/10.1080/21645515.2018.1462639

20. Chughtai, A.A., Wang, Q., Dung, T.C., Macintyre, C.R.: The presence of fever in adults with influenza and other viral respiratory infections. Epidemiol. Infect. **145**(1), 148–155 (2017)

21. Spinou, A., Birring, S.S.: An update on measurement and monitoring of cough: what are the important study endpoints? J. Thorac. Dis. **6**(Suppl 7), S728 (2014)

22. Chan, T.V.: The patient with sore throat. Medical Clinics **94**(5), 923–943 (2010)

23. O'Driscoll, B.R., Murphy, P., Turkington, P.M.: Acute monitoring of patients with chronic respiratory disease during hospital admission. Clin. Med. **12**(1), 79 (2012)

24. Mejia, F., et al.: Oxygen saturation as a predictor of mortality in hospitalized adult patients with COVID-19 in a public hospital in Lima. Peru. PloS one **15**(12), e0244171 (2020)

25. Qadir, F.I., et al.: The relationship between CT severity infections and oxygen saturation in patients infected with COVID-19, a cohort study. Ann. Med. Surg. **76**, 103439 (2022)

26. Davidson, J.A., Warren-Gash, C.: Cardiovascular complications of acute respiratory infections: current research and future directions. Expert Rev. Anti Infect. Ther. **17**(12), 939–942 (2019)

27. Tharakan, S., Nomoto, K., Miyashita, S., Ishikawa, K.: Body temperature correlates with mortality in COVID-19 patients. Crit. Care **24**, 1–3 (2020)

28. Sharma, P., Hui, X., Zhou, J., Conroy, T.B., Kan, E.C.: Wearable radio-frequency sensing of respiratory rate, respiratory volume, and heart rate. NPJ Digit. Med. **3**(1), 98 (2020)

29. Nanchen, D.: Resting heart rate: what is normal? Heart **104**(13), 1048–1049 (2018)

30. Turner, R.D., Birring, S.S.: Measuring cough: what really matters? J. Thorac. Dis. **15**(4), 2288 (2023)

31. Schelfhout, J., et al.: Validation and meaningful change thresholds for an objective cough frequency measurement in chronic cough. Lung **200**(6), 717–724 (2022)

32. Holt, K.J., Smith, J.A.: How often do healthy people cough? Respir. Res. **24**(1), 275 (2023)

33. Weng, L.M., Su, X., Wang, X.Q.: Pain symptoms in patients with coronavirus disease (COVID-19): a literature review. J. Pain Res. **14**, 147–159 (2021)

Investigation of the Impact of a Passive Shoulder Exoskeleton on the Shoulder Range of Motion: A Preliminary Study

Tiejun Ma[ID], Erik Jonathan[ID], and Shuping Xiong[✉][ID]

Department of Industrial and Systems Engineering, Korea Advanced Institute of Science and Technology (KAIST), Daejeon, Republic of Korea
{matj,erikjonath,shupingx}@kaist.ac.kr

Abstract. This study presents a pilot experiment to systematically explore the influence of exoskeleton supportive force, exoskeleton physical design, and external loads on the user's shoulder range of motion (ROM). A within-subjects two-factor factorial design was applied to assess ROM changes under nine experimental conditions (3 exoskeleton settings × 3 loads). The exoskeleton settings were varied among three levels: without exoskeleton as the baseline (NoExo), with a force-on exoskeleton (the supportive force of the exoskeleton was turned on; ExoWithForce), and with a force-off exoskeleton (the supportive force of the exoskeleton was turned off; ExoNoForce). Three different loads (0, 3, and 6 kg) were tested under each exoskeleton setting. Nine healthy young male subjects voluntarily participated and their ROMs in shoulder flexion/extension (FLEX), vertical abduction/adduction (VABD), and horizontal abduction/adduction (HABD) were recorded via a motion capture system. The results showed that the exoskeleton setting significantly influenced the shoulder ROM in the VABD but not that in the HABD and FLEX. Meanwhile, load significantly limited the shoulder ROMs of FLEX, VABD, and HABD. No statistical significance was observed for the interaction effect between load and exoskeleton setting on the ROMs of the shoulder. Notably, compared to the No Exo condition, the mean ROM of VABD of the ExoNoForce and ExoWithForce conditions was lower. There was no significant difference between the ExoNoForce and ExoWithForce conditions of VABD. These findings suggest that while the physical design of the exoskeleton and external load can limit shoulder ROM, the supportive force could partially offset this effect.

Keywords: Industrial exoskeleton · Range of motion · Load · Ergonomics

1 Introduction

Over the years, work-related musculoskeletal disorders (WMSDs) have been imposing heavy burdens on society, leading to a growing interest in the industrial use of exoskeletons to prevent them (Weston et al., 2022). For example, wearing a passive upper-lib exoskeleton EksoVest for repetitive industrial tasks reduced the muscle activity by almost

V. G. Duffy (Ed.): HCII 2024, LNCS 14709, pp. 219–230, 2024.
https://doi.org/10.1007/978-3-031-61060-8_16

37% (Blanco et al., 2022). Despite the benefits offered by exoskeletons, several studies have reported that they can alter the range of motion (ROM) which may introduce potential challenges for the workers (Baltrusch et al., 2019; Perez et al., 2019; Luque et al., 2020). For example, Cardoso et al. (2020) found that an exoskeleton limited movement and could hinder the execution of the task, as the participants reported the perception of ROM reduction and movement restriction with the Laevo exoskeleton.

Maintaining an appropriate ROM is important for several reasons. First, it is essential for tasks that require high flexibility and agility (Kermavnar et al., 2021). A reduced ROM thus may hinder the ability to perform tasks and limit the overall workplace productivity. For example, Park et al. (2022) observed that individuals wearing a back-support exoskeleton exhibited prolonged reaction time, hindered hip flexion kinematics during reactive stepping, and reduced hip flexion. Consequently, this reduction in hip flexion led to decreased peak knee flexion velocity, knee ROM, and step length, which together contribute to compromised balance recovery. The back-support exoskeleton also resulted in a reduction of postural balance during bipedal standing (Park et al., 2021). Additionally, a proper ROM is important for users to avoid awkward posture. Limited ROM may restrict the choices of working postures, potentially leading to the adoption of uncomfortable positions and increased risk of WMSDs. Thus, it is crucial to understand the effects of exoskeletons on the changes of users' ROM (Ma et al., 2023).

There are several potential explanations for the exoskeleton-induced changes in ROM. First, the industrial exoskeleton can alleviate user fatigue by providing additional support (De Bock et al., 2023). This support may enable workers to maintain a higher lifting capability, potentially increasing their overall ROM. However, due to the physical design of exoskeletons, the agility and flexibility of workers can be limited (Li et al., 2018), impeding their free movements. So far, the impact of exoskeletons on the ROM remains largely unexplored. Specifically, current research lacks an in-depth examination of these mechanisms independently. In addition, it is crucial to account for the impact of external loads in studies of changes in ROM due to industrial exoskeletons, especially the upper body exoskeletons in which the presence of loads or tools is common. Understanding how external loads influence ROM is highly relevant for a comprehensive analysis of exoskeleton mechanisms.

Therefore, as a preliminary step to explore the mechanisms of ROM changes due to the use of industrial exoskeletons, this study presents a pilot experiment to systematically examine the effects of the physical design and supportive forces of an exoskeleton as well as external loads on the user's shoulder ROM.

2   Methods

2.1   Participants

A total of nine voluntary subjects from the local community participated in this experiment. The age, weight, and height of these subjects were 25.44 ($\pm$ 2.60) years, 74.38 ($\pm$ 8.49) kg, and 1.79 ($\pm$ 0.05) m, respectively. None of the subjects reported any history of musculoskeletal disorders within the last five years. The protocol of this experiment (KH2023–140) was approved by the Institutional Review Board at the Korea Advanced

Institute of Science and Technology. Written informed consents were obtained from all subjects.

2.2 Exoskeleton

The industrial exoskeleton used in this study was the CDYS shoulder support exoskeleton (Crimson Dynamics Technology, Dalian, China), as shown in Fig. 1. This passive exoskeleton is designed to support the frequent arm-lifting tasks in the automobile and aircraft industries, shipyards, construction, and agriculture. The total weight of this exoskeleton is 2.6 kg. The exoskeleton is connected to the users through two arm cuffs, one waist strap, and several trunk belts. This exoskeleton can provide different levels of assistance from the torque generators mounted at the waist strap. The exoskeleton settings (EXO) were altered across three levels: without exoskeleton as baseline (NoExo), with a force-on exoskeleton (the supportive force of the exoskeleton was turned on; ExoWithForce), and with a force-off exoskeleton (the supportive force of the exoskeleton was turned off; ExoNoForce). The comparison between the NoExo and the ExoNoForce conditions aimed to elucidate the impact of the exoskeleton physical design. Similarly, the comparison between the ExoWithForce and the ExoNoForce conditions was to investigate the effect of supportive forces/moments.

Fig.1. The CDYS shoulder support exoskeleton

2.3 Experimental Design and Procedure

A within-subject two-factor factorial design was applied to assess the ROM changes under nine experimental conditions consisting of three exoskeleton settings (NoExo,

ExoWithForce, and ExoNoForce) and three different external loads (0, 3, and 6 kg). The presentation order of the conditions was randomized. Written informed consents were obtained from the subjects after a brief introduction to the experiment. Then, a period of five to ten minutes was given to allow the familiarization with the exoskeleton and the ROM tasks. After the measurement of the body segment lengths of the subjects, they were equipped with sensors from the Xsens MVN motion capture system (Xsens, Enschede, the Netherlands). The subjects were then instructed to conduct the three ROM tasks outlined below under the nine experimental conditions (Fig. 2). In the ExoNoForce and ExoWithForce conditions, the exoskeleton was fitted and adjusted to the subjects following the guidelines from the manufacturer. Sufficient break was given in between the conditions.

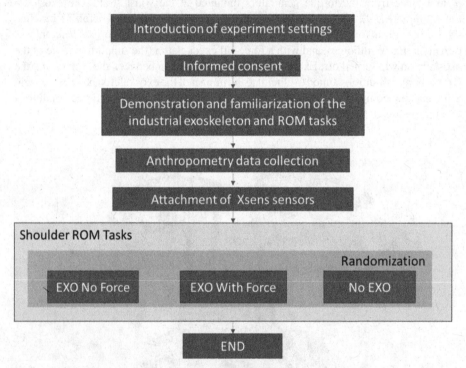

Fig.2. Overall experimental flowchart. The three load conditions of the shoulder ROM tasks were assigned in random orders within each EXO setting condition.

The three shoulder ROMs tasks (Fig. 3) conducted by each subject were: vertical abduction/adduction (VABD), flexion/extension (FLEX), and horizontal abduction/adduction (HABD).

- Shoulder VABD: The subject started at an initial position of standing upright with the dominant arm and hand straightened, leveled with the shoulder, and parallel to the coronal plane. The load was passed to the subject by the experimenter. The dominant arm was first abducted upwards along the coronal plane to its limit, then adducted as parallel and as close to the coronal plane as possible to its limit, and eventually brought back to the initial horizontal position. This exercise was repeated for five times

- Shoulder FLEX: The subject started at an initial position of standing upright with the dominant arm and hand straightened along the trunk and the thumb pointed forward. The load was passed to the subject by the experimenter. The dominant arm was first flexed upwards parallel to the sagittal plane to its limit, then extended posteriorly to its limit, and eventually brought back to the initial position. This exercise was repeated for five times.

- Shoulder HABD: The subject started at an initial position of standing upright with the dominant arm and hand straightened, leveled with the shoulder, and parallel to the coronal plane. The load was passed to the subject by the experimenter. Along this horizontal plane, the dominant arm was first adducted or flexed towards the non-dominant side to its limit, and then abducted or extended backwards posteriorly to its limit. It was eventually brought back to the initial position. This exercise was repeated for five times.

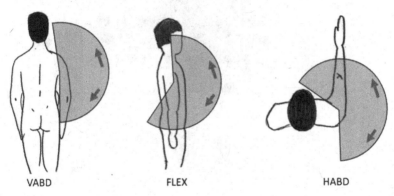

Fig.3. Three shoulder ROMs tasks

2.4 Instrumentation and Outcome Measures

The whole-body motions were measured during the three ROM tasks. The whole-body no-hands kinematics was measured by the Xsens MVN system (Fig. 4). This system used for this experiment consisted of 15 inertial measurement units. The standard Xsens MVN calibration procedure was followed. The data was recorded over the whole movement sequence of trials with the Xsens MVN Analyze software version 2018.2. The data of each experimental trial was later transferred to the Python and MATLAB and used for the calculation of shoulder ROM. Repeated measures analysis of variance (ANOVA) was conducted on the measured data of the shoulder VABD, FLEX, and HABD to test for significance. The mean ROM was calculated as the difference between the trimmed means of the upper limit and lower limit. As each condition was repeated for five times, the average values of the upper limit and lower limit were obtained from the remaining three measurements after the elimination of the maximums and minimums.

Fig.4. Wearable Xsens MVN system for measuring subject's shoulder ROMs

3 Results

The exoskeleton settings significantly influenced the shoulder ROM of VABD [$F_{(2,64)}$ = 3.770, p = 0.028], but not the FLEX [$F_{(2,64)}$ = 1.637, p = 0.202] and HABD [$F_{(2,64)}$ = 1.428, p = 0.247]. Increased load significantly limited the shoulder ROMs in VABD [$F_{(2,64)}$ = 11.885, p < 0.001], FLEX [$F_{(2,64)}$ = 11.287, p < 0.001], and HABD [$F_{(2,64)}$ = 28.372, p < 0.001]. In addition, no statistical significance was observed for the interaction effect between load and exoskeleton setting on the ROMs of the shoulder [VABD, $F_{(4,64)}$ = 0.710, p = 0.588; FLEX, $F_{(4,64)}$ = 0.535, p = 0.711; HABD, $F_{(4,64)}$ = 0.013, p = 0.999]. These results are presented in detail below.

3.1 The Effect of Exoskeleton Setting

For the VABD task, the ExoWithForce condition significantly decreased the mean ROM of shoulder by 12.13° as compared to the NoExo condition; no significant difference was found between the ExoNoForce and the ExoWithForce conditions due to variation (Fig. 5). For the FLEX and HABD, no significant difference was found in any pairwise comparison among the three conditions. However, the FLEX task exhibited a similar non-significant trend to that of the VABD. Specifically, the mean ROM of the ExoNoForce and ExoWithForce conditions were the lowest two among the three EXO conditions, while the mean ROM of the NoExo condition was the highest. Regarding the HABD, the mean ROM was lower in the ExoWithForce and ExoNoForce conditions than the NoExo condition, and the mean of the ExoNoForce condition was the lowest among the three EXO conditions.

3.2 The Effect of Load

The load resulted in significant effects on all three tasks (Fig. 6). As the load increased from 0 kg to 3 kg and from 3 kg to 6 kg, the mean ROMs of the shoulder VABD, FLEX, and HABD all decreased gradually. This decrease was statistically significant between 0 kg and 6 kg for VABD, FLEX, and HABD, and between 3 kg and 6kg for VABD, FLEX and HABD. Specifically, the mean ROMs in 0 kg and 6 kg for VABD were respectively 156.19 and 131.94°. As the load increased from 0 kg to 6 kg, the mean ROM for FLEX decreased from 163.93° to 134.21°. Regarding the HABD, the mean ROM decreased for 45.92° when the load was increased from 0 kg to 6 kg. The mean ROM of VABD, FLEX, and HABD were respectively decreased for 13.23, 16.80, and 28.76° as the load increased from 3 kg to 6 kg. A significant difference was also found between 0kg and 3 kg in HABD. The mean HABD ROM of 0 kg was 106.64°, while that of 3 kg was 89.47°. Also, the differences between 0 kg and 3 kg were smaller than the differences between 3 kg and 6 kg for VABD, FLEX, and HABD.

3.3 The Interaction Effect

There was no significant interaction effect of load and exoskeleton setting on any of the three shoulder ROM tasks (Fig. 7). For the HABD, all three load conditions exhibited a similar trend with the ROMs of the 0 kg and 3 kg being higher than that of the 6 kg. A similar trend between 0 kg and 3 kg was also found in the VABD and FLEX.

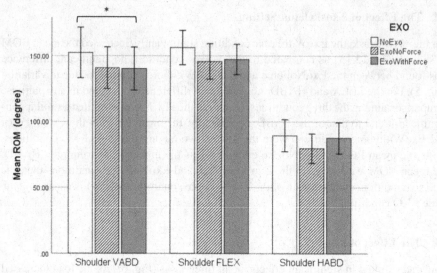

Fig.5. The mean ROMs of the three ROM tasks across the three EXO conditions. Data are presented as means with error bars indicating 95% confidence intervals. The statistically significant difference is indicated by the connecting line.

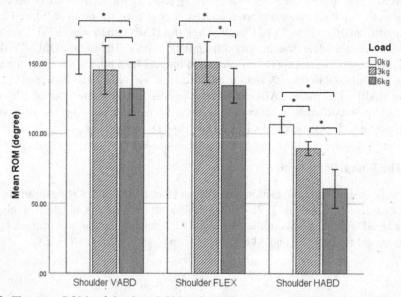

Fig.6. The mean ROMs of the three ROM tasks under three loads (0, 3, and 6 kg). Data are presented as means with error bars indicating 95% confidence intervals. Statistically significant differences are indicated by the connecting lines.

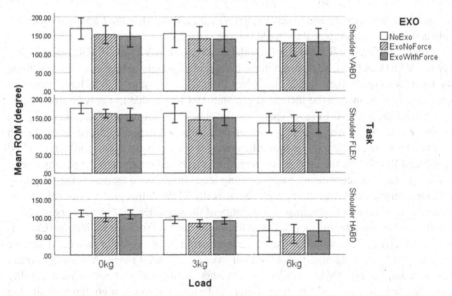

Fig. 7. The mean ROMs of the three ROM tasks across the EXO and load conditions. Data are presented as means with error bars indicating 95% confidence intervals. No statistical significance was found.

4 Discussion

Regarding the exoskeleton settings, compared to the NoExo condition, the ExoWithForce condition had significantly lower ROMs in the VABD; although no significant difference was observed, the same trend was seen in the FLEX. These results agree with a previous study (Hakansson et al., 2021) which reported decreases of ROM in shoulder extension and adduction with four passive shoulder exoskeletons (ShoulderX, EksoVest, Skelex and Paexo) during ROM testing. Similarly, the decreases of ROM in shoulder flexion and abduction were also observed with a passive upper extremity exoskeletal vest (Kim et al., 2018). In the ExoNoForce, the presence of the exoskeleton might have acted as an additional load, resulting in decreased shoulder ROMs. The physical design of the exoskeleton might have introduced unintended friction or resistance for the shoulder movements (Chander et al., 2019). In addition, the presence of the exoskeleton might have influenced the proprioception or perceived limits of joint movement (Bosch et al., 2016; Elprama et al., 2023), resulting in the subconscious choice of a conservative ROM for safety and comfort. Notably, in the VABD and FLEX ROMs, the effect of supportive force was less pronounced than that of the physical design. As the supportive force in the upper and lower limits of the VABD and FLEX plane was negligible, there was no significant change after the supportive force was turned on. Another noteworthy observation was that the ROMs in the HABD of the ExoWithForce condition were higher than those in the ExoNoForce condition. This might indicate that a supportive force could enhance the ROMs in the HABD. An explanation would be that the supportive force might have partly or fully compensated for the additional gravity force resistance caused by the exoskeleton entity and loads (De Vries et al., 2019). Also, the ExoWithForce may help achieve the stability of the shoulder joint.

Load significantly limited the shoulder ROMs in the VABD, FLEX, and HABD. For the VABD and FLEX, this may have been due to gravity acting as a resistant force for wearers to reach their upper and lower limits. The muscles had to have increased activation in response to the increased gravitational forces due to loads (Antony et al., 2010). The motion had to stop when the muscles were not capable of generating the required force. Moreover, excessive muscular exertion led to quick fatigue during which the muscles were unable to generate sufficient force (Enoka et al., 2008) and thus resulted in reduced ROMs. On the other hand, regarding the HABD, although the gravity due to loads was not a direct resistant force, holding loads might have increased the fatigue in shoulder muscles and thus indirectly decreased the ROM in this plane. For example, an excessive load might compromise the stability of the shoulder joint of a user conducting a horizontal motion, requiring additional muscular exertion for its stabilization (Chowdhury et al. 2018). This would cause an early occurrence of muscular fatigue, disabling the muscles from sustaining the movement over an extended range. Also, users would tend to reduce their ROMs for safety reasons when the muscular forces for joint stability were insufficient. Lastly, the increased inertia of increased loads might have resulted in additional challenges for the shoulder joint movements, contributing to the reduction of the shoulder ROMs in all three tasks.

No statistical significance was observed for the interaction effect between load and exoskeleton setting on the shoulder ROMs. The lack of significant effects between loads and EXO in all three shoulder ROMs suggested that the impacts of the external load and exoskeleton setting might act independently of each other. As it was also observed, the external load resulted in changes in the shoulder ROMs consistently across exoskeleton setting conditions. The increase or decrease of load may not substantially alter the impact of the EXO.

This pilot study is subject to certain limitations, which will be addressed in future research endeavors. Firstly, the sample size of the present study was relatively small (nine subjects), which poses challenges to the generalizability of the findings. Additionally, the study observed a brief testing duration of five repetitions for each condition of the ROM tasks. This temporal restriction could impact the applicability of the findings to the long-term effects of exoskeletons on shoulder ROMs. Another noteworthy limitation is that all subjects were young students with no prior experience in the tested tasks, deviating from the target users of industrial exoskeletons. To enhance the reliability of findings regarding the effectiveness of the industrial exoskeleton, future tests should involve industrial workers as subjects.

5   Conclusions

In conclusion, this study explored the impact of a passive shoulder exoskeleton on the ROM of the user's shoulder joints, with the consideration of the factors of supportive force, physical design, and external load. The findings suggest that while the physical design of the exoskeleton and external load could reduce shoulder ROM, supportive forces could partially offset this effect. This preliminary investigation demonstrates the complex interplay of factors that influence the range of motion of industrial exoskeleton users and could contribute to improved design of occupational exoskeletons.

Acknowledgments. This research was supported by the National Research Foundation of Korea (NRF) funded by the Ministry of Science and ICT (NRF-2022R1F1A1061045, NRF-2022M3J6A1063021).

Disclosure of Interests. The authors have no competing interests to declare that are relevant to the content of this article.

References

Antony, N.T., Keir, P.J.: Effects of posture, movement and hand load on shoulder muscle activity. J. Electromyogr. Kinesiol. **20**(2), 191–198 (2010)

Baltrusch, S., Van Dieën, J., Bruijn, S., Koopman, A., Van Bennekom, C., Houdijk, H.: The effect of a passive trunk exoskeleton on metabolic costs during lifting and walking. Ergonomics **62**(7), 903–916 (2019)

Blanco, A., Catalán, J.M., Martínez-Pascual, D., García-Pérez, J.V., García-Aracil, N.: The effect of an active upper-limb exoskeleton on metabolic parameters and muscle activity during a repetitive industrial task. IEEE Access **10**, 16479–16488 (2022)

Bosch, T., van Eck, J., Knitel, K., de Looze, M.: The effects of a passive exoskeleton on muscle activity, discomfort and endurance time in forward bending work. Appl. Ergon. **54**, 212–217 (2016)

Cardoso, A., Colim, A., Sousa, N.: The effects of a passive exoskeleton on muscle activity and discomfort in industrial tasks. In: Arezes, P.M., et al. (eds.) Occupational and Environmental Safety and Health II. SSDC, vol. 277, pp. 237–245. Springer, Cham (2020). https://doi.org/10.1007/978-3-030-41486-3_26

Chander, D.S., Cavatorta, M.P.: Modelling friction at the mechanical interface between the human and the exoskeleton. Int. J. Human Factors Model. Simul. **7**(2), 119–136 (2019)

Chowdhury, S.K., Nimbarte, A.D., Hsiao, H., Gopalakrishnan, B., Jaridi, M.: A biomechanical shoulder strain index based on stabilizing demand of shoulder joint. Ergonomics **61**(12), 1657–1670 (2018)

De Bock, S., et al.: Passive shoulder exoskeleton support partially mitigates fatigue-induced effects in overhead work. Appl. Ergon. **106**, 103903 (2023)

De Vries, A., De Looze, M.: The effect of arm support exoskeletons in realistic work activities: a review study. J. Ergon **9**(4), 1–9 (2019)

Elprama, S.A., Bock, S.D., Meeusen, R., Pauw, K.D., Vanderborght, B., Jacobs, A.: Design and implementation requirements for increased acceptance of occupational exoskeletons in an industrial context: a qualitative study. Int. J. Human–Comput. Interact 1–16 (2023)

Enoka, R.M., Duchateau, J.: Muscle fatigue: what, why and how it influences muscle function. J. Physiol. **586**(1), 11–23 (2008)

Hakansson, N.A., Jorgensen, M., Desai, J., Hodson, A., Madden, T.: Range of motion from four passive shoulder exoskeleton. In: The XXXIIIrd Annual Occupational Ergonomics and Safety Conference, Virtual Conference, Sep 16–17 (2021)

Kermavnar, T., de Vries, A.W., de Looze, M.P., O'Sullivan, L.W.: Effects of industrial back-support exoskeletons on body loading and user experience: an updated systematic review. Ergonomics **64**(6), 685–711 (2021)

Kim, S., Nussbaum, M.A., Esfahani, M.I.M., Alemi, M.M., Jia, B., Rashedi, E.: Assessing the influence of a passive, upper extremity exoskeletal vest for tasks requiring arm elevation: part II–unexpected" effects on shoulder motion, balance, and spine loading. Appl. Ergon. **70**, 323–330 (2018)

Li, H., Cheng, W., Liu, F., Zhang, M., Wang, K.: The effects on muscle activity and discomfort of varying load carriage with and without an augmentation exoskeleton. Appl. Sci. **8**(12), 2638 (2018)

Luque, E.P., Högberg, D., Pascual, A.I., Lämkull, D., Rivera, F.G.: Motion behavior and range of motion when using exoskeletons in manual assembly tasks. In: Proceedings of the SPS2020: Swedish Production Symposium, vol. 13, p. 217 (2020)

Ma, T., Zhang, Y., Choi, S.D., Xiong, S.: Modelling for design and evaluation of industrial exoskeletons: a systematic review. Appl. Ergon. **113**, 104100 (2023)

Park, J.-H., Kim, S., Nussbaum, M.A., Srinivasan, D.: Effects of two passive back-support exoskeletons on postural balance during quiet stance and functional limits of stability. J. Electromyogr. Kinesiol. **57**, 102516 (2021)

Park, J.-H., Lee, Y., Madigan, M.L., Kim, S., Nussbaum, M.A., Srinivasan, D.: Wearing a back-support exoskeleton impairs single-step balance recovery performance following a forward loss of balance–an exploratory study. J. Biomech. **144**, 111352 (2022)

Perez Luque, E.: Evaluation of the Use of Exoskeletons in the Range of Motion of Workers. Dissertation, University of Skövde, School of Engineering Science (2019)

Weston, E.B., Alizadeh, M., Hani, H., Knapik, G.G., Souchereau, R.A., Marras, W.S.: A physiological and biomechanical investigation of three passive upper-extremity exoskeletons during simulated overhead work. Ergonomics **65**(1), 105–117 (2022)

User Assessment of Passive Exoskeleton in Manual Material Handling

Arnold Nieto[1], Hardik Vora[1], Fatemeh Davoudi[1,2](✉) 🄳, and Armin Moghadam[3]

[1] Machine Learning & Safety Analytics Lab, School of Engineering, Santa Clara University, Santa Clara, CA 95053, USA
{anieto,hvora,fatemeh.davoudi}@scu.edu

[2] Department of General Engineering, Santa Clara University, Santa Clara, CA 95053, USA

[3] Department of Technology, College of Engineering, San Jose State University, San Jose, CA 95192, USA
armin.moghadam@sjsu.edu

Abstract. Manual material handling (MMH) tasks, involving activities like lifting, carrying, and holding various loads, contribute significantly to lower back fatigue, pain, injuries, and musculoskeletal disorders in occupational settings. To address these challenges, passive back-supporting industrial exoskeletons (BExo) have been introduced as assistive technologies to mitigate ergonomic risks associated with MMH tasks. This study evaluates the acceptance of BExos during MMH tasks in laboratory conditions, providing insights from users' perspectives. The results, showing consistently reduced physical discomfort scores across tasks, emphasize the efficacy of the back-supporting exoskeleton in alleviating perceived effort during manual material handling. Notable reductions in discomfort, especially in critical areas like the lower back, upper back, shoulders, and knees during the box-carrying task, highlight the targeted impact of the exoskeleton on essential anatomical regions. Positive user perceptions underscore the utility of the exoskeleton in alleviating fatigue, promoting ergonomic posture, and serving as a comfortable and wearable assistive technology. These findings offer insights for safety practitioners and human factors experts, suggesting the potential applicability of the back exoskeleton in diverse occupational tasks and settings.

Keywords: Exoskeleton · Safety · Ergonomics · Fatigue · Users and Workplace

1 Introduction

Manual material handling (MMH) tasks are prevalent, physically demanding activities in many occupational settings such as manufacturing, warehouse operations, logistics, construction, and agriculture. These physically demanding activities involve lifting, pushing, pulling, carrying, and holding diverse loads, contributing to a substantial physical workload in these settings [1]. Engaging in manual material handling (MMH) tasks often imposes significant compression on the back, constituting a primary risk factor for occupational injuries. This heightened pressure on the back underscores the importance of addressing ergonomic considerations and implementing proper lifting techniques to mitigate the potential for work-related injuries.

© The Author(s), under exclusive license to Springer Nature Switzerland AG 2024
V. G. Duffy (Ed.): HCII 2024, LNCS 14709, pp. 231–242, 2024.
https://doi.org/10.1007/978-3-031-61060-8_17

Musculoskeletal disorders (MSDs) stand out as the primary cause of non-fatal injuries and contribute substantially to the number of days-away-from-work across industries. These disorders consist of a range of conditions affecting the muscles, bones, tendons, ligaments, and other elements of the musculoskeletal system. In particular, back injuries alone constitute a significant portion, accounting for 17% of all MSDs [2]. The prevalence of these injuries underscores the need for comprehensive strategies in occupational health and safety, emphasizing preventive measures and ergonomic interventions to reduce the incidence of MSDs, enhance workplace well-being, and minimize the associated economic impact. Efforts aimed at addressing the specific challenges posed by back injuries can play a pivotal role in fostering a healthier and more productive workforce [3].

MMH tasks are considered the foremost contributor to occupational lower back fatigue, pain, and injuries, necessitating a concentrated research focus on intervention strategies and innovative technologies [4]. The primary objective is to mitigate the risk and severity of back injuries associated with MMH tasks and cultivate a workplace environment that prioritizes ergonomic considerations. Employing a research-driven methodology, this initiative seeks to elevate occupational safety through the formulation and implementation of measures designed to alleviate the physical strain associated with MMH tasks.

The focus on interventions and technologies aims to specifically address the inherent ergonomic challenges of MMH, with the ultimate objective of creating a safer and more supportive work environment. This effort aims to promote the overall well-being of workers and reduce the occurrence of incapacitating back-related issues, to create healthier and more sustainable workforce.

Among these technologies are industrial exoskeletons designed to support the back, that have been recently introduced as a new tool for reducing the risk of lower back injuries [5, 6], and are gaining recognition as effective ergonomic interventions for mitigating the risk of back injuries in workplace settings [7, 8]. Exoskeletons, alternatively referred to as Exosuit or wearable robots, are easily deployable wearable devices designed to alleviate fatigue and strain [9, 10]. Within the passive back-support exoskeleton, torque generators utilize gas springs for force generation, offering torque transfer capabilities intended to alleviate the workload on the back during various MMH activities performed by users [11, 12]. By doing so, they play a crucial role in preventing injuries to the body parts subjected to the most stress during routine workplace activities [9].

While prior research has offered valuable insights into the potential application of exoskeletons in different occupational settings, a more comprehensive investigation is required to thoroughly assess various aspects of their integration, especially in roles that routinely involve MMH tasks. Recognizing the pivotal role of user posture in the successful adoption of exoskeletons, this study aims to examine the influence of a back support exoskeleton on postures during MMH tasks [13, 14].

1.1 Objective of the Study

Despite the existing literature, several aspects of exoskeleton adaptation, particularly their impact on reducing task exertion across various body parts, remain inadequately explored. Additionally, the acceptance and willingness of users to wear exoskeletons are pivotal factors for real-world utilization, yet few studies have comprehensively examined multiple criteria such as users' trust in this technology and their willingness to use it as impactful equipment.

In an effort to address this research gap, our study conducts a comparative analysis of users' assessments of a back-supporting exoskeleton during a series of Manual Material Handling (MMH) tasks, comparing scenarios with and without the use of exoskeletons. The anticipated outcomes aim to provide valuable insights into the effects of exoskeleton usage on critical factors such as comfort, fatigue, and usability. By analyzing these various aspects, our research seeks to contribute to practical understanding of the role and impact of exoskeletons in enhancing user experience and performance during manual material handling tasks.

2 Methodology

In this study, we designed an occupational experiment simulating most common manual material handling tasks, along with a survey questionnaire. The designed experiments involved a series of standard occupational MMH tasks for participants, followed by the completion of a questionnaire. The survey aimed to evaluate participants' perspectives on the potential impact of a supportive assistive technology, like a back exoskeleton, on their physical fatigue. Additionally, it sought to gather participants' insights into their overall attitudes toward exoskeleton usage. The study was conducted in accordance with the Declaration of Helsinki, and approved by the Institutional Review Board and the Office of Research Compliance and Integrity of Santa Clara University (No: 23-11-2076). Informed consent was obtained from all participants involved in the study prior to each experiment.

2.1 Experimental Set-Up

In this experimental setup, the Ottobock BackX industrial passive back-supporting exoskeleton (BExo) was used. Participants were enlisted to execute simulated MMH tasks in accordance with the provided guidelines.

The experimental procedures involved a series of tasks performed by participants with and without the BExo. Initially, participants engaged in walking, carrying a box, and lifting a box without the assistance of the BExo. The walking segment extended for a duration of two minutes, followed by carrying a 15.6-pound box for two sets of three repetitions and lifting the box for two sets of three repetitions. The table height, where participants placed the box during lifting, was set at 90 cm. The carrying distance for the box spanned from point A to point B in the laboratory, covering a distance of 2.6 m. The BExo and the box used in the study are shown in Fig. 1.

Before conducting the trial, the subjects were familiarized with the protocol and equipment. Each participant was provided with a consent form, allowing sufficient time for reading and making an informed decision regarding their participation. Subsequently, all participants willingly agreed to participate in the trial and signed the consent form.

Following the completion of the tasks, participants were administered a survey questionnaire for feedback. Participants were informed that they could withdraw from the experiment at any point without facing any penalties, although all participants successfully completed all assigned tasks. To ensure participant well-being, sufficient intervals were incorporated to facilitate recovery from any potential fatigue from the preceding phase of the experiment.

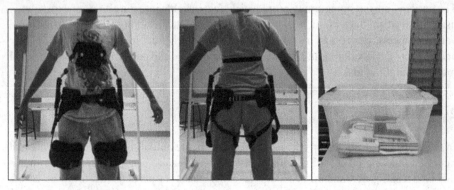

Fig. 1. Participant wearing the BExo; (a) front schematic (b) back schematic (c) box used

2.2 Participants and Data Collection

Eighteen college students volunteered for this study, ensuring gender balance with nine males and nine female participants. Participants were explicitly informed of their right to withdraw from the experiment at any point without any penalties, and all participants successfully completed the experiments. The average age of participants was 19.6 years, with a standard deviation of 2.27 years.

To assess user acceptance of BExo, the Borg Rating of Perceived Exertion (RPE) scale was employed [15]. Following ach experimental session, participants completed a survey questionnaire utilizing the Borg RPE, offering insights into discomfort levels, feelings of physical stress, and fatigue across various body parts during MMH tasks with and without the BackX exoskeleton. Additionally, users provided feedback on the exoskeleton's utility in alleviating fatigue, promoting a more ergonomic posture, and serving as a comfortable and wearable assistive technology. The entire experimental procedure lasted between 35 to 45 min.

3 Results

This section presents the comprehensive findings from our investigation into users' perceptions of the physical exertion associated with the back exoskeleton. Beyond assessing the physical strain, we looked into multiple criteria, evaluating users' trust in the exoskeleton, its influence on ergonomic task performance, overall comfort and wearability, and users' broader assessment of its contribution to the successful completion of various MMH tasks. This approach allows us to describe and evaluate user experiences, providing valuable insights into the alleviation of physical exertion as well as the overall effectiveness and acceptance of the exoskeleton across a spectrum of crucial factors.

3.1 Exertion and Exo Support

The impact of BExo on the overall perceived discomfort is illustrated in Fig. 2. In order to assess the statistical significance of the difference in the total discomfort between the two conditions (exo and no-exo), a Tukey test (at $\alpha = 0.05$) was conducted for the support variable, which includes two levels: exo and no-exo. Significantly different levels are identified by distinct letters.

The Tukey test results for mean comparison reveal a noteworthy reduction in the average sum of perceived discomfort across various tasks, task types, and body parts when participants wore BExo. Specifically, the mean discomfort level for the no-exo condition is 16.23 (A), while for the exo condition, it is 9.56 (B). The distinct letters indicate a statistically significant reduction in the average perceived discomfort from 16.23 to 9.56 with the presence of the exoskeleton during trials. This underscores the efficacy of BExo in decreasing the overall perceived exertion.

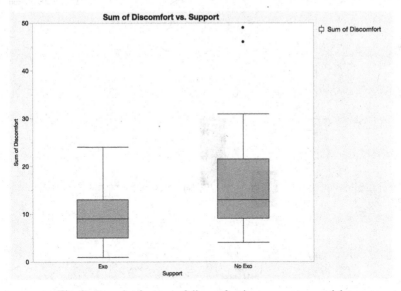

Fig. 2. Box plot for sum of discomfort in exo vs. no exo trial.

3.2 Exertion and MMH Tasks

The impact of BExo on the overall perceived discomfort during MMH tasks in both exo and no-exo experimental conditions in shown in Fig. 3. To evaluate the statistical significance of the disparity in total discomfort between the two conditions, exo and no-exo, a Tukey test (at $\alpha = 0.05$) was conducted for the MMH task variable, with three levels: carrying the box, lifting the box, and walking. Distinct letters in Table 1 denote significantly different levels. The results from the Tukey test are given in Table 1.

Table 1. Statistical Difference in Exo vs No-Exo Scenarios using Tukey Test

Task/Support	*Mean	Mean RPE
Lift- No Exo	A	21.00
Lift- Exo	B	12.00
Carry- No Exo	A	19.60
Carry- Exo	A	12.30
Walk- No Exo	A	8.10
Walk- Exo	B	4.40

* Levels not connected by same letter are significantly different.

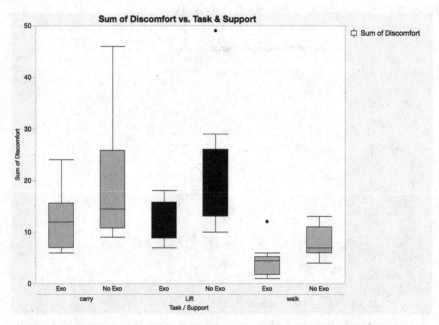

Fig. 3. Box plot for sum of discomfort in exo vs. no exo trial based on MMH task.

The mean comparison reveals a statistically significant reduction in the average sum of perceived discomfort during lifting and walking activities between the exo and no-exo trials. Specifically, the average rate of perceived exertion decreased by 9 points (42%) for the lifting task and by 4 points (50%) for the walking task. Although the average total discomfort rate reduced from 19.6 to 12.3 due to wearing the BExo during the carrying task, this difference was not statistically significance. This emphasizes the efficacy of BExo in decreasing the overall perceived exertion in specific MMH tasks. These findings offer valuable insights into how and for what assignments BExo could be optimally employed to maximize health benefits for workers engaged in MMH tasks across diverse industries.

3.3 Physical Exertion in Box-Carry Task

This section evaluates the outcomes related to the rate of perceived exertion (RPE), or physical discomfort, encountered by participants during the course of the experiments. The participants engaged in a variety of MMH tasks, both with and without the assistance of the BExo. Irrespective of the specific task, the findings consistently indicate that the exoskeleton effectively lowered the RPE scores for all participants across all completed tasks.

Examining the box-carrying task, as shown in Fig. 4, a conspicuous reduction in the aggregate discomfort across diverse body parts is evident with the BExo. Noticeable reductions were observed in the lower back, upper back, shoulders, and knees. In contrast, minimal alterations in the discomfort level were discernible for the feet, elbow, neck, ankle, and wrist when comparing experiments conducted with and without the exoskeleton. However, no discernible change in discomfort was observed in the chest region during the execution of the box-carrying task, irrespective of the presence or absence of the exoskeleton.

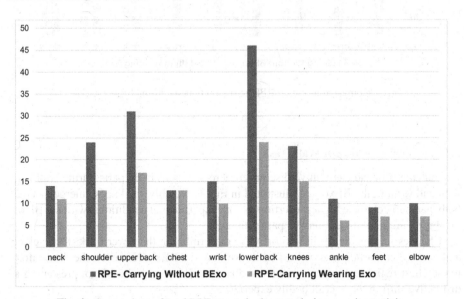

Fig. 4. Comparison of total RPE across body parts during carrying activity

3.4 Physical Exertion in Box-Lift Task

As illustrated in Fig. 5, the lifting task without the exoskeleton (exo) revealed the highest reported discomfort in the lower back, knees, and upper back. However, a noteworthy reduction in discomfort for these specific body parts was observed when participants repeated the lifting task while wearing the BExo. The feet remained the least affected, exhibiting consistently low discomfort in both scenarios.

It is crucial to emphasize that, regardless of the subtle nature of the differences, all body parts showed reduced exertion when tasks were performed wearing the BExo. This observation underscores the positive impact of the BExo on mitigating discomfort and exertion across various anatomical regions during lifting tasks.

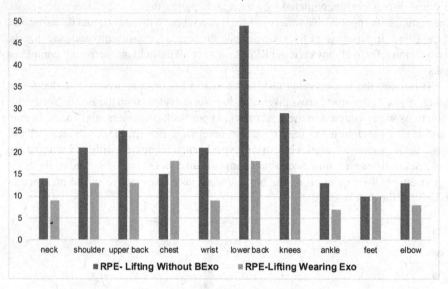

Fig. 5. Comparison of total RPE across body parts during lifting activity

3.5 Physical Exertion in Walk Task

The outcomes of the cumulative discomfort across various body parts during walking, with and without the BExo, are illustrated in Fig. 6. Notably, the knees emerged as the body part subject to the highest exertion in both experimental conditions, with the BExo exhibiting minimal impact on this particular area.

Changes in the sum of discomfort were discernible in the lower back, feet, ankle, and neck when participants walked while wearing the BExo. However, the discomfort in the chest region exhibited an increase during walking with the BExo, presenting a distinctive shift in the overall bodily experience.

3.6 Other Evaluation Criteria in BExo

In order to gain insights into the potential acceptance of exoskeletons as assistive technology in workplaces involving MMH tasks, participants were surveyed and asked to score the exoskeleton on various criteria, ranging from trustworthiness to overall contribution. The criteria included participants' trust in the exoskeleton, the ergonomic impact it

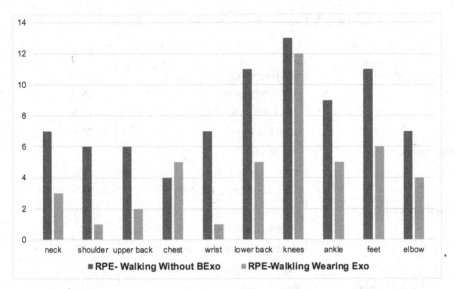

Fig. 6. Comparison of total RPE across body parts during walking activity.

had on task performance, the comfort level experienced while wearing it, and the overall contribution to completing tasks with reduced fatigue and physical exertion. Participants were asked to give a score based on 1 to 10 for each criterion. The criteria asked the below questions:

- Trustworthiness: how much trust they have in this exoskeleton to use as part of their job;
- Ergonomic Impact: How they rate the impact of the exo on helping them do the given task in an ergonomic manner;
- Comfort level: How comfortable they feel while doing the given tasks wearing the exo;
- Overall contribution: How they perceive overall helpfulness of the exoskeleton in completing the given task with less fatigue and physical exertion;

The analysis results, presented in Table 2 shed light on the participants' perceptions of the BExo. A significant 88% of participants regarded the exoskeleton as trustworthy for use in their jobs, with only 22% expressing low trust in the technology. From an ergonomic perspective, all participants found the BExo to be impactful, improving their posture in an ergonomic-friendly manner. Specifically, 61% noted a high impact on posture improvement, while 39% described the ergonomic impact as slightly to moderately helpful.

Turning to comfort and wearability, 50% of participants found the BExo very comfortable to wear, while 44% rated it as slightly to moderately uncomfortable. Only a minimal 1% reported finding the exoskeleton very uncomfortable. In terms of overall helpfulness and impact, all participants unanimously described the exoskeleton as a beneficial assistive technology. Specifically, 50% rated it as very helpful, 28% as moderately helpful, and only 22% as slightly helpful.

Table 2. Overall Assessment of BExo Contribution

Criteria	Scales	Percent
Trustworthiness	very trustworthy	39%
	moderately trustworthy	28%
	somewhat trustworthy	11%
	slight low trust	22%
Ergonomic Impact	very helpful	33%
	moderately helpful	28%
	slight to moderate helpful	39%
Comfort Level	very comfortable	44%
	slightly comfortable	6%
	slight to moderate uncomfortable	44%
	very uncomfortable	1%
Overall Contribution	Very Helpful	50%
	Moderately helpful	28%
	Slightly helpful	22%
	Very Helpful	50%

4   Discussion and Conclusion

This study aimed to thoroughly investigate the usability and effectiveness of a commercial industrial back exoskeleton by analyzing users' perceptions of the rate of perceived exertion during a series of manual material handling tasks conducted in controlled laboratory conditions. The results consistently indicated a reduction in the rating of physical discomfort scores across all tasks, highlighting the effective impact of the back-supporting exoskeleton in alleviating perceived effort for participants.

Notably, during the box-carrying task, there was a significant reduction in discomfort across critical body parts, including the lower back, upper back, shoulders, and knees, while minimal alterations were observed in discomfort for the feet, elbow, neck, ankle, and wrist, with no discernible change in the chest region. These findings underscore the visible alleviation of discomfort in crucial anatomical areas facilitated by the BExo during specific manual material handling tasks, contributing to the ergonomic evaluation of its efficacy.

Similarly, during the lifting task, the exoskeleton demonstrated a significant decrease in discomfort in the lower back, knees, and upper back, emphasizing its efficacy in mitigating discomfort during lifting activities. Regardless of subtle differences, all body parts experienced reduced exertion when using the exoskeleton, indicating its positive impact on mitigating exertion across diverse anatomical regions during lifting tasks. The observed variation in levels of discomfort during walking further contributes to our understanding of the exoskeleton's targeted effects on different body areas, offering valuable insights into its potential implications in various ambulatory activities.

Moreover, users provided a positive perception of the exoskeleton, citing its usefulness in alleviating fatigue, contributing to a more ergonomic posture, and being a comfortable and wearable assistive technology. These results offer valuable insights for safety practitioners and experts in human factors and ergonomics, suggesting the potential applicability of the BExo across various occupational tasks and settings. Additionally, the findings encourage further consideration of design modifications to address weaknesses and enhance the overall accessibility and acceptance of passive back-supporting exoskeletons in diverse work environments.

As a limitation of the study, it is important to acknowledge that the research was conducted in a controlled laboratory environment, and real-world factors in dynamic workplaces might influence the exoskeleton's performance and users' perception of the exoskeleton differently. Future directions for research could involve longitudinal studies in actual workplace settings to provide a more comprehensive understanding of the long-term usability and effectiveness of the back exoskeleton in diverse occupational contexts.

Acknowledgments. We thank the students who volunteers to participate in this research and provide their feedback.

Disclosure of Interests. The authors have no competing interests to declare that are relevant to the content of this article.

References

1. Schwartz, M., Desbrosses, K., Theurel, J., Mornieux, G.: Using passive or active back-support exoskeletons during a repetitive lifting task: influence on cardiorespiratory parameters. Eur. J. Appl. Physiol. **122**(12), 2575–2583 (2022). https://doi.org/10.1007/s00421-022-05034-x
2. Iranzo, S., et al.: Assessment of a passive lumbar exoskeleton in material manual handling tasks under laboratory conditions. Sensors 22(11) (2022). https://doi.org/10.3390/s22114060
3. Ralfs, L., Hoffmann, N., Glitsch, U., Heinrich, K., Johns, J., Weidner, R.: Insights into evaluating and using industrial exoskeletons: summary report, guideline, and lessons learned from the interdisciplinary project "Exo@ Work." Int. J. Ind. Ergon. **97**, 103494 (2023). https://doi.org/10.1016/j.ergon.2023.103494
4. Golabchi, A., Han, S., Fayek, A.R., Student, P.D.: A fuzzy logic approach to posture-based ergonomic analysis for field observation and assessment of construction manual operations. https://mc06.manuscriptcentral.com/cjce-pubs
5. Park, J.H., Lee, Y., Madinei, S., Kim, S., Nussbaum, M.A., Srinivasan, D.: Effects of back-support exoskeleton use on lower limb joint kinematics and kinetics during level walking. Ann. Biomed. Eng. **50**(8), 964–977 (2022). https://doi.org/10.1007/s10439-022-02973-6
6. Park, H., Kim, S., Lawton, W., Nussbaum, M.A., Srinivasan, D.: Effects of using a whole-body powered exoskeleton on physical demands during manual handling. In: Proceedings of the Human Factors and Ergonomics Society Annual Meeting, vol. 64, no. 1, pp. 888–889 (2020)https://doi.org/10.1177/1071181320641211

7. Kazerooni, H., Tung, W., Pillai, M.: Evaluation of trunk-supporting exoskeleton. In: Proceedings of the Human Factors and Ergonomics Society Annual Meeting, vol. 63, no. 1, pp. 1080–1083 (2019). https://doi.org/10.1177/1071181319631261

8. Nazari, F., Mohajer, N., Nahavandi, D., Khosravi, A., Nahavandi, S.: Applied exoskeleton technology: a comprehensive review of physical and cognitive human-robot interaction. IEEE Trans Cogn Dev Syst **15**(3), 1102–1122 (2023). https://doi.org/10.1109/TCDS.2023.3241632

9. Golabchi, A., Jasimi Zindashti, N., Miller, L., Rouhani, H., Tavakoli, M.: Performance and effectiveness of a passive back-support exoskeleton in manual material handling tasks in the construction industry. Constr. Robot. **7**(1), 77–88 (2023). https://doi.org/10.1007/s41693-023-00097-4

10. Toxiri, S., et al.: Back-support exoskeletons for occupational use: an overview of technological advances and trends. IISE Trans Occup Ergon Hum Factors **7**(3–4), 237–249 (2019). https://doi.org/10.1080/24725838.2019.1626303

11. Golabchi, A., Miller, L., Rouhani, H., Tavakoli, M.: Impact of passive back-support exoskeletons on manual material handling postures in construction. In: Proceedings of the International Symposium on Automation and Robotics in Construction, International Association for Automation and Robotics in Construction (IAARC), pp. 359–366 (2022). https://doi.org/10.22260/isarc2022/0050

12. Madinei, S., Alemi, M.M., Kim, S., Srinivasan, D., Nussbaum, M.A.: Biomechanical evaluation of passive back-support exoskeletons in a precision manual assembly task: 'expected' effects on trunk muscle activity, perceived exertion, and task performance. Hum. Factors **62**(3), 441–457 (2020). https://doi.org/10.1177/0018720819890966

13. van Sluijs, R.M., Wehrli, M., Brunner, A., Lambercy, O.: Evaluation of the physiological benefits of a passive back-support exoskeleton during lifting and working in forward leaning postures. J. Biomech. **149**, 111489 (2023). https://doi.org/10.1016/j.jbiomech.2023.111489

14. Lazzaroni, M., et al.: Back-support exoskeleton control strategy for pulling activities: design and preliminary evaluation. Designs **5**(3), 39 (2021). https://doi.org/10.3390/designs5030039

15. Williams, N.: The borg rating of perceived exertion (RPE) scale. Occup. Med. **67**(5), 404–405 (2017). https://doi.org/10.1093/occmed/kqx063

Enhancing Episodic Future Thinking in Children with ADHD: A Virtual Reality Gaming Therapy Approach

Li Zheng[1], Mei Si[2(✉)], Aihua Cao[3], and Tingting Ma[1,2,3]

[1] Rensselaer Polytechnic Institute, Troy, NY 12180, USA
xiaozl02@hotmail.com
[2] Shandong University of Arts, Jinan, China
meisi.g@gmail.com
[3] Qilu Hospital of Shandong University, Jinan, China

Abstract. Attention Deficit/Hyperactivity Disorder (ADHD) affects a significant number of children worldwide, impacting their learning and social interactions. Current treatments primarily focus on medication and behavioral therapies, with recent Virtual Reality (VR) games targeting executive function training. Episodic Future Thinking (EFT) refers to the cognitive ability to project oneself into the future to envision potential outcomes based on past experiences. Most existing VR games for ADHA overlook the potential of Episodic Future Thinking (EFT) to enhance decision-making and behavioral control. This work addresses this gap by developing VR-based EFT games. These games aim to simulate real-life scenarios within a virtual playground, teaching children with ADHD essential skills such as turn-taking, respecting personal space, and patience through interactive modules like Turn-Taking, Maintaining Personal Space, and Patience Practice. This innovative approach promises to enhance the current ADHD treatment landscape by offering a more engaging, effective, and holistic method for managing the disorder's symptoms. In this work, we review relevant literature, detail our current game design, and outline plans for future evaluations.

Keywords: Episodic Future Thinking · VR Games · ADHD

1 Introduction

Attention Deficit/Hyperactivity Disorder (ADHD) is a common childhood psychological and behavioral disorder with symptoms like excessive distractibility, high activity levels, impulsivity, and impaired impulse control. These symptoms significantly affect children's learning and social interactions and can persist into later life stages, though some symptoms may diminish over time.

Global ADHD prevalence was estimated at 5.29% by Polanczyk et al. in 2007 [1], and later revised to 7.2% by Thomas et al. in 2015 [2], indicating an increase in diagnoses. Geographical variations are notable, with a 5.9% prevalence in Italian children [3], 5.5% in Spanish children with variations across age groups [4], and 5.7% in Indian children

V. G. Duffy (Ed.): HCII 2024, LNCS 14709, pp. 243–255, 2024.
https://doi.org/10.1007/978-3-031-61060-8_18

[5]. In the United States, 9.8% of children aged 3 to 17 were diagnosed with ADHD between 2016 and 2019 [6].

ADHD is categorized into three subtypes: predominantly inattentive, predominantly impulsive, and combined. The hyperactive/impulsive subtype tends to be less severe compared to the more severe inattentive subtype. The combined subtype encompasses a broader range of more complex symptoms. Symptoms of hyperactivity/impulsivity are associated with neurodevelopmental delays, whereas inattentive symptoms reflect deviations in neurodevelopment, manifesting as distractibility or difficulty retaining attention. This project focuses on mitigating symptoms in children with the predominantly hyperactive/impulsive subtype. We aim to develop virtual reality games as a therapeutic tool, leveraging their proven efficacy in educational settings to address ADHD symptoms. Additionally, we plan to incorporate Episodic Future Thinking (EFT) as the core strategy in our game design to support symptom alleviation.

1.1 Related Work

This section delves into the current landscape of research on ADHD treatment, exploring various methodologies and their outcomes.

1.2 Medication Therapy and Physical Therapy

Medications have been effective in improving behavior, academic performance, and social adaptation in children with ADHD, with success rates ranging from 50% to 90%. Methylphenidate, a medication used globally for over 60 years, shows positive effects on hyperactivity, impulsivity, and inattention. However, a study by Li [9] found that the impact of methylphenidate on the height, weight, BMI, and nutritional intake of children with ADHD persists over time. This is mainly due to its appetite-suppressing effect, which leads to reduced energy intake and increased dopamine levels, potentially hindering growth hormone secretion and cartilage tissue growth. As a result, some patients and parents may be cautious about medication use.

Common physical therapies include [7]: Electroencephalogram (EEG) biofeedback: Involves monitoring different brain wave characteristics, such as alpha, theta, and beta waves, to analyze activity levels in various brain areas. In this intervention, children with ADHD must maintain their attention while watching monotonous animations or playing games, while doctors monitor changes in their brain wave patterns using EEG biofeedback devices. Sandplay therapy: Rooted in the "World Technique" concept developed by British pediatrician M. Lowenfeld, it uses toys to explore children's inner worlds and resolve underlying thoughts. For children with ADHD, sandplay therapy can help address internal conflicts and modify external behavioral problems. Behavioral therapy: Based on behavioral learning theory, it focuses on developing adaptive behavioral responses through appropriate training. Common techniques include positive reinforcement, negative reinforcement, time management, incremental learning, self-monitoring, social skills training, and the use of time reminders. Executive function training: Particularly emphasizes the executive abilities of children with ADHD. These individuals often have deficits in inhibitory control, working memory, and spatial perception. Methods of executive function training include cognitive training games, working memory training, attention training, decision-making training, and inhibitory control training.

Despite extensive research into genetics, environment, cognitive neurological deficits, and brain mechanisms, ADHD's exact causes remain unclear. Traditional treatments combine medication and behavioral therapies but have limitations like medication side effects, limited behavioral improvements, time consumption, and environmental constraints. Virtual reality technology offers a promising alternative, providing more effective and safer simulations of realistic life scenarios [8].

1.3 Virtual Reality Games for Children with ADHD

The therapeutic potential of electronic game therapy for improving symptoms in children with ADHD has gained empirical support. In a seminal 2013 study, Gazzaley from the University of California, San Francisco, utilized the "Neuroracer" video game in a six-week regimen to enhance cognitive attention in older adults. The study concluded that the observed improvement in attention among the elderly participants was linked to enhanced cognitive control facilitated by improved brain network functions. Building upon this, Akili Interactive, a venture co-founded by Gazzaley, developed "EndeavorRX" - a therapeutic electronic game targeted at enhancing working memory and attention in children with ADHD. This innovation marked the first electronic game to receive FDA approval for ADHD treatment [10]. The evolution of virtual reality (VR) technology has catalyzed research into VR game applications for training and treating children with ADHD. In 2020, Bioulac and his research team implemented an attention-sustaining task within a VR classroom setting. This task required children with ADHD to accurately complete designated activities amidst various sensory distractions. The findings indicated notable symptomatic improvement over traditional medication treatment. A preference for VR games, as opposed to conventional video games, has been observed among children with ADHD [11]. VR technology's integration with interactive testing offers the benefits of reducing external distractions, prolonging attention spans, and aiding in ADHD rehabilitation [12, 13]. Crucial to this approach are the methods of observing behavior in VR environments to identify deficits [11] and the application of skills acquired in VR to real-world scenarios [14].

Most VR games designed for ADHD training are simulations of traditional executive function training for affected children. For example, in EndeavorRX, a seemingly straightforward design belies its complexity. Players navigate a boat and concurrently engage in battles with monsters. This dual-task gameplay is strategically developed to stimulate the prefrontal cortex, thereby targeting and enhancing the self-control capabilities of the child players. This approach mirrors the underlying principles utilized in conventional executive function training, where similar methodologies are applied to develop cognitive control.

Recently, therapy based on Episodic Future Thinking (EFT) has gained traction as an innovative approach for treating mental health disorders. Despite its growing application, its potential in ADHD treatment has yet to be investigated, motivating our research in this area.

2 Episodic Future Thinking

Episodic Future Thinking (EFT) originated from Canadian psychologist and neuroscientist Endel Tulving. His memory theory divides memory into explicit (declarative) memory and semantic memory [15]. Semantic memory represents our general knowledge of the world [16], while explicit memory involves recalling past experiences and re-experiencing them psychologically. Based on this framework, projecting an individual's recollections into future events, allowing for the pre-experience of these events, is known as Episodic Future Thinking [16]. This anticipatory thinking about the future can influence an individual's decision-making regarding upcoming events. EFT is a cognitive process that enables individuals to predict and plan for the future by subjectively re-creating and simulating future events, thereby influencing decision-making. Widely applied in psychotherapy, behavioral change, and health promotion, EFT, as a beneficial cognitive tool, helps patients develop a positive outlook for the future and set goals.

Forming memories of past experiences to generate anticipatory judgments about future behavioral outcomes is an important ability for human survival. For a mentally healthy normal person, basic future imaginative thinking usually starts to develop around the age of 5 [17]. Although EFT capabilities develop during childhood in individuals with normal development, studies have found deficits in imagination among patients with Autism Spectrum Disorder (ASD) [18]. Additionally, generating future scenarios requires the recombination of past events and needs more cognitive resources than recalling past events [19]. As a common childhood psychiatric disorder, ADHD, although not specifically supported by literature, is indicated by Taurines' research [20] to have a high degree of overlap with autism, which is also part of the spectrum of psychiatric disorders. At the same time, Dennis [21] emphasized that children with ADHD experience difficulties in "executive functions," specifically manifesting as a lack of planning, organization, and the ability to conceptualize future actions. Therefore, our medical team believes, based on case study analyses, that patients with ADHD also exhibit deficits in Episodic Future Thinking (EFT) capabilities, as evidenced by impulsive behaviors that do not consider consequences.

Currently, there is a substantial amount of research on using EFT for the treatment of individual mental illnesses, primarily based on its impact on future decision-making. Boyer was the first to link episodic future thinking with decision-making, emphasizing the importance of vivid and imaginative foresight in the decision-making process [22]. EFT plays a guiding role in individual behavioral decisions and can also influence decisions that are maladaptive to individual development. For example, Impulsive Eating and Obesity Obese individuals exhibit higher delay discounting and a significant correlation with food addiction [23]. In recent studies, obese individuals were asked to observe images of their weight increase and decrease, and to predict the future consequences of their current dietary behavior before choosing food. The results showed a significant increase in the choice of low-fat foods after such predictions [24]. Individuals with alcohol dependence show significantly higher delay discounting compared to the normal population [25]. Furthermore, heavy drinkers exhibit higher delay discounting than light drinkers [26]. Studies indicate that episodic anticipation can significantly reduce delay discounting in alcohol-dependent individuals in cross-temporal decisions, and this reduction in delay discounting persists in the repetition of episodic anticipation tasks [27]. Tobacco Dependence research shows that the delay discounting of individuals dependent on tobacco is higher than that of non-smokers [28]. Episodic anticipation can significantly reduce their delay discounting [29, 30], enhancing self-control over tobacco and reducing smoking behavior [31, 32]. Procrastination is a common problem behavior that spans various times and contexts, reducing individual health, work efficiency, academic performance, and psychological well-being. Typically, individuals develop aversion to a specific task before formally starting it, leading to the choice to postpone the task. This negative emotion is the result of the individual's anticipation, simulation, and imagination of the impending behavior [33, 34]. Experiments by Feng's research team found that anticipatory imagery has a directional impact on procrastination, separating the impact of anticipatory imagery of the procrastination process and results, while also examining the role of emotions triggered by anticipatory imagery in procrastination behavior [35]. Regardless of whether individuals have high or low procrastination tendencies, anticipatory imagery of the task process tends to exacerbate procrastination, while anticipatory imagery of the task results tends to alleviate it. The emotions (annoyance or pleasure) generated in the imagination process significantly predicted changes in procrastination behavior. The results affirmed that emotions and anticipatory imagery are key factors affecting procrastination, and skillfully manipulating anticipatory imagery of different task components can effectively intervene in procrastination behavior.

Although the impact of anticipatory imagination on decision-making is supported by various studies, the relationship between EFT and decision-making is not consistent and is influenced by modulating factors such as age, working memory capacity, and self-relevance [36]. Regarding age, older individuals find it more difficult to imagine detailed scenarios and produce fewer details compared to younger individuals [37]. In terms of working memory, Lin and Epstein [38] found that the impact of future thinking on delay discounting is moderated by working memory capacity, with higher working memory capacity associated with lower delay discounting in cross-temporal decision-making. Self-relevance, compared to non-self-relevant events, episodic future thinking is more sensitive to self-relevant events, leading to better foresight. Additionally, the foresight for self-relevant events and the intensity of individual emotional experiences positively correlate with a stronger preference for delayed rewards [39].

Furthermore, the impact of episodic future thinking on cross-temporal decision-making is also influenced by individual psychological mechanisms. These mechanisms include emotional valence, subjective perception of time distance, and the weighting of delayed rewards [36]. Emotional valence, or the emotional reaction of an individual to events, affects delay discounting: positive events reduce delay discounting, negative events increase it, and neutral events have no significant effect [40–42]. Subjective perception of time distance refers to an individual's perception of the length of time, influenced by emotional states and the self-relevance of events. Under positive emotions, individuals pay less attention to time perception, while negative emotions increase attention to time, affecting the choice of immediate rewards [16, 36, 40, 43–45]. The weighting of delayed gains is related to the individual's level of cognitive frameworks, with higher-level cognitive frameworks tending to emphasize the importance of delayed choices, while lower-level cognitive frameworks emphasize the importance of immediate choices [46]. These factors collectively influence the psychological process of individuals when facing choices, affecting their decisions between immediate and delayed rewards.

A related concept, Self-Future [47], focuses on the processes and outcomes of envisioning one's future self, suggesting that a stronger connection to one's future self-promotes healthier lifestyle choices [48, 49]. This connection underscores the broader impact of future-oriented thinking on behavior and decision-making, expanding the application of EFT principles in mental health and lifestyle improvement.

EFT offers exciting potential in mental health but hasn't yet been applied to treat ADHD in children, a novel approach our project is eager to explore. Traditional ADHD treatments mainly focus on executive functions, overlooking the benefits of EFT models to alleviate symptoms. Collaborating with the team at Qilu Hospital in Jinan, China, this project aims to introduce a groundbreaking ADHD treatment using VR games for EFT cognitive training, aiming to avoid the side effects typical of conventional ADHD medications. This innovative method marks a significant advancement in ADHD therapy, utilizing technology to enhance mental health care for children. The game design is aimed at improving measurements by SNAP-IV (Swanson, Nolan, and Pelham - Version IV), a tool that assesses ADHD symptoms and oppositional defiant behavior through parent and teacher evaluations, ensuring a targeted therapeutic approach [50]. This project will measure the effectiveness of our method by comparing pre- and post-intervention data at the Children's Neurorehabilitation Center of Qilu Hospital, showcasing the potential of VR-based EFT training in transforming ADHD treatment.

3   Research Question(S)

The proposed investigation centers on the potential of Virtual Reality (VR)-based Episodic Future Thinking (EFT) games to ameliorate symptoms of Attention Deficit Hyperactivity Disorder (ADHD) in children. By harnessing VR's immersive qualities, this project aims to foster cognitive and behavioral advancements in this demographic. The research is structured around several pivotal questions:

- How does VR-based EFT game design influence ADHD symptom severity as measured by SNAP-IV and other ratings before and after intervention?
- What are the specific cognitive and behavioral changes observed in children with ADHD following EFT game intervention?
- Do improvements in ADHD symptoms following EFT game intervention persist over time, and what factors influence long-term outcomes?
- How do children with ADHD interact with the EFT game, and what game design elements are most effective in engaging them?
- What are the parents' and teachers' perceptions of the effectiveness and applicability of VR-based EFT games for managing ADHD symptoms?

By focusing on these key areas, the study aims to thoroughly assess the impact of VR-based EFT games as a novel therapeutic approach for ADHD, exploring not only immediate but also long-term benefits and the broader implications for treatment personalization and real-world application.

4   Methodology

This project aims to address self-control and anticipatory decision-making using
Episodic Future Thinking (EFT) within a virtual reality environment. After discussions
within the project team, an initial design for a virtual playground scenario was developed,
specifically targeting school-aged children and replicating the dynamics of a real playground. Based on the SNAP-IV scale and typical behaviors observed in children with
impulsive ADHD, this design phase includes interactive components such as "Turn-
Taking," "Maintaining Personal Space," and "Patience Practice." The outcomes of the
discussions on the game design concept for this project will be presented, showcasing
the strategic approach to enhancing self-control and decision-making skills in children
with ADHD through immersive VR experiences (Fig. 1).

Fig. 1.   Screenshot from the game -- Turn-Taking

4.1   Crafting Behavioral Interventions in Games

The project implements three intervention mechanisms in the VR game to help children
with ADHD improve their anticipatory decision-making and self-control:

- Turn-Taking: In this module, participants learn the value of turn-taking as they wait in
  line for playground equipment like slides and swings. NPCs queue before the player,
  demonstrating patience and adherence to queuing rules. This module aligns with the
  SNAP-IV scale's assessment of queuing adherence and utilizes EFT capabilities to
  foster anticipatory decision-making.
- Maintaining Personal Space: This module requires players to avoid physical contact
  with NPCs. Should contact occur, a visual alert (such as a red circle) and a saddened
  expression from the NPC, accompanied by a sound alert, will signal the breach.
  This scenario is inspired by the Rutter Children's Behavior Questionnaire's inquiries
  into physical conflicts, aiming to teach players to respect personal space, thereby
  enhancing EFT skills and anticipatory behaviors.
- Patience Practice: This module teaches the importance of delayed gratification
  through activities requiring waiting periods, such as air rifle shooting and ladder

climbing. Players learn to remain in designated waiting areas until it's their turn, with early departure prompting a restart of the wait, reinforcing patience and strategic thinking.

These interventions are designed to closely simulate real-life playground interactions and their consequences, providing meaningful feedback for children in the VR setting. After development, we'll test these games using VR headsets, specifically opting for the PICO brand in our evaluations.

4.2 VR Game Development Plan

To bring these interactive designs to life, this project will use Unity3D for programming and Maya for modeling and animations, integrating AI for dynamic sound effects and voiceovers. The games will be rigorously debugged using Pico glasses, ensuring a seamless VR experience. These development tools will allow for the creation of immersive and engaging game environments where children can practice and internalize behavioral interventions effectively.

5   Assessment

The evaluation of VR-based EFT interventions for children with ADHD will be conducted at the Youngsters' ADHD Research Center of Qilu Hospital, Shandong University, with 50 children diagnosed with ADHD participating. These children will receive a detailed diagnostic evaluation using multiple tests to provide a comprehensive understanding of their ADHD symptoms, as recommended by Dr. Cao's team. This process is designed to identify both immediate and potential long-term effects of the interventions.

The participants will be split into two groups for different training schedules: one will engage in an intensive 12-day holiday program combining VR therapy with traditional executive function training, where each child will use the game for 30 min daily. The second group will join a 3-month spring or autumn program, training three times a week, with each session also lasting 30 min. Cognitive, behavioral, and EFT abilities will be assessed before and after the training to measure the interventions' impact.

To deepen our analysis, we will conduct observations and field studies to capture the experiences of both the children and their parents with the VR games. Additionally, we plan to explore the possibility of a long-term study to evaluate the sustained effects of these interventions, with the goal of incorporating these findings into future research.

A variety of scales will be employed to ensure a thorough assessment, offering a detailed perspective on how effectively the interventions address cognitive, behavioral, and emotional challenges faced by children with ADHD. This evaluation will also provide insights into the practical applications of VR-based EFT games, as reported by both participating children and their parents. The selected scales and their specific areas of focus will encompass:

- Achenbach Child Behavior Checklist (CBCL): Assesses emotional and behavioral problems.
- Strengths and Difficulties Questionnaire (SDQ): Measures psychological attributes.

- Rutter Children's Behavior Questionnaire (Parent Form): Identifies behavioral and emotional issues.
- Vanderbilt ADHD Diagnostic Rating Scale (VADRS - Parent Form): Evaluates ADHD symptoms and coexisting conditions.
- Weiss Functional Impairment Rating Scale (WFIRS-P - Parent Version): Gauges the impact of ADHD on daily functioning.
- Stroop Test: Tests attention and executive functioning.
- Attention Divided Test: Assesses the ability to focus and divide attention.
- Spatial Location Memory Span Test: Measures working memory capacity.
- Executive Function Assessment Form: Evaluates executive functioning skills.
- DSM-V Assessment: Provides a standard diagnostic evaluation for ADHD.
- Audio-Visual Integration Continuous Processing Test: Assesses sustained attention and sensory integration.
- SNAP-IV Assessment: Assesses ADHD symptoms and oppositional defiant behavior.

6 Potential Impact

This project has the potential to positively impact children with ADHD, society, and the academic community.

Societal Impact. The use of VR games incorporating Episodic Future Thinking (EFT) for ADHD treatment brings broad societal advantages. This approach can boost public health by cutting ADHD-related costs, alleviating stress on families and schools, and enhancing the well-being of those affected. Additionally, it can improve ADHD children's social skills and behavior management, thus mitigating conflicts within families and schools and fostering social cohesion. From an economic perspective, this method has the potential to lower the long-term expenses associated with unemployment and criminal activities stemming from behavioral issues. Moreover, applying EFT and VR in treating ADHD encourages innovation in technology and healthcare, expanding treatment options for other mental and behavioral disorders. Crucially, the success of these treatments can heighten ADHD awareness and acceptance by dispelling myths and promoting broader societal understanding.

Impact on Children with ADHD. VR and EFT treatments significantly benefit children with ADHD by enhancing their foresight, decision-making, and self-regulation. These VR games create an engaging environment that boosts focus and attention, strengthens executive functions such as planning and problem-solving, and facilitates simulated social interactions to improve communication skills and social integration. For some, these games offer a compelling medication-free treatment option, providing a safe space for behavioral experimentation. This multifaceted approach not only addresses ADHD symptoms but also broadly improves children's quality of life and overall well-being.

Academic Impact. The integration of Episodic Future Thinking (EFT) and virtual reality (VR) games into ADHD treatment promises significant future impacts across a variety of academic fields. In the realm of game studies, this approach motivates the development of both educational and therapeutic games, challenging designers to unlock the full potential of gaming for learning and healing. For psychologists, it opens new pathways for understanding the unique behaviors and needs of children with ADHD, leading to more innovative and effective treatments. Psychiatry stands to benefit from enhanced diagnostic and treatment methodologies, broadening the scope for addressing ADHD and related mental health conditions. In the sectors of medicine and public health, this innovative treatment strategy holds the potential to alleviate the public health impact of ADHD by providing more targeted and effective interventions. This interdisciplinary strategy not only advances the treatment of ADHD but also promotes growth and innovation in related academic disciplines such as game design, psychology, psychiatry, and public health, marking a step forward in the holistic approach to mental health care.

7 Discussion and Future Work

Current research on EFT therapy for children with ADHD is in its initial stages. Leveraging virtual reality (VR) technology, we present a highly adaptable, engaging, and flexible treatment approach tailored to meet individual needs. We plan to further develop VR games by enhancing interactivity and realism, thereby providing an immersive virtual environment that effectively fosters cognitive, social, and emotional development in children with ADHD. Future studies will delve into the specific mechanisms by which EFT improves executive functions in these children, including its impact on brain activity and cognitive abilities, validated through neuroimaging studies and cognitive-behavioral assessments. Additionally, by expanding the sample size and employing a diverse set of assessment tools, coupled with long-term follow-up studies, we aim to explore the sustained effects of these interventions and evaluate their integration into family and school settings for feasibility and effectiveness.

Recognizing the pivotal role of family and community in supporting the development of children with ADHD, future efforts will involve creating guidance materials and training workshops to educate parents and teachers on the application of EFT interventions within VR games in daily life. This initiative is designed to provide a more supportive growth environment for children with ADHD, while also exploring the potential of EFT interventions in treating other cognitive and behavioral disorders such as Autism Spectrum Disorder and anxiety. Through these comprehensive efforts, we not only aim to improve the quality of life for children with ADHD but also contribute innovative therapeutic methods and tools to the field of mental health, advancing more precise and customized intervention strategies in clinical settings.

References

1. Polanczyk, G., De Lima, M.S., Horta, B.L., et al.: The worldwide prevalence of ADHD: a systematic review and metaregression analysis. Am. J. Psychiatry **164**(6), 942–948 (2007)
2. Thomas, R., Sanders, S., Doust, J., et al.: Prevalence of attention-deficit/hyperactivity disorder: a systematic review and meta-analysis. Pediatrics **135**(4), e994–e1001 (2015)
3. Reale, L., Bonati, M.: ADHD prevalence estimates in Italian children and adolescents: a methodological issue. Ital. J. Pediatr. **44**(1), 108 (2018)
4. Canals Sans, J., Morales Hidalgo, P., Roigé Castellví, J., et al.: Prevalence and epidemiological characteristics of ADHD in pre-school and school-age children in the province of Tarragona. Spain J. Attention Disord. **25**(13), 1818–1833 (2021)

5. Joshi, H.M., Angolkar, M.: Prevalence of ADHD in primary school children in Belagavi city, India. J. Attention Disord. **25**(2), 154–160 (2021)
6. Rui, M. (Ed.): New Study: Asian American Children Least Likely to Receive Mental Health Treatment. China Daily, June 14, 2023 (2023)
7. Shi, T.K., Wang, F.H.: Identification and Intervention Treatment of ADHD Children. Chemical Industry Press, Beijing (2019)
8. Bioulac, S., Micoulaud-Franchi, J.A., Maire, J., Bouvard, M.P., Rizzo, A.A., Sagaspe, P., et al.: Virtual remediation versus methylphenidate to improve distractibility in children with ADHD: a controlled randomized clinical trial study. J. Atten. Disord. **24**, 326–335 (2020)
9. Rong, L., Ninan, L., et al.: Effect of methylphenidate hydrochloride prolonged-release tablets on the growth of children with attention deficit hyperactivity disorder. Chinese J. Child Health Care, **31**(7) (2023)
10. Emily, W.: First video game to treat disease gains FDA okay. Nat. Biotechnol. **38**, 1224–1225 (2020)
11. Pollak, Y., Weiss, P.L., Rizzo, A.A., Weizer, M., Shriki, L., Shalev, R.S., et al.: The utility of a continuous performance test embedded in virtual reality in measuring ADHDrelated deficits. J. Dev. Behav. Pediatr. **30**, 2–6 (2009)
12. Parsons, T.D., Bowerly, T., Buckwalter, J.G., Rizzo, A.A.: A controlled clinical comparison of attention performance in children with ADHD in a virtual reality classroom compared to standard neuropsychological methods. Child Neuropsychol. **13**, 363–381 (2007)
13. Gaitatzes, A., Papaioannou, G., Christopoulos, D.: Virtual reality systems and applications. In: Proceedings of the ACM symposium on Virtual reality software and technology. 2006 Nov 1–3; Limassol, Cyprus (2006)
14. Riva, G., Mantovani, F., Gaggioli, A.: Presence and rehabilitation: toward secondgeneration virtual reality applications in neuropsychology. J. Neuroeng. Rehabil. (2004)
15. Tulving, E.: Précis of elements of episodic memory. Behavioral Brain Sci. **7**(2), 223–268 (1984)
16. Tulving, E.:On the uniqueness of episodic memory. In: Nilsson, L., Markowitsch, H.J., (eds.) Cognitive Neuroscience of Memory, pp. 11–42. Hogrefe & Huber (1999)
17. Atance, C.M., Meltzoff, A.N.: My future self: young children's ability to anticipate and explain future states. Cogn. Dev. **20**, 341–361 (2005)
18. Feller, C., Dubois, C., Eliez, S., Schneider, M.: Episodic future thinking in autism spectrum disorder and 22q11.2 deletion syndrome: association with anticipatory pleasure and social functioning. J. Autism Dev. Disord. **51**(12), 4587–4604 (2021)
19. Addis, D.R., Wong, A.T., Schacter, D.L.: Remembering the past and imagining the future: common and distinct neural substrates during event construction and elaboration. Neuropsychologia **45**(7), 1363–1377 (2007)
20. Taurines, R., Schwenck, C., Westerwald, E., et al.: ADHD and autism: differential diagnosis or overlapping traits? A selective review. ADHD Atten. Def. Hyp. Disord. **4**, 115–139 (2012)
21. Thompson, D.: More Links Seen Between Autism, ADHD. HealthDay. Web. http://consumer.healthday.com/kids-health-information-23/attention-deficit-disorder-adhd-news-50/more-links-seen-between-autism-adhd-679518.html. Accessed 26 Aug 2013
22. Boyer, P.: Evolutionary economics of mental time travel? Trends Cogn. Sci. **12**(6), 219–224 (2008)
23. Vanderbroek-Stice, L., Stojek, M.K., Beach, S.R.H., Vandellen, M.R., MacKillop, J.: Multidimensional assessment of impulsivity in relation to obesity and food addiction. Appetite **112**, 59–68 (2017)
24. Segovia, M.S., Palma, M.A., Nayga, R.M., Jr.: Can episodic future thinking affect food choices? J. Econ. Behav. Organ. **177**, 371–389 (2020)
25. Field, M., Christiansen, P., Cole, J., Goudie, A.: Delay discounting and the alcohol stroop in heavy drinking adolescents. Addiction **102**(4), 579–586 (2007)

26. Amlung, M., Vedelago, L., Acker, J., Balodis, I., MacKillop, J.: Steep delay discounting and addictive behavior: a meta-analysis of continuous associations. Addiction **112**(1), 51–62 (2017)

27. Mellis, A.M., Snider, S.E., Deshpande, H.U., LaConte, S.M., Bickel, W.K.: Practicing prospection promotes patience: repeated episodic future thinking cumulatively reduces delay discounting. Drug Alcohol Depend. **204**, 107507 (2019)

28. Bickel, W.K., Koffarnus, M.N., Moody, L., Wilson, A.G.: The behavioral and neuroeconomic process of temporal discounting: a candidate behavioral marker of addiction. Neuropharmacology **76**, 518–527 (2014)

29. Aonso-Diego, G., Gonzalez-Roz, A., Krotter, A., Garcia-Perez, A., Secades-Villa, R.: Contingency management for smoking cessation among individuals with substance use disorders: in-treatment and post-treatment effects. Addict. Behav. **119**, 106920 (2021)

30. Chiou, W.B., Wu, W.H.: Episodic future thinking involving the nonsmoking self can induce lower discounting and cigarette consumption. J. Stud. Alcohol Drugs **78**(1), 106–112 (2017)

31. Stein, J.S., Sze, Y.Y., Athamneh, L., Koffarnus, M.N., Epstein, L.H., Bickel, W.K.: Think fast: rapid assessment of the effects of episodic future thinking on delay discounting in overweight/obese participants. J. Behav. Med. **40**(5), 832–838 (2017)

32. Stein, J.S., Wilson, A.G., Koffarnus, M.N., Daniel, T.O., Epstein, L.H., Bickel, W.K.: Unstuck in time: episodic future thinking reduces delay discounting and cigarette smoking. Psychopharmacology **233**(21–22), 3771–3778 (2016)

33. Zhang, S., Feng, T.: Cognitive neural mechanisms and genes of procrastination: a multidimensional study on behavior-brain-genes. Adv. Psychol. Sci. **25**(3), 393–403 (2017)

34. Zhang, S., Feng, T.: Decision model of procrastination. Psychol. Sci. **40**(5), 1242–1247 (2017)

35. Wei, J.M., Feng, T.Y.: The effect of episodic future thinking on procrastination: the dissection effect of contents of task. J. Psychol. Sci. **49**(3), 619–625 (2019)

36. Gao, X., Liu, R.: Imagining the future: mechanisms of scenario foresight for intertemporal decision-making. Chinese J. Appl. Psychol. **28**(3), 333–343 (2022)

37. Acevedo-Molina, M.C., Novak, A.W., Gregoire, L.M., Mann, L.G., Andrews-Hanna, J.R., Grilli, M.D.: Emotion matters: the influence of valence on episodic future thinking in young and older adults. Conscious. Cogn. **85**, 103023 (2020)

38. Lin, H., Epstein, L.H.: Living in the moment: Effects of time perspective and emotional valence of episodic thinking on delay discounting. Behav. Neurosci. **128**(1), 12–19 (2014)

39. Benoit, R.G., Gilbert, S.J., Burgess, P.W.: A neural mechanism mediating the impact of episodic prospection on farsighted decisions. J. Neurosci. **31**(18), 6771–6779 (2011)

40. Barsics, C., Van der Linden, M., D'Argembeau, A.: Frequency, characteristics, and perceived functions of emotional future thinking in daily life. Q. J. Exp. Psychol. **69**(2), 217–233 (2016)

41. Busby Grant, J., Wilson, N.: Manipulating the valence of future thought: the effect on affect. Psychol. Rep. **124**(1), 227–229 (2020)

42. Zhang, S., Peng, J., Qin, L., Suo, T., Feng, T.: Prospective emotion enables episodic prospection to shift time preference. Br. J. Psychol. **109**(3), 487–499 (2018)

43. Buhusi, C.V., Meck, W.H.: Interval timing with gaps and distracters: evaluation of the ambiguity, switch, and time-sharing hypotheses. J. Exp. Psychol. Anim. Behav. Process. **32**(3), 329–338 (2006)

44. Meck, W.H., Macdonald, C.J.: Amygdala inactivation reverses fear's ability to impair divided attention and make time stand still. Behav. Neurosci. **121**(4), 707–720 (2007)

45. Yang, L., Yan, S.: Temporal discounting and its impact on intertemporal decision-making. Acta Psychol. Sin. **48**(4), 362–370 (2016)

46. Trope, Y., Liberman, N.: Temporal construal. Psychol. Rev. **110**(3), 403–421 (2003)

47. Pronin, E., Ross, L.: Temporal differences in trait self-ascription: when the self is seen as an other. J. Pers. Soc. Psychol. **90**(2), 197 (2006)

48. Urminsky, O.: The role of psychological connectedness to the future self in decisions over time. Current Dir. Psychol. Sci. **26**(1), 34–39 (2017)
49. Gabriele, O., Sevincer, A., Gollwitzer, T., Peter, M.: The Psychology of Thinking about the Future. Guilford Publications(2018)
50. Hall, C.L., et al.: The validity of the SNAP-IV in children displaying ADHD symptoms. Assessment **27**(6), 1258–1271 (2020)

User Experience, Communication, and Collaboration

Lean Six Sigma to Improve Customer Service Processes: A Case Study

Genett Isabel Jiménez-Delgado[1]([✉]) [iD], Hugo Hernandez-Palma[2] [iD],
Nadia León Castro[3,4], Anderson Nieto-Granados[5], Dairo Novoa[6],
and Jairo Martinez Ventura[7]

[1] Department of Industrial Engineering, Institución Universitaria de Barranquilla IUB,
Barranquilla, Colombia
gjimenez@unibarranquilla.edu.co
[2] Faculty of Engineering, Industrial Engineering Program, Corporación Universitaria
Iberoamericana IBERO, Bogotá, Colombia
hugo.hernandez@ibero.edu.co
[3] Faculty of Economic Sciences, Universidad de la Costa CUC, Barranquilla, Colombia
nleon1@cuc.edu.co, nleon-ca27454@universidadean.edu.co
[4] Doctorate of Project Management, Universidad EAN, Bogotá, Colombia
[5] Faculty of Engineering, Corporación Universitaria Iberoamericana IBERO, Bogotá, Colombia
anderson.nieto@ibero.edu.co
[6] Management of Tourism Enterprises Program, Universidad del Atlántico, Barranquilla,
Colombia
aironovoa@mail.uniatlantico.edu.co
[7] Facultad Ciencias Económicas, Corporación Universitaria Latinoamericana CUL,
Barranquilla, Colombia
academico@ul.edu.co

Abstract. The customer service process is crucial to the success of any company, both manufacturing and services, regardless of its size and nature, due to direct contact with the customer before, during, and after the sale of products or services. In the current changing and complex context, a good product or service is not enough; it must be complemented with agile response times, the ability to resolve doubts, concerns, and problems, as well as personalized and friendly attention, which can improve or worsen the customer's perception of quality. Therefore, companies focus their operations on providing the best customer experience, from design to after-sales service. On the other hand, the COVID-19 pandemic intensified the use of non-face-to-face channels such as websites, chats, and telephone lines. These constitute communication channels with quick and convenient access, allowing customers to inquire about the products. Products or services of a company without having to travel to the offices or units, which is why it is necessary to improve the quality of the response and customer service continually. In this context, the Lean Six Sigma methodology is a valuable tool to improve efficiency and quality in customer service processes. This paper presents the application of Lean Six Sigma methodology to improve the time and quality of attention to a service company's non-face-to-face channel "telephone line" in a low- and medium-income country. The study problem focuses on long waiting times and the quality of care received. To address this problem, implementing the Lean Six Sigma methodology

V. G. Duffy (Ed.): HCII 2024, LNCS 14709, pp. 259–278, 2024.
https://doi.org/10.1007/978-3-031-61060-8_19

is proposed by identifying the activities that do not add value to waiting times and that impact the quality of the customer service process. This methodology was carried out through the identification of critical processes, the measurement of waiting times and service quality, the analysis of the data obtained, and the implementation of process improvements. The results show essential improvements in process times, mainly in call waiting times. This systematic, data-driven approach leads to greater operational efficiency and strengthens the relationship between the company and its customers, driving long-term loyalty and retention.

Keywords: Lean Six Sigma (LSS) · Service sector · Quality service · Complaints · Response time

1 Introduction

According to the World Bank [1], the service sector has experienced faster growth than the manufacturing industry in developing economies. For example, in 2019, the services sector represented 55% of GDP and 45% of employment in developing economies, while in developed economies, this sector represented 75% of GDP, on average. In 2022, the services sector recorded an average increase of 3.9% in job creation, with a proportion of employment and GDP of 60% in Latin America and the Caribbean. On the other hand, the services sector has been dynamic in innovation and the adoption of technologies, allowing it to access new markets through digital interaction with customers and even address the complexities imposed by the COVID-19 pandemic regarding isolation and interruption in face-to-face operations through migration to non-face-to-face customer service channels.

Despite the importance of the service sector in economies, it is exposed to challenges such as high competition, changes in customer needs, and market instability, which companies in the industry must address to provide not only quality products and services that respond to customer needs and with added values, but also a superior customer service experience that manages not only to attract customers but also their loyalty over time, which is why it is vital to maintaining your satisfaction [2]. In this regard, McDermott [3] mentions that offering mediocre service is a high-impact risk for companies, and this intensified during and after the Covid-19 pandemic, changing the way customers interact and their needs; they are now less compassionate and more critical of the care they receive. In a recent customer experience trends study, more than 60% of customers will defect after a bad experience, so fewer and fewer customers are willing to endure frustrating experiences. On the other hand, the same study revealed that 64% of managers stated that customer service positively impacts the growth of organizations, and 60% indicated that it influences improving customer loyalty. On the other hand, current trends in customer service demand continuous improvement of quality over quantity. In this sense, clients expect omnichannel service, faster waiting and service times, service without reprocesses, resolution of problems and concerns, comfort, empathy, and permanent and personalized support from advisors, which for clients represents a high-quality service [2]. In this sense, service quality becomes relevant for companies that want to differentiate themselves from their competitors. It requires organizations to adopt continuous improvement methodologies and techniques, both hard and soft, to make their processes more robust, adding value and adapting to changing customer needs and expectations.

One of the methodologies that has captured the attention of academics, scientists, and businesspeople to improve service quality is Lean Six Sigma, which is not only a quantitative methodology with a technical purpose but is conceived as a strategy to enhance the quality of service. High-value business to improve efficiency, profitability, quality, and stakeholder interaction [4]. In this regard, different research and theoretical and practical studies have been developed regarding implementing continuous improvement methodologies applied to the service sector, such as Lean Six Sigma, initially used in the manufacturing industry [5–9], but with an exciting development in the service sector. In this sense, research has focused on identifying critical factors for implementing Lean Six Sigma in the service sector [10] and the practical implementation of Lean Six Sigma in different service companies [11–14]. The advantages of the Lean Six Sigma methodology in the service sector include improved performance, employee participation [15], increased efficiency of procedures, and improved quality of products and services [16]. Hence, applying the Lean Six Sigma methodology in service companies and enhancing customer service is essential and relevant.

This paper proposes the implementation of Lean Six Sigma to improve quality in the customer service process of a large service company, oriented towards reducing customer service times and improving the customer satisfaction indicator. Customer, with an impact on the company's reputation. The papers presented in Sect. 2 are the literature review of Lean Six Sigma in customer service. Then, Sect. 3 presents the methodology framework. Section 4 details the results and discussion of the Lean Six Sigma implementation. Finally, conclusions and future works are explained in Sect. 5.

2 Literature Review

This section presents articles or research projects related to the proposed implementation of the Lean Six Sigma Methodology to improve the time and quality of customer service process in a company of services. You will better understand common challenges, best practices, and lessons learned by analyzing previous research, case studies, and experiences related to implementing Lean Six Sigma in the customer service and customer service space.

The research project is based on the problems expressed by the members who participated in the in-depth measurement focus group by Circular 2023–0003 Member Voice Measurement, which was carried out to investigate the population's dissatisfaction with the service provided. Through non-face-to-face channels such as the telephone line and identifying complaints/claims with this service. In this regard, [17] highlights that the Six Sigma methodology provides solutions to short-term repetitive problems through a robust customer-focused and process-centered design, with quality being one of the main factors for customer satisfaction. On the other hand, [5] highlights that Lean is a philosophy and management model focused on minimizing losses in production and service systems and maximizing the creation of value for the customer. According to [18], Six Sigma is a work methodology focused on the client; it allows optimizing and seeking opportunities for improvement by restructuring processes to make them more efficient, agile, and of quality.

[19] over time, companies focus on a framework of continuous improvement due to the extraordinary market demands and customers. Therefore, methodologies such as Six Sigma and Lean have been incorporated as an organizational strategy in large, medium, or small companies, from the public or private sector, obtaining great benefits in terms of efficiency and effectiveness in the short or medium term. In this sense, as highlighted by [20], Lean Six Sigma (LSS) is an alternative that helps close the gaps of operational inefficiencies, as it is a methodological framework that helps in the decision-making process at the managerial level by identifying factors that do not add value in processes. [21] expresses how the Lean Six Sigma tool allows for defining, measuring, analyzing, improving, and controlling processes, a methodology that has not been expanded to other areas or departments in the company or regardless of the focus of said company, believing in the basis that this tool can only focus on production.

According to [22], the Lean Six Sigma methodology focuses on reducing waiting times and errors in processes, increasing efficiency and production in the department, which translates into decreased operating costs. The application of this tool allows an improvement in the company, attracting customers and controlling processes, streamlining service, and reducing waiting time. The research developed by [24–26], and [23] explains in detail what the Lean Six Sigma methodology is and how it can help organizations improve their performance and competitiveness. Likewise, they highlight the success of implementing LSS in various productive sectors such as health, higher education institutions, or customer service companies.

Next, the key concepts were defined to imply terms related to this project, by quality management and the provision of services, giving an everyday basis of understanding to address the interpretation of the project:

- Lean Manufacturing: According to [27], this philosophy originated in Japan and is based on the continuous improvement of processes. It uses different production systems that promise to pave the way to guarantee no unexpected failures and optimize the resources it allocates. The companies.
- Six Sigma: [28] defines the Six Sigma approach as a continuous improvement strategy for production and service processes through the application of different statistical tools in the management of the quality philosophy in search of the efficiency and effectiveness of a company.
- Lean Six Sigma: [22] defines Lean Six Sigma as the integration of two methodologies that significantly impact industries, aiming to improve the quality of products and services, as well as the performance of the company, contributing in different ways. Six Sigma enhances capacity in the flows that add value to the product. Lean Manufacturing is responsible for eliminating that which does not add value to the product and service.
- Services: According to [29], A service is an action or set of activities intended to satisfy a specific customer need, providing an immaterial and personalized product. In other words, a service is an intangible product that meets customer needs through customized activities.
- Quality of Service: It is based on knowledge of the client's needs and exceeding their expectations with the specific service. [30] defines service quality as the direct

relationship with customer satisfaction because users exposed to quality services generate greater satisfaction and complacency.

- Complaint: According to External Circular 008 of 2020 Family Subsidy Superintendency [31], a complaint manifests dissatisfaction with a specific collaborator's performance while providing a service.
- Claim: External Circular 008 of 2020 Family Subsidy Superintendence [31] defines a claim as the dissatisfaction that a person formulates with a current legal breach or expression of dissatisfaction made to an Organization concerning listening to the voice of its clients or the process itself by PQRSF
- Attention Time: [32] defines service time as the period that elapses from when a customer initiates a request or query until they receive a response or solution from the company.
- Responsiveness: [32] expresses that responsiveness is the willingness and ability of a company to help its customers and provide them with fast and quality service.
- DMAIC Cycle: According to [33], the DMAIC Cycle is a methodology used in Six Sigma to improve the quality of business processes. DMAIC is an acronym that stands for Define, Measure, Analyze, Improve, and Control and represents the five critical steps of the methodology. This approach has been used successfully in various industries, including financial services, manufacturing, and healthcare, to identify and solve quality problems and improve processes. Each step of the DMAIC cycle uses multiple tools and techniques to resolve issues effectively.
- Family Compensation Fund: according to [34], "Family Compensation Funds are private, non-profit entities subject to State surveillance through the Family Subsidy Superintendency, an entity attached to the Ministry of Job.

In summary, according to [35], Lean Six Sigma is a methodology that combines the Lean philosophy with the versatile tools of Lean and the Six Sigma continuous improvement system. This merger seeks to optimize processes and statistically control critical points to improve the productivity and profitability of a company. Its approach focuses on eliminating obstacles that prevent products or services from satisfying customer requirements and reducing defects or failures in the value chain. The implementation of the Lean Six Sigma Methodology leads to a reduction in production costs, which increases efficiency and profits. Additionally, it changes organizational culture by basing decisions on qualitative information supported by evidence rather than intuition. This methodology seeks continuous improvement and allows us to identify and eliminate unnecessary processes, reduce waiting times, and improve customer satisfaction. This methodology can be applied in multiple production sectors, with proven optimization results, as in the research carried out by [36–39].

3 Methodology

The methodological design of this study has a descriptive scope, quantitative approach, and transversal design to improve service times and the quality perceived by users in the customer service process through non-face-to-face channels via telephone. The proposed methodology is based on the combination of the steps of the Lean Manufacturing methodology (Diagnosis, Identification, and Analysis of MUDA, Improvement States) with the stages of the implementation of Six-Sigma continuous improvement programs known as DMAIC (Define, Measure, Analyze, Improve, and Control). The integration of these two methodologies can reduce times and improve quality indices in the processes, especially in a complex environment such as the service sector, in which, due to the high component of interaction and human behavior, unpredictability occurs in the process of service provision and customer service, as well as the ability to identify root causes and establish improvement plans [40]. The following integrated three-step methodology is proposed (See Fig. 1).

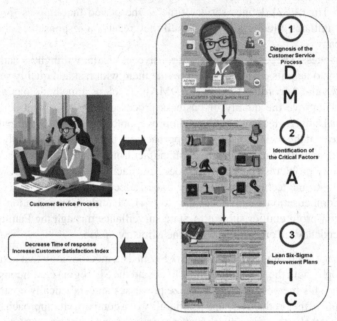

Fig. 1. Methodological Framework Lean Six-Sigma for reducing times and increasing the quality in Customer Service Process.

Step 1. *Diagnosis of the Customer Service Process.* In this first stage, the Project Charter was defined, the process mapping was carried out using the SIPOC diagram, and the needs, drivers, and critical quality factors were defined through the Voice of Customer Diagram (VoC), process data was collected to develop Value Stream Mapping and evaluate quality indicators and service times through data analytics and a Six Sigma process capacity study.

Phase 2. *Identification of Critical Factors:* In this phase, the critical factors or MUDA that impact non-face-to-face customer service via telephone line were identified by applying techniques and procedures of the Lean Six Sigma methodology. The cause-effect diagram and the 7 Lean waste technique were used in this sense.

Phase 3. *Lean Six-Sigma Improvement Plans:* In this stage, based on the identification and analysis of the critical factors of the process, the improvement plan was designed based on quality tools or Six Sigma, to improve the user service process through 5WH

Improvement plans. Finally, a control plan was established based on variable control charts and indicators to maintain the improvements obtained after implementing the improvement plans.

4 Results

4.1 Diagnosis of the Customer Service Process

This Research presents the case of a service organization with more than 50 years in the market dedicated to providing services for Workers and their families, such as educational services, financial services, recreation services, social programs, and housing subsidies, among others, being the second-leading company in its market segment. In addition to meeting the demands and requirements of its users (companies and Workers), this organization must comply with current state regulations for providing services for workers and companies, regarding compliance with both financial and operational indicators and customer satisfaction. In this regard, this company must maintain a minimum customer satisfaction percentage of 95%, for which different factors can affect the customer's perception of the service. One of these critical factors is related to the attention received by the user in the other service channels (in-person, telephone, and digital), which, due to the pandemic, experienced significant growth given the circulation restrictions. Confinement and in-person service have changed how we relate to and serve customers, including non-face-to-face channels. Therefore, it is vital for companies to continuously monitor and improve the customer satisfaction indicator because failure to comply with this indicator leads to establishing Improvement plans before the corresponding government agencies with legal, economic, and reputational effects. Likewise, service times in non-face-to-face channels affect the quality of the service provided, since the longer the wait and service time, the lower the customer satisfaction will be, affecting indicators of retention of current clients and acquisition of new clients.

Initially, a Lean Six-Sigma work team was formed, led by an external Black Belt with more than ten years of experience in LSS projects, three Green Belts from the Quality and Continuous Improvement area of the company, the Head of the Logistics Department, as responsible for the service process in non-face-to-face channels and the logistics professional. The objectives were established: i) increase the percentage of customer satisfaction in the attention of non-face-to-face telephone line channels and ii) reduce the attention times of the non-face-to-face telephone line channels, the different actors involved in the project, such as the logistics area, the quality and continuous improvement area and the users of the services, as well as the scope, limitations, execution time and resources for the project. The Project Charter was socialized to senior management, obtaining its approval for execution. It was subsequently communicated to the work team and staff in the areas involved to establish commitments for the effective implementation of the methodology. For this case, the customer service process via telephone for the provision of financial services was analyzed, which presented problems in service times and unfavorable ratings in customer satisfaction surveys in the user service component. Next, the Voice of Customer technique defined the needs, drivers, and critical quality factors. (VoC), as seen in Fig. 2.

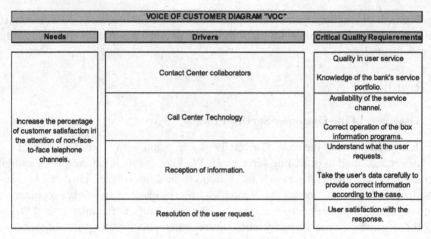

Fig. 2. Voice of Customer Diagram.

Subsequently, the SIPOC diagram of the non-face-to-face customer service process was designed, including those of suppliers, inputs, activities of the process, outputs, and customers (See Fig. 3).

SIPOC DIAGRAM OF NON-FACE-TO-FACE CUSTOMER SERVICE PROCESS					
Suppliers	**Inputs**	**Activity**	**Processes**	**Outputs**	**Customers**
Customers	Request for telephone attention.	Call Reception	1. The user dials the green service line or the national line of Company to obtain information regarding the services offered or response to any concern.	Customer served.	Customers
			2. The user listens to the pre-recorded information by Company: "Welcome to XYZ Company, an entity monitored by the Supersubsidio; if you know the extension number, enter it now..."	Request, Complaint, Claim, Suggestion or Congratulations attended.	Logistics Department
			3. User marks the option of the query they wish to make.		Quality and Improvement Department
	Call statistics and menu options.		4. Once the option is marked, listen carefully to the alternatives offered by the selected service and select the one of interest.		Goverment (reports)
Application MI Fone	Home menu PBX voice.	Data Registration and Query Resolution	5. The user's call is received.	Telephone service statistical report	
			6. The user's request is listened to, and the user's registration is performed.		
			7. The information (Subsidies, Financial Services, and general Sports Services) is provided according to the user's requirements, taking into account the frequently asked questions bank published on the Website. Suppose the user requires more detailed information about events, sports, recreation, etc. Call transfer is made to the area in charge.		
			8. Suppose the user is required to file a PQRSF. In that case, the Contact Center Customer Service Advisor listens to the user and, according to what is filed, indicates whether it is a request or request for information, complaint, claim, suggestion, or congratulation and registers it in the application. of "PQRSF", informing the user of the filing and response time by what is described in the Customer Experience Measurement Manual.		
			9. When the response corresponds to a specific person who cannot be found, you should find out what they need and try to channel the request to another person. If it is impossible to provide this support, the message must be sent to the official in charge by telephone.		
		Ending Call	10. End the call with the user cordially, remembering the Company service channels.		

Fig. 3. SIPOC diagram for the non-face-to-face customer service process in a service company.

Then, data was collected corresponding to the times of the customer service process for financial services and critical service quality indicators, such as the customer satisfaction index regarding the Call Center service and the rate of answered calls. These data allowed us to develop the Value Stream Mapping of the current process and use data analytics to evaluate the current behavior of the process times and calculate the process capacity under Six Sigma. Figure 4 shows the current Value Stream Mapping of the process.

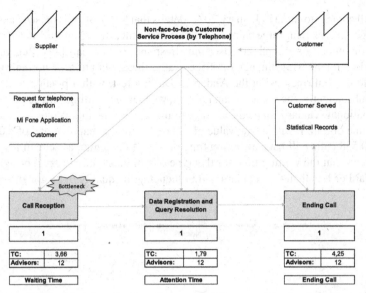

Fig. 4. Value Stream Mapping for Non-face-to-face Customer Service Process in Financial Services (by Telephone Channel).

The VSM findings reveal a CT = 9.7 min from when the customer initiates the call until their request is answered. In addition, the VSM makes it possible to identify the stages of the process that represent bottlenecks due to time delays and that can generate customer dissatisfaction. In this sense, the time of the call reception stage, in which the user must listen to prerecorded information, is the bottleneck stage of the process, both in terms of efficiency and in terms of quality in customer service, which was corroborated by data analysis and process capacity, as well as with the analysis of crucial service quality indicators.

One of the critical points of the process is the waiting time, which is one of the factors of user dissatisfaction, which affects the rating of the service and the attention received. For a more detailed analysis of the critical stage, a statistical analysis of the waiting times was carried out for the calls received from Financial Services, initially, with an analysis of the normality of the data and subsequently, through an analysis of capacity for telephone attention of the service, these analyzes were carried out with the help of the Minitab 17® statistical package.

For the capacity analysis of waiting times, the data obtained from the process is compared against a reference value, a national or international standard, to determine if the waiting times comply with these standards. When reviewing the international regulations regarding waiting times, it was found that, in Spain, the Customer Service Services Law was approved in April 2023, which regulates essential aspects of customer service, such as waiting times. Waiting, personalized care, rights expansion, and robotic care regulation, among others [41]. One of the most notable aspects of this new law is limiting the maximum waiting time on a customer service call to three (3) minutes for general information, complaints, and after-sales services. In addition, the new law, which will come into force in January 2024, details that "95% of calls must be answered, on average, in less than three minutes." After that time, the agent will not be able to hang up the phone on the phone. User must respond to their call [42]. Regarding the waiting time for housing financial services calls, the assumption of normality of the data could be confirmed using the Anderson-Darling test, with a p-value > 0.05 (See Fig. 5) Subsequently, the capacity analysis shows that the waiting time is greater than the international standard, since the average of the data is 3.66 min versus the maximum waiting time of 3 min, with a Cpk value of -0.66, this means that of a total of 1,000,000 calls, 980,538 calls will have a waiting time of more than 3 min, as seen in Fig. 6. The above shows that the waiting time for this type of call must be improved, bringing it to the standard or less than the standard and influencing the quality of customer service.

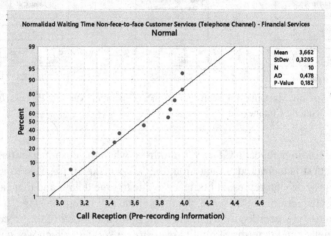

Fig. 5. Normality Test of Waiting time non-face-to-face Customer Service (Telephone Channel) - Financial Services.

On the other hand, the quality indicators of the process that account for opportunities for improvement in the call reception stage were analyzed. Firstly, information on the customer satisfaction indicator was analyzed for telephone attention to financial services customer requirements, corresponding to the first six months. Although the indicator is at 96.43%, the number of users who rated the telephone service as Regular or Bad is of particular importance since out of a total of 491 surveys, 21 clients rated the service as Regular and seven as Bad, as shown in Fig. 7. When analyzing the causes of these ratings, the users surveyed stated that their dissatisfaction was mainly due to the waiting times for the call to be attended to by an advisor, as well as the quality of the information received and attention to calls.

In addition, the data from the answered calls indicator was analyzed, providing valuable information on performance and efficiency in managing telephone interactions, as seen in Table 1.

In the period analyzed, 1,503 answered calls were recorded (27% of the total calls). This indicator reflects the number of calls in which Contact Center agents managed to establish a connection and provide service or resolve user queries. On the other hand,

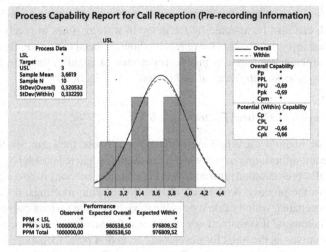

Fig. 6. Process Capability Report for Call Reception (Pre-recording Information) and Waiting time non-face-to-face Customer Service (Telephone Channel) - Financial Services.

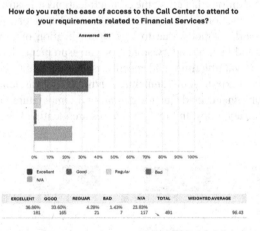

Fig. 7. Member voice measurement survey results - Financial Services (I Sem 2023)

Table 1. Center Answered Calls Indicator

Indicator	D1	D2	D3	D4	Total
Answered calls	98	497	453	455	1503
Unanswered calls	217	606	2561	743	4127
Total	315	1103	3014	1198	5630

4,127 unanswered calls were observed (73% of the total calls). This data is significant since it indicates the number of calls that were not answered by the agents or left unanswered, which can also be affected by the delay in waiting times in receiving the call and prerecorded information. The above results show the need to thoroughly analyze the causes of the efficiency and quality problems detected to establish the most appropriate action plans for process improvement and customer satisfaction.

4.2 Identification of Critical Factors

Considering the findings identified in the diagnosis process, the Lean Six-Sigma team collected relevant information to analyze the causes that impacted the high waiting times in receiving calls, pre-recorded information in the customer service process and identified the MUDAS in the process. As a result of the Project team meetings, a Cause-Effect Diagram was prepared, which made it possible to visualize the various causes that could contribute to members' dissatisfaction with the non-face-to-face telephone line service. This structure serves as the basis for developing an action plan, focusing on addressing identified causes and improving the efficiency and effectiveness of the service. The results of the cause-effect diagram show that the critical factors are associated with the equipment due to technical problems in the telephone system (faults in the calling software, weather conditions that affect the communications infrastructure) from human talent due to lack of personnel, lack of motivation and lack of training in customer service; from the work methods, due to lack of application of care protocols in the different channels, and lack of supervision; from measurement, due to the absence of indicators to measure waiting times and specific aspects of quality in telephone service and due to internal and external environmental conditions such as demanding customers, stressful work environment, inadequate lighting, and temperature conditions and lack of workplace welfare activities. In Fig. 8 the causes are identified using the cause-effect diagram.

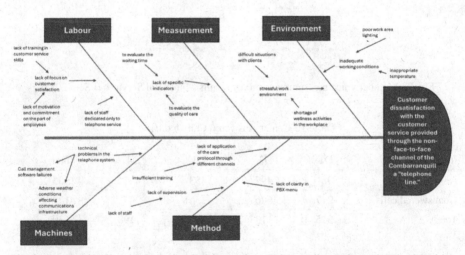

Fig. 8. Cause-and-effect analysis for Call Reception (Pre-recording Information) and Waiting time non-face-to-face Customer Service (Telephone Channel) - Financial Services

In addition to identifying the causes of influence on the inefficiency of the process, the waste or MUDA relevant to the process was identified. In the current context of the company and the service sector, attention through non-face-to-face channels such as the "telephone line" has become significant in customer satisfaction. For this reason, the LSS team used the "7 wastes" technique to identify and eliminate activities that do not add value, thus promoting substantial improvements in the efficiency and quality of the service. This analysis seeks to determine precisely which waste plays a determining role in the non-face-to-face channel service process, specifically the "telephone line" for service in Financial Services. This tool allows you to optimize operational efficiency and increase the general quality of customer service. A more agile, precise, and focused service is encouraged by identifying and eliminating waste directly affecting the user experience. In Fig. 9, the main categories and Description of the MUDAs identified are observed, which correspond mainly to the categories of Waiting, Overproduction, Defects, Motion, and Skills.

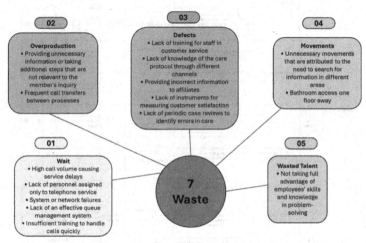

Fig. 9. MUDAs Identification for Call Reception (Pre-recording Information) and Waiting time non-face-to-face Customer Service (Telephone Channel) - Financial Services

4.3 Lean Six-Sigma Improvement Plans

In this last stage, the specific actions to be implemented were established during three months to evaluate the effectiveness of the adopted strategies. To this end, the LSS team structured a 5W2H Action Plan focused on attacking the causes and waste identified in the analysis stage, assigning those responsible, dates, and resources, which was socialized and approved by Senior Management to its execution. Different company areas participated in this plan, such as Logistics Management, Human Resources, Planning, and Financial Management. The plans include actions such as i) training programs in customer service, motivational and employee recognition programs, ii) training to improve adherence to customer service protocols, iii) hiring of two advisors, iv) new call time control software, v) training in handling clients and challenging situations, vi) improvement of lighting, ventilation and access to bathrooms, among others. The details of the action plan are shown in Fig. 10.

Aspects to improve	Causes	Improvement actions	Responsible	Start date	End Date	Means of Verification (Evidence)	USD costs
Improve waiting times and quality in the non-face-to-face channel of the Combarranquilla Family Compensation Fund telephone line.	Lack of focus on customer satisfaction	Implement training programs in customer service skills and focus on customer satisfaction such as courses in Sena for: Effective communication, customer service techniques, handling of complaints and claims, etc..	HR department / Logistics Management Department	Start I quarter of 2024	Month expired at the close of the I Quarter 2024	Training and development program records.	$ 360
		Include motivation and recognition programs for good work by publishing recognition pieces through welfare networks and the corporate intranet.	HR department / Logistics Management Department	Start I quarter of 2024	Month expired at the close of the I Quarter 2024	Motivation and recognition programs implemented.	$ 360
	Unnecessary movements attributed to the need to seek information in other areas	Training on the procedures stipulated for the services, to reinforce weak points and minimize unnecessary movements	Logistics Management Department / Planning Department	Start I quarter of 2024	Month expired at the close of the I Quarter 2024	Attendance record	$ 21
	Lack of staff dedicated only to telephone service	Hiring 2 supernumerary people to cover telephone service in high seasons.	Logistics Management Department	Start I quarter of 2024	Month expired at the close of the I Quarter 2024	Contracts made	$ 580
	Lack of specific indicators to evaluate waiting time and quality of care	Implement the proposed indicators in the development of this project.	Logistics Management Department	Start I quarter of 2024	Month expired at the close of the I Quarter 2024	Defined and improved indicators.	$ 75
		In 2024 it will implement a new time control software with the provider Movistar called One Inbox, which promises to provide indicators of online waiting time, service time, corporate email control, etc.	Logistics Management Department	Start I quarter of 2024	Month expired at the close of the I Quarter 2024	One Inbox System Registration	$ 7,500
	Stressful work environment	Provide specialized training in handling difficult situations with clients, such as customer management courses.	HR department / Logistics Management Department	Start I quarter of 2024	Month expired at the close of the I Quarter 2024	Training records in handling difficult situations.	$ 2,640
		Introduce wellness activities in the workplace to reduce stress and improve the work environment, such as: Active Breaks, healthy snacks and motivational talks.	HR department / Logistics Management Department	Start I quarter of 2024	Month expired at the close of the I Quarter 2024	Implementation of well-being activities. (Graphic record - Attendance Record)	$ 75
	Inadequate working conditions (temperature and lighting)	Prepare a visit schedule for maintenance technicians specialized in equipment such as air conditioning.	Unit Coordination / Logistics Management Department	Start I quarter of 2024	Month expired at the close of the I Quarter 2024	Schedule	$ 31
		Conduct periodic surveys to obtain staff opinion on temperature and its impact on work performance.	Logistics Management Department / Planning Department	Start I quarter of 2024	Month expired at the close of the I Quarter 2024	Survey results	$ 31
		Conduct individual interviews or group sessions with employees to understand their needs and preferences regarding temperature and lighting.	Logistics Management Department / Planning Department	Start I quarter of 2024	Month expired at the close of the I Quarter 2024	Chat group results	$ 31
	Bathroom access to a remote floor	Find solutions to facilitate access to the bathroom, such as assigning the bathroom only to cashier employees, and assigning a new one for planetarium customers.	Unit Coordination / Logistics Management Department	Start I quarter of 2024	Month expired at the close of the I Quarter 2024	Graphic Registration	$ -
	Technical problems in the telephone system	Implement measures to resolve technical problems in the telephone system and ensure its correct operation, such as a red light that allows determining the efficiency of the network. (Green light: Functional, Orange light: Alert, Red light: No network).	System Department / Logistics Management Department	Start I quarter of 2024	Month expired at the close of the I Quarter 2024	Resolution of technical problems and their documentation.	$ 1,250
	Adverse weather conditions affecting communications infrastructure	Develop a contingency plan to face adverse weather conditions that may affect communications infrastructure.	Planning Department / Logistics Management Department / System Department	Start I quarter of 2024	Month expired at the close of the I Quarter 2024	Contingency plan for adverse weather conditions.	$ 21
	Lack of application of the attention protocol of the different channels	Reinforce the application of the care protocol through different channels to guarantee consistent care, through different training groups, to avoid interrupting care. Additionally, reinforce the inclusive care protocol with collaborators..	HR department / Planning Department / Logistics Management Department	Start I quarter of 2024	Month expired at the close of the I Quarter 2024	Training report	$ 94
	Lack of supervision	Establish effective supervision systems to guarantee compliance with protocols and quality of care.	Logistics Management Department	Start I quarter of 2024	Month expired at the close of the I Quarter 2024	Implementation of effective supervision systems.	$ 628
	Lack of clarity in PBX menu	Review and improve clarity in the PBX menu to make it easier for customers to navigate.	Logistics Management Department	Start I quarter of 2024	Month expired at the close of the I Quarter 2024	Documented improvements to PBX menu clarity.	$ 10
						Total	$ 13,706

Fig. 10. Lean Six-Sigma Improvement Plants.

After the first two months of implementation, the LSS team collected data on the times of the intervention process to evaluate the effectiveness of the actions taken and, if the time reduction was not achieved, take new actions to close the project—Gap in waiting time in receiving calls and in the process cycle. The monitoring results showed a significant improvement in both the waiting time for receiving the call and the process cycle time. In this sense, the waiting time for receiving the call and pre-recorded information went from 3.66 min to 2.55 min (a reduction of 30.32%). Regarding the process cycle time (CT), it went from 9.7 min to 7.75 min (a decrease of 20.1%) since the improvement actions not only impacted the "waiting time for call reception" but also impacted the "Data Registration and Query Resolution" stages and in the "Ending Call" stage. In Fig. 11, the improvement in the Value Stream Mapping of the process is observed, and in Fig. 12, the reduction in time in the critical stage of Call Reception is evident.

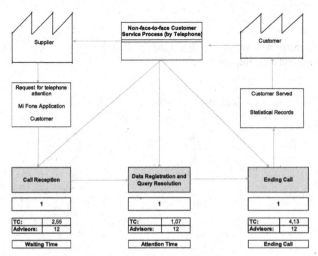

Fig. 11. Improved Value Stream Mapping for Non-face-to-face Customer Service Process in Financial Services (by Telephone Channel).

Another of the results obtained was the improvement in the Process Capacity index, which went from a Cpk = -0.66 to a Cpk = 3.58, which means that the users of the Telefonica line channel will not have to wait more than 3 min while they receive the pre-recorded information and are redirected to a service advisor, as shown in Fig. 13.

Finally, a control plan was proposed to maintain the improvements achieved by implementing the LSS methodology. In this sense, the measurement of process times through I-MR control letters was integrated into the company's quality management system for better monitoring and timely action in the event of deviations (Fig. 14).

Likewise, the LSS team proposed a set of indicators based on the Customer Satisfaction survey to improve the monitoring and evaluation of the process, facilitating the analysis of data both in real-time and through historical data, which offers not only an instantaneous view of the quality of care received by the user but also provides a perspective over time, allowing trends, patterns, and areas of opportunity to be identified. Table 2 shows the proposed indicators.

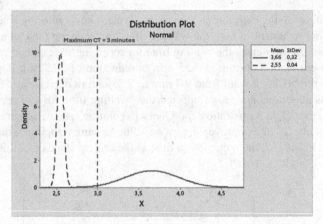

Fig. 12. The comparison between waiting time in Call Reception (before implementation improvement plans and after improvement). ·

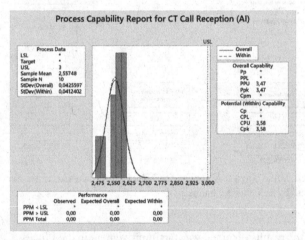

Fig. 13. Improvement of Process Capability for Call Reception (Pre-recording Information) and Waiting time non-face-to-face Customer Service (Telephone Channel) - Financial Services.

5   Conclusions and Future Work

This paper presents the application of the integrated Lean Six Sigma methodology to improve user service times and quality in the customer service process through non-face-to-face channels (telephone lines) in a large service company. Integral for the worker, specifically for answering calls from users of financial services. As the main contribution of the study, there is the proposal of a methodological approach that provides short and long-term improvements in the services sector, which, given its complexities, requires the use of robust, practical tools and methodologies that combine quantitative analysis with making strategic decisions to improve processes, oriented towards customer and stakeholder satisfaction continuously.

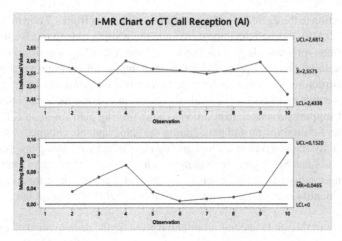

Fig. 14. I-MR control chart for monitoring the CT after project finalization

Table 2. Proposal Indicators

Indicator	Description	Type	Frequency	Source Data	Responsible	Goal
Customer satisfaction rate	Measures the level of customer satisfaction with the service received	Quality	Quarterly	Post-call surveys	Customer Service Professional Logistics Professional	>97%
Quality of Information Provided (QIP)	Measures the accuracy and relevance of the information provided by the advisor during the call	Quality	Quarterly	Post-call surveys	Customer Service Professional Logistics Professional	>97%
Query resolution	Measures the ability of advisors to resolve queries	Quality	Quarterly	Post-call surveys	Customer Service Professional Logistics Professional	>97%

With the development of the integrated LSS methodology, significant results were obtained in terms of reducing process times and adopting comprehensive improvement plans incorporated into the company's quality management system. Through a 3-step methodological approach, the stages of the Six-Sigma DMAIC cycle were combined with the stages of the Lean Manufacturing methodology. One of the main results obtained was the reduction in the cycle time of the process, which went from 9.7 min to 7.75 min (a decrease of 20.1%), through the improvement in the waiting time to receive the call and the information—pre-recorded, from 3.66 to 2.55 min (30.32% reduction). In addition, improvement strategies were proposed that cover components for improving the techno-logical infrastructure, improving adherence to user service protocols, training advisors in customer service and handling difficult situations, improving locating conditions and the hiring of support personnel, in addition to a monitoring plan based on control charts and indicators for monitoring and maintaining the achievements obtained. These strate-gies significantly impacted the time and quality perceived by the company's customers. In addition, the Lean Six Sigma methodology is a beneficial approach to improving the processes and quality of customer service in any company because this methodology allows us to identify unnecessary processes and variables that interrupt the correct flow of service.

The results of this study become an essential point for the development of new studies both in the company under study of this research, extending the field of application to other services, and in other organizations in the service sector. In addition, future studies can address the factors for the successful implementation or barriers to implementing Lean Six Sigma improvement programs, as well as the impact of these programs on labor, health and safety, and innovation, among others. Finally, other research can address the joint implementation of LSS with different techniques such as Multi-criteria decision-making, simulation, machine learning, and industry 4.0/5.0 to demonstrate the potential and tangible benefits for companies, expanding the horizon of research opportunities and application in the actual field of the Lean Six-Sigma methodology.

References

1. Gill, I.: At your service? Developing economies bet on service industries for growth. https://blogs.worldbank.org/voices/your-service-developing-economies-bet-service-industries-growth. Accessed 29 Feb 2024
2. Kowalik, K.: Six Sigma as a method of improving the quality of service process. Prod. Eng. Arch. **19**, 10–15 (2018). https://doi.org/10.30657/pea.2018.19.03
3. McDermott, A.: El año del crecimiento basado en el servicio de atención al cliente (2023). https://www.zendesk.es/blog/2022-the-year-of-customer-service-led-growth/. Accessed 29 Feb 2024
4. Banuelas, A.: A strategy of survival. Manuf. Eng. **80**(3), 119–121 (2001)
5. Jimenez, G., et al.: Improvement of productivity and quality in the value chain through lean manufacturing - a case study. Procedia Manuf. **41**, 882–889 (2019). https://doi.org/10.1016/j.promfg.2019.10.011
6. Rodrigues, J., Sá, J.C., Silva, F.J., Ferreira, L.P., Jimenez, G., Santos, G.: A rapid improvement process through "Quick-Win" lean tools: a case study. Systems **8**, 55 (2020). https://doi.org/10.3390/systems8040055
7. Azevedo, J., Sá, J., Santos, G., Cruz, F., Jimenez, G., Silva, F.: Improvement of production line in the automotive industry through lean philosophy. Procedia Manuf. **41**, 1023–1030 (2019)
8. Sá, J.C., et al.: Assessing the impact of lean tools on production and safety by a multicriteria decision-making model and statistical analysis: a case study in textile sector. In: Stephanidis, C., et al. (eds.) HCII 2021. LNCS, vol. 13097, pp. 616–638. Springer, Cham (2021). https://doi.org/10.1007/978-3-030-90966-6_42

9. Jiménez-Delgado, G., et al.: Implementation of Lean Six Sigma to improve the quality and productivity in textile sector: a case study. In: Duffy, V.G. (ed.) HCII 2023. LNCS, vol. 14028, pp. 395–412. Springer, Cham (2023). https://doi.org/10.1007/978-3-031-35741-1_30
10. Tsironis, L., Psychogios, A.: Road towards Lean Six Sigma in service industry: a multi-factor integrated framework. Bus. Process. Manag. J. **22**(4), 812–834 (2016). https://doi.org/10.1108/BPMJ-08-2015-0118
11. Alhuraish, I., Robledo, C., Kobi, A.: A comparative exploration of lean manufacturing and six sigma terms of their critical success factors. J. Cleaner Prod. **164**, 325–337 (2017)
12. Uluskan, M.: A comprehensive insight into the Six Sigma DMAIC Toolbox. Int. J. Lean Six Sigma **7**(4), 406–429 (2016). https://doi.org/10.1108/IJLSS-10-2015-0040
13. Ortiz-Barrios, M., Coba-Blanco, D., Jiménez-Delgado, G., Salomon, V.A.P., López-Meza, P.: Implementation of Lean Six Sigma to lessen waiting times in public emergency care networks: a case study. In: Stephanidis, C., et al. (eds.) HCII 2021. LNCS, vol. 13097, pp. 83–93. Springer, Cham (2021). https://doi.org/10.1007/978-3-030-90966-6_7
14. Ortíz-Barrios, M., McClean, S., Jiménez-Delgado, G., Martínez-Sierra, D.E.: Integrating Lean Six Sigma and discrete-event simulation for shortening the appointment lead-time in gynecobstetrics departments: a case study. In: Duffy, V.G. (ed.) HCII 2020. LNCS, vol. 12199, pp. 378–389. Springer, Cham (2020). https://doi.org/10.1007/978-3-030-49907-5_27
15. Lubowe, D., Blitz, A.: Driving operational innovation using Lean Six Sigma. Bus. Perform. Manag. **6**(3), 10–15 (2008)
16. Engelund, E.H., Breum, G., Friis, A.: Optimisation of large-scale food production using lean manufacturing principles. J. Foodservice **20**(1), 4–14 (2009)
17. Navarro Albert, E., Gisbert Soler, V., Pérez Molina, A.I.: Metodología E Implementación De Six Sigma. 3C Empresa: Investigación y pensamiento crítico **6**(5), 73–80 (2017). https://doi.org/10.17993/3cemp.2017.especial.73-80
18. Socconini, L., Escobedo, E.: Lean six sigma green belt: paso a paso (2021)
19. Guerrero Moreno, D.R., Silva Leal, J.A., Bocanegra-Herrera, C.C.: Revisión de la implementación de Lean Six Sigma en Instituciones de Educación Superior. Ingeniare. Revista chilena de ingeniería **27**(4), 652–667 (2019). https://doi.org/10.4067/S0718-33052019000400652
20. García Camús, J.M.: Lean Six Sigma Startup Methodology (L6SSM): una metodología general de innovación de la calidad aplicada a los sectores de la producción y servicios. Universidad Rey Juan Carlos (2015)
21. Jurado, E.A., Naranjo, K.A.: Propuesta para implementar lean seis sigma en el departamento de servicio al cliente en una empresa del sector retail. Universidad de La Salle, p. 59 (2019)
22. Tafernaberri, E., Gisbert Soler, V., Molina Pérez, A.I.: La importancia de Lean Six Sigma en las organizaciones (2016)
23. Caro Teller, J.M., et al.: Implementación Lean Six Sigma en la mejora del circuito de dispensación de medicación. J. Healthc. Qual. Res. **35**(6), 364–371 (2020). https://doi.org/10.1016/j.jhqr.2020.04.005
24. Guerrero Moreno, D.R., Silva Leal, J.A., Bocanegra Herrera, C.C.: Revisión de la implementación de Lean Six Sigma en Instituciones de Educación Superior Implementation of Lean Six Sigma in Higher Education Institutions: a comprehensive review. Revista chilena de ingeniería **27**(4), 652–667 (2019)
25. Vasquez Aleman, M.: Propuesta de Mejora en el Proceso de Gestión del Area de Servicio al Cliente y Gestión de Cobro de REFINANCIA Colombia Utilizando la Metodología Lean Six Sigma. Universidad Católica de Colombia (2019)
26. Carrillo Landazábal, M.S., Alvis Ruiz, C.G., Mendoza Álvarez, Y.Y., Cohen Padilla, H.E.: Lean manufacturing: 5 s y TPM, herramientas de mejora de la calidad. Caso empresa metalmecánica en Cartagena, Colombia. SIGNOS - Investigación en sistemas de gestión **11**(1), 71–86 (2019). https://doi.org/10.15332/s2145-1389-4934

27. Morales Londoño, N., Carrillo Landarzabal, M.S., Castillo Salgado, B.L.: Propuesta metodológica en la implementación del enfoque itls para la contribución a la calidad y a la mejora continua. SIGNOS - Investigación en sistemas de gestión **12**(2), 111–123 (2020). https://doi.org/10.15332/24631140.5940

28. Miranda, M., Tapia, L., Romero, M., Chiriboga, P.: La calidad de los servicios y la satisfacción del cliente, estrategias del marketing digital. Ciencias técnicas y aplicadas **7**(4), 1430–1446 (2021). http://dominiodelasciencias.com/ojs/index.php/es/index. https://orcid.org/0000-0002-5408-1200

29. Izquierdo Espinoza, J.R.: La Calidad De Servicio En La Administración Pública. Horizonte Empresarial **8**(1), 425–437 (2021). https://doi.org/10.26495/rce.v8i1.1648

30. Supersubsidio. Circular Externa 008 de 2020 Superintendencia del Subsidio Familiar. https://ssf.gov.co/ Accessed 13 Oct 2020

31. Loaiza Vasquez, W.E., Guatumillo Freire, E.L., Jiménez Silva, W.R.: Impacto de un chat conversacional en la atención al cliente de las empresas de servicios de la provincia de Tungurahua. Uniandes EPISTEME **7**, 177–191 (2020). https://revista.uniandes.edu.ec/ojs/index.php/EPISTEME/article/view/1665/1106

32. Torres Oviedo, J.K.: Metodología para implementar marcos ágiles en los equipos de servicio al cliente especializados en quejas y reclamos. Universidad Santo Tomás (2023)

33. Henao, M.L.: Cajas de Compensación Familiar (2001)

34. Fuster Rojas, L.: Impacto de las metodologias Lean Service, Lean Six Sigma y Lean Management en el sector consultoría y servicio. Pontificia Universidad Católica del Perú (2020)

35. Benalcázar, A.: Propuesta de aplicación de la metodología Lean Six Sigma para mejorar la eficiencia de los procesos productivos en la Empresa 'Tejidos Parwall. Universidad Tecnica del Norte (2021). http://repositorio.utn.edu.ec/bitstream/123456789/11057/4/04IND2 97TRABAJOGRADO.pdf

36. Quishpe, F.J., Arroyo Morocho, F.: Analysis and optimization in the production of cardboard pac-kaging, using value stream mapping I En la producción de envases de cartón, empleando el value stream mapping. Universidad y Sociedad **13**(3), 536–542 (2021)

37. Fons Jareño, I.: Implantación de la metodología Lean Seis Sigma en un proceso de mantenimiento aeronáutico (2020)

38. Hofmann, G.A.A., de Souza, H.A.: Application of total quality management tools in the risk analysis of pathologies in steel-structured buildings. Ingeniare **30**(4), 745–759 (2022). https://doi.org/10.4067/S0718-33052022000400745

39. Rodríguez Cruz, J.S., Verde Castro, E.A.: Herramientas de LEAN MANUFACTURING para reducir desperdicios en la empresa de calzado Kalia. Universidad Privada Antenor Orrego (2022). https://orcid.org/0000-0001-5952-0535

40. Li, N., Laux, C.M., Antony, J.: How to use lean Six Sigma methodology to improve service process in higher education: a case study. Int. J. Lean Six Sigma **10**(4), 883–908 (2019). https://doi.org/10.1108/IJLSS-11-2018-0133

41. Hernandez, J.: «Tiempo máximo que me podrán dejar en espera en una llamada a la atención al cliente» (2023)

42. Anzola, P.: «Tres minutos de espera máxima al teléfono y atención personalizada: qué cambia con la nueva Ley de Atención al Cliente» (2023)

Lean Philosophy "Quick Wins": A Case Study in a Non-alcoholic Beverage Company

Genett Isabel Jiménez-Delgado[1]([✉]) [iD], Hugo Hernandez-Palma[2,4] [iD],
Bellanith Lucena-León Castro[3,4], and Yesith Ternera-Muñoz[5]

[1] Department of Industrial Engineering, Institución Universitaria de Barranquilla IUB,
Barranquilla, Colombia
gjimenez@unibarranquilla.edu.co

[2] Faculty of Engineering, Industrial Engineering Program, Corporación Universitaria
Iberoamericana IBERO, Bogotá, Colombia
hugo.hernandez@ibero.edu.co

[3] International Business Program, Corporación Universitaria Americana, Barranquilla,
Colombia
bellanithlucena@americana.edu.co

[4] Doctorate of Project Management, Universidad EAN, Bogotá, Colombia
bleonca36518@universidadean.edu.co

[5] Department of Computer Science and Electronics, Universidad de la Costa CUC,
Barranquilla, Colombia
yternera@cuc.edu.co

Abstract. The non-alcoholic beverage industry stands out as one of the fastest-growing agroindustrial sectors, despite the difficulties generated by the COVID-19 pandemic, with optimistic projections in the coming years. Its importance lies in the economic, productive, and social contribution and the social responsibility programs companies carry out for their interest groups. However, the industry faces challenges such as competition, government restrictions related to the environment, quality and safety of products and processes, and product diversification due to changes in consumer demand for more natural products. Therefore, companies in the non-alcoholic beverage sector must establish and implement appropriate strategies to maintain the quality of their products, optimize costs, and satisfy continuous and changing customer requirements. The present study presents the application of the Lean Manufacturing methodology as a philosophy of continuous improvement aimed at achieving early victories in terms of quality and productivity. It costs through three-phase methods, which consisted of 1) diagnosis of the current state of the production line, 2) identification of the types and sources of waste that affect the efficiency and quality of the process, 3) Action Plan and implementation of appropriate Lean Manufacturing techniques and, 4) Evaluation of the impact of the improvement proposal on time, cost, quality, and customer satisfaction indicators. The case study is presented in the process of changing the flavor of a non-alcoholic beverage company, which is of high value in Latin America and is part of one of the largest companies worldwide. The results evidenced significant improvements in time lost due to flavor change, which went from 234 min to 170 min, decreased costs due to a reduction in time lost in flavor

V. G. Duffy (Ed.): HCII 2024, LNCS 14709, pp. 279–294, 2024.
https://doi.org/10.1007/978-3-031-61060-8_20

change went from USD 258,750 to USD 203,500, and improvement in a corporate culture focused on quality and continuous improvement, with an impact on reducing non-value added times or waste times.

Keywords: Lean Philosophy · Lean Manufacturing · Kaizen · SMED · Non-alcoholic beverage company

1 Introduction

The non-alcoholic beverage industry includes companies that produce and sell drinking products that don't contain alcohol. This includes bottled water, coffee, tea, soft drinks, juices, and other products. The wide variety of products with non-alcoholic content has contributed to the sustained growth of the sector, reflected in its contribution to the economy, job creation, and the reduction of social gaps. Despite the difficulties experienced by the non-alcoholic beverage industry during the COVID-19 pandemic, with a decrease of 100 billion dollars in global revenue, the trend in the market remains buoyant. It has growth prospects for the next few years [1]. For example, the non-alcoholic beverage market in 2022 grew by more than 7% in volume in 10 of the largest markets around the world, with a market value exceeding USD 11 billion [2]. The growth expectations of the non-alcoholic beverage sector are positive, with a forecast of global revenue in the market of 0.3 trillion dollars between 2023 and 2027, which represents an increase of 20.69%, reaching a growth indicator of 1.74 trillion dollars in 2027 [3]. Likewise, the non-alcoholic beverage category is expected to represent more than 90% of the total growth of the beverage category in the coming years [2].

Despite sustained growth, the non-alcoholic beverage industry faces serious challenges, such as increasing costs for producers and the introduction of regulatory changes, for example, healthy taxes, transparency in nutritional information, levies on plastics single-use, changes in consumer preferences towards low-sugar beverages, intense competition and increase in emerging beverage brands, adoption of sustainable practices regarding packaging, production, distribution, and use of resources, innovation, and differentiation of the product portfolio, the interruption of global supply chains generated by external situations and the technological challenges in the adoption of emerging technologies, such as artificial intelligence and automation. Addressing these challenges requires the development of strategic approaches that include constant innovation, attention to market trends, commitment to sustainability, and the application of continuous improvement methodologies in processes to detect inefficiencies and establish technical interventions. Technological, procedural, and human that add value and guarantee the sector's sustained growth.

The Lean philosophy, or Lean Manufacturing, is a management approach originating in the manufacturing sector. Still, given its benefits and impacts, it has scaled various industries such as fishing industry [4], metalworking [5], automotive [6], textile [7, 8], health [9, 10] among others. The Lean philosophy focuses on maximizing value for the customer while minimizing waste and misused resources, improving efficiency, quality, and cost indicators, generating added value, and promoting innovation and sustainability. Using the Lean philosophy, the flows of the value chain processes can be diagnosed, evaluated, and intervened to eliminate bottlenecks, delays, and activities that do not add value, ensuring that products or services flow Efficiently from the raw material to the end customer. In addition, the Lean philosophy is oriented towards creating a culture of continuous improvement, where each employee is committed to efficiency, quality, and customer satisfaction through a diverse set of specific tools and techniques, such as Kaizen, Just-in-time, and visual management systems, among others.

This paper proposes using Lean philosophy to achieve early victories in cycle times (CT) and costs in a sizeable non-alcoholic beverage company, providing a valuable framework for strategic decision-making. It is operational in other industries and extendable to different economic sectors. This paper is organized as follows. Section 2 presents the literature review of Lean philosophy in the manufacturing sector. Section 3 details the methodology. Section 4 presents the results and discussion of the Lean philosophy application. Finally, conclusions and future studies are detailed in Sect. 5.

2 Literature Review

This section presents articles or research projects related to the proposed implementation of the Lean Six Sigma Methodology to improve the time and quality in a non-alcoholic beverage company with more than 119 years of experience in the Colombian beverage market, and one of the main industrial organizations in Latin America. The company grew and expanded throughout the country and later partnered with other national and international companies. Thus, it increased its production capacity by using the plants of the three companies and managed to cover the national territory [11, 12]. It has been identified that several production processes need to be optimized.

This section develops the state-of-the-art, accumulated knowledge of a specific area to know the evolution and development achieved in the area to be studied. In other words, it is a study of information collected on a particular topic [13].

Firstly, [14] in his thesis, he developed the objective of proposing a process improvement using Lean Manufacturing tools in the yogurt production line of a Dairy Company in the city of Arequipa. For this, an export-factor or non-experimental methodology was applied because the information was collected and analyzed without manipulating any situation and observing the natural behavior of the company's yogurt production line. As a result, the study and strategic plan were obtained, identifying points of improvement and improvement proposals, considering data collection. The application of Lean Manufacturing stands out as a contribution, as well as the proposal of indicators, as a guide for this research project. Likewise, [15] the thesis raised the general objective to increase the level of service offered to clients below the minimum required 95% using the methodology chosen.

Likewise, [16] in their thesis developed the general objective of an improvement proposal for the production process of Red Globe table grapes by implementing the Lean Manufacturing methodology and reducing process times, considering the scope of this study from the selection process to the labeling of boxes of Red Globe table grapes for export. In a similar sense, [17], in their thesis, set the objective of presenting an improvement proposal to optimize the production process in a baking company by applying the Lean Manufacturing tool. Regarding the methodology, they applied non-experimental research with a descriptive design.

On the other hand, [18] proposed the general objective of implementing lean manufacturing methodologies to optimize the results of the weighing process of the company's laboratories in the chemical sector thesis. The methodology used was non-experimental with a qualitative case study. Likewise, [19]executed the general objective of applying lean manufacturing to improve efficiency in the bottling line of the wine industry. The methodology used had a sequential and evidentiary quantitative approach with an explanatory method focused on investigating the causes and effects that caused the deficiencies in the bottling line. Also, [20], in his industrial engineering thesis, proposed as a general objective to develop a proposal for the implementation of the SMED methodology around the injection of PVC accessories to increase the availability of the equipment of the company Mexichem Perú. [21–23] present success stories of implementing Lean Manufacturing in different companies in the productive sector.

Following the same order of ideas, different topics related to quality management and continuous improvement in organizations were addressed in this work. To this end, the main theoretical approaches that support these themes were reviewed, considering the following order:

- Waste: Waste is all those activities that do not add value to the product or service offered to the customer and generate unnecessary costs for the company. These can be different types: overproduction, transportation, waiting time, excess processes, inventory, movements, product defects, and underutilized personnel [24]. Thus, the efficiency and profitability of the company can be improved by offering a quality product or service that satisfies the customer's needs and expectations.
- Kaizen is a Japanese word that means "change for the better" or "improvement." It is a philosophy and methodology that seeks to improve the quality and productivity of organizations through the active participation of all its members, from top management to rank-and-file employees, through the idea that small incremental changes can generate a significant impact over time [24, 25]
- Lean Manufacturing: LM is a simple, profound, and practical work methodology that has its origin in Japan, focused on increasing productive efficiency in all processes by implementing the Kaizen management philosophy or continuous improvement in time, space, waste, inventory, and defects, involving the worker and generating in them a sense of belonging by being able to participate in the process of proposing their ideas on how to do things better. Likewise, this methodology is based on the principle that everything can be done better and that processes must be adjusted to customer demand, eliminating everything that does not add value and optimizing the use of resources. It uses various tools such as Value Stream Mapping, Kanban, 5S, SMED, TPM, Poka Yoke, and Karakuri [8].
- Optimization of processes: Process optimization consists of improving the efficiency and effectiveness of the organizational system. This can be achieved by identifying and eliminating unnecessary steps, automating repetitive tasks, and using tools and technologies that improve communication and collaboration. Therefore, process optimization can reduce costs, improve quality, and increase customer satisfaction [26].
- SMED: Quick tool change (SMED) is a lean production technique that reduces the time it takes to change tools or settings on a machine. This can be achieved by

classifying tool-changing steps into internal and external, with the former being those that can be completed while the machine is running and external steps, which must be achieved when the machine is off. By identifying and reducing internal steps, SMED can help companies improve flexibility, quality, and productivity [27].

The application of Lean Manufacturing in food and beverage companies has optimized processes and improved productivity at all levels. [28] in their research, they looked for which Lean tools Malaysian companies have used, finding that the preferred one is Kaizen, while SMED did not show favorable results [29] their study determined that the application of Lean Manufacturing, in addition to reducing waste in the food and beverage production processes in canned food, made it possible to optimize procedures. Other success stories of the implementation of Lean Manufacturing can be presented in the studies carried out by [30–34].

3 Methodology

To decrease the Cycle Time (CT) and costs for retards in process in the non-alcoholic beverage industry, the following three-step methodology is proposed to apply the Lean Philosophy "Quick wins" (See Fig. 1).

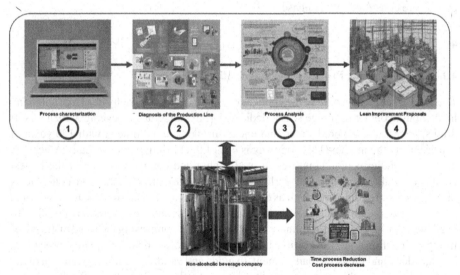

Fig. 1. Proposed Lean Philosophy for decreasing times and costs in the non-alcoholic beverage industry

Phase 1. *Process Characterization*: In this phase, the endogenous and exogenous variables and interest groups of the production process are identified, and the activities of the process are visualized through the use of the SIPOC Diagram and the Value Chain diagram.

Phase 2. *Diagnosis of the Production Line*: For this stage, data is collected on the process times of the production line, and the cycle time is calculated, as well as the value-added time and the non-added value time, using Value Stream Mapping, comparing the times. They were obtained with the cycle time adjusted to the demand or Takt Time.

Phase 3. *Analyze*: At this stage, the critical activities of the process that generated bottlenecks and economic losses for the process were identified. Additionally, the leading causes of waste or MUDA in the process were identified, and the cost of waste and its impact on profitability was calculated. This stage is highly significant in the Lean philosophy since, through identifying the leading waste and its causes, the most appropriate intervention strategies were established using both Lean Manufacturing tools and management strategies. This phase used cause-effect analysis and TIMWOODS technique (Transport, Inventory, Motion, Waiting, Overproduction, Over Processing, Defects, and Skills).

Phase 4. *Improve*: Considering the previous diagnosis and analysis of the process, specific intervention plans focused on technical improvements, procedures, and employee training to reduce time and costs during knowledge changes in the production line. Subsequently, the implementation of the improvement plans was monitored, which made it possible to identify the "quick wins" in the process regarding the reduction of process time, non-added value times, and costs due to loss of time in the process. The company's team of experts, the Integration of Lean Manufacturing tools, and 5WH improvement plans were consulted in this phase.

4 Results

4.1 Define Phase 1. Process Characterization

This study presents the case of the application of the Lean philosophy in a large company in the non-alcoholic beverage sector dedicated to manufacturing beverages such as soft drinks, juices, tea, flavored water, and energy drinks, among others, with 120 years of experience in the market. This company is one of the leading brands in Latin America's low- and middle-income countries. It is also an allied company of one of the largest companies in the segment in the world, such as PepsiCo. Currently, there are deficiencies in the beverage bottling line, such as delays in process times and costs due to loss of time in the process, which affects the efficiency of the process and the generation of profits. To begin the Project, an interdisciplinary team was formed, comprising the Head of the juice-filling production line, production line operators, professionals in quality processes, human talent, and financial management, to guide and validate the implementation of the Lean philosophy and integrate it into the corporate culture. The internal Work team had the support of external experts in the Lean Manufacturing methodology and continuous improvement tools. As the first sub-stage of phase 1, the company's production lines were analyzed to identify the line with the most significant lost time. The initial diagnosis results showed that production line No. 11 had the highest lost times, mainly due to pipe cleaning activities due to flavor changes in the production line, this being the line selected for the study, as shown In Fig. 2. These preliminary findings require the company's intervention, with substantial technical, human, and administrative changes, to improve lost time and maximize the company's financial indicators.

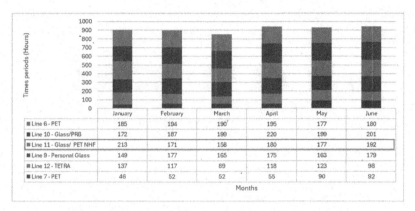

	January	February	March	April	May	June
■ Line 6 - PET	185	194	190	195	177	180
■ Line 10 - Glass/PRB	172	187	199	220	199	201
■ Line 11 - Glass/ PET NHF	213	171	158	180	177	192
■ Line 9 - Personal Glass	149	177	165	175	163	179
■ Line 12 - TETRA	137	117	89	118	123	98
■ Line 7 - PET	46	52	52	55	90	92

Months

Fig. 2. Lost Time (total plant per line).

As a second sub-stage, the stakeholders involved directly or indirectly in the Project were established, which may be positively affected and whose needs were considered to improve the production line. These stakeholders included shareholders, consumers, and clients., employees, suppliers, community surrounding the company, government, and environment, with whom the following expected benefits were defined: i) reduce non-added value times or lost times in the production line, ii) reduction in costs operations due to loss of time in the process, iii) reduction in the percentage of non-conforming products, and iv) increase in social responsibility actions. These objectives were shared with senior management, the interdisciplinary team, and collaborators for final approval. As a third sub-stage, the SIPOC diagram of the production line was prepared with details of suppliers, inputs, critical stages of the process, output, and customers (Fig. 3).

4.2 Diagnosis of the Production Line

In this Second phase, the current process's Value Stream Mapping (VSM) was prepared, considering the stages identified in the SIPOC diagram. To prepare the VSM, information about the process was collected regarding the number of shifts, working hours, ineffective time, available time, gross production, number of machines, percentage of machine operation, actual production, percentage of defects, product change time, and number of operators, daily demand and lead time. Then, the main process metrics such as cycle time, Value Added Time (TVA), Non-Value Added Time (TNVA), Total Time (TT), Touch Time (TOU), and Takt Time were calculated, which represent the value flow of the production process as seen in Fig. 4. The results of the VSM show a total time of 526 min, of which 491 min correspond to non-added value time (145 min of pasteurization step and 185 min of Juice Filling step), and 35.05 min to value time. Added, with a Touch Time value of 6.67%, which means that of the total process time, only that percentage is used to add value to the product.

In addition, a time adjusted to demand or Takt Time of 0.048 min/kg was obtained. Takt Time is the maximum time that can be invested in the process for each kilogram of juice drink to satisfy customer demand. Therefore, if customer demand increases or available time decreases, Takt time will be affected, and the production process must be

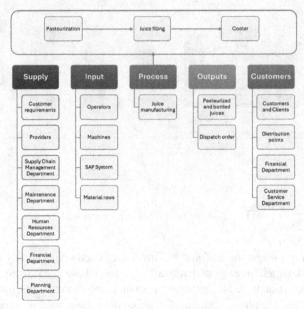

Fig. 3. SIPOC diagram for the production line juice manufacturing in non-alcoholic beverage industry.

adjusted to avoid delays or waste. On the other hand, the VSM identified the stages of the value chain that represent bottlenecks and those with the highest percentage of defective products. In this sense, the pasteurization and juice-filling stages are the production process bottlenecks, and juice-filling also presents the highest rate of faulty products (d = 5%). The previous results show the need to analyze the causes that affect lost time or non-added value and the inefficiency of the production process.

4.3 Analyze Phase

After the results were obtained in the diagnostic stage, we analyzed the root causes of the delays in the process, represented in high times of non-added value. Initially, the internal activities of the process that contribute to the increase in non-added value time were analyzed. In this sense, the activities that generate the most significant loss of time on the production line are flavor change (51.2%), filling (9.0%), equipment cleaning (8.6%), and blowing (6.4%), for which while interdisciplinary project team focused on the loss of time due to flavor change.

Subsequently, meetings were held with the work team and operators to establish the leading causes of time losses in the production line and in flavor change activities, which affect the pasteurization and juice filling processes and, therefore, the production process. The results revealed that the causes of the lost time in the flavor change are the following: lack of supervision by analysts regarding alarms or failures of the pasteurization equipment, lack of technicians in the installation of fake bottles, lack of technicians in the disassembly of false bottles, The "2- Post-prod-soda" recipe of the pasteurizer is not optimized, the activities for the installation of false bottles exceed the time, the

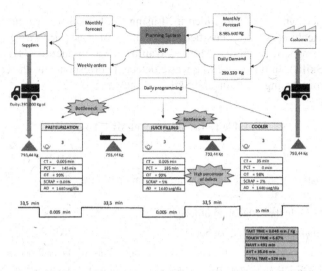

Fig. 4. Value Stream Mapping for the production line juice manufacturing in non-alcoholic beverage industry.

activities for the disassembly of false bottles and lubrication exceed the required time, the on and off setting control parameters are not set, the steam valve control parameters are not set, the soda pump is incorrectly located, there is no ladder, the fat machine has an obsolete technology and the filler constantly runs out of lubrication. Based on these identified causes, the Ishikawa diagram shown in Fig. 5 was created.

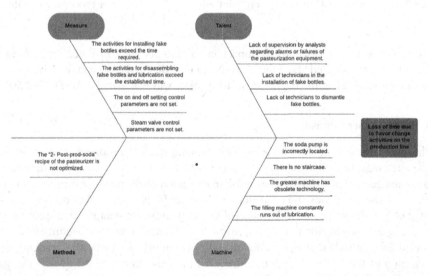

Fig. 5. Cause-and-effect analysis for the production line juice manufacturing in non-alcoholic beverage industry.

On the other hand, the causes identified using the Ishikawa Diagram through the TIMWOODS technique were classified into sources of waste according to the Lean philosophy (Transport, Inventory, Motion, Waiting, Overproduction, Overprocessing, Defects, and Skills). In this sense, the waste detected corresponds to the categories of Waiting, Overprocessing, Motion, and Skills, as shown in Table 1.

Table 1. Identification of MUDAS

Cause	MUDA Type
Lack of supervision by analysts regarding alarms or failures of the pasteurization equipment	Skills
Lack of technicians in the installation of fake bottles	Skills
Lack of technicians to dismantle fake bottles	Skills
The "2- post-prod-soda" recipe of the pasteurizer is not optimized	Over Processing
The activities for installing fake bottles exceed the time required	Waiting
The activities for disassembling false bottles and lubrication exceed the established time	Waiting
The on and off setting control parameters are not set	Over Processing
Steam valve control parameters are not set	Over Processing
The soda pump is incorrectly located	Motion
There is no staircase	Motion
The grease machine has obsolete technology	Over Processing - Waiting
The filling machine constantly runs out of lubrication	Over Processing - Waiting

Finally, the cost of waste and its impact on profitability was calculated. In this sense, information was collected about the costs of lost time due to flavor change activities lost in the process, which at the beginning of the project was calculated at USD 258,750.

4.4 Improvement Phase

In this phase, the causes identified in the analysis stage were considered, as well as their classification according to the type of Lean waste, to select the most appropriate Lean waste management measures and establish intervention plans to reduce the time lost due to flavor change activities and costs due to lost time. In this regard, the following Lean strategies were implemented: i) Creation of a work team for the continuous improvement of the KAIZEN production line, ii) Improvement of internal activities to reduce lost time (post-production soda recipe, installation and disassembly of fake bottles, tracking and monitoring of the pasteurization machine), iii) implementation of the SMED (Single Minute Exchange of Die) methodology to reduce the time and resources necessary to make flavor changes on the production line. This strategy included the development of training activities for employees, the adjustment of the steam valve, the reduction of unnecessary cold-water time and rapid dosing of soda in the process, the adjustment of the pump on and off parameters. of soda, the relocation of the soda pump to speed up interventions in case of failures and reduce the time lost due to lack of dosage (see Fig. 6.), the reduction in the number of external sprays for cooling, the implementation of a checklist for the assembly and disassembly of false bottles, with assignment of those responsible, increase in the frequency of oil lubrication, as well as the acquisition of a higher technology grease machine as seen in Fig. 7., of an additional ladder, to support the cleaning tasks and the installation of an alarm and remote screen on the pasteurizer near the filler to quickly identify equipment failures and carry out interventions promptly (see Fig. 8).

Fig. 6. Relocation of the soda dosing pump, to facilitate intervention, cleaning and maintenance tasks.

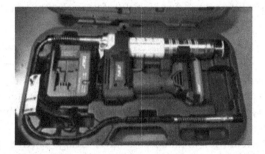

Fig. 7. Purchase of a higher technology grease machine

After 3-month implementation of technical, human, and process strategies, quick wins were obtained that show the importance of using continuous improvement philosophies with Lean. Firstly, the progressive reduction of lost time on the production line associated with flavor change activities is observed from the initial diagnosis to the third month of implementation, in which 12 production cycles were completed. From 234 to 170 min, a reduction of 27.35%, as seen in Fig. 9.

In addition, the Improved Value Stream Mapping was developed (see Fig. 10), in which a slight decrease in the cycle time is observed in the pasteurization and juice filling stages and a 1% reduction in the percentage of defective products in the juice filling stage. When analyzing the VSM in detail, it is evident that one of the primary

Fig. 8. Installation of remote screen and alarm in the pasteurization machine

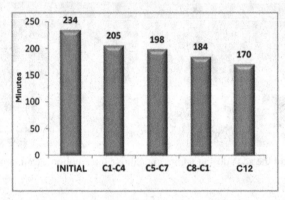

Fig. 9. The comparison between lost times initial (before implementation improvement plans) and after improvement.

early victories is associated with the reduction of times due to changes in the product, in which cleaning activities due to a change in flavor intervene. In this sense, the product change times for the pasteurization stage were reduced by 17.2%, going from 145 min to 120 min, while the product change time for the Juice Filling stage obtained a reduction of 13.5%, going from 185 min to 160 min, as seen in Table 2.

As a result of the reduction in time lost to flavor change activities in the juice manufacturing line, the second early victory was the reduction in costs due to lost time in flavor change activities, with a decrease in costs of 21.35%, going from USD 258,750 to USD 203,500, as seen in Fig. 11.

However, more improvement cycles are required with the Lean philosophy to improve cycle times and non-added value times in the different lines and stages of the productive process, to increase productivity, improve quality, and achieve the continuous satisfaction of its clients and interest groups as well as the financial sustainability of the company.

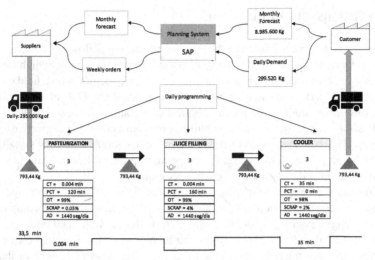

Fig. 10. Improved Value Stream Mapping for the production line juice manufacturing in non-alcoholic beverage industry.

Table 2. Comparison Product change time (min)

Activity	Product Change Time (min)		
	Before Lean	After Lean	% Reduction
Pasteurization	145	120	17,2%
Juice Filling	185	160	13,5%

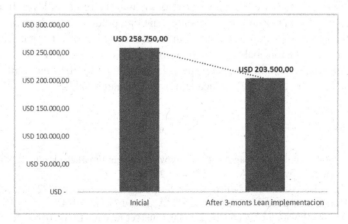

Fig. 11. Cost reduction in lost time due to flavor change.

5 Conclusions and Future Work

This paper presents the application of the lean manufacturing philosophy to obtain quick wins in productivity and costs in a non-alcoholic beverage company, which has been successfully implemented in various industrial and service sectors, with a field of action still being developed in the non-alcoholic beverage industry. One of the significant contributions of this study is the methodological contribution to the sector under study since it shows the application of the Lean philosophy from a practical perspective focused on the needs of the business and its interest groups. It considers this industry's challenges, such as high competitiveness, emerging competitors, product diversification, resource optimization, and the development of clean operations.

This project was developed in a large company in the non-alcoholic beverage sector, recognized in Latin America and is an ally of one of the most valuable companies in the segment. Significant results were obtained through a 4-phase methodology, which combined technical and process elements and human and administrative elements. A first early Victory was the reduction in the times lost in the process, mainly attributed to the times lost by flavor change activities, whose times went from 234 min to 170 min. The Second Early Victory reduced costs due to decreased time lost in flavor change, from USD 258,750 to USD 203,500. The third early victory obtained was incorporating a corporate culture oriented on quality and continuous improvement through permanent training in continuous improvement tools and Lean tools, as well as the formation and formalization of work teams focused on reducing non-value added time or waste time.

The results of the Lean philosophy give rise to the development of new projects for the continuous improvement of companies, extending its application to other industrial and service sectors to evaluate their productivity, quality, and profitability impact. However, future studies could focus on studying other implications of the Lean philosophy and its quick-wins at the environmental level, occupational health and safety, and organizational climate, which are still under development at the research level. In addition, other studies can focus on adopting strategies that can potentiate the benefits of Lean, such as industry 4.0 / 5.0, project management, the adoption of quantitative methods and multi-criteria decision-making, sustainability, and social responsibility. Corporate, among others, would expand the spectrum of opportunities for the Lean philosophy in the industrial, commercial, services, academic, and research fields.

References

1. Statista, Non-alcoholic Beverages. https://www.statista.com/markets/415/topic/997/non-alc oholic-beverages/#overview. Accessed 29 Feb 2024
2. Dingwall, K.: The No-Alcohol Drinks Market Surpassed $11 Billion In 2022, The No-Alcohol Drinks Market Surpassed $11 Billion in 2022. Accessed 29 Feb 2024
3. Ridder, M.: Worldwide non-alcoholic beverage market revenue from 2016 to 2027. https://www.statista.com/forecasts/1206691/market-value-non-alcoholic-beverages-worldwide. Accessed 20 Feb 2024
4. Jimenez, G., et al.: Improvement of productivity and quality in the value chain through lean manufacturing - A case study. Procedia Manuf. **41**, 882–889 (2019). https://doi.org/10.1016/j.promfg.2019.10.011

5. Rodrigues, J., Sá, J., Silva, F.J.G., Ferreira, L.P., Jimenez, G., Santos, G.: A rapid improvement process through "Quick-Win" lean tools: a case study. Systems **8**, 55 (2020). https://doi.org/10.3390/systems8040055

6. Azevedo, J., Sá, J., Santos, G., Cruz, F., Jimenez, G., Silva, F.: Improvement of production line in the automotive industry through lean philosophy. Procedia Manuf. **41**, 1023–1030 (2019)

7. Sá, J.C., et al.: Assessing the impact of lean tools on production and safety by a multicriteria decision-making model and statistical analysis: a case study in textile sector. In: Stephanidis, C., Duffy, V.G., Krömker, H., Nah, F.-H., Siau, K., Salvendy, G., Wei, J. (eds.) HCII 2021. LNCS, vol. 13097, pp. 616–638. Springer, Cham (2021). https://doi.org/10.1007/978-3-030-90966-6_42

8. Jiménez-Delgado, G., et al.: Implementation of Lean Six Sigma to improve the quality and productivity in textile sector: a case study. In: Duffy, V.G. (ed.) HCII 2023. LNCS, vol. 14028, pp. 395–412. Springer, Cham (2023). https://doi.org/10.1007/978-3-031-35741-1_30

9. Ortiz-Barrios, M., Coba-Blanco, D., Jiménez-Delgado, G., Salomon, V.A.P., López-Meza, P.: Implementation of Lean Six Sigma to lessen waiting times in public emergency care networks: a case study. In: Stephanidis, C., et al. (eds.) HCII 2021. LNCS, vol. 13097, pp. 83–93. Springer, Cham (2021). https://doi.org/10.1007/978-3-030-90966-6_7

10. Ortíz-Barrios, M., McClean, S., Jiménez-Delgado, G., Martínez-Sierra, D.E.: Integrating Lean Six Sigma and discrete-event simulation for shortening the appointment lead-time in gynecobstetrics departments: a case study. In: Duffy, V.G. (ed.) HCII 2020. LNCS, vol. 12199, pp. 378–389. Springer, Cham (2020). https://doi.org/10.1007/978-3-030-49907-5_27

11. Postobon. "¿Quiénes somos?". https://appurl.io/yuinfAlONW. Accessed 24 Aug 2023

12. Postobon. "Informe de sostenibilidad: Avanzar hacia un mundo sostenible". https://appurl.io/rkGiY6bGDI. Accessed 09 June 2023

13. Molina Montoya, N.P.: "¿Qué es el estado del arte?," Ciencia & Tecnología para la Salud Visual y Ocular, no. 5, p. 73 (2005). https://doi.org/10.19052/sv.1666

14. Huertas Soria, M.L.: Propuesta de mejora de procesos utilizando herramientas de lean manufacturing en la línea de producción de yogurt de una empresa láctea de la ciudad de Arequipa (2019)

15. Gonzales, V., John, W., Gonzales, W.J.V., De, P.: Propuesta de mejora de procesos en la producción de bebidas alcohólicas utilizando herramientas del Lean Manufacturing (2023)

16. Valderrama, M.: Propuesta de mejora para la reducción de tiempos en el proceso productivo para uvas de mesa variedad Red Globe aplicando herramientas Lean Manufacturing. Universidad Peruana de Ciencias Aplicadas (UPC), p. 258 (2018)

17. Fiorella, K.: Propuesta para optimizar el proceso de producción en una empresa panificadora aplicando lean manufacturing. Universidad Peruana de Ciencias Aplicadas (UPC) (2021). https://repositorioacademico.upc.edu.pe/handle/10757/656057

18. Acevedo Ramírez, L.M., Rodríguez Pérez, W.P.: Propuesta de implementación de herramientas Lean Manufacturing. Caso de estudio: Laboratorios de pesaje una empresa del sector químico en Guarne Antioquia. Universidad ECCI (2021)

19. Vasquez, P.: Aplicación de herramientas de Lean Manufacturing para mejorar la eficiencia en la Línea de Embotellado en una industria vitivinícola. Universidad Ricardo Palma (2021). https://repositorio.urp.edu.pe/bitstream/handle/20.500.14138/4619/M-ECOL-T030_46021444_MMARINSANCHEZUlert.pdf?sequence=1

20. Manyari Taipe, E.O.: Propuesta De Implementación De La Metodología Smed En El Área De Inyección De Accesorios De Pvc, Para Incrementar La Disponibilidad De Los Equipos De La Empresa Mexichem Perú, El Agustino-2019 (2020). https://orcid.org/0000-0002-7266-4290

21. Rahmanasari, D., Sutopo, W., Rohani, J.M.: Implementation of lean manufacturing process to reduce waste: a case study. In: IOP Conference Series: Materials Science and Engineering, vol. 1096, no. 1, p. 012006 (2021). https://doi.org/10.1088/1757-899x/1096/1/012006

22. Abu, F., Gholami, H., Zameri Mat Saman, M., Zakuan, N., Streimikiene, D.: The implementation of lean manufacturing in the furniture industry: a review and analysis on the motives, barriers, challenges, and the applications. J. Clean Prod. **234** (2019). https://doi.org/10.1016/j.jclepro.2019.06.279

23. Kovacs, G.: Application of lean methods for improvement of manufacturing processes. Acad. J. Manuf. Eng. **15**(2) (2017)

24. Aguirre Alvarez, Y.: Análisis de las herramientas Lean Manufacturing para la eliminación de desperdicios en las Pymes. Universidad Nacional de Colombia (2015)

25. Rodriguez, J.: Método Kaizen: definición, pasos y ejemplos. https://bit.ly/448WUyj. Accessed 15 Mar 2022

26. Martinez Tubay, H.T., Alexandra, M., Rivas, A.: Optimización de procesos de control de inventarios en bodegas de Industrial Juvenalis S.A. Universidad de Guayaquil (2016). http://repositorio.ug.edu.ec/bitstream/redug/19240/1/LAFRANQUICIACOMOPLANDENEGOCIOSALTERNATIVAPARAELEMPRENDIMIENTOENELECUADOR.pdf

27. Almomani, M.A., Aladeemy, M., Abdelhadi, A., Mumani, A.: A proposed approach for setup time reduction through integrating conventional SMED method with multiple criteria decision-making techniques. Comput. Ind. Eng. **66**(2) (2013). https://doi.org/10.1016/j.cie.2013.07.011

28. Khusaini, N.S., Jaffar, A., Yusoff, N.: A survey on lean manufacturing tools implementation in Malaysian food and beverages industry using Rasch model. Adv. Mat. Res. **845**, 642–646 (2014). https://doi.org/10.4028/www.scientific.net/AMR.845.642

29. Norman, A.A.P., Kuncorosidi, Rosmalia, R.: Application of lean manufacturing in the canned food and beverage industry: literature review. Diskursus Ilmu Manajemen STIESA (Dimensia) **19**(1), 115–140 (2023). https://ojs.stiesa.ac.id/index.php/dimensia

30. Riad Bin Ashraf, S., Rashid Mahi, M., Mynur Rashid, M., Harunur Rashid, A.R.M.: Implementation of 5S methodology in a food & beverage industry: a case study. Int. J. Eng. Technol. **4**(3), 1791–1796 (2017). www.irjet.net

31. Nomikou, M.G., Konstantinou, P.: The combination of lean manufacturing methodology and innovation in the beverage business. In: 1st International Conference on Sustainable Chemical and Environmental Engineering, Athens, pp. 184–185 (2022)

32. Chen, X., Tobias, V.: Implementation of the manufacturing execution system in the food and beverage industry. J. Food Eng. **278** (2020). https://doi.org/10.1016/j.jfoodeng.2020.109932

33. Lopes, R.B., Freitas, F., Sousa, I.: Application of lean manufacturing tools in the food and beverage industries. J. Technol. Manag. Innov. **10**(3), 120–130 (2015). https://doi.org/10.4067/s0718-27242015000300013

34. Cabrera, J.L., Corpus, O.A., Maradiegue, F., Álvarez Merino, J.C.: Improving quality by implementing lean manufacturing, SPC, and HACCP in the food industry: a case study. S. Afr. J. Ind. Eng. **31**(4), 194–207 (2020). https://doi.org/10.7166/31-4-2363

User Demand-Oriented Evaluation of Outdoor Unit of Air Conditioner

Weilin Liu and Chunfeng Xu[✉]

Qingdao University of Technology, Shandong 266520, China
xuchunfeng202@163.com

Abstract. Whether the design of outdoor air conditioning units can meet the actual needs of users and provide them with a good user experience directly affects product sales and subsequent user loyalty to the product and even the brand. A method for evaluating outdoor unit of air conditioner is proposed from the perspective of meeting user expectations. Evaluation indicators from four aspects: cost, achievable functionality, intelligence, and appearance. Firstly, based on the investigation and analysis of the target users of outdoor air conditioning units, four evaluation indicators are given. Then, the Analytic Hierarchy Process is applied to weight the evaluation indicators and determine the importance of each evaluation indicator. Finally, the TOPSIS method is applied to calculate the evaluation values of different schemes, achieving quantitative evaluation of different schemes. In the research case of A Company's air conditioning B outdoor unit development project, the evaluation values of the alternative solutions were calculated to be 54.25%, 66.16%, and 41.70%, respectively. Finally, M2 was selected as the optimal solution. The engineering practice also verified the evaluation method proposed in this article and achieved good results.

Keyword: User Demand-oriented · Air conditioning outdoor unit · Analytic Hierarchy Process · TOPSIS

1 Introduction

With the ongoing deterioration of global climate conditions, the intensification of high temperature weather events, and the gradual shift in the global consumer market towards customer-centricity, air conditioning enterprises are facing an increasingly competitive environment. To effectively respond to diverse user needs and market demands, enterprises must swiftly acquire competitive advantages through product innovation. The innovative design of air conditioning products presents significant opportunities for enterprises within this complex and dynamic competitive landscape. Pre-evaluation of innovative design schemes plays a crucial role in the product development process before formal prototype production as it aids in assessing the overall achievement of design objectives [1]. Furthermore, consumers (i.e., users) hold considerable influence over air conditioning product designs. Therefore, technological innovation should be considered alongside user-centered design principles during product development to meet actual

V. G. Duffy (Ed.): HCII 2024, LNCS 14709, pp. 295–307, 2024.
https://doi.org/10.1007/978-3-031-61060-8_21

user requirements. Creating a positive user experience and subsequently enhancing satisfaction have become pivotal starting points for evaluating innovative design schemes during the research and development stage of air conditioning products. This study focuses on outdoor units—an essential component of air conditioning systems—and proposes an evaluation method for designing such units to support scientific assessment of innovative product designs by air conditioning enterprises.

The air conditioner outdoor unit is an important part of the split air conditioner and plays an important role in providing users with a comfortable microclimate. Under the guidance of user needs, purposeful evaluation and selection of multiple options for outdoor unit alternative designs can highlight product advantages and characteristics and achieve product innovation. In current practice, the design of outdoor units is mainly carried out by the product R&D department by combining the knowledge and experience of technology and R&D personnel to independently design product solutions. The design solution takes functional realization as the core goal. As the level of homogeneity of product functions becomes higher and higher, users pay more attention to whether the products can bring them a better experience when choosing to buy air-conditioning products. Therefore, with the introduction of advanced design concepts such as "user-centered", "emotional design" and "perceptual design", and their application in practice have become more and more prominent (such as Apple's user experience design, Mitsubishi Motors Perceptual driving platform design), more and more companies are beginning to think about how to integrate users' real needs (functional and emotional) into product design. It is necessary and meaningful to fully consider user needs in the design of air conditioner outdoor units.

In the product design stage, many design plans are usually generated. The evaluation of design plans is to evaluate multiple alternatives and select the design plan that best meets the requirements. In recent years, with the continuous development and evolution of product evaluation methods, many scholars have begun to develop a series of evaluation methods based on traditional product evaluation methods that are more suitable for modern multi-attribute characteristics. For example, Fang Hui [2] combined rough set theory with the uncertainty language multi-attribute decision-making method to construct an evaluation model suitable for product design solutions; Zhai et al. [3] used rough sets to express the uncertainty of information and combined it with gray Correlation methods are combined to evaluate alternatives; Lin Xiaohua et al. [4] proposed a multi-objective decision-making model for product collaborative innovation programs based on fuzzy theory, which quantified and improved the evaluation indicators in the evaluation system. Hu Shan et al. [5] used a weighting method that combined the analytic hierarchy process and the entropy method to evaluate the design of the guide cane. Zhang yinglong et al. [6] used AHP, TOPSIS and GRA methods to construct a TOPSIS-GRA evaluation model, calculate the relative fit level between office seats and ideal solutions, and evaluate and optimize design solutions. After generating a set of feasible solutions according to the genetic algorithm, Huang et al. [7] used fuzzy back propagation (BP) neural network algorithm to evaluate the solution set. Lai [8] proposed a new method of user-oriented design, using perceptual engineering to extract experimental samples, and finally determining the best combination of product form and product color based on neural network theory. The evaluation of these methods is objective and scientific.

However, few existing research results are aimed at air-conditioning product design solutions, and the evaluation index system for air-conditioning outdoor unit design solutions that considers the actual needs of users is not clear. Existing research results are in there is still a lot of room for improvement in solving the problem of outdoor unit design evaluation.

Therefore, this article starts from the user demand orientation and selects the outdoor unit of company A as a case. On the basis of accurately identifying the user's needs for outdoor unit products, it combines the analytic hierarchy process and the approximate ideal solution ranking method to complete the design stage of the air conditioner outdoor unit. Plan evaluation provides new ideas and method reference for the multi-factor evaluation of outdoor unit design plans [9].

2 Air Conditioning Outdoor Unit Evaluation Method

2.1 Establishment of Evaluation Index Matrix

Firstly, n evaluation indicators of the outdoor unit design scheme are extracted through user demand investigation, and the evaluation index matrix Y is formed according to m sample data of the selected n evaluation indicators.

$$Y = \begin{bmatrix} Y_{11} & Y_{12} & \cdots & Y_{1n} \\ Y_{21} & Y_{22} & \cdots & Y_{2n} \\ \vdots & \vdots & \vdots & \vdots \\ Y_{m1} & Y_{m2} & \cdots & Y_{mn} \end{bmatrix} \tag{1}$$

Then, the samples are standardized to eliminate the original dimensions of each indicator, making them comparable and forming a new matrix X.

$$\overline{Y_j} = \frac{1}{m} \sum_{i=1}^{m} Y_{ij} \quad (j = 1, 2, \cdots, n) \tag{2}$$

$$S_j^2 = \frac{1}{m-1} \sum_{i=1}^{m} (Y_{ij} - \overline{Y_j})^2 \quad (j = 1, 2, \cdots, n) \tag{3}$$

$$X_{ij} = \frac{Y_{ij} - \overline{Y_j}}{S_j} \tag{4}$$

$$X = \begin{bmatrix} X_{11} & X_{12} & \cdots & X_{1n} \\ X_{21} & X_{22} & \cdots & X_{2n} \\ \vdots & \vdots & \vdots & \vdots \\ X_{m1} & X_{m2} & \cdots & X_{mn} \end{bmatrix} \tag{5}$$

2.2 Applying Hierarchical Analysis to Determine the Weights of Evaluation Indicators

AHP method has the advantages of classifying evaluation indicators and stratifying them step by step. It can build an evaluation index system composed of target layer, criterion layer and index layer from top to bottom. Meanwhile, it can make use of the influence degree of lower index on adjacent upper index to assign weight to evaluation index.

First, the judgment matrix scale is determined. The binary comparison method is used to compare the indicators of the same layer in pairwise, and the indicators are assigned values from 1 to 9 according to their relative importance, as shown in Table 1.

Table 1. Comparison Scale

scale	hidden meaning	scale	hidden meaning
1	The two elements are of equal importance in comparison	7	The former is more strongly important than the latter when comparing the two elements
3	The former is slightly more important than the latter when comparing the two elements	9	The former is extremely more important than the latter when comparing the two elements
5	When comparing the two elements, the former is significantly more important than the latter	2, 4, 6, 8	Intermediate values of the above adjacent judgments
countdown	The two elements are compared, with the latter having a higher importance scale than the former		

Next, construct the judgment matrix. Let m elements (programs or goals) on a criterion there is relative importance, according to Table 1, the ith element (i = 1, 2, … ,m) and other elements two by two comparison of the judgment, the relative importance of the scale for aij (j = 1, 2, …, m), the construction of the m-order matrix used to solve the elements on a criterion of the priority of the weight, which is called the weight resolution judgment matrix, referred to as A = (aij) m n. It is called the weight resolution judgment matrix, or judgment matrix for short, notated as A = (aij) m × n.

After that, to find the normalized relative importance of each element with respect to a certain element (criterion, etc.) in the subsuperior layer.

$$W_i = \left(\prod_{j=1}^{n} a_{ij} \right)^{\frac{1}{n}} \tag{6}$$

$$W_i^0 = \frac{W_i}{\sum_i W_i} \tag{7}$$

Then, the consistency test of the judgment matrix of each stratum is carried out to find λmi: Since the judgment matrix is affected by the different degrees of multi-layer indicators and the subjective experience of the decision maker interferes, it is inevitable that there is an error. Therefore, in order to avoid the error is too large, resulting in the judgment results deviate from the objective reality, need to judgment matrix consistency test. Where: C.R. is the consistency ratio; C.I. is the consistency index, n is the order of the judgment matrix; R.I. is the random consistency index, when the order of the judgment matrix were 1, 2, ..., 14, through the table to determine the R.I. If C.R. < 0.1, the judgment matrix is considered to be through the consistency test. Otherwise, the matrix should be re-compare the value, until it passes the consistency test. Comparison of values until the consistency test is passed.

$$\lambda_{mi} = \frac{\sum\limits_{j=1}^{n} a_{ij} W_j}{W_i} \tag{8}$$

$$\lambda_{\max} \approx \frac{1}{n} \sum\limits_{i=1}^{n} \lambda_{mi} \tag{9}$$

Calculate consistency indicator C.I and consistency ratio C.R.

$$C.R. = \frac{C.I.}{R.I.} < 0.1 \tag{10}$$

$$C.I. = \frac{\lambda_{\max} - n}{n - 1} \tag{11}$$

Find the corresponding average random consistency indicator R.I (Table 2).

Table 2. Scale of comparison

n	1	2	3	4	5	6	7	8	9	10	11	12	13	14
R.I	0	0	0.52	0.89	1.12	1.26	1.36	1.41	1.46	1.49	1.52	1.54	1.56	1.58

Finally, the calculation of the relative weight or importance vector W of the indicators is carried out by the summation method (arithmetic average method). That is, the elements of A are normalized by column, and then the normalized columns are summed, and the summed vector is divided by n to obtain the weight vector.

$$Wi = \frac{1}{n} \sum\limits_{j=1}^{n} \frac{aij}{\sum\limits_{k=1}^{n} akj} \qquad (i = 1, 2, \cdots, n) \tag{12}$$

$$W = (W1, W2, ..., Wn) \tag{13}$$

2.3 Application of TOPSIS Analysis to Calculate the Closeness of Evaluation Schemes

The basic principle of the Approximate Ideal Solution Ranking Method (TOPSIS) [10–12] is to set the positive and negative ideal solutions of the programs, and rank them according to the size of the distance of the programs to be selected to the positive and negative ideal solutions. The positive ideal solution is a virtual optimal solution, in which all evaluation indexes are optimal values, while the negative ideal solution is a virtual worst solution, which contains evaluation indexes that are the worst values. If the solution to be selected is the closest to the positive ideal solution and at the same time the farthest from the negative ideal solution, the solution is the optimal solution, and vice versa is the worst solution.

Since the actual evaluation indexes have different outlines and units and are not comparable, the evaluation indexes need to be non-outlined first to eliminate the non-metricity of the indexes.

$$Z = Y'W = \begin{bmatrix} Y'_{11} & Y'_{12} & \cdots & Y'_{1n} \\ Y'_{21} & Y'_{22} & \cdots & Y'_{2n} \\ \vdots & \vdots & \vdots & \vdots \\ Y'_{m1} & Y'_{m2} & \cdots & Y'_{mn} \end{bmatrix} \begin{bmatrix} W_1 & 0 & \cdots & 0 \\ 0 & W_2 & \cdots & 0 \\ \vdots & \vdots & \vdots & \vdots \\ 0 & 0 & \cdots & W_n \end{bmatrix} = \begin{bmatrix} Z_{11} & Z_{12} & \cdots & Z_{1n} \\ Z_{21} & Z_{22} & \cdots & Z_{2n} \\ \vdots & \vdots & \vdots & \vdots \\ Z_{m1} & Z_{m2} & \cdots & Z_{mn} \end{bmatrix} \quad (14)$$

In the formula, wj is the weight of the jth indicator.

$$Z_j^+ = \left\{ (\max(Z_{ij}), j \in J^*), (\min(Z_{ij}), j \in J^-) \right\}$$
$$Z_j^- = \left\{ (\min(Z_{ij}), j \in J^*), (\max(Z_{ij}), j \in J^-) \right\} \quad (15)$$

In the formula, J* is the set of effectiveness indicators (the larger the value of the indicator, the better); J− is the set of cost-based indicators (the smaller the value of the indicator, the better).

Then, the distance to the positive ideal point Si+ and the distance to the negative ideal point Si− are calculated for each program.

$$S_i^+ = \sqrt{\sum_{j=1}^{n} (Z_{ij} - Z_j^+)^2}, i = 1, 2, 3 \cdots, m$$

$$S_i^- = \sqrt{\sum_{j=1}^{n} (Z_{ij} - Z_j^-)^2}, i = 1, 2, 3 \cdots, m$$
$$(16)$$

Finally, the relative closeness Ci of each scheme is calculated and ranked according to the magnitude of the relative closeness of each scheme, the larger the value the better, and the optimal solution of the index layer is found.

$$C_i = \frac{S_i^-}{S_i^+ + S_i^-} (i = 1, 2, 3 \cdots, m) \quad (17)$$

2.4 Conducting Optimal Comprehensive Evaluation

Multiply the closeness matrix C of the evaluation object to the positive ideal solution and the corresponding indicator weight vector W to get the comprehensive evaluation result vector M. The optimal solution is determined according to the final evaluation value of each program, i.e., the maximum value of the final evaluation value is the optimal solution for the overall program decision.

$$M = W \times C \tag{18}$$

3 Example Application

3.1 Case Overview - Company A Air Conditioner Outdoor Unit B

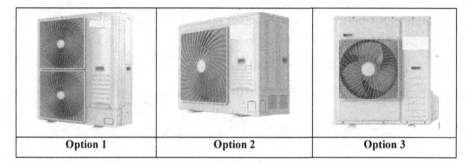

Option 1	Option 2	Option 3

Fig. 1. Alternative design options for air conditioning

Company A launched a comfort air conditioner B for the domestic home decoration area, which can be used in family living rooms. The split air conditioner has a cooling capacity of 7200W, which meets the national energy efficiency certification standards and can be used in the T1 working environment in mainland China. There are three options for the design of its outdoor unit (see Table 3). The first alternative is with a height of 1170 mm. It adopts a double-fan appearance to achieve large air volume heat dissipation. It has a hidden stop valve installation and connection method. The overall appearance is relatively wide and thick. It can be installed in four directions and has optional intelligent control. The second alternative is a height of 845 mm, with a single fan appearance, large air volume design, wider width, hidden stop valve installation and connection method, the overall appearance is relatively solid, and can be installed in three directions, with optional Equipped with an intelligent controller; the third alternative is with a height of 970 mm, which can be completely installed under the outdoor window sill. It adopts a single fan appearance and an open stop valve installation and connection method. The overall appearance is relatively solid and can be installed in three directions. Comes with optional smart controller (Fig. 1).

3.2 Selection of Evaluation Indicators

By collecting comments about outdoor units from the comments about air conditioners on JD.com, Gome and other platforms, and combi on this, a level 2 user questionnaire was designed and surveyed in the form of options. Through random distribution of paper questionnaires in offline physical stores such as Gome and Suning, a total of 162 copies were distributed and 161 were recovered. After screening, 1 invalid questionnaire was eliminated, and the final number of valid questionnaires was 160, with an effective rate of 98.75%. The basic distribution of the surveyed population: there are more males, 60 people, accounting for 37.5%, and 100 females, accounting for 62.5%, and the proportion of males is low; in terms of age, they are basically distributed in the 31–45 age group, the largest number of people are those aged 36–40, followed by those aged 31–35, accounting for 23.75%, while the proportion of those aged 45 and above is lower, indicating that the purchasing crowd is relatively young. In terms of academic qualifications, the largest number of people are 56 with bachelor's degrees, accounting for 35%. Among them, the number of people with master's degrees and doctoral degrees are 43 and 13 respectively, indicating that the purchasers have higher academic qualifications. The number of married people is 146, and the number of unmarried people is 14, indicating that more purchasers are getting married and starting a business (Fig. 2).

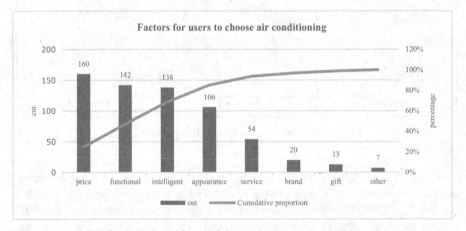

Fig. 2. Statistics of factors for users to choose air conditioners

The key factors for users to choose air conditioning are price, function, intelligence, and appearance, accounting for a total of 85.31%; The overall price, optional parts, and installation prices in the price factor account for a total of 81.25%; The functional factors include fast cooling and fast heating, self-cleaning, variable frequency, and air volume, accounting for a total of 89.58%; Among the intelligent factors, visualization, multi-dimensional control, and online upgrading account for a total of 87.5%; Among the appearance factors, appearance screws, built-in stop valves, number of fans, aspect ratio, and multi-directional installation account for a total of 89.58%. The final evaluation index system includes four dimensions (i.e. price, functionality, intelligence, and appearance), as well as 15 indicators, as shown in Fig. 3.

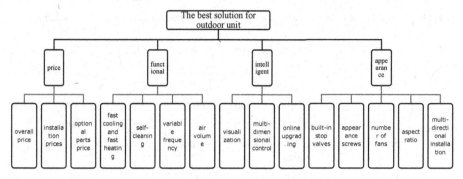

Fig. 3. Evaluation index system of outdoor unit

For the overall outdoor unit of the air conditioner, the first thing that is perceived is the appearance, that is, the appearance and design layout of the product, which is specifically divided into the aspect ratio of the outdoor unit, the number of fans, whether the connection stop valve is built-in, and the number and appearance screws. The directionality of connection and installation will affect the overall beauty of the product. In addition to the aspect ratio requirements, attention should be paid to the control of height dimensions. In the current design of high-rise residential buildings, the outdoor unit is generally installed below the window. Therefore, when designing the size of the outdoor unit, it should be avoided to block the view of the window and affect the user's use.

Secondly, in addition to the basic cooling and heating functions, the functional configuration of the outdoor unit of the air conditioner also involves users' requirements for new functions, such as rapid cooling and rapid heating, outdoor unit self-cleaning, variable frequency environmental protection and large air volume.

In terms of intelligence, air conditioners should now pay more attention to visual control, so that more young users can like it. Multiple interaction methods enable the use of line controllers, remote controls and mobile APPs, which are convenient and smart. For remote start, you can turn on the air conditioner in advance when you go home and achieve zero waiting. Online upgrades allow users to have a clearer understanding of the product during use, and can be maintained remotely if problems arise, saving time on on-site maintenance.

In terms of price, the overall analysis is carried out from three dimensions: the price of the complete machine with basic configuration, the installation price and the price of some optional parts. Outdoor units can be more competitive in the market if they can achieve high performance at a reasonable and advantageous price.

Table 3. Evaluation indicators and alternatives for air conditioning outdoor unit schemes

Target layer A	Criterion layer B	Subcriterion layer C	Scheme 1	Scheme 2	Scheme 3
The best solution for outdoor unit	Price	overall price	1120	890	1030
		installation prices	210	186	198
		optional parts price	390	280	200
	Function	fast cooling and heating	Support	Nonsupport	Support
		self-cleaning	240	310	280
		variable frequency	R32	R32	R410A
		air volume	7000	8000	6000
	Intelligent	visualization	Support	Support	Nonsupport
		multi-dimensional control	Support	Support	Nonsupport
		online upgrading	Support	Support	Nonsupport
	Appearance	built-in stop valves	Support	Support	Nonsupport
		appearance screws	22	20	18
		number of fans	double	single	single
		aspect ratio	0.75	0.48	0.36
		multi-directional installation	Multiple	Multiple	One way

3.3   Determine the Weight of Indicators

First, the AHP was used to construct the A-B judgment matrix of the target layer for the criterion layer, and a total of 61 experts including technical review experts, product managers, marketing managers, professional engineers, process engineers, and test and evaluation engineers of the company's professional technical committee were selected as the survey objects, score according to the comparison scale, and the statistical results are shown in Table 4.

Table 4. A-B judgment matrix

A	B1	B2	B3	B4	weight	normalized weight
B1	1.00	3.00	1.00	1.00	3.00	29.73%
B2	0.33	1.00	0.33	0.33	0.04	9.91%
B3	1.00	3.00	1.00	0.50	1.50	25.00%
B4	1.00	3.00	2.00	1.00	6.00	35.36%

To test the consistency of A-B judgment matrix, from the weight vector, we can get $\lambda\text{max} = 4$, $CI = 0.020145$, and checking the table, we know that $RI = 0.89$, so that $CR = CI/RI = 0.022634 < 0.1$, satisfying the consistency test. Therefore, the weight vector $W0 = [0.2973, 0.0991, 0.2500, 0.3536]$ is within the error range and acceptable. Similarly, the weight coefficients of the evaluation indicators in the indicator layer can be derived.

$W_1 = [0.4286, 0.1429, 0.4286]$
$W_2 = [0.3284, 0.0848, 0.2431, 0.3437]$
$W_3 = [0.2599, 0.4126, 0.3275, 0.3437]$
$W_4 = [0.0989, 0.1883, 0.2261, 0.2984, 0.1883]$

3.4 Calculation of Indicator Closeness

Construct a judgment matrix for the evaluation indicators and perform dimension elimination processing to obtain the matrix:

$$Y' = \begin{pmatrix} 0.92 & 1.00 & 1.05 & 0.58 & -1.04 & 0.58 & 0.00 & 0.58 & 0.58 & 0.58 & 0.58 & 1.00 & 1.15 & 1.10 & 0.58 \\ -1.06 & -1.00 & -0.10 & -1.15 & 0.95 & 0.58 & 1.00 & 0.58 & 0.58 & 0.58 & 0.58 & 0.00 & -0.58 & -0.25 & 0.58 \\ 0.14 & 0.00 & -0.94 & -0.58 & 0.09 & -1.15 & -1.00 & -1.15 & -1.15 & -1.15 & -1.15 & -1.00 & -0.58 & -0.85 & -1.15 \end{pmatrix}$$

$$Z = Y'W$$

The evaluation indicators include the price of the whole machine, the installation price, the price of optional parts, the number of screws on the appearance, the number of fans and the aspect ratio, the smaller the better, rapid cooling and rapid heating, self-cleaning, air volume, control visualization, and multi-control. It can be upgraded online, has a built-in stop valve, and can be installed in multiple directions. The bigger the better, the better. It calculates the positive and negative ideal solutions, as well as the distance between the evaluation object and the ideal solution:

$$S^+ = \begin{Bmatrix} 1.7321 \ 1.1180 \ 0.0000 \ 1.0000 \\ 0.4211 \ 1.0850 \ 1.0850 \ 1.0000 \\ 0.7877 \ 0.5000 \ 0.4286 \ 1.0880 \end{Bmatrix}$$

$$S^- = \begin{Bmatrix} 0.0000 \ 1.5000 \ 1.7321 \ 2.0000 \\ 1.5281 \ 1.7321 \ 1.7321 \ 1.5321 \\ 1.1845 \ 1.1518 \ 0.0000 \ 1.0000 \end{Bmatrix}$$

3.5 Evaluation of the Selection of the Optimal Design Scheme

According to the formula $C_i = \frac{S_i^-}{S_i^+ + S_i^-}(i = 1, 2, 3 \cdots, m)$, the matrix C of the closeness is constructed as:

$$C = \begin{Bmatrix} 0.0000 \ 0.5729 \ 1.0000 \ 0.6667 \\ 0.7840 \ 0.6148 \ 0.6148 \ 0.6049 \\ 0.6006 \ 0.6973 \ 0.0000 \ 0.4789 \end{Bmatrix}$$

Finally, based on the weights of the guideline layer indicators, the combined superiority of the three programs is calculated as:

$$M = (0.5425, 0.6616, 0.4170)$$

In summary, the overall superiority of the design scheme is 47.29%, 71.38% and 38.72%, and the three schemes are ranked as follows: scheme 2 > scheme 1 > scheme 3. Therefore, scheme 2 is the optimal scheme.

4 Conclusion

This article proposes an evaluation method for air conditioner outdoor units that considers the real needs of users, and applies this method to the evaluation of air conditioner outdoor units of Company A. The results achieved: ① Constructed a systematic and hierarchical air conditioner including 15 indicators Evaluation index system for outdoor unit design. This index system can point out the direction for the optimal design of outdoor units. Among them, price, function, intelligence and appearance are the four key aspects that users currently use to evaluate the design of air conditioner outdoor units; ② Established an evaluation index system based on The outdoor unit evaluation method of AHP-TOPSIS can provide method support for subsequent outdoor unit evaluation, and can also provide reference for the design evaluation of similar outdoor unit products; ③ For the case of company A's outdoor unit B, after model calculation, three The comprehensive superiority of the outdoor unit scheme is 54.25%, 66.16%, and 41.70% respectively, that is, scheme 2 is better than scheme 1 and scheme 3, and scheme 2 is determined to be the optimal scheme. Engineering practice results show that the market response to the product design of Plan 2 was good after it was launched. 23,900 units were sold that year and the cost was reduced by 6.008 million. This proves the effectiveness of this research result and can achieve scientific and reasonable selection of air-conditioning outdoor unit product design solutions.

References

1. Li, X., Zhou, D.: Research on design evaluation process and methods for the whole process of enterprise product development. Sci. Technol. Progress Countermeasures **35**(24), 144–149 (2018)
2. Fang, H., Tan, J., Yin, G., Li, Z.: Design program evaluation based on multi-attribute decision making with improved uncertainty language. Comput. Integrated Manuf. Syst. **15**(07), 1257–1261+1269 (2009)
3. Zhai, L.Y., Khoo, L.P., Zhong, Z.W.: Design concept evaluation in product development using rough sets and grey relation analysis. Expert Syst. Appl. **36**(3), 7072–7079 (2009)
4. Lin, X., Feng, Y., Tan, J., et al.: Product conceptual program evaluation based on improved DEMATEL-VIKOR hybrid model. Comput. Integr. Manuf. Syst. **17**(12), 2552–2561 (2011)
5. Hu, S., Liu, J.: Application of fuzzy comprehensive evaluation method in product design program decision-making. Mach. Des. **37**(01) (2020)
6. Zhang, Y.L., Zhang, H.K., Cheng, Z.L.: Application of AHP-TOPSIS-GRA method in the evaluation of office chair design options. J. Forestry Eng. **7**(4), 181–186 (2022)

7. Huang, H.Z., Bo, R., Chen, W.: An integrated computational intelligence approach to product concept generation and evaluation. Mech. Mach. Theory **41**(5), 567–583 (2006)
8. Lai, H.H., Lin, Y.C., Yeh, C.H., et al.: User-oriented design for the optimal combination on product design. Int. J. Prod. Econ. **100**(2), 253–267 (2006)
9. Yang, F.Q., Lin, Z.: Application of ANP-SWOT model in the construction of safety culture on university campuses. Saf. Environ. Eng. **27**(5), 147–152 (2020)
10. Wang, P.: Multi-attribute product decision model for approximating ideal solution and its application. Ind. Technol. Econ. (03), 89–90 (2003)
11. Wang, Y.: System Engineering. Machinery Industry Press, Beijing (2015)
12. Tan, Y.: Quantitative Analysis Methods. Renmin University of China Press, Beijing (2015)

Research on Interface Optimization of Mobile Shopping APP for the Elderly Based on Improved FMEA

Weilin Liu , Fei Wang^(✉) , and Yawei Xue

School of Management Engineering, Qingdao University of Technology, Qingdao 266520,
People's Republic of China
844412316@qq.com

Abstract. The purpose of this study is to improve the satisfaction of elderly user with the interface of mobile shopping apps and optimize the user experience. Firstly, the confusion and problems of the elderly when using mobile shopping APP were understood through interview and observation method, and the potential failure mode was found by using improved FMEA (Failure Mode and Effects Analysis), and the causes and consequences of the potential failure mode were analyzed. Then, a questionnaire survey was conducted to record severity (S), occurrence (O), and detection (D) ratings of relevant potential failure modes, and calculate the ERPN index to identify areas that require improvement. Finally, according to the identified problem points, the feasible suggestions for interface optimization are proposed. Taking the elder mode of Taobao APP as an example, by using the improved FMEA analysis method to find out the problems caused by the elderly when applying the interactive interface and put forward suggestions for improvement, it can not only provide a reference for the future design of such interactive interface, but also optimize the user experience of the elderly and improve their satisfaction.

Keywords: Elderly and innovation · Improved FMEA · Potential failure mode · Mobile shopping APP · Taobao APP elderly mode

1 Introduction

According to statistics, the global elderly population (aged 60 and above) has reached 1 billion in 2019 and will increase to 2–2.1 billion in 2050, accounting for 22% of the global population. China has entered an aging society. The size of the elderly population will be 264 million in 2020 and may reach 480 million in 2050, accounting for more than 30% of China's total population and more than 20% of the global elderly population [1]. Compared with young people, elderly people have obvious differences in physiological function and psychological state, which leads to more errors in interactive interface operation for elderly people than young people. Therefore, it is necessary to conduct differentiated research and age-friendly modifications in human-computer interaction based on the physiological and psychological characteristics of the elderly. Currently,

© The Author(s), under exclusive license to Springer Nature Switzerland AG 2024
V. G. Duffy (Ed.): HCII 2024, LNCS 14709, pp. 308–319, 2024.
https://doi.org/10.1007/978-3-031-61060-8_22

there are few relevant studies on the actual needs of the elderly, and drawbacks have been gradually exposed in the process of human-smartphone interaction. Particularly with the development of e-commerce, the frequency of elderly online shopping is increasing, but the lengthy shopping process and complex operation interfaces often lead to confusion and poor user experience for the elderly.

With the implementation of the "Aging Population Strategy" in China, the Ministry of Industry and Information Technology issued the "Special Action Plan for Aging and Barrier-Free Transformation of Internet Applications" in December 2020, which has greatly promoted the aging transformation of mobile applications. Many mobile shopping apps have also launched versions specifically designed for older adults, commonly known as "elderly versions" or "care versions". These age-appropriate versions generally feature enlarged font size, contrasting colors, and simplified interfaces to facilitate the use of older adults. However, due to the lack of research, these types of app interfaces have posed various problems for elderly users. Therefore, appropriate methods are needed to explore and improve the problems caused by the elderly when using mobile shopping apps and make improvements to enhance their satisfaction and optimize user experience. This article will analyze the elderly mode launched by Taobao APP, the leading product in the current mobile shopping APP. Based on the analysis results, it will propose optimization suggestions and offer valuable insights for future patterns and versions of mobile apps targeted at the elderly.

2 Literature Review

Currently, in the field of interface design optimization research for the elderly in China: in 2022, Zhou investigated the user experience of the elderly using Taobao from three aspects: interactive experience, emotional experience, and value of use, and proposed design optimization strategies [2]; in 2022, Yun et al. analyzed the interaction characteristics and requirements of the elderly using online shopping software, summarized the interface design principles and design points to improve the user experience of the elderly [3]; in 2018, Liu evaluated and predicted the perceived usability of the homepage interface of shopping websites for elderly users using a combination of subjective evaluation scales and objective eye-tracking measurements, which can accurately and effectively predict the perceived usability of the homepage interface of a shopping website for elderly users [4]. In the use of FMEA analysis method: in 2021, Li et al. proposed a research method based on Failure Modes and Effects Analysis (FMEA) and Fault Tree Analysis (FTA) to improve the satisfaction of the elderly car interfaces and design car interfaces suitable for the elderly [5]; in 2010, Liu et al. proposed a quantitative usability evaluation method based on FMEA to solve the problem that existing methods only evaluate the overall availability of products. Based on common availability evaluation methods, the task set of products is evaluated from effectiveness, efficiency, and subjective satisfaction, and the usability level of the product is calculated [6].

In foreign research, various experts and scholars have put forward their own views on the interface design optimization for elderly users. In 2023, Tsujikawa et al. designed a user-friendly offline robot based on the TCD telephone conversation database, aiming to provide certain psychological support for elderly people living alone. The effectiveness of the robot was verified through experiments with participants involved in the design [7]. In 2023, Ghorayeb et al. collected the needs of elderly people through interviews, observations, and other methods, and designed a smart home display interface through collaborative design by participants and authors [8]. In 2020, Restyandito et al. took elderly people in a Brazilian city as a sample, and demonstrated the importance of elderly people clearly identifying the user's movements in the house through completing tasks using a control system designed by the authors. The findings could help improve elderly people's interaction with smart home systems [9]. In 2020, Bong et al. believed that nostalgic interfaces can promote the elderly's understanding of knowledge. Therefore, they designed, developed, and evaluated an application with a nostalgic interface for the elderly to help them learn new technologies better and more intuitively [10].

The above-mentioned literature represents only a part of the research on interface design optimization for the elderly. However, it is evident that in the current research, the studies on the interface of mobile shopping apps mainly propose optimization suggestions from the perspective of interactive features. There is relatively less systematic analysis of the problems that occur in the entire shopping process during the use of the app. At the same time, Failure Modes and Effects Analysis (FMEA) has been proven to be an effective method to analyze the whole process from the beginning of APP use to the completion of the final task, and discovering the problems that occur during the use of the product. The improved FMEA method used in this paper eliminates the drawbacks of multiplying numerical values in FMEA, making the measurement scale more scientific. It also allows for determining the relative importance of each indicator, making the ranking results more accurate and the sorting process more convenient. Therefore, this paper will use the improved FMEA analysis method to explore potential failure modes in the process of mobile shopping for the elderly, and thus provide certain references for the aging adaptation and interface optimization design of mobile shopping apps.

3   Research Method

FMEA (Failure Mode and Effects Analysis) is an analysis tool proposed by the American aerospace industry in the 1960s. This method is used in the design phase of a product or related system to analyze the various components and branches of engineering products or systems. Identify potential failure modes and analyze their potential consequences and causes in order to react early and improve the quality and safety of the product or system. The main steps involve expert group discussions to identify potential failure modes. A certain number of participants complete related tasks and then rate the severity (S), occurrence (O), and detection (D) of potential failure modes on a scale of 1–10 using a corresponding scoring table through methods such as questionnaires. The Risk Priority Number (RPN) is obtained by multiplying these ratings. If RPN $\geq$ 125, the potential failure mode may cause dangerous consequences, and corrective measures should be taken. If RPN $<$ 125, it indicates that the potential failure mode does not require immediate improvement, but if S $>$ 8, corrective action should still be taken [16]. In order to enhance the evaluation capability of FMEA, Kuei-Hu Chang et al. proposed an improved FMEA method in 2012. This modification involved assigning weights (WS, WO, WD) to severity (S), occurrence (O), and detection (D) respectively, and adjusting the calculation of the Enhanced Risk Priority Number (RPN) to index risk priority index. That is, ERPN = 3WS × S + 3WO × O + 3WD × D, reducing the redundancy of the Risk Priority Number and improving the accuracy of the evaluation results [11].

In the process of analyzing the interface of mobile shopping apps using the improved FMEA analysis method, the analysis steps are as follows:

1. Pre-preparation. First, a group of experts is convened, and the number of experts is controlled to 5–7 people. Secondly, a certain number of elderly subjects were selected, the number of which was fixed at 3–6, and the proportion of those who had used the interactive interface analyzed should be the same as that of those who had not used it. Using interview and observation methods, the whole process of using mobile shopping APP was recorded by video and other means when the elderly used the APP. After that, the expert team analyzed and discussed the use of mobile shopping apps by the elderly through video or record files before the study, and identified the problems caused by the use of mobile shopping apps by the elderly.
2. Identify potential failure modes. A sufficient number of elderly people should be selected as subjects, the number of subjects should not be less than 10, and the subjects here should not be repeated with the subjects in the preliminary preparation. Under the auspices of the experimenter, all subjects were asked to complete the tasks determined in advance, such as completing a series of purchase tasks by operating the mobile shopping APP. After that, various problems that occurred during the completion of the task were recorded and combined with the conclusions drawn by the expert team in the preliminary preparation to identify all potential failure modes.
3. Analyze causes and consequences. After identifying all potential failure modes, the expert team should analyze the causes and consequences of the potential failure modes according to the whole process of the subjects completing the shopping operation, and make an improved FMEA analysis table.
4. Calculate index risk priority number. The scores of severity (S), occurrence (O) and detectability (D) of each potential failure mode were collected for all experimental subjects through a questionnaire survey, and the threshold values of the three values were 1–10. Severity refers to the degree of impact on the user if the potential failure mode occurs. Occurrence degree refers to the frequency of the potential failure mode in the process of using the mobile shopping APP. Detection refers to whether the user can identify the occurrence of the potential failure mode. Next, the expert group proposes weights for the three scores and substitutes them into the formula to calculate the ERPN value.
5. Propose improvement suggestions. All potential failure modes with ERPN ≥ 19.8 (S = 5, O = 5, D = 5) and S > 8 were selected, and suggestions for improvement and optimization were put forward respectively.

4 Case Study

4.1 Research Product Profile

Currently, there has been a gradual increase in the mobile shopping app models for the elderly. Among them, Taobao, as a leading online shopping app, has a large number of customers. On October 12, 2021, Taobao officially announced that it would launch the "elderly mode" in the latest version. Taobao's official introduction states that the platform's aging-friendly transformation (i.e., the introduction of the elderly mode) mainly focuses on three aspects: simplified information, enlarged fonts, and the addition of a voice assistant. These features make it easier for the elderly to access product information and engage in barrier-free online shopping. Open the Taobao APP, click "Mode Switch" in the "Settings" in the upper right corner of "My Taobao", and you can see the selection page of "Standard mode" and "Elderly Mode". After checking "Elderly Mode", you can enter the mode.

According to statistics, as of January 2022, the monthly active number of middle-aged and elderly users of Taobao has reached 140 million. The launch of the elderly mode can make it easier for the elderly to shop online. However, currently, the elderly mode of various apps on the market is generally simple to enlarge the font and simplify the interface, without truly improving the interaction interface based on the needs of the elderly, lacking in personalization. Such interaction interfaces not only fail to bring convenience to the elderly but also make it more difficult for them to operate, reducing the elderly's user experience. Therefore, this article will conduct an improved Failure Modes and Effects Analysis (FMEA) on Taobao's Elderly Mode, identify potential failure modes affecting the elderly's usage, and propose optimization suggestions to provide certain references for the subsequent design of relevant elderly modes for elderly users.

4.2 Research Process

Pre-preparation. First, three subjects were selected to use the elderly mode of the Taobao app for shopping. The three subjects included an elderly person with over a year of experience in using the elderly mode of the Taobao app, an elderly person who had just started using the elderly mode of the Taobao app, and an elderly person who had never used any relevant shopping app before. Subsequently, through the method of observation, visits were made to the homes of the three elderly individuals to observe and record the issues they encountered while using the elderly mode of the Taobao app. Interviews were also conducted to understand the confusion experienced by the elderly participants after using the elderly mode of the Taobao app. Finally, a five-person expert panel was established, which included professional app designers, human factors engineering university professors and students, relevant design professionals, and elderly individuals with significant experience in using mobile apps. In the early stage of the study, the expert panel analyzed and discussed the usage and confusion of the elderly mode of the Taobao app among the three subjects. Finally, the problems that the elderly are prone to when using this model are studied and discussed.

Identify Potential Failure Modes. Ten elderly individuals from Jiaozhou, Qingdao, Shandong Province were selected as subjects (the 10 subjects were different from the 3 subjects in the pre-preparation phase). There were 5 male and 5 female subjects, all aged 60 and above. Among them, 4 individuals had previous experience using the Elderly Mode of the Taobao app, with over a year of operational experience, 3 had just started using the Elderly Mode of Taobao for 1 to 3 months, and the remaining 3 had never used any relevant shopping app. The 10 subjects were required to complete the research tasks individually without any other interference. The tasks included the following steps: first, the subjects opened the Taobao app, which had already been switched to the elderly mode by the experimenter. Second, the subjects searched for the word "books" in the search bar and selected a book they liked from the search results to open and browse. Third, they were to purchase the book and complete the payment. After the payment was completed, they were to return to the main page. During the task, the experimenter recorded any usage problems encountered by the participants, and combined with the analysis of the expert panel in the pre-preparation phase, potential failure modes were determined, as shown in Table 1.

Table 1. Potential failure mode of Taobao APP elder mode

Error number	potential failure mode
A1	Cannot find the search bar
A2	Can not see the price and the number of buyers
A3	Do not understand the meaning of navigation bar
A4	Unable to find the required icon
A5	Cannot see the "User Assurance" location content clearly
A6	Unable to contact customer service
A7	Not sure how to proceed to the next step

Analysis of Causes and Consequences. The expert panel was convened again to analyze the potential failure modes identified from the subjects' experiences. The panel combined the analysis from the pre-preparation phase with their own experiences to discuss the causes and consequences of each potential failure mode. This was done to propose optimization measures based on the causes and consequences.

Calculation of Index Risk Priority Number. A questionnaire survey was distributed to the 10 subjects to investigate the severity (S), occurrence (O), and detection (D) of the problems encountered during the operation. The score range was 1–10, with 1 being the lowest and 10 being the highest. As the elderly have a relatively lower understanding ability, the questionnaire presented the three professional terms in a relatively simple language to prevent abnormal values arising from their lack of understanding. Furthermore, according to the discussion of the expert panel, the weights of severity (S), occurrence (O), and detection (D) were determined as WS = 0.4, WO = 0.35, and WD = 0.25, respectively. The collected S.O.D values are shown in Table 2. The average values of the three numbers were calculated and recorded in Table 3. The index risk priority number (ERPN) was calculated using the formula, and the improved FMEA analysis table was completed for improvement. To ensure data accuracy, the calculated ERPN values were rounded to one decimal place.

Propose Improvement Suggestions. When ERPN $\geq$ 19.8 (S = 5, O = 5, D = 5), it is necessary to propose improvement measures or optimizations. According to Table 3,

Table 2. Improved FMEA test score table

Error number	A1			A2			A3			A4			A5			A6			A7		
subject	S	O	D	S	O	D	S	O	D	S	O	D	S	O	D	S	O	D	S	O	D
subject1	2	3	6	7	3	2	8	8	7	8	4	7	8	9	8	8	6	4	4	3	4
subject2	2	1	1	1	1	5	6	5	6	5	5	7	5	6	6	6	7	5	6	5	5
subject3	2	7	7	8	3	2	4	7	7	3	7	6	8	4	3	2	7	7	4	7	3
subject4	1	5	5	3	4	5	8	4	5	5	6	7	8	7	6	6	8	8	8	4	5
subject5	1	5	6	5	6	6	5	8	7	6	7	7	7	7	4	4	8	8	8	7	7
subject6	2	7	6	7	6	4	8	6	6	3	7	7	6	7	5	5	7	6	6	8	7
subject7	1	1	4	3	3	1	2	4	9	5	4	4	9	5	5	7	6	2	7	3	4
subject8	2	8	8	6	7	7	6	8	7	6	6	8	7	7	7	8	8	6	6	6	8
subject9	2	7	7	4	8	7	9	8	9	6	6	8	7	7	9	6	9	9	7	6	6
subject10	2	8	9	7	5	7	6	6	8	4	8	8	6	7	6	7	8	7	9	8	8

except for the two potential failure modes A1 and A2, the ERPN of the remaining five potential failure modes are all greater than 19.8. Therefore, improvement suggestions will be proposed for these five potential failure modes [17].

1. For potential failure mode A3, it is caused by the lack of clear definition in the navigation bar on the homepage of the Taobao app's elderly mode. As shown in Fig. 1, the "Guardian Health" in the homepage navigation bar is not clearly defined, so the elderly do to not understand the meaning of this position. The original intention of this position is to represent recommended drugs with high sales or essential for the elderly. Therefore, it is suggested to change the "Guardian Health" to "Medicine Section" so that the elderly can more easily understand the intended meaning of the navigation bar [15].
2. Potential failure mode A4 refers to the inability of elderly individuals to find the icons they need on the homepage. As shown in Fig. 2, the homepage of standard mode of Taobao app contains icons such as "Tmall Supermarket" and "Tao Xianda", which are frequently clicked by users during the purchase process. However, in the elderly mode, there are only icons such as "Coin Redemption" and "Fruit Collection", which not only cannot play a relevant role in the purchase of products by the elderly, but also may sometimes mislead the elderly to produce wrong operations. Therefore, to address this potential failure mode, it is suggested to transfer high-frequency icons such as "Tmall Supermarket" that are frequently clicked by elderly individuals to the elderly mode and remove other icons that may cause confusion.
3. For potential failure mode A5, it is caused by the small font size of "User Protection". When users browse products, the user protection enjoyed by the purchase of this product will be displayed in the box, and all the contents of the protection will be displayed after clicking (see Fig. 3 and Fig. 4). The information typically includes details such as whether the product is eligible for a no-reason return or if it includes

Table 3. Improved FMEA analysis table

Error number	Potential failure mode	Potential failure mode consequences	Severity (S)	Potential failure mode cause	Occurrence (O)	Detection (D)	Index risk priority number (ERPN)
A1	Cannot find the search bar	Unable to complete the next action	1.7	The search bar is too small	5.2	5.9	14.6
A2	Can not see the price and the number of buyers	Not familiar with product information	5.1	The interface color is not clearly distinguished	4.6	4.6	18.9
A3	Do not understand the meaning of navigation bar	Poor user experience	6.2	The navigation bar is not clearly defined	6.4	7.1	34.0
A4	Unable to find the required icon	Further operating difficulty	5.1	The icons that users need are not on the home page	6	6.9	26.1
A5	Cannot see the "User Assurance" location content clearly	Unable to understand the required information	7.1	The "User Protection" content font is too small	6.6	5.9	40.4
A6	Unable to contact customer service	Causes users to feel anxious	5.9	The "Customer Service" icon is too small	7.4	6.2	36.1
A7	Not sure how to proceed to the next step	Unable to complete product purchase	6.5	Lack of guidance and prompting	5.7	5.7	31.1

shipping insurance, which is crucial information for users before making a purchase and directly impacts their purchase intent. However, the elderly due to their unique physical abilities, may have difficulty reading this content due to the small font size. Therefore, it is necessary to enlarge and bolden the font at the "User Protection" location, making it easier for elderly individuals to understand the rights and protections associated with their purchases [12].

4. For potential failure mode A6, it is caused by the "Customer Service" icon being too small, leading to some elderly individuals being unable to find it. When elderly

Fig. 1. Homepage of Taobao APP elderly mode

Fig. 2. Homepage of Taobao APP standard mode

individuals seek to understand product details, they may not necessarily navigate to the product details page but instead prefer to contact customer service for information.

Currently, the "Customer Service" icon is too small, causing frustration for elderly individuals if they cannot locate it and directly impacting their user experience with the app. To make it easier for elderly individuals to find the "Customer Service" icon, it is recommended to enlarge the icons at the bottom of the interface, allowing elderly individuals to quickly locate the position of the icon and complete their purchase more efficiently, thereby enhancing the user experience for elderly users [13].

5. When the elderly use Taobao APP, not all of them have the experience of purchasing products using mobile apps, which will lead to the elderly who have just come into contact with Taobao APP and do not know how to place an order to purchase products, resulting in the potential failure mode of A7. To address this issue, the Taobao app's elderly mode should provide appropriate guidance based on the user's experience. For instance, when a new mobile number is used to register on the Taobao app, the app should detect this and provide guidance to the new user through text and arrows, approximately three to five times, before ceasing further guidance. Additionally, a "guide" icon can be added to the interface, allowing elderly users to click on it when they are unable to complete a purchase, thereby facilitating the purchasing process [14].

Fig. 3. Product Browsing Interface

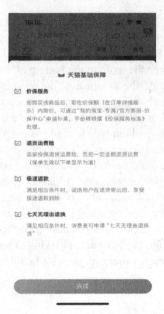

Fig. 4. "User Protection" Details

5   Conclusion

This article is aimed at the elderly, using the improved FMEA analysis method to analyze the interface of mobile shopping apps. Through the improved FMEA analysis of the elderly mode of the leading mobile shopping app, Taobao, it is found that elderly users may encounter potential failure modes such as cannot find the search bar, cannot see the price and the number of buyers, do not understand the meaning of navigation bar, unable to find the required icon, cannot see the "User Assurance" location content clearly, unable to contact customer service and not sure how to proceed to the next step. The ERPN values of the potential failure modes are calculated, and corresponding optimization solutions are proposed for failure modes with ERPN $\geq$ 19.8, which provides a practical reference for improving the satisfaction and user experience of the elderly when using shopping apps. Improved FMEA not only identifies potential failure modes throughout the process of using mobile shopping apps but also analyzes the causes and consequences of failure modes, so as to make the improvement suggestions for app interface optimization more effective. In the follow-up study, more targeted interface optimization will be carried out on the proposed suggestions, and optimized interface will be designed, so as to better improve the satisfaction of elderly users when using mobile shopping apps and enhance user experience.

Acknowledgments. This study was funded by Undergraduate Teaching Reform and Research Project at Qingdao University of Technology (grant number F2023-117).

Disclosure of Interests. The authors have no competing interests to declare that are relevant to the content of this article.

References

1. Hu, Z., Peng, X.Z., Wu, Y.S.: China plan for actively responding to population aging. Soc. Sci. China (9), 46–66+205 (2022)
2. Zhou, C.: Research on the design optimization of mobile shopping APP based on the user experience of the elderly. Ind. Eng. Des. **4**(05), 67–73 (2020)
3. Yun, Z., W, K.X.: Research on the design of online shopping interface for the elderly under the guidance of science and technology for the elderly. Design **35**(21), 111–113 (2022)
4. Liu, C.: Research on the usability of shopping website interface design considering the characteristics of elderly user. Northeastern University (2021)
5. Li, Y.F., Chen, Z.Y.: Research on human-computer interface design of elderly cars based on FMEA and FT. Packaging Eng. **42**(06), 98–105 (2021)
6. Liu, H., Liu, H.S.: Using FMEA's product usability evaluation method. Ind. Eng. J. **13**(03), 47–50 (2010)
7. Tsujikawa, S., Tsutsui, H., Honda, Y.: Development and application of a communication robot to improve the emotional state of elderly living alone. Univ. Access Inf. Soc. 1–8 (2023)
8. Ghorayeb, A., Comber, R., Gooberman-Hill, R.: Development of a smart home interface with older adults: multi-method co-design study. JMIR **6**(1) (2023)
9. Restyandito, Febryandi, Nugraha, K.A., Sebastian, D.: Mobile social media interface design for elderly in Indonesia. In: Stephanidis, C., Antona, M., Ntoa, S. (eds.) HCII 2020. CCIS, vol. 1294, pp. 79–85. Springer, Cham (2020). https://doi.org/10.1007/978-3-030-60703-6_10
10. Bong, W.K., Maußer, F., van Eck, M., De Araujo, D., Tibosch, J., Glaum, T., Chen, W.: Designing nostalgic tangible user interface application for elderly people. In: Miesenberger, K., Manduchi, R., Covarrubias Rodriguez, M., Peňáz, P. (eds.) ICCHP 2020. LNCS, vol. 12377, pp. 471–479. Springer, Cham (2020). https://doi.org/10.1007/978-3-030-58805-2_56
11. Chang, K.H., Chang, Y.C., Lai, P.T.: Applying the concept of exponential approach to enhance the assessment capability of FME. J. Intell. Manuf. **25**, 1413–1427 (2014)
12. Li, J.H., Shen, K.Y., Xu, Y.: Research on the design of vehicle-mounted human-computer interaction interface. Packaging Eng. **44**(14), 145–151+169 (2023)
13. Tang, F.L.: Research on the design of medical APP interactive interface for aging based on geriatric cognitive characteristic. Internet Weekly (07), 62–64 (2023)
14. Li, Z.J., Bai, S.: Research on the interaction design of aging smart pill box based on improved FME. Packaging Eng. **44**(08), 225–233+252 (2023)
15. Mao, S., Xiao, L.: Research on WeChat visual improvement design for elderly user groups. Packaging Eng. **41**(04), 177–181+251 (2020)
16. Wang, Y., Wang, R.Z.: Prevention model of library internal human factors design based on improved FMEA: a case study of Tianjin University of technology. New Century Libr. (08), 57–61 (2019)
17. Han, Y.J., Yin, C., Peng, Y.F.: Online shopping service error prevention model based on FME. Ind. Eng. Manag. **22**(05), 114–119+127 (2017)

Exploration of User Experience in Virtual Reality Environment. A Systematic Review

Olaoluwa Oyedokun[✉], Mohammed Alkahtani, and Vincent G. Duffy

Purdue University, West Lafayette, Indiana 47907, USA
{ooyedoku,alkahtan,duffy}@purdue.edu

Abstract. Virtual Reality (VR) is a computer-generated simulation that immerses users in a three-dimensional environment, often using a head-mounted display and motion tracking technology. It aims to replicate or simulate real and imaginary worlds, allowing users to interact with and navigate through these environments. VR finds applications in gaming, training, education, healthcare, design visualization, and virtual tourism, providing immersive and realistic experiences. Technology is continually evolving, with the potential to revolutionize various industries and how people engage with digital content. The evolving advancement in virtual reality is creating more rooms for immersive interactive options for the users. This technology is gradually taking over different aspects of human computer interaction, therefore the need to understand the user experience of this technology is of great interest to researchers in this field.

Keywords: User Experience · Virtual Reality · Applied Ergonomics

1 Introduction and Background

Virtual Reality (VR) has emerged as a transformative technological frontier, reshaping the way we perceive and interact with the digital realm. Through the seamless integration of advanced hardware and immersive software, virtual reality transcends traditional boundaries, transporting individuals into artificial yet astonishingly realistic environments. This groundbreaking technology holds the promise of revolutionizing various industries, from entertainment and education to healthcare and beyond, as it continues to redefine the very fabric of human experience. In the realm of virtual reality, the lines between the physical and virtual worlds blur, offering a captivating journey into realms limited only by imagination and innovation.

The emergence in popularity that Virtual Reality (VR) is currently experiencing marks a significant resurgence, akin to a technological renaissance, as highlighted by Kim et al. (2020). This revival is not merely a fleeting trend but a paradigm shifts in how we engage with digital content and experiences. At its core, VR is defined by a computer-generated, three-dimensional digital environment that goes beyond traditional two-dimensional interfaces. This immersive technology is characterized by its ability to seamlessly blend computer-generated elements with real-world sensations, creating an

V. G. Duffy (Ed.): HCII 2024, LNCS 14709, pp. 320–338, 2024.
https://doi.org/10.1007/978-3-031-61060-8_23

environment that users perceive as authentic and interactive. (Jayaram, Connacher, & Lyons, 1997; Jerald, 2015; Pan-telidis, 1993; Pratt, Zyda, & Kelleher, 1995).

The essence of VR lies in its capacity to provide users with a sense of presence, allowing them to feel as though they are physically present within the digitally con-structed environment. This sense of presence is achieved through a combination of advanced hardware, such as headsets and motion controllers, and sophisticated soft-ware that enables realistic simulations and interactions. As users don VR headsets, they are transported into alternate realms, transcending the limitations of traditional screens, and bringing about an unparalleled level of immersion. The multifaceted nature of VR extends its applicability across diverse domains, including but not limited to entertain-ment, education, healthcare (Curtis et al., 2021), and business. In entertainment, VR offers a revolutionary approach to gaming and storytelling, where users become active participants in the narrative, navigating and influencing the virtual world around them. In education, VR provides immersive learning experiences, enabling students to explore historical events, scientific phenomena, or artistic creations as if they were physically present. The healthcare industry leverages VR for therapeutic purposes, creating sim-ulated environments to assist in rehabilitation, treat phobias, or even simulate complex medical procedures for training purposes. In the business realm, VR is transforming the way professionals collaborate and train, fostering virtual meetings, and facilitating realistic simulations for skill development.

As VR gains traction, it not only redefines how we interact with technology but also opens new possibilities for innovation. The ongoing advancements in VR hardware, soft-ware, and content creation are propelling this technology into new realms of possibility, promising an era where the virtual and physical worlds converge seamlessly, creating a paradigm shift that extends far beyond the realms of conventional computing. Using google ngram to show the relationship between usability, user experience and virtual in response to the emergence of virtual reality as seen in Fig. 1.

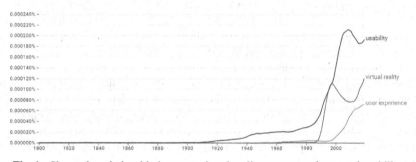

Fig. 1. Shows the relationship between virtual reality, user experience and usability.

2 Related Topics

2.1 Background and Significance

In the wake of industry 4.0 which is seeking avenues to enhance and accelerate the traditional development of workflows using automation, and modern communication (Safikhani et al., 2022). Industry 4.0, often referred to as the fourth industrial revolution, represents a paradigm shift characterized by the fusion of digital technologies, data analytics, artificial intelligence, and the Internet of Things (IoT) to create smart, interconnected systems. In this context, VR serves as a catalyst for redefining not only how industries operate but also how individuals engage with their work environments. The integration of VR technologies into Industry 4.0 initiatives introduces a dynamic dimension to traditional workflows by providing immersive, interactive, and efficient solutions. Automation, a cornerstone of Industry 4.0, is complemented by VR's ability to create virtual environments where automated processes can be simulated, optimized, and fine-tuned before implementation in the physical realm.

Modern communication, another key element of Industry 4.0, is elevated to new heights with VR. Virtual Reality facilitates remote collaboration and communication by enabling individuals to interact within shared virtual spaces, transcending geographical boundaries. Professionals can engage in virtual meetings, collaborative design sessions, and training simulations, fostering a level of connectivity and engagement that traditional communication methods struggle to achieve. Moreover, the immersive nature of VR contributes to enhanced training programs within Industry 4.0 frameworks. Workers can undergo realistic simulations of complex tasks, machinery operations, or emergency scenarios, improving skill acquisition and reducing the learning curve associated with new technologies. This not only ensures a more competent workforce but also minimizes the risks associated with on-the-job training in high-stakes environments.

The connection between a digital model and other areas of technological innovation is described as digital twin (Dawood et al., 2020). They posited that the sluggish integration of these technologies into Architectural, Engineering, and Construction (AEC) projects stems from the absence of a comprehensive study examining the cost-benefit analysis of such technologies. To address this, they conducted a survey involving 158 industry professionals to evaluate the present status and future expectations of Virtual Reality (VR) and Augmented Reality (AR). The results reveal that virtual environments find primary application in residential and commercial projects. Furthermore, industry experts anticipate a significant surge in the adoption of augmented reality technologies in the next 5 to 10 years. Notably, the study indicates that the older generation expresses greater confidence in the prospects of VR/AR based on their findings (Noghabaei et al. 2020).

This revolution of industry 4.0 is not only making changes in the construction industry but also has its footprint in tourism (Hung et al., 2022). According to (Clarke & Bowen, 2018; Cohen, 1972) tourism has been characterized as comfort of the old versus the search of the new. In both situations users are looking to explore places they have not seen before, but with the introduction of VR in tourism, people do not have to physically travel to these places to experience this thing. To commence, assuming the Virtual Environment (VE) is well-crafted, Virtual Reality (VR) can extend its reach to locations that are not easily accessible. Consequently, the potential danger and risk of accidents are entirely mitigated (Cheong, 1995; Guttentag, 2010; Lee & Kim, 2021). Following this, VR tourism offers significant conveniences and eliminates various hassles, including visitor harassment, traffic issues, and unnecessary time consumption. Last but certainly not least, VR allows for the creation of experiences within a controlled environment. Every variable within the VE can be adjusted, proving particularly advantageous for designing highly personalized travel experiences (Cheong, 1995).

The health industry is gradually experiencing an increase in the use of virtual reality as a means of educating about healthcare and brought about new learning opportunities (Shin 2017). In healthcare VR is used to integrate sound, graphics, and other sensory inputs to create a computer-generated world the users in the healthcare industry can interact with and to make it easier to entertain (Gregg and Tarrier 2007). Computer-based simulations are frequently employed as educational tools in healthcare practice, as highlighted by (Bracq, Michinov, and Jannin 2019a). Notably, this technology finds application in nursing education, as evidenced by studies conducted by (Foronda et al., 2017; Irwin and Coutts 2015; Koivisto et al. 2018; Padilha et al. 2019; Lelardeux et al., 2017; Verkuyl et al., 2017).

In using this VR technology, one common factor is present which is hand gesture. The prevalent virtual reality (VR) configuration for achieving a heightened sense of immersion and interactivity involves pairing a head-mounted display (HMD) with handheld controllers (Jacobsen et al., 2022). As a result, this setup has been widely utilized across various domains, including entertainment, education, industry, research, and even clinical fields (Melo 2020). Despite the growing prevalence of hand gestures, certain difficulties associated with their implementation can contribute to an unfavorable user experience in virtual reality (VR) applications. Problems may arise from tracking system issues, leading to imprecise hand tracking, incorrect segmentation of hands, and ultimately, a misinterpretation of gestures (Yan et al., 2020). Additionally, employing hand gestures may impede the ability to perform other tasks concurrently, such as direct interaction with objects. Excessive reliance on hand gestures can elevate cognitive load and result in increased physical fatigue (Yan et al., 2020) (Fig. 2).

2.2 Research Questions and Organization of the Report

Although a conventional literature review frequently yields valuable insights, it may overlook crucial information or recent trends, occasionally due to the researcher's limitations. The inherent constraints of this approach prompted the formulation of the research question for this report:

Research Question- What insights can be traced and what information can be gathered using a systematic literature review based on articles retrieved through a bibliometric and content analysis approach to discover methods to improve user experiences in virtual reality during trainings and learning opportunities?

This report begins with the sourcing process, involving the identification and collection of over a thousand articles through diverse bibliometric and content analysis techniques and tools, drawing data from multiple sources. The subsequent section of the report delves into the analysis of the various obtained articles.

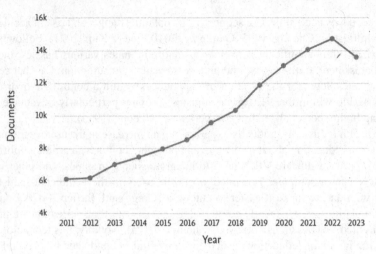

Fig. 2. Shows trends of word engagement.

3 Procedure – Article Search, Identification, and Collection

This section below itemizes the steps used in gathering, identifying, and collecting articles making use of the bibliometric and content analysis techniques.

3.1 Step 1: Identification of Articles from Various Databases and Books

The aim of the first step is to familiarize ourselves with the general topic of user experience and look for articles in the various databases and textbooks on the topic of user experience.

The table below describes the top cited articles from Google Scholars, Research Gate, Scopus, Web of Science, and Springer using the key word "User Experience" that are of great importance and selection of relevant chapters from the textbook Handbook on Human Factor and Applied Ergonomics, which is chapter 37, User Experience and Usability (Table 1).

3.2 Step 2: Articles Search Using Harzing and Visualizing with VOSviewer

The aim of step 2 is to commence the use of bibliometric and content analysis tools in aiding our searching process for finding relevant articles. This process was used because other researchers have made use of Harzing software and VOSviewer in their research (Kanade& Duffy, 2022). For this initial search was carried out using Harzing's Publish or Perish (Windows GUI Edition 8.9.4538.8589). Harzing allows the search of multiple data base for articles that a researcher is looking for, (i.e., Google Scholars, Web of Science etc.) but for the purpose of this research and bibliometric content analysis, we used Harzing to get metadata of google scholar and we could sort it by Author's or Sources order. For this step, what used the keyword "User Research" to get data from

Table 1. Summary of top cited articles in user experience

Author	References	Source
Kumar, S Stecher, G Li, M Knyaz, C Tamura, K	MEGA X: Molecular evolutionary genetics analysis across computing platforms	Scopus
Moher, David; Liberati, Alessandro; Tetzlaff, Jennifer;	Preferred Reporting Items for Systematic Reviews and Meta-Analyses: The PRISMA Statement	Web of Science
Siar Sarferaz	Compendium on Enterprise Resource Planning User Experience	Springer
Marc Hassenzahl Noam Tractinsky	User experience - a research agenda	Google Scholar
Hima Jonnalagadda	A Proposal: Human Factors Related to the User Acceptance Behavior in Adapting to New Technologies or New User Experience	ResearchGate

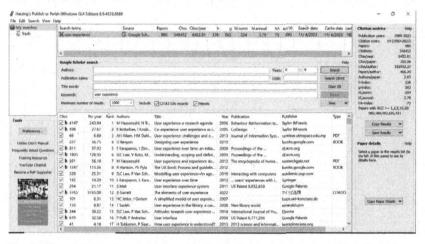

Fig. 3. Shows the output results from Harzing software using keyword User Experience

Harzing and the data was exported as a txt file to be used in other content analysis software (Fig. 3).

The data obtained from this software served as the foundation for conducting a comprehensive content analysis, enabling the identification of key trends and insights within the research domain. Subsequently, this valuable information was harnessed to generate graphical representations, specifically graphs, that visually showcase the leading conferences and influential authors in this space. Figures 4 and 5, as presented herein, offer a detailed breakdown of the findings, providing a nuanced and insightful view of most cited authors and top conferences where articles about user experience is sourced.

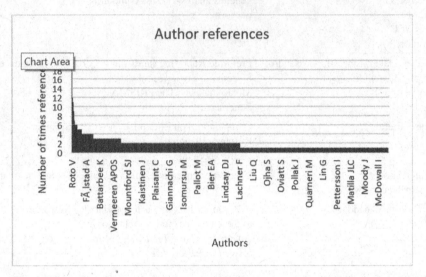

Fig. 4. Hierarchy of most cited authors graphically represented using Microsoft excel.

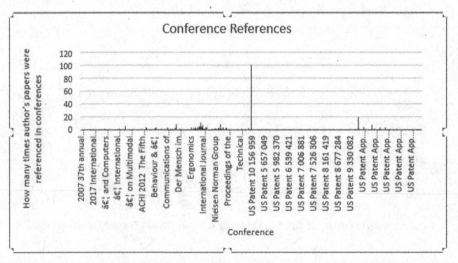

Fig. 5. Hierarchy of conference where these papers were presented graphically represented using Microsoft excel.

The number of articles found using Harzing software were 998, the searched files was exported to a txt file that can be by another bibliometric content analysis software called

VOSviewer. The data that was retrieved from Harzing was cleaned up using BibExcel (Version 2016–02-20) arranging the data in the name of the authors as seen in Fig. 6. BibExcel is a software tool designed for bibliometric analysis and data extraction from bibliographic databases. It is commonly used in the field of scientometrics and bibliometrics to analyze citation patterns, co-authorship networks, and other bibliographic data. BibExcel is particularly well-known for its ability to process bibliographic information from reference files and generate various types of output for further analysis.

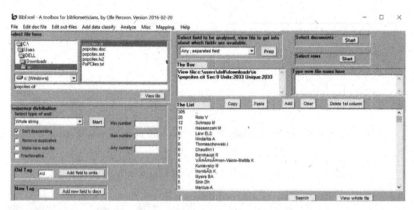

Fig. 6. Using BibExcel to format the information retrieved through Harzing software.

VOSviewer is a software tool designed for visualizing and exploring bibliometric networks. It is commonly used in the field of scientometrics to analyze and represent the relationships between scholarly publications, authors, and keywords. The tool employs a variety of visualization techniques to present complex bibliometric data in an accessible and meaningful way. VOSviewer can be utilized to create maps that illustrate the connections between different research areas, highlight key authors, and identify clusters of related publications. By employing color-coding and size adjustments, it helps users quickly grasp the significance and impact of specific elements within the network.

VOSviewer, a powerful tool for bibliometric analysis, played a crucial role in scrutinizing the data extracted through Harzing. In this analytical process, the articles were systematically organized into various clusters, with the categorization driven by a combination of co-citation and co-authorship patterns. This approach allowed for the identification of interconnected networks and relationships within scholarly literature.

Moreover, the analysis extended beyond citation and authorship metrics, as certain articles were further segmented into distinct clusters based on thematic cohesion and subject-related associations among them. This nuanced approach provided a more comprehensive understanding of the underlying patterns and connections present in the research landscape, offering valuable insights into the interplay of ideas and collaborative networks within the academic realm (Fig. 7 and Table 2).

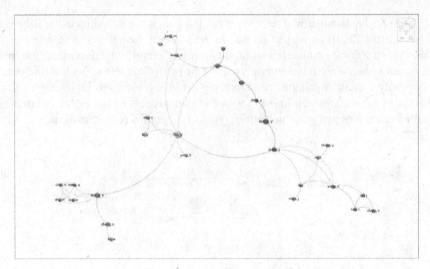

Fig. 7. Cluster of articles authors in VOSviewer content visualization

Table 2. Cluster identified from VOSviewer with Authors.

Cluster 1	Cluster 2	Cluster 3	Cluster 4
Kim, Y.	Jerald, J.	Pantelidis, V	Pratt.

3.3 Step 3: Expanded Bibliometric Search Using Scopus

The objective of incorporating Scopus into the search for additional articles was to extend the scope beyond the findings obtained through Harzing in step 2. This was done to yield additional results and gain insights into broader trends within the public. Commencing the content analysis, we utilized the same keyword, "User Experience," to retrieve results from Scopus. The search spanned from 1996 to 2022, generating a total of 164,665 documents. This timeframe was deliberately selected to delve into the early stages of user experience, particularly in connection with aviation design and not really in virtual reality user experience.

The decision to focus on this period aimed to sift through the initial developments of user experience, which were predominantly linked to aviation design. The search outcome proved to be highly informative, revealing that over 10 thousand articles were published annually about User Experience. This number of articles seems fit as an emerging topic to discuss and research about it. Figure 8 depicts a graph illustrating the emergence of user experience as a prominent topic, evident in the sporadic annual increase in publications.

Two articles were selected from this database and other articles citing this two papers were looked into to get relating topics from it (Table 3).

Table 3. Summary of articles selected from Scopus database.

Article title	Authors	Database	Why selected
Immersive virtual reality for extending the potential of building information modeling in architecture, engineering, and construction sector	Safikhani, S., Keller, S., Schweiger, G., & Pirker, J	Scopus	It was relevant to the topic in discuss
Clinical Virtual Simulation in Nursing Education: Randomized Controlled Trial	Padilha, J., P. Machado, A. Ribeiro, and J. Ramos	Scopus	It was relevant to the topic in discuss

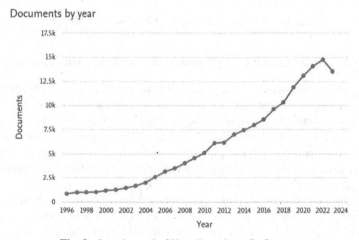

Fig. 8. Search trend of User Experience in Scopus.

Additionally, the insights derived from Scopus highlight the presence of burgeoning themes within the realm of User Experience. This discernible trend suggests that User Experience is increasingly becoming a focal point of discussion at numerous conferences, drawing the attention and participation of computing scientists with varied backgrounds and expertise. The gradual integration of this emerging topic into the discourse of conferences across disciplines underscores its growing significance and relevance. This not only reflects the dynamic nature of User Experience but also emphasizes its multidimensional impact on the field, fostering meaningful conversations among professionals from diverse backgrounds.

Details concerning User Experience, providing additional context and valuable information to supplement the findings presented in the main body of the document. This supplementary material aims to enrich the reader's grasp of the evolving landscape of User Experience and its implications across different spheres of research and practice.

Documents per year by source

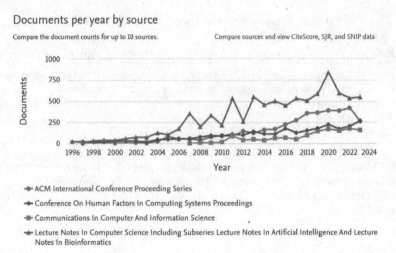

Compare the document counts for up to 10 sources.   Compare sources and view CiteScore, SJR, and SNIP data

-◆- ACM International Conference Proceeding Series

-◆- Conference On Human Factors In Computing Systems Proceedings

-■- Communications In Computer And Information Science

-▲- Lecture Notes In Computer Science Including Subseries Lecture Notes In Artificial Intelligence And Lecture Notes In Bioinformatics

Fig. 9. Conference search of User Experience in Scopus.

3.4 Step 4: Articles Search Using Scopus and Visualizing with CiteSpace

The aim of this fourth step is to use Scopus bibliometric that was gathered through step 3 and use a different content analysis tool to create a data visualization, in the process observe new patterns to aid our search in finding relevant articles. This was achieved using CiteSpace. CiteSpace allows researchers to explore and visualize the relationships among scholarly papers, authors, and keywords based on citation patterns. It's often employed in bibliometric analysis to identify emerging trends, key contributors, and the evolution of research topics within a specific field.

The utilization of visualizations significantly contributes to the deepening of our understanding of the intellectual landscape within a particular field of study. These visual aids not only facilitate the identification of influential works but also unveil intricate patterns of collaboration and the flow of information among researchers.

During our exploration, two specific articles were deliberately selected owing to their close alignment with the focus of our research. Despite this intentional selection, our analysis extended beyond these articles, allowing us to construct a comprehensive summary table that captures the essence of clusters characterized by substantial size. This broader approach ensures a more encompassing perspective, encompassing a diverse range of literature and contributing to a holistic view of the intellectual terrain in our research domain. For this report, we only presented 10 out of the 36 clusters summarized (Table 4).

The primary objective is to illustrate the interconnected nature of these articles through the utilization of the clustered system in CiteSpace. Additionally, the aim is to highlight the robustness of the interconnections within each conference and their correlation with the strength of individual study areas. Figure 10 visually represents the interconnectedness of each topic area. These supplementary visuals provide further insights into the findings of the content analysis, specifically enhancing our understanding of the intricacies within the realm of User Experience. The results from CiteSpace

Table 4. Summary of articles from cluster generated by CiteSpace.

ClusterID	Size	Silhouette	Label (LSI)	Label (LLR)	Label (MI)	Average Year
0	21	0.853	user experience	psychometric user experience model (23.41, 1.0E-4)	hedonic user experience qualities (1.08)	1967
1	16	0.918	defining user experience goal	industrial system (21.08, 1.0E-4)	mobile augmented reality (1.27)	2011
2	13	1	user experience	user experience evaluation practice (24.77, 1.0E-4)	smart device (0.11)	2010
3	5	1	investigating users' experience on social media ads: perceptions of young users	young user (9.36, 0.005)	user experience (0.08)	2016
4	5	0.966	can users embed their user experience in user-generated images? evidence from jd.com	com (9.36, 0.005)	user experience (0.08)	2019
5	5	1	evaluating user experience of augmented reality eyeglasses	augmented reality eyeglasses (11.09, 0.001)	user experience (0.09)	2013
6	5	0.932	developing user-centered libraries	engagement walking (12.16, 0.001)	holistic approach (0.11)	2013
7	4	1	exploratory analysis of differences between social experience design and user experience design	social experience design (9.36, 0.005)	user experience (0.08)	2011
8	4	0.988	developing a ux kpi based on the user experience questionnaire	user experience questionnaire (11.09, 0.001)	user experience (0.09)	2015
9	4	1	quality of user experience in 5g-vanet	quality (8.32, 0.005)	user experience (0.09)	2014
10	4	1	enhancing user experience in fashion m-retail: mapping shopping user journey using google analytics, eye tracking technology and retrospective think aloud interview	using google analytics eye tracking technology (8.45, 0.005)	user experience (0.07)	2019

also shows that research topics of User Experience on Virtual reality ranking number, sustaniate the research question of User Experience in Virtual Reality as an emerging topic.

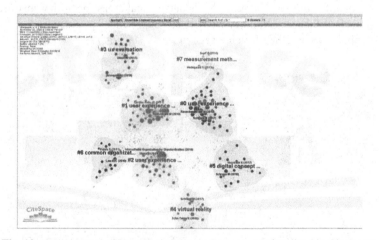

Fig. 10. Search trend of User Experience in Scopus and visualized in CiteSpace.

User Experience in virtual reality shows significant growth, as it relates to several areas of study and training process. Since this technology is making waves and changing most learning process from traditional learning style and the introduction of gamification in the learning process, human factor researchers and researchers are looking at understanding how the experiences gained by users in the virtual world will be applicable to real life scenarios.

3.5   Step 5: Articles Search Using Web of Science

Engaging in a systematic literature review is a comprehensive process that involves scouring diverse databases to not only discern the existing body of research but also to pinpoint gaps within the specified research domain. In the fifth step of this meticulous process, we conducted a targeted search using the keyword "User Experience" with the goal of uncovering articles and exploring topic areas that contribute to the development of emerging technologies and the creation of user-friendly experiences within virtual environments.

Despite encountering some familiar authors whose work had been previously identified in other databases our attention remained steadfast on the core objective: identifying subject areas where User Experience emerges as a central focus of research interest. This strategic search provided valuable insights into the interconnectedness and continuity of research efforts across various databases. To offer a more nuanced view, a breakdown of the search keywords is shown in Table 5, specifically showcasing subject areas where User Experience is at the forefront of ongoing research endeavors. This visual representation not only highlights the prevalence of User Experience as a focal point but also identifies the key contributors and thought leaders in the exploration of user experiences within the expansive landscape of virtual reality. The inclusion of such detailed information enriches our understanding of the current state of research in this dynamic field and aids in the identification of emerging trends and critical areas for further investigation. Searching Web of Sciences with key word "User Experience" produced a result of over 140, 61 publications and the break are seen in Fig. 9 (Fig. 11).

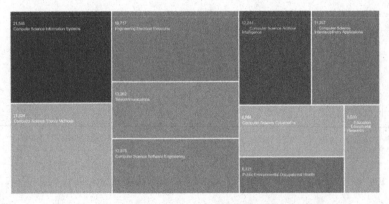

Fig. 11. Search trend of User Experience in web of sciences.

3.6   Step 6: Articles Search Using Springer

The purpose of this step is to broaden the scope of our investigation by incorporating the resources available on the Springer database. Our goal is to identify potential contributions that can augment the existing body of research or address gaps within the current research area. A targeted exploration within this database reveals that the predominant topics center around User Experience in Virtual Reality, particularly in the context of tourism. The selected articles from this database play a crucial role in expanding our understanding of Virtual Reality's applications. Specifically, they highlight that Virtual Reality is not confined solely to the realm of tourism but can be leveraged in various aspects of learning. This discovery introduces a nuanced perspective, emphasizing the versatility and multifaceted potential of Virtual Reality technology.

By incorporating insights from Springer, we not only enrich the depth of our research findings but also underscore the diverse applications and evolving landscape of Virtual Reality. This expansion broadens the narrative surrounding the role of Virtual Reality in different domains, offering a more comprehensive view that encompasses both tourism and educational contexts.

3.7   Step 7: Articles Search Using ResearchGate

In this phase, we searched ResearchGate. ResearchGate is a social networking platform tailored for researchers, scholars, and scientists. Established in 2008, it serves as a hub for academic professionals to create profiles, share publications, and connect with peers. The platform emphasizes collaboration by providing features such as publication sharing, collaboration opportunities, and a questions-and-answers section. Researchers can track the impact of their work through metrics and analytics, and the site also offers job postings for academic and research positions. Due to the advantage of ResearchGate been a social networking of researchers, it is easier to find what researchers are discussing in different subject areas of research. For this searched using the keyword User Experience and we were able to pick a quality topic on healthcare, where User Experience in immersive world of virtual reality has been used as a training tool.

3.8   Step 8: Summary of Searches and Articles

After concluding the search of all 25 articles, it is paramount to understand where each of the articles from picked and the search terms used in each of the databases. In Table 5, a recap of the search terms, database and the number of articles picked from the database was mentioned.

Table 5. Summary of articles from all the databases.

Search Terms	Database	Number of Articles
User Experience	Google Scholar/Harzing	10
User Experience	Scopus	8
User Experience	Web of Science	5
User experience	Springer	1
User Experience	ResearchGate	1

4   Results and Analysis

The session consists of two phases, the first phase is comprising of a content analysis involving the word cloud which was generated using the 25 articles that used in this report. The second phase is synthesizing where each of these articles has in common and how each of them has been able to leverage this emerging technology in different fields of study.

4.1   Content Analysis

In this section, we analyzed the 25 articles that we selected from the 5 databases. To do this, we used a software called NVivo. NVivo provides a platform for organizing and coding qualitative data, enabling users to identify patterns, themes, and trends within the information they have collected. It supports a variety of data types and formats, allowing users to import, organize, and analyze their data efficiently. Researchers often use NVivo in fields such as social sciences, psychology, anthropology, market research, and other disciplines where qualitative analysis is crucial for understanding complex phenomena.

Furthermore, the word cloud in Fig. 10 shows the prominent key words that are present in the papers that are read and the metadata that retrieved from Scopus, while using NVivo to analyze the entire documents. The most frequent words from each of these articles are highlighted in orange colors which are learning, virtual, reality, user research and experience. The word cloud information was filtered to (Fig. 12).

4.2   Synthesis Analysis Phase – User Experience in Virtual Reality

Throughout this process, we successfully identified the correlations among all the articles, shedding light on the collective findings that contribute to answering the research question: how hand gestures have influenced user experience in virtual environments. Each of these articles has provided valuable insights into the intricate relationship between virtual environments, user experience, and learning outcomes. While the existing literature has offered valuable perspectives on the broader impact of virtual environments on user experience and learning, it is evident that more dedicated research is warranted in the specific domain of hand gestures. The articles reviewed have laid a foundation by emphasizing the significance of virtual environments, but there remains

Fig. 12. NVivo output from the selected 25 articles

a distinct need for further exploration and understanding of the nuanced role that hand gestures play in shaping user experiences within these environments.

In essence, this analysis has not only synthesized existing knowledge on the broader topic but has also identified a focused area—hand gestures—where additional research efforts can significantly contribute to advancing our understanding of how users interact and learn within virtual spaces. This recognition of an ongoing research frontier underscores the dynamic nature of the field and highlights opportunities for future investigations and advancements.

5   Discussion

Virtual reality has emerged as a crucial component of learning experiences, particularly in the contemporary era characterized by rapid technological advancements. The selected articles collectively demonstrate significant promise in leveraging cutting-edge technology to enhance learning outcomes. The impact of virtual reality extends beyond the realm of education, influencing various industries.

The table below provides a summary of industries where user experience in virtual reality is prominently featured in this report (Table 6):

Table 6. Summary of industries and emerging use of Virtual reality.

Industry	Article mention of Virtual Reality User Experience
Education	Emphasis on virtual reality's role in enhancing learning outcomes
Healthcare	Applications of virtual reality in medical training and patient care
Tourism	Utilization of virtual reality to enhance travel experiences

This summary underscores the diverse impact of virtual reality across multiple sectors, showcasing its potential to revolutionize various aspects of learning and industry practices. The articles selected offer insights into the transformative effects of virtual reality, paving the way for continued exploration and adoption of this technology across different domains.

6 Future Work

The exploration and enhancement of User Experience in virtual reality are poised for more extensive research and development. Anticipated advancements in technology, particularly the creation of innovative head-mounted displays by engineers and developers, signal a forthcoming revolution. The transformative experiences realized in this context are expected to extend to various other realms within virtual reality.

While our primary focus in this investigation delved into the realms of health, education, and tourism, it is noteworthy that breakthroughs are also occurring in the realm of entertainment. This expansion of virtual reality experiences is evident in groundbreaking research initiatives, some of which have received recognition and awards from the National Science Foundation (NSF), highlighting the breadth and significance of ongoing advancements in this dynamic field. For example, there was a project for those will mobility impairment person, where a researcher is creating an experience where this category of people could experience what Virtual Environment feel. More trending topics on Virtual Reality is available on NSF award page (https://www.nsf.gov/awards earch/simpleSearchResult?queryText=user+experience+in+virtual+reality+).

References

Bracq, M.-S., Michinov, E., Jannin, P.: Virtual reality simulation in nontechnical skills training for healthcare professionals. Simul. Healthc. J. Soc. Simul. Healthc. **14**(3), 188–194 (2019). https://doi.org/10.1097/SIH.0000000000000347

Cheong, R.: The virtual threat to travel and tourism. Tour. Manag. **16**(6), 417–422 (1995). https://doi.org/10.1016/0261-5177(95)00049-T

Clarke, J., Bowen, D.: Repeat tourists and familiar place formation: conversion, inheritance and discovery. J. Destin. Mark. Manag. **20**(3), 100605 (2021). https://doi.org/10.1016/j.jdmm.2021.100605

Cohen, E.: Toward a sociology of international tourism. Soc. Res. **39**(1), 164–182 (1972). https://www.jstor.org/stable/40970087

Curtis, R., et al.: Improving user experience of virtual health assistants: scoping review. J. Med. Internet Res. **23**, e31737 (2021). https://doi.org/10.2196/31737

Dawood, N., Pour Rahimian, F., Seyedzadeh, S., Sheikhkhoshkar, M.: Enabling the development and implementation of digital twins. In: Proceedings of the 20th International Conference on Construction Applications of Virtual Reality (2020)

Foronda, C., et al.: Virtually nursing: emerging technologies in nursing education. Nurse Educ. **42**(1), 14–17 (2017). https://doi.org/10.1097/NNE.0000000000000295

Gregg, L., Tarrier, N.: Virtual reality in mental health. Soc. Psychiatry Psychiatr. Epidemiol. **42**, 343–354 (2007). https://doi.org/10.1007/s00127-007-0173-4

Guttentag, D.A.: Virtual reality: applications and implications for tourism. Tour. Manag. **31**(5), 637–651 (2010). https://doi.org/10.1016/j.tourman.2009.07.003

Hung, P.K., Liang, R.H., Ma, S.Y., Kong, B.W.: Exploring the experience of traveling to familiar places in VR: an empirical study using google earth VR. Int. J. Hum.–Comput. Interact. 1–23 (2022).

Irwin, P., Coutts, R.: A systematic review of the experience of using second life in the education of undergraduate nurses. J. Nurs. Educ. **54**(10), 572–577 (2015). https://doi.org/10.3928/014 84834-20150916-05

Jacobsen, L.F., Krogsgaard-Jensen, N.M., Peschel, A.O.: Shopping in reality or virtuality? A validation study of consumers' price memory in a virtual vs. physical supermarket. Foods **11**(14), 2111 (2022). https://doi.org/10.3390/foods11142111

Jayaram, S., Connacher, H.I., Lyons, K.W.: Virtual assembly using virtual reality techniques. Comput.-Aided Des. **29**(8), 575–584 (1997). https://doi.org/10.1016/S0010-4485(96)00094-2

Jerald, J.: The VR Book: Human-Centered Design for Virtual Reality. Morgan & Claypool, New York, NY (2015)

Kanade, S.G., Duffy, V.G.: Use of virtual reality for safety training: a systematic review. In: Duffy, V.G. (eds.) Digital Human Modeling and Applications in Health, Safety, Ergonomics and Risk Management. Health, Operations Management, and Design. HCII 2022. LNCS, vol. 13320, pp. 364–375. Springer, Cham (2022). https://doi.org/10.1007/978-3-031-06018-2_25

Kim, Y.M., Rhiu, I., Yun, M.H.: A systematic review of a virtual reality system from the perspective of user experience. Int. J. Hum.-Comput. Interact. **36**(10), 893–910 (2020)

Koivisto, J.-M., Haavisto, E., Niemi, H., Haho, P., Nylund, S., Multisilta, J.: Design principles for simulation games for learning clinical reasoning: a design-based research approach. Nurse Educ. Today **60**, 114–120 (2018). https://doi.org/10.1016/j.nedt.2017.10.002

Lee, W.J., Kim, Y.H.: Does VR tourism enhance users' experience? Sustainability **13**(2), 806 (2021). https://doi.org/10.3390/su13020806

Melo, M., Goncalves, G., Monteiro, P., Coelho, H., Vasconcelos-Raposo, J., Bessa, M.: Do multisensory stimuli benefit the virtual reality experience? A systematic review. IEEE Trans. Vis. Comput. Graph. **28**(01), 1428–1442 (2020). https://doi.org/10.1109/tvcg.2020.3010088

Noghabaei, M., Heydarian, A., Balali, V., Han, K.: Trend analysis on adoption of virtual and augmented reality in the architecture, engineering, and construction industry. Data **5**(1), 26 (2020)

Padilha, J., Machado, P., Ribeiro, A., Ramos, J.: Clinical virtual simulation in nursing education: randomized controlled Trial. J. Med. Internet Res. **21**(3), e11529 (2019). https://doi.org/10.2196/11529

Pantelidis, V.S.: Virtual reality in the classroom. Educ. Technol. **33**(4), 23–27 (1993)

Pons Lelardeux, C., Panzoli, D., Lubrano, V., Minville, V., Lagarrigue, P., Jessel, J.-P.: Communication system and team situation awareness in a multiplayer real-time learning environment: application to a virtual operating room. Vis. Comput. **33**(4), 489–515 (2017). https://doi.org/10.1007/s00371-016-1280-6

Pratt, D.R., Zyda, M., Kelleher, K.: Virtual reality: in the mind of the beholder. Computer **28**, 17–19 (1995)

Safikhani, S., Keller, S., Schweiger, G., Pirker, J.: Immersive virtual reality for extending the potential of building information modeling in architecture, engineering, and construction sector: systematic review. Int. J. Digit. Earth **15**(1), 503–526 (2022)

Shin, D.-H.: The role of affordance in the experience of virtual reality learning: technological and affective affordances in virtual reality. Telemat. Inform. **34**, 1826–1836 (2017). https://doi.org/10.1016/j.tele.2017.05.013

Verkuyl, M., Romaniuk, D., Atack, L., Mastrilli, P.: Virtual gaming simulation for nursing education: an experiment. Clin. Simul. Nurs. **13**, 238–244 (2017). https://doi.org/10.1016/j.ecns.2017.02.004

Yan, Y., Shi, Y., Yu, C., Shi, Y.: HeadCross: exploring head-based crossing selection on head-mounted displays. Proc. ACM Interact. Mob. Wearable Ubiquit. Technol. **4**(1), 1–22 (2020). https://doi.org/10.1145/3380983

Autonomous Video Transmission and Air-to-Ground Coordination in UAV-Swarm-Aided Disaster Response Platform

Chengyi Qu[1]([✉]) [iD], Paulo Drefahl[1] [iD], Wenbin Guo[2] [iD], and Hong Wang[3]

[1] Florida Gulf Coast University, Fort Myers, FL 33965, USA
{cqu,pdrefahl}@fgcu.edu
[2] University of Florida, Gainesville, FL 32611, USA
wenbin.guo@ufl.edu
[3] Chang'an University, Shanxi 710064, China
hong.wang@chd.edu.cn

Abstract. Unmanned Aerial Vehicles (UAVs), or drones with cameras, are crucial for environmental awareness in applications like smart agriculture, border security, and disaster response. Building realistic UAV testbeds for novel network control algorithms is challenging due to time constraints and regulatory limitations. To develop an autonomous air-to-ground coordination platform, in this paper, we introduce a UAV-swarm-aided Disaster Response Platform (DRP) that simulates video transmission and coordination that integrates simulation for both drones and networks, allowing experimentation with protocols (HTTP/TCP, UDP/RTP, QUIC) and video properties (codec, resolution). Our design combined human-centered interaction principles, prioritizing user experience and indicating multi-modal interactions. In addition, our approach utilizes trace-based experiments to demonstrate its effectiveness in delivering video quality (e.g., PSNR) aligning with real-world measurements, while in the meantime validating model accuracy. Evaluation results demonstrate that our intelligent video transmission and air-to-ground coordination strategies present reasonable video quality under measurement of subjective and objective metrics, and in the meantime achieve $\approx$ 85% accuracy with dynamic decision-making with competitive time efficiency and energy savings ($\approx$ 18% gain) compared to on-boarding only. Implementing these strategies in UAV-swarm-aided DRPs significantly enhances overall response efficiency, ensuring the safety of lives and property.

Keywords: Drone-Ground Interaction Platform · Disaster Response Platform · Video Transmission · Air-to-ground Coordination

1 Introduction

Unmanned Aerial Vehicles (UAVs) play a crucial role in diverse applications, including smart farming, public safety, emergency medical services, and package

V. G. Duffy (Ed.): HCII 2024, LNCS 14709, pp. 339–355, 2024.
https://doi.org/10.1007/978-3-031-61060-8_24

delivery. These drones empower computer systems, including Ground Control Stations (GCS), to actively manage their location, leading to coordinated efforts that significantly enhance environmental situational awareness [12]. As illustrated in Fig. 1, these systems commonly incorporate air-to-ground wireless links, establishing connections between the edge network, Unmanned Aerial Vehicles (UAVs), and Ground Control Stations (GCS). Compared to a single-UAV operation, a UAV-swarm-aided operation shows the efficiency and robustness of the system [2]. The networking architecture typically involves setting up peer-to-peer or centralized-control communication networks with two primary modes including i) Air-to-Air, and ii) Air-to-Ground.

In addition, the application of geospatial video analytics with UAV-swarm in various domains is widespread, involving intricate data processing pipelines to extract environmental situational awareness from videos captured from diverse perspectives. However, the deployment of realistic UAV swarm testbeds with appropriate network edge-communication protocols is currently a time-consuming and costly endeavor. This challenge arises from constraints such as ensuring safe operation, managing limited energy resources, and navigating government regulation restrictions [13]. Furthermore, constructing UAV swarm testbeds for high-scale experiments poses additional difficulties, particularly in creating repeatable and reproducible experiments for testing major hypotheses. The complexities involved in achieving these objectives further contribute to the overall challenges in advancing geospatial video analytics with UAV technology [16].

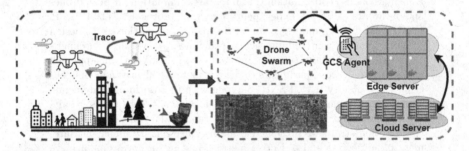

Fig. 1. Overview of converting from single UAV operation into UAV-swarm aided operation system with Air-to-Ground Coordination.

Traces derived from UAVs during video analytics simulations, offer real-time opportunities for experimentation with edge-cloud configurations, diverse UAV mobility models, and control connection status between devices and infrastructure. These traces enable adaptation and policy experiments in video analytics based on network performance measurements, incorporating Human-Computer Interaction (HCI) concepts to enhance user experience and system usability [8]. In the realm of UAV-swarm-aided geospatial video analytics algorithms, network simulations involve setting up multi-UAV configurations with custom wireless communication and network links (air-to-air; air-to-ground), along with mobility routing protocols. Moreover, despite the availability of effective UAV simulations for measuring flight movements, battery life, and application performance, they often lack integration with relevant network simulators. Conversely, powerful network simulators exist but lack the necessary features to realistically address UAV-specific issues at a high scale [1,11]. The joint design of UAV and network simulations, incorporating HCI principles, offers significant benefits to experimenters. It allows for testing various system configurations, such as network security protocols [9], and implementing different air-to-ground coordination strategies before actual deployment in the field. This synergistic approach enhances the efficiency and effectiveness of experiments in UAV-swarm-aided configuration testing, ensuring a user-centric and user-friendly system design.

This paper investigates state-of-the-art approaches to advanced UAV-swarm-aided Disaster response Platforms (DRPs), focusing on trace generation for (a) network communication between UAV-swarm edge-server architectures and (b) computation in UAV video analytics across multiple application scenarios. Addressing knowledge gaps identified in the literature survey, we propose a trace-based DRP design utilizing NS-3 [6]. Our design integrates UAV-swarm-aided simulations within a hierarchical UAV configuration, covering wide-area search drones and intelligence-gathering drones, to serve applications requiring geospatial environmental situational awareness, with a thoughtful consideration of Human-Computer Interaction (HCI) concepts.

The hierarchical UAV platform involves collaboration between low-cost and high-cost drones using a geo-location service to provide a 'common operating picture' for decision-makers. Our innovative approach synergizes network and drone simulators/emulators, demonstrating apparent benefits in trace-based simulations involving realistic drone video analytics pipelines. Videos and traces generated from our platform can integrate various drone configurations, wireless communication links (air-to-air; air-to-ground), and mobility routing protocols. Utilizing our UAV-swarm-aided DRP implementation, we conduct experiments with real-world UAS traces, encompassing diverse mobility models, geospatial link information, and video analytics measurements. This research not only advances the understanding of UAV simulation capabilities but also emphasizes a user-centric approach through the incorporation of HCI concepts in DRP design.

The remainder of the paper is organized as follows: In Sect. 2, we describe the UAV-swarm-aided disaster response platform design in detail. Section 2.2 details our model strategies related to video transmission and coordination to achieve air-to-ground communication. Section 4 describes the platform experiment results and salient findings. Lastly, Sect. 5 concludes the paper.

2   UAV-Swarm-Aided DRP Design and Modeling

In this section, we initiate our exploration by offering a comprehensive overview of our platform, meticulously outlining each component intricately linked to its functionality. To ensure a thorough analysis and to present a holistic view of our output processes, we delve into the specifics of air-to-ground video transmission and coordination modeling, providing detailed descriptions of the design and operational intricacies.

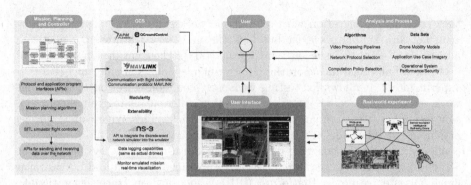

Fig. 2. User has interaction with the components of the Air-to-Ground Coordinator. Analysis and processes are done based on the outputs from the video transmission. The emulator is integrated with a real-world experiment component, and its functionality should include the emulation of any MAVLink-compatible vehicle.

2.1   Design Overview

Figure 2 provides an overview of our proposed solution approach, specifically focusing on an Air-to-ground Coordination scenario within Disaster Response Processes (DRP). Our approach incorporates *system* awareness (e.g., energy levels), *mobility* awareness (e.g., ground sensor location, UAV trajectory), and *environmental* awareness (e.g., physical obstacles, wind intensity) modeling. This comprehensive awareness modeling guides learning-based video transmission and offloading strategies intelligently and jointly.

In our hierarchical UAV system connected to the edge, we deploy both low-capability search UAVs, covering extensive geographic areas, and high-capability intelligence gathering UAVs for fine-grained surveillance in targeted regions. These UAVs can be deployed both in the field and within a network-embedded UAV simulator. Human operators effectively control UAV swarms through a single orchestration end-point, enabling interactive and coordinated operations among the UAV swarms for streamlined management.

Moreover, the synergistic operation of UAVs and network emulators offers benefits to human operators, including the ability to (a) test various system configurations on the networking side and (b) implement different flight algorithms before deploying them in disaster-stricken areas. This approach enhances the efficiency and adaptability of disaster response operations through the integration of intelligent UAV swarms and network emulation capabilities.

In conjunction with the human-centered interaction graphical user interface (GUI) design, our approach incorporates open-source API design to establish connectivity with the NS-3 network simulation platform, as documented in [11]. The integration of Mission, Planning, and Controller components facilitates the dissemination of detailed flight information to GCS operators, enabling them to make informed pre-flight decisions. Throughout the take-off phase, operators can leverage our proposed user interface system, outlined in Fig. 2, to perform additional operations. Notably, the user interface supports the concurrent oper-ation of multiple drones within a single page, with each interaction manifesting in real-world drone flights. Furthermore, the system captures and logs datasets, storing them in files for subsequent analyses and operations.

2.2 Air-to-Ground Video Transmission and Coordination Modeling

In this section, we detailed our video transmission approach between air-to-ground, considering various video transmission protocols and network setups. After that, we discuss the coordination of drones and GCS to provide a bet-ter transmission environment by briefly introducing the orchestration between multi-drones and GCS in the disaster response management scenario.

Video Transmission Modeling: In response to user specifications, we will organize diverse solutions into categorized lists, addressing various aspects. The categories encompass a range of protocols, video codecs, and video resolutions. Each category comprises distinct options, including (i) Network protocols, offer-ing choices among HTTP, TCP, UDP, RTP, and QUIC; (ii) Video Properties, with a selection between H.265 HEVC (High-Efficiency Video Coding) and H.264 AVC (Advanced Video Coding) for video codec; and allowing choices between 720p, 1080p, and 2K for video resolution.

To enhance predictive modeling, we correlate Application-layer and Transport-layer Protocols with video transmission properties, encompassing net-work protocol, video codec, and video resolution. In practical scenarios, the unpredictable wireless environment poses challenges in precisely anticipating net-work conditions during drone flights. Furthermore, rapid changes in network pro-tocols aligned with environmental situational awareness requirements may occur along the flight paths. Consequently, selecting network protocols and video prop-erties at the commencement of a drone flight assumes paramount importance. Given the absence of detailed information on network and video codec selec-tion in the comprehensive dataset of detailed video transmissions captured by drones, we conducted additional video transmission tasks within our proposed user interface platform. Specifically, for each trace obtained from the dataset, varied combinations of network and video properties were employed to generate outputs, such as 1080p video encoded with H.265 under HTTP/TCP commu-nication, and subsequent observations of the results were made. The flowchart depicted in Fig. 3 delineates the decision-making process employed in the selec-tion of network protocols and video properties. The evaluation of the modeling incorporates both Peak Signal-to-Noise Ratio (PSNR) as an objective criterion and Mean Opinion Scores (MOS) as a subjective criterion. Comprehensive details of the evaluation results are available in Sect. 4.3.

Air-to-Ground Coordination Modeling: To streamline these processes, we bifurcate collaboration and orchestration into two distinct phases: the pre-application analysis phase and the real-time in-application prediction phase. The initial step involves gathering traces from diverse scenarios under both Disaster response (DR) setups. For each DR scene, we execute benchmark video streaming

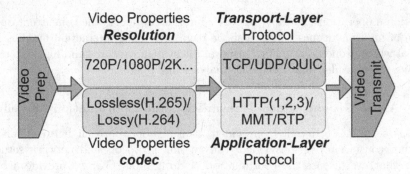

Fig. 3. Flowchart detailed the process of selecting network protocols and video properties using our GUI platform. The GUI provides detailed output on the video component, supporting multiple UAV video transmissions with the same configurations.

analytics to simulate performance across three execution categories: local execution (on a single UAV), edge server execution (complete resource offloading onto the edge server), and UAS-swarm-Server collaboration execution (leveraging joint learning-based computation offloading approach [3] for task distribution). The benchmarking encompasses network protocols and video properties as detailed in the previous section. Thresholds, derived from DR scene analysis results, factor in crucial metrics like recognition accuracy, map-generating rate, and DR scene response time. The outcomes of policy-based decisions are then applied to each UAV for subsequent deployment.

While the utilization of benchmark analysis results optimizes performance and facilitates policy-based decisions in the UAV-swarm-aided with Edge server, i.e., air-to-ground collaboration, there arises a necessity to dynamically orchestrate the operational processes by predicting traces and making advanced decisions during operations. In response, we propose a Deep Q-Network (DQN)-based trajectory prediction algorithm, generating predictive traces for each moving UAV. This DQN trajectory prediction algorithm is applied to each UAV involved in task sharing across various mobility models [5], such as random waypoints, Gauss-Markov, and mission-plan-based. The precise trajectory predictions are distributed for each DR scene, and decisions are guided by policy-based collaboration strategies. To implement this, each *wide-area search UAV* and *multi-sensor intelligent gathering UAV* embed (as described in the right-hand side of the Fig. 2) reference weights from the learning output of the DQN algorithm. To enhance the prediction procedure, we compare several DQN methods, including DQN, Double-DQN, and Duelling-DQN. The evaluation output (see Sect. 4.3), encompassing network performance and overall gains, is discernible across the various DQN methods listed.

3 UAV-Swarm-Aided Disaster Response Platform User Interface Design

In this section, we describe the user interface design of our proposed UAV-swarm-aided DRP. In detail, we delve into the detailed description of the open-sourced user interface, highlighting components related to human-centered interaction strategies. Finally, we introduce the software components and dependencies that have been employed in designing the platform.

3.1 User Interface Design and HCI Components

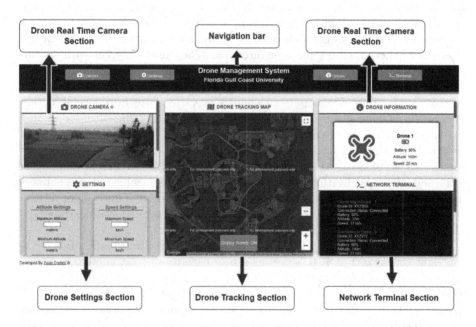

Fig. 4. Snapshot of the initial dashboard in the DRP Graphical User Interface (GUI), Highlighting Key Elements and Functionalities. Exploration of all the techniques and SPA design patterns, including (from left to right) i) drone cameras, ii) navigation bar, iii) drone information details, iv) general settings, v) tracking map, and vi) network terminal.

In the realm of UAV management, the integration of HCI principles and advanced GUI design is paramount for elevating user experience and ensuring system usability across diverse devices. Detailed analysis of Fig. 4 spotlighting the distinctive features of the software UI and its design patterns, with a particular emphasis on responsiveness, clarity, and adaptability. These qualities collectively contribute to an efficient and user-friendly interface tailored for controlling and monitoring drones.

A significant challenge associated with software of this nature, dealing with substantial amounts of UAV-related data and variables, lies in presenting this information in an accessible and user-friendly manner. Constantly exploring information visualization concepts [15]. The data must be readily available for monitoring by the GCS Agent or individuals using the software, ensuring UAVs are performing optimally and extracting valuable insights from the received information. The first design pattern that emerges is the *Single Page Application (SPA)* [14], coupled with a *modal* or *"lightbox"* technique.

SPA consolidates all pertinent information onto a single webpage, eliminating the need for users to navigate through multiple pages. This approach provides a comprehensive view of i) drone cameras, ii) navigation bar, iii) drone information details, iv) general settings, v) tracking map, and vi) network terminal. By optimizing resource loading and dynamically updating content, SPAs significantly reduce loading times, ensuring quick and efficient access to critical information [14]. In conjunction with SPA, the incorporation of Modal Design Patterns further enhances the user interface. When users interact with specific elements, such as a drone camera or network terminal, a modal overlay extends the relevant section, offering detailed information, charts, or controls related to that drone. This design pattern enables users to delve into specific details without navigating away, fostering a more immersive and efficient interaction.

These interactions are made possible by various UI elements seamlessly integrating HCI principles to ensure optimal user experience and system operability across diverse devices. At the top of Fig. 4, the Navigation Bar presents clear icons and labels, facilitating intuitive interaction. Recognizable buttons enhance user navigation, focusing on specific sections when pressed. This design, responsive across platforms, allows for effortless navigation through various functionalities, aligning with the SPA pattern.

The primary drone information is housed in the Drone Information Box at the top right corner of Fig. 4. It serves as a user-friendly display, emphasizing easy comprehension of drone details such as battery status, drone ID, altitude, coordinates, etc. Hover-over tooltips and touch interactions on mobile devices enable quick exploration. Responsive design ensures a seamless experience, expanding upon interaction to provide users with a comprehensive view of all connected devices. This aligns with the SPA pattern, consolidating information for a unified and accessible display.

Crafted for diverse devices, the Settings Interface within the bottom right corner of Fig. 4 allows users to customize drone parameters effortlessly. Whether adjusting sliders on a computer or using touch controls on mobile devices, the design ensures optimal interaction and adaptability, reflecting the SPA pattern's responsiveness. The expandable settings box accommodates varying input requirements, enhancing the precision of user inputs and aligning with the Modal Design Pattern.

To track drones, a Drone Tracking Map was implemented, prominently displayed at the center of the application (Fig. 4). It facilitates interactive HCI and integrates drone locations using an API from Google Maps and a real-time server that retrieves coordinates from the drones. The ability to manipulate the map through a mouse or touch gestures on mobile devices ensures user-friendly navigation. Responsive design empowers users to actively control drone icons, fostering situational awareness. Features such as map navigation, linking drones to the information box, and toggling drone locations align with the SPA and Modal Design Patterns. Functioning as a system log display, the Network Terminal Box ensures transparent HCI. Located at the bottom right of the page (Fig. 4), responsive design and clarity in presenting information make it suitable for effective monitoring and troubleshooting. Users can scroll through logs on computers, and touch interactions facilitate navigation on iPad, allowing the terminal to expand and scroll through even on mobile devices. The expandable terminal box provides a comprehensive view of real-time updates from the drones, demonstrating a seamless integration of HCI principles and UI design elements. This UAV-swarm-aided DRP is open-source and can be downloaded and inspected at the GitHub repository [4].

3.2   Software Components and Dependencies

In terms of the software components and dependencies used to develop this DRP, each component has undergone a rigorous requirements-gathering process and multiple design iterations to facilitate the Human-Computer Interaction (HCI) aspects, providing operators with an intuitive platform for efficient drone oversight and control. The front-end utilizes a combination of HTML, CSS, JavaScript, and complementary frameworks such as Bootstrap. This amalgamation forms the backbone of the software's user interface, enabling seamless access and navigation through various sections, as highlighted in the Navigation Bar (see Table 1). Bootstrap enhances the responsiveness of the navigation bar, aligning with the software's commitment to optimal user experience.

The Drone Camera Box, a focal point of the user interface, leverages several technologies to deliver a rich and responsive experience. Real-time video communication is achieved through WebRTC [7], utilizing a back-end API in JavaScript to handle protocols for receiving live video feeds from drones. The HTML5 video element and JavaScript animations contribute to toggling functionalities and displaying a recording indicator. This integration aligns with the software's emphasis on clear communication of the camera's status.

The Drone Tracking Map Box, crucial for real-time drone location monitoring, harnesses the power of the Google Maps API along with JavaScript, HTML, and CSS. This combination allows the presentation of real-time drone positions on an interactive map. Animations enhance user engagement, facilitating intuitive navigation through the map and dynamic control of drone display. This technological synergy, outlined in Table 1, underscores the software's scalability and its ability to enable real-time tracking possibilities in the future.

To monitor real-time updates about individual drones, a Drone Information Box has been developed, facilitated by HTML, CSS, and JavaScript. The seamless integration of these technologies ensures a user-friendly display of critical information, promoting easy comprehension across devices. Information requests

Table 1. Overview of System Components with Descriptions and Main Functionalities. All are displayed in SPA pattern with boxes that are dynamically extended based on Ground Control Operators (users) interaction.

Component	Description
Frontend Application	User interface for interacting with the drone management system.
Navigation Bar	Navigation bar for easy access to different sections of the software.
Drone Camera Box	Displays live video feed from the drone camera, toggle functionality, and recording indicator.
Drone Tracking Map Box	Shows a map with real-time drone positions, toggle display button.
Drone Information Box	Displays real-time information about individual drones.
Settings Box	Allows users to configure various drone parameters such as altitude, speed, rotation, and camera settings.
Network Terminal Box	A terminal-like box for displaying system logs and messages.
Animation Script	Responsible for animating drones on the map and providing dynamic visual feedback.
Backend node.js	Manages data, handles user requests, and communicates with drones and external systems.
Stylesheets	CSS files for styling the user interface.
Drone Communication	Integration with drones for real-time data exchange

ping through an API in the Node.js backend at specific intervals to ensure the accuracy of the displayed data. Hover-over tooltips and touch interactions enhance the responsiveness of this component, contributing to an efficient and transparent operational environment.

In software development, the ability to interact with settings and platform specificity is crucial. Hence, a Settings Box has been added, designed for configuring various drone parameters, utilizing HTML, CSS, and JavaScript. This technology functions in synchrony with the Network Terminal Box. Together, they allow users to input and handle configurations with ease while observing real-time responses and updates from the drones.

In summary, the technological components detailed in this section form a robust foundation for the DRP user interface. Through meticulous requirements gathering and iterative design, the front end employs a blend of HTML, CSS, JavaScript, and supportive frameworks like Bootstrap. This amalgamation serves as the backbone, ensuring an intuitive platform for Ground Control Operators to oversee and control drones efficiently.

4   Platform Experiment Results and Findings

In this section, we first provide the experiment setups with both simulation and real-world setups. To evaluate our performance in the DRP, we provide several experiments under both simulator and real-world setups considering various metrics in terms of time efficiency and energy-saving. Objective and subjective results related to video transmission are also provided to evaluate the human-center interaction principles.

4.1   Experiment Setups

In this experiment setups, we consider both simulator and real-world experiments. To emulate the streaming process among UAVs and the Edge server, we utilized FFmpeg to systematically configure raw data into videos, employing different codecs (h.264, h.265) and setting various video resolutions (720×480, 1280×720, 1920×1080), all at a constant 25 FPS. This effort resulted in the generation of 100 distinct videos. Subsequently, these videos were executed on a Nvidia Jetson Xavier NX using the YoloV8 [17] model to perform real-time object detection. The output included key confidence data and processing speed. In the context of our network performance evaluation, we implemented a network offloading strategy for drone swarms utilizing TCP video streaming. The streams were limited by different bit rates (500kbs, 1mbs), resulting in $\approx$ 500 unique streaming situations.

In terms of the real-world experiments, we conducted data collection from a multi-hierarchical drone configuration using centralized-control communication networks, considering various mobility models and varying fleet sizes. Each drone is operated by one Ground Control Station (GCS), and all traces and computation processes are centrally controlled by a single edge server. To streamline our experiments, we focused on two aspects of data: drone video capture data and drone trace data.

For drone video capture data in the real-world experiment category, we gathered 30 video clips from three types of drones (two Skydio 2+ drones, two Parrot Anifa AI drones, and one Parrot Anifa USA drone). Each drone had three different mobility settings: mission-based plan model, Gaussian-Markov model, and random model. Drone video clips were transmitted to GCS via a simple, reliable, and widely available data link, such as IEEE 802.11. Metrics were calculated based on both video codec type and video resolution.

In terms of drone flight trace gathering, we utilized real-world experiments to generate fleets of 2 and 4 drones. Traces were formatted as JSON files and stored in a NoSQL database. Metrics were calculated on (i) the goodput through a network monitor at a GCS and (ii) detailed flight traces information, including longitude, height, speed (mph), and ascent (feet). For every millisecond, one throughput data point was sent from the drones to the GCS for recording and archival purposes.

4.2   Evaluation Metrics Discussion

In evaluating video transmission results, a comprehensive assessment involves both subjective and objective metrics. Subjective evaluation, conducted through a Mean Opinion Score (MOS) questionnaire, captures users' perceptions and experiences across key categories such as visual presentation, sound quality, smooth playback, absence of freezes, and overall satisfaction. MOS provides a qualitative measure, allowing users to express their opinions and preferences on the multimedia content. This human-centric approach is crucial for understanding the real-world impact of video transmission on user satisfaction. Detailed topics, example questions, and the number of questions list can be found in Table 2.

On the other hand, incorporating objective metrics is essential for a more technical and quantitative assessment. Peak Signal-to-Noise Ratio (PSNR) serves as an objective metric, measuring the quality of the transmitted video signal by evaluating the difference between the original and received signals. PSNR offers a numerical representation of video fidelity, providing insights into the technical performance of the transmission.

The synergy between subjective MOS evaluations and objective PSNR metrics is beneficial for a holistic understanding of video transmission quality. While MOS captures the user's perceptual experience, PSNR quantifies the technical aspects, ensuring a well-rounded evaluation. Combining both subjective and objective assessments enhances the robustness of the evaluation process, facilitating a comprehensive analysis that considers both user satisfaction and technical quality. This dual approach is pivotal for addressing diverse aspects of video transmission, ultimately leading to more informed decisions and improvements in multimedia delivery systems.

Table 2. Questionnaire detailed topics, example questions, and the number of questions list for video transmission results.

Catgory	Topic	Question Example - No. of Questions
1	Visual Presentation	How satisfied with video clarity? (1-5) - 5
2	Sound Quality	How clear is the audio? (1-5) - 3
3	Smooth Playback	Rate video smoothness (1-5) - 2
4	Absence of Freezes	Any interruptions or freezes? (1-4) -3
5	Effectiveness	Satisfied with absence of disruptive elements? (1-5) - 2
6	Other Issues	Notice any concerns? Specify. −1
7	Overall Satisfaction	Rate overall satisfaction (1–5). - 1

The evaluation metrics for our HCI user interface and Air-to-Ground Coordination system again encompass both subjective and objective measures to ensure a comprehensive understanding of performance. To evaluate the user interface experience, we rely on feedback from GCS agents, treating their opinions as subjective metrics. Our open-source UI, freely accessible on community discussion boards and regularly updated logs on GitHub, encourages transparency and collaboration, fostering a participatory environment. We have specifically engaged Missouri Soybean field farmers and Florida citrus farmers, providing them with open access to the UI and collecting their opinions to enhance usability.

In terms of objective metrics, we focus on network performance and energy efficiency. Network performance is evaluated through latency and end-to-end delay, measuring the operational efficiency of communication between the GCS agent and the drone. This ensures that real-time data transmission is efficient and responsive. For air-to-ground coordination, we consider optimal scheduling time and energy consumption rate. The former ensures effective coordination timing, optimizing the communication between the air and ground components. Meanwhile, the latter quantifies energy usage for coordination relative to energy usage for flight, providing insights into the system's overall energy efficiency.

The ongoing collection of opinions from farmers reflects our commitment to iterative improvement based on user feedback. The combination of subjective and objective metrics in our evaluation approach ensures a well-rounded understanding of the HCI and Air-to-Ground Coordination system, paving the way for continual enhancements to meet user needs and optimize system performance.

4.3   Evaluation Experiments and Findings

Table 3. Various experiment comparison results (subjective: MOS and objective: PSNR) in terms of the video transmission. Comparison methods include real-world experiments (using built-in video transmission), SITL experiments [10] (based on simulator and traces), DroneNet-Sim [11], our proposed platform, and oracle (original video source).

Experiments	MOS							PSNR
Real-World	3.5 ± 0.75	2.5 ± 0.5	1.9 ± 0.25	1.8 ± 0.5	1.6 ± 1.5	1.8 ± 0.6	2.1 ± 0.8	28 ± 5
SITL	2.3 ± 0.75	3.2 ± 0.5	3.0 ± 0.2	3.2 ± 0.5	3 ± 0.27	3.5 ± 0.7	3.8 ± 0.3	26 ± 10
DroneNet-Sim	3.5 ± 0.6	4.2 ± 0.2	4.0 ± 0.15	4.1 ± 0.1	4.2 ± 0.5	**4.5 ± 0.2**	4.3 ± 0.3	30 ± 5
Ours	**4 ± 0.5**	**4.8 ± 0.2**	**4.5 ± 0.3**	**4.8 ± 0.2**	**4.6 ± 0.2**	4.3 ± 0.1	**4.5 ± 0.5**	**40 ± 10**
Oracle	4.5 ± 0.5	4.7 ± 0.25	4.8 ± 0.12	4.7 ± 0.15	4.4 ± 0.6	4.8 ± 0.1	4.6 ± 0.35	N/A

Table 3 presents a comparative analysis of various image processing methods, including our own, evaluated through Mean Opinion Score (MOS) and Peak Signal-to-Noise Ratio (PSNR) metrics across diverse disaster response scenarios. As we can observe from the results, our method consistently outperforms Real-World, SITL, and DroneNet-Sim counterparts considering both MOS and PSNR values. This superiority is evident not only in terms of higher subjective and objective image quality but also in showcasing lower variability. Across diverse scenarios, our method demonstrates an overall MOS measurement of 4.5 ± 0.5, surpassing Real-world (2.1 ± 0.8), SITL (3.8 ± 0.3), and DroneNet-Sim (4.3 ± 0.3). In terms of the objective metrics PSNR, our video transmission output again outperformance other comparison methods with an overall of 35–45 PSNR that highlights the robust and consistent empirical performance of our method. Notably, our approach closely approaches the Oracle with minimal differences, indicating image quality on par with the theoretical best in the evaluated context. In conclusion, the proposed method excels in both perceived and measured image quality, surpassing counterparts and approaching the optimal quality represented by the Oracle.

The evaluation results presented in Fig. 5 illustrate the performance of our air-to-ground coordination solution implemented in the Air-to-Ground Coordinator User interface, as detailed in the Method section. Based on the collected data, we draw the following conclusions:

Observation 1: Our coordination scheme, leveraging air-to-ground coordination, demonstrates superior performance compared to local execution and the Q-learning-based QL-JTAR [3] solution, particularly in scenarios with low Air-to-Ground ratios. Figure 5a highlights that our approach aligns with Offload Only, where human operators fully coordinate, resulting in a noteworthy improvement of up to 15% in scheduling make-span compared to offload-only schemes (and achieving $\approx$ 85% accuracy with dynamic decision-making). Random offloading exhibits erratic behavior with significant variance, while the scheduling time remains consistently optimal for exclusive local UAV processing, preventing ground queue buildup. In contrast, QL-JTAR shows inefficiency, requiring approximately 800 s in all experiments, particularly proving ineffective for low ratios. Our experimental focus on low Air-to-Ground ratios underscores the excellence of our approach in such scenarios.

Observation 2: Our air-to-ground coordination approach surpasses Random offloading and Local Only execution in terms of energy consumption, providing considerable energy savings (approximately 18% gain) compared to on-boarding only, in addition to offering reasonable energy savings relative to the QL-JTAR solution. As demonstrated in Fig. 5b, the energy consumption rate sharply increases with rising Air-to-Ground ratios for Local Only and Random offloading strategies. However, our approach consistently maintains a lower energy consumption rate than these methods, albeit slightly higher than the Offload Only scheme. This discrepancy is justifiable as the Offload Only scheme only considers transmission energy, excluding video processing energy. Nevertheless, the energy difference between our approach and the Offload Only scheme remains relatively small. Considering our approach's up to 40% improvement in scheduling time over the Offload Only scheme, it becomes evident that our method excels when both time and energy considerations are taken into account.

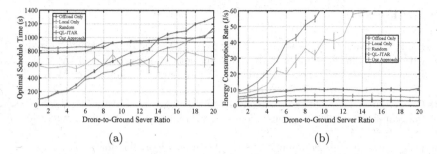

Fig. 5. Various comparisons of air-to-ground coordination strategies have been conducted, encompassing Offload Only (fully coordinated by human operators), exclusive local execution (UAV only), a random approach, the QL-JTAR learning-based approach, and our air-to-ground coordination approach. The results are presented in terms of (a) the correlation between increasing Air-to-Ground ratio (UAV swarm size: human operator) and optimal schedule time (in seconds) and (b) the relationship between Air-to-Ground ratio and the average energy consumption per UAV (in Joules).

5   Conclusion

In this paper, we discuss the role of UAV-swarm-aided in diverse applications and their impact on environmental situational awareness, the complexities associated with constructing UAV testbeds, and highlights the difficulties in achieving repeatability and reproducibility. To address these challenges, we investigate state-of-the-art approaches in advanced UAV simulators, proposing a trace-based simulation design utilizing NS-3. The hierarchical UAV-swarm-aided platform, involving collaboration between low-cost and high-cost drones, demonstrates the synergistic benefits of integrating network and drone simulators. The implemented simulator, designed with Human-Computer Interaction (HCI) principles, advances the understanding of UAV simulation capabilities and emphasizes a user-centric approach. Based on the experiments with real-world UAV traces, encompassing diverse mobility models and video analytics measurements, our platform not only contributes to advancing UAS technology but also prioritizes user experience and system usability in the design of simulators. Futures works can be

Acknowledgments. This study was funded by Florida Gulf Coast University (FGCU) U.A. Whitaker College of Engineering Head Start Funding. We extend our thanks to Alicia Esquival from the University of Missouri-Columbia for her insightful ideas regarding user interface design. Their contributions have greatly enriched the development and design aspects of our project. **Disclosure of Interests:** The authors have no competing interests to declare that are relevant to the content of this article.

References

1. Baidya, S., Shaikh, Z., Levorato, M.: Flynetsim: An open source synchronized UAV network simulator based on ns-3 and ardupilot. In: Proceedings of the 21st ACM International Conference on Modeling, Analysis and Simulation of Wireless and Mobile Systems, pp. 37–45 (2018)
2. Chemodanov, D., Qu, C., Opeoluwa, O., Wang, S., Calyam, P.: Policy-based function-centric computation offloading for real-time drone video analytics. In: 2019 IEEE LANMAN
3. Dab, B., Aitsaadi, N., Langar, R.: Q-learning algorithm for joint computation offloading and resource allocation in edge cloud. In: 2019 IFIP/IEEE IM, pp. 45–52. IEEE (2019)
4. Drefahl, P.: UAV-swarm-aided disaster response platform source code. https://github.com/PauloDrefahl/Drone-Management-Software
5. Duong, T.Q., et al.: UAV caching in 6G networks: a survey on models, techniques and applications. Phys. Commun. **51**, 101532 (2022)
6. Fontes, H., Campos, R., Ricardo, M.: Improving the ns-3 tracebasedpropagation-lossmodel to support multiple access wireless scenarios. In: Proceedings of the 10th Workshop on Ns-3, p. 77-83. WNS3 '18, Association for Computing Machinery, New York, NY, USA (2018). https://doi.org/10.1145/3199902.3199912, https://doi.org/10.1145/3199902.3199912
7. Jedari, B., Premsankar, G., Illahi, G., Di Francesco, M., Mehrabi, A., Ylä-Jääski, A.: Video caching, analytics, and delivery at the wireless edge: a survey and future directions. IEEE Commun. Surv. Tutorials **23**(1), 431–471 (2020)
8. Kashef, M., Visvizi, A., Troisi, O.: Smart city as a smart service system: Human-computer interaction and smart city surveillance systems. Comput. Hum. Behav. **124**, 106923 (2021)
9. Morel, A.E., Ufuktepe, D.K., Ignatowicz, R., Riddle, A., Qu, C., Calyam, P., Palaniappan, K.: Enhancing network-edge connectivity and computation security in drone video analytics. In: 2020 IEEE Applied Imagery Pattern Recognition Workshop (AIPR), pp. 1–12. IEEE (2020)
10. Qays, H.M., Jumaa, B.A., Salman, A.D.: Design and implementation of autonomous quadcopter using SITL simulator. Iraqi J. Comput., Commun., Contr. Syst. Eng. **20**(1), 1–15 (2020)
11. Qu, C., Morel, A.E., Dahlquist, D., Calyam, P.: Dronenet-sim: A learning-based trace simulation framework for control networking in drone video analytics. In: Proceedings of the 6th ACM Workshop on Micro Aerial Vehicle Networks, Systems, and Applications, pp. 1–6 (2020)
12. Qu, C., Sorbelli, F.B., Singh, R., Calyam, P., Das, S.K.: Environmentally-aware and energy-efficient multi-drone coordination and networking for disaster response. IEEE Transactions on Network and Service Management (2023)
13. Ramisetty, R.R., Qu, C., Aktar, R., Wang, S., Calyam, P., Palaniappan, K.: Dynamic computation off-loading and control based on occlusion detection in drone video analytics. In: Proceedings of the 21st International Conference on Distributed Computing and Networking, pp. 1–10 (2020)
14. Scott Jr, E.A.: SPA Design and Architecture: Understanding single-page web applications. Simon and Schuster (2015)
15. Sedrakyan, G., Mannens, E., Verbert, K.: Guiding the choice of learning dashboard visualizations: Linking dashboard design and data visualization concepts. J. Comput. Lang. **50**, 19–38 (2019)

16. Tmušić, G., et al.: Current practices in UAS-based environmental monitoring. Remote Sens. **12**(6), 1001 (2020)
17. Ultralytics: Yolov8 document. https://docs.ultralytics.com/

Point Target Detection for Multimodal Communication

Hannah VanderHoeven$^{(\boxtimes)}$ (iD), Nathaniel Blanchard(iD),
and Nikhil Krishnaswamy(iD)

Colorado State University, Fort Collins Co 80523,, USA
{hannah.vanderhoeven,nathaniel.blanchard,
nikhil.krishnaswamy}@colostate.edu

Abstract. The future of multimodal communication between humans and AIs will rest on AI's ability to recognize and interpret non-linguistic cues, such as gestures. In the context of shared collaborative tasks, a central gesture is deixis, or pointing, used to indicate objects and referents in context. In this paper, we extend our previously-developed methods for gesture recognition and apply them to a collaborative task dataset where objects are frequently indicated using deixis. We apply gesture detection to deictic gestures in the task context and use a "pointing frustum" to retrieve objects that are the likely targets of deixis. We perform a series of experiments to assess both the quality of gesture detection and optimal values for the radii of the conical frustum, and discuss the application of target detection using pointing to multimodal collaborative tasks between humans and computers.

Keywords: Deictic gesture · Gesture semantics · Multimodal dialogue

1 Introduction

As artificial intelligence becomes more ubiquitous and sophisticated, users will increasingly expect computers to behave more like humans. This includes the capacity to understand not only common input modalities like language, but also non-linguistic modalities such as gestures. A critical component of multimodal human-human interaction is deictic gesture (pointing), and therefore accurate identification of pointing targets in real time is an important feature for multimodal language understanding and human-computer interaction. By using pointing vectors to aid in identifying targets in three-dimensional space, the semantic denotata intended by a user can be extracted from a video stream. In addition, when combined with other features, such as speech, the data extracted can further aid the overall understanding of how humans are communicating with one another or with an intelligent system. For the most accurate analysis and seamless use, correctly and consistently identifying people, gestures, and their intended semantic targets in real time is vital. We previously developed a pipeline to automatically detect preparatory, "stroke," and recovery phases of gestures [26], based on the gesture semantics previously developed by the

V. G. Duffy (Ed.): HCII 2024, LNCS 14709, pp. 356–373, 2024.
https://doi.org/10.1007/978-3-031-61060-8_25

community [1,9,18]. Our method showed promising results in automatic identification of complex multi-frame gestures in real time, with lower computational overhead than competing approaches.

In this paper, we incorporate this model into a pipeline that detects the semantic target of pointing gestures, specifically. This serves as a direct operationalization of the pointing cone semantics of Kranstedt et al. [13], among others. We demonstrate this capability in the context of a small group task where people communicate with each other using both gesture and language [10]. To effectively extract instances of pointing and the associated targets from a small group scenario, a few things must be considered. First, accurate gesture detection on a per-participant basis is necessary to consistently match the pointing vector with who is communicating. Second, precision errors can occur when a single vector is used to select objects, since it is unlikely that the objects and vector line up perfectly. To account for this, a "pointing frustum" is formed around the pointing vector to create a "detection" region in three-dimensional space. Objects that intersect with this region, based on the center of the object are selected as targets on interest [12]. As pointing specificity degrades with distance from the pointer to the target but is still interpretable by other humans at a distance [25], selecting the most fitting near and far base radii for the pointing frustum is important to correctly identify intended targets in a small space, without selecting unintended targets. We compare an automatic pointing detection method with a human-annotated ground truth, and frustum radii to determine the feasibility of point and target detection of small objects. We establish a novel baseline for object selection in a joint situated task using deictic gesture only, and in the process expose how challenging automatic inference of indicated objects in a collaborative setting can be, due to variation across individuals and groups in communication and deictic strategies. We discuss how target objects detected through pointing can then provide important context to the automated understanding and interpretation of interactions in a small group task, and how additional features might help add more context to overcome inaccuracies.

2   Related Work

In various human computer interaction studies, pointing is a common gesture used to indicate the intended target of a user or study participant. Use of pointing for deixis spans many different languages and cultures [11], making it an ideal gesture to be integrated with HCI systems. Pointing may be used to execute hardware commands or interact with a user interface [7]. Pointing is also an important feature of small group communication especially when combined with speech, as it allows individuals to ground their utterances to the physical environment around them, which adds critical context. For example, any use of demonstratives ("this one," "those," etc.) to refer to physical entities must almost necessarily be coupled with a deictic gesture to be interpretable.

While pointing can add useful context to communication, relying only on non-verbal deictic gesture, such as pointing, does not always guarantee accurate target selection. Various experiments have been run to determine the potential increase in accuracy of pointing when combined with other features, such as speech [5]. In the mentioned study researchers experimented the effectiveness of single plane pointing in an augmented reality, from various perspectives, with and without speech. Participants were required to either point at or "identify" (with pointing and speech) an intended target from various perspectives. They found that combining speech and gesture, accuracy was increased, however there were still errors selecting the intended target.

In [16], participants interacted with a virtual avatar using a combination of gesture and speech in a shared construction task. Subjects were placed in one of four conditions that varied the information presented to them and the presence of physical cues in the environment that served as distractors. It was found that users adapted the direction of their deixis toward the correct target region, except in cases when explicitly misleading information about the role of the surrounding physical environment was presented.

These studies and more follow from a history of gesture semantics that continues traditions of viewing gesture as either *simulated action* [6,19] or a general mode of reference [4,28]. Lascarides and Stone [18] interpret gesture on the basis of the co-perception of gesture and denotatum. This is critical for deictic gesture in particular as the use of deictic gesture G presupposes that its interpretation function $[\![G]\!]$ is also co-perceptible by the intended recipient of the gesture. Given the typical use of deixis as an indicator of physical items, $[\![G]\!]$ readily resolves to an item in the environment under this model. The gesture abstract meaning representation (GAMR) language that we leverage in this paper [3] also builds directly on Lascarides and Stone's division of deictic and iconic gestures [17].

van der Sluis and Krahmer [25] studied deixis in the context of multimodal referring expressions and found a main effect of distance. The decreased specificity of pointing over distance can be modeled as a "cone" *a la* Kranstedt et al. [12]—a volume narrower at the vertex (the pointing digit) and wider as distance from the digit increases. In this paper we experiment with a "pointing *frustum*" (viz. a cone with the tip truncated) to create a region of detection around the pointing vector. This combined with other features in a multimodal system may further improve the accuracy of pointing as a means to select the intended target.

3   Methodologies

In this section we introduce our dataset, and the tools and methods used in our experiments.

3.1   Weights Task Dataset

The Weights Task Dataset [10] (WTD) is a collection of audiovisual recordings of a collaborative problem solving (CPS) task. Groups of 3 work together to determine the weights of various small colored blocks using a tabletop balance scale. The data comprises 10 groups, each including videos from 3 Azure Kinect

RGBD cameras at different angles [2]. The participants do not know that weights of the blocks follow an instance of the Fibonacci sequence, where each block is the combined weight of the previous two smaller blocks. At the end of the task the group is asked to determine the weight of one mystery block which, according to the pattern, is the combined weight of the previous two blocks. The dataset totals approximately 4 h of recordings. Figure 1 shows an example still from Group 1 and Group 2 of the Weight Task Dataset.

Fig. 1. Sample stills from Groups 1 and 2 of the Weights Task Dataset.

This dataset contains many different forms of real-world multimodal communication in the course of the task-oriented collaboration, including but not limited to speech, gesture, body language, and gaze. While these features exist in each of the ten groups, the exact language and gestures used to communicate can vary, often widely, between groups and even participants. In the domain of deixis alone, for example, specific deictic gestures might range from gesturing to a target with the entire hand to using one or more fingers, or even an object like a pen, giving us diverse, challenging and realistic data to experiment with. Additionally, the blocks themselves are quite small, at 1.5" (38.1 mm) or 2" (50.8 mm) on a side, in a working space (table and chairs) that is approximately 5' × 5' (1.52 m × 1.52 m). Naturally, pointing with the fingers only (rather than extending the entire arm) is the most common form of deictic gesture used to indicate targets in this dataset. Thus pointing is an important feature that can be used to select the intended target; deixis might be used to indicate objects that are the subject of a current question or subgoal, or used to draw attention of other group members to specific items, meaning that it is a potentially important predictor of how the collaborative task will unfold. Referring back to Fig. 1, in both examples participants are seen gesturing to a specific block, using deictic pointing gestures.

Data Preprocessing. A few data prepossessing steps were required in order to test our proposed target selection solution using the WTD. Human-annotation of frames in which pointing gestures occurred were gathered for a subset of groups. This process involved manually stepping through each frame and marking a participant ID[1] along with the start and stop frame for each deictic gesture. For each manually annotated frame we also saved the block's color, quaternion describing its location, location in 3D Cartesian space, and 2D bounding box information. This gave us a maximally precise object location in each frame against which to assess the quality of object selection with automated deixis detection compared to a human-annotated ground truth. From there we ran a linear interpolation algorithm to fill in the object locations for the intervening video frames. Figure 2 shows an example of the target blocks on the scale, with and without the overlaid 2D bounding box drawn from the manual annotations. Because of the time required to annotate each video, only a representative subset of groups were selected for our experiments.

Fig. 2. Target blocks, with and without bounding box overlay.

3.2   Robust Gesture Recognition

In order to accurately determine both when a participant is pointing, and the intended target of that point within in a scene, certain specific information needs to be extracted from the video frame. Gesture recognition has previously been treated as data-hungry computer vision problem [21], and while sophisticated approaches like vision transformers remain state of the art, a high-throughput experimental scenario like ours demands a more lightweight solution. In [8] we demonstrated that our robust gesture recognition pipeline [26] displayed competitive performance with much larger models on the gestures of interest in the WTD using only automatically-extracted 6 degrees of freedom joint positions instead of full pixel or depth channels.

Our method consists of a pipeline to automatically detect *preparatory*, *stroke*, and *recovery* phases of gestures, using joint positions automatically extracted from the video signal before classification [26]. Design choices when developing that framework were based on the gesture semantics previously defined by the community [1,9,18] (namely Kendon's pre-/post-stroke *hold* formulation). Here,

---

[1] Participants are conventionally indexed 1–3 from left to right in the video frame.

we leverage that system to aid in determining when someone is pointing in order to determine targets of interest in 3D space. Our pipeline which consists of three stages—a static classification model, movement segmentation algorithm, and phase breakdown—distills videos down to "key frames," which we define as the union of the pre-stroke, stroke, and post-stroke phases, where the most of the semantically significant movement for a gesture takes place. In this use case, these key frame span the semantically significant movement of pointing gestures. Figure 3 shows the gesture detection pipeline, with the addition of our steps taken for point based target detection.

The static classification model recognizes the general static shape of complex gestures when in a *hold* phase. The movement segmentation routine aids in breaking down a video into segments of similar movements. The phase breakdown uses the classification model and video segments to identify and classify the segments and frames that are in a *hold* phase, and thus most semantically significant, or adjacent to the most semantically-significant frames.

We hypothesize that for deictic gestures such as pointing, the "key frames" dictate when a participant is not just pointing but also pointing toward the intended target, thus lining up the object, reference point (in this case, the body), and the frame of reference [20]. Using the output of our gesture detection pipeline, we can determine which frames are candidates for containing pointing gestures, and determine from there determine the intended target.

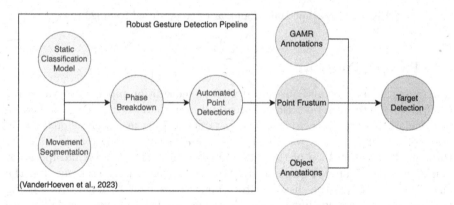

Fig. 3. Complex gesture and target detection pipeline. Items within the box denote components already established in VanderHoeven et al. (2023) [26].

3.3   MediaPipe

As mentioned, our recognition pipeline depends on automatically-extracted joint positions rather than raw pixels, and these must be extracted using some off-the-shelf software. Hand detection tools, such as MediaPipe, an open source library developed by Google [29], support such gesture recognition methods by performing this automatic extraction (see Fig. 4). These joint positions, or *landmarks*, of detected hands [29] can then be used to train custom gesture recognition models such as ours with a wide range of applications.

MediaPipe has a few limitations that need to be overcome to handle more complex scenarios with multiple participants. While MediaPipe has the ability to return multiple hands from a single frame, the ordering of the hands is not consistent and can vary frame to frame. Because of this, participants' hands can be mixed up, leading to inconsistent hand tracking. In Sect. 3.5 we detail how we handled this issue.

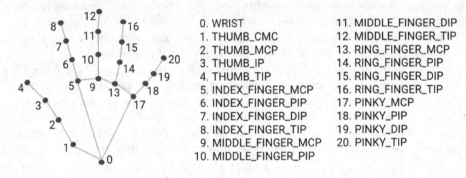

Fig. 4. MediaPipe Hand Landmarks (reproduced from [29]).

3.4   Pointing Frustum

Leveraging MediaPipe and our robust gesture recognition pipeline, we can identify frames of interest for deictic gestures, and from there use the hand landmarks to calculate a pointing vector to identify target objects in a scene. For the purposes of our experiments we calculate our pointing vector by extending a ray through the base and tip of the index finger, comprising the MediaPipe landmarks at index 5 and 8, respectively. We then extend the vector out into the environment 5 times the distance from finger base joint to fingertip, starting from the tip of the index finger (joint 8). Figure 5 shows the joints used to create the pointing vector relative to the MediaPipe landmarks.

When using a vector embedded within a single plane to detect targets of interest, it is very unlikely that the vector and object of interest will line up perfectly. Because of this, we use a "pointing frustum" to create a target detection region. A frustum is a geometric shape resembling a cone, where a radius value is set for the top and bottom of the cone. By using a pointing frustum we can specify a "near" (or top) radius at the tip of the index finger and "far" (or bottom) radius at the end of the pointing vector to allow increased

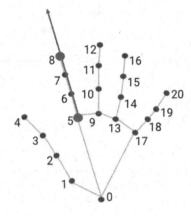

Fig. 5. Pointing vector relative to MediaPipe landmarks.

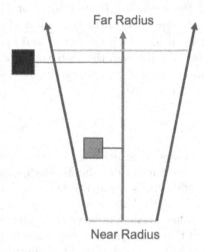

Fig. 6. Top down view of the pointing frustum. The red block is an example of an object that falls *outside* the detection region, the green block is an example of an object that falls *inside* the detection region and would be marked a target of interest (Color figure online).

granularity when experimenting with detection regions. This reproduces the pointing cone semantics of [12], and makes it extensible to allow for different levels of imprecision at distance. Figure 6 shows a top down view of the frustum, noting that in a real scenario, the frustum is a three-dimensional volume with circular cross-sections. The red block in the figure denotes a target object outside the detection region, whereas the green box is an example of a target of interest. We determine if a target is in the detection region by first finding the location of the target perpendicular to the vector, outlined in Fig. 7. From there we can find the radius of the frustum at that point and determine if the center

$$\vec{P} = p2 - p1$$
$$\vec{B} = p3 - p1$$
$$\vec{A} = \frac{\vec{B} \cdot \vec{P}}{\|\vec{P}\|^2} \vec{P} \qquad (1)$$
$$x = p1 + \vec{A}$$

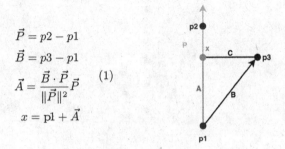

Fig. 7. Calculation of pointing vector target, where P represents the pointing vector, $p3$ represents the center of a target object, and x represents $p3$ projected onto P

of the object is within that radius. This process is depicted in Fig. 7 and Eq. 1. x denotes the center of the candidate target object projected onto the pointing vector (P). $r_d = r_n + \frac{r_f - r_n}{\|P\|} \|A\|$ gives the radius of the pointing frustum at distance $\|A\|$ from the "near" plane (where r_n and r_f are the near and far radii, respectively). If the distance from the center of the candidate target to its projection x is less than or equal to r_d, the candidate lies within the pointing frustum and is considered "retrieved."

3.5 Azure Landmarks

In order to implement gesture recognition on multiple participants, additional assurances needed to be built on top of the MediaPipe hand recognition [26]. MediaPipe includes the ability to track multiple hands but does not guarantee the order of the returned hands. This means that participants' hands can get mixed up (for instance, if they overlap, or leave the frame and return), leading to incorrect assignment and therefore gesture classifications and attributions. For instance if participant 1 is pointing at the blue block, but the gesture is associated with participant 2, the result would be inaccurate representations of gestures within the scene. We therefore took the locations of joints on the bodies of the different participants, which were extracted from the depth video stream (see Fig. 8). Using these, we calculated a bounding box on each of the participants' hands, to allow MediaPipe to retrieve the hand joints from a localized area. By tracking the bounding box to the wrist joint according to Azure, we could more consistently associate hands (and thus complex gestures and movements) with a participant.

Fig. 8. Azure body landmarks overlaid on a frame.

3.6 Depth Information

In addition to body landmark locations, the Azure SDK facilitates retrieving framewise depth information. This depth information is saved as grayscale Z-coordinate values for each pixel in field of view, measured in millimeters. Figure 9 shows an example depth frame, with a semi-opaque overlay of the RGB data. The depth information allowed us to convert hand landmarks and object locations between two-dimensional and three-dimensional space, thus allowing us to create a pointing vector, and detect targets in three-dimensional space.

3.7 GAMR

Ground truth target object annotations are provided in the WTD in the form of Gesture Abstract Meaning Representation (GAMR) annotations [3]. GAMR annotations comprise up of four main parts, the gesture type, gesturer, semantic content, and addressee. For the purposes of our experiments we focus only on the *deictic* gesture type, or gestures that refer to a location by pointing. Figure 10 shows an example of a pointing gesture referencing a block. ARG0 denotes the gesturer, ARG1 the semantic content of the gesture and ARG2 is the addressee or intended recipient. Figures 11 and 12 show examples of GAMR annotations from the WTD. Note that in, e.g., Fig. 11, the gesturer (ARG0) is participant_1 and semantic content of the gesture (ARG1) is the blue_block. We used this information in conjunction with the targets selected by intersection with the pointing frustum to verify if object selections were correct.

Fig. 9. Azure Depth Data with RGB overlay

```
(d / deixis-GA
    :ARG0 (g / gesturer)
    :ARG1 (b / block)
    :ARG2 (a / addressee))
```

Fig. 10. Deixis GAMR template according to [3].

Fig. 11. Group 1 deixis GAMR example

4   Experiments

Our experimental protocol involved assessing the values of near and far frustum radii that provided the best possible and most consistent object selection across multiple groups. Relevant video frames that were tested against included those which were annotated with GAMR type `deixis-GA`, and had been annotated as containing a point gesture, or the gesture recognizer detected one. From there

Fig. 12. Group 2 deixis GAMR example.

we assessed which objects intersected the pointing frustum. Per-frame recall, precision, and F1 were calculated against the ARG1 of the GAMR annotation. This repeated for each relevant frame and we kept a running average for each metric across the entire video. In order to determine the number of correct inferences and type I or type II errors based on selected blocks, we created the following guidelines using the GAMR annotations:

- If ARG1 is a single block, if the selected block matches the annotation, it is considered a true positive. If selected blocks do not match the annotation, they are considered false positives.
- If ARG1 is a combination of blocks, such as when the GAMR annotations did not specify a single block as the denoted target, but rather a set, each selected block that matches a block in ARG1 is considered a true positive. Selected blocks not contained in ARG1 are considered false positives.
- If a block included in ARG1 is not selected, it is considered a false negative.

The subset of groups we evaluated against included groups 1, 2, 4, and 5 of the WTD (see Sect. 3.1).

5   Results and Discussion

Table 1 shows the average F1, recall and precision across all 4 videos for different combinations of radii, assessed against both the human-annotated pointing frames and those retrieved by the automated gesture detection. It is worth noting the variability in F1 scores; in many cases the standard deviation is almost the same as the average. This indicates the challenge in selecting a single set of frustum radii for the most effective target selection. Additionally, the F1 scores over the the human-annotated frames and the automatically selected frames are generally very similar, showing that our automated pipeline's frame selection achieves similar results when compared to human annotators.

Table 1. Average target detection F1 for human annotated and automatically detected frames from groups 1, 2, 4 and 5.

Near	Far	μ Human F1	σ Human F1	μ Auto F1	σ Auto F1
20	50	0.187	0.170	0.185	0.192
30	60	0.213	0.175	0.199	0.191
40	70	0.282	0.254	0.275	0.278
50	80	0.349	0.235	0.338	0.274
60	90	0.401	0.216	0.384	0.267
70	100	0.417	0.207	0.404	0.260
80	110	0.420	0.210	0.404	0.261
90	120	0.418	0.206	0.400	0.261
100	130	0.416	0.195	0.396	0.253

The relatively high standard deviations shown in Table 1 indicate the variation present across groups in the dataset. We also present group-wise results showing the average metrics across all frames vs. the radius sizes. This provides additional granularity in determining the most effective radius combination on a per group basis, as opposed to selecting and testing radius combinations one at a time.

Fig. 13. Incremental radius step example, Group 1.

Figures 13 and 14 show examples of the incremental radius steps, and show how as the size of the pointing frustum grows, as the detected targets change.

Fig. 14. Incremental radius step Example, Group 2.

Blocks outlines in green indicate those selected as targets of pointing. Red indicates those not selected. Note that in Fig. 14, as the radius grows the green block is the only one ever selected. This is because the remaining blocks are resting on the paper behind the scale, and are therefore behind the origin of the pointing vector and the frustum's near plane.

Figures 15a–15d show experimental results across a range of different near and far radius combination for each group, averaged across all relevant frames of the video. We compare metrics over those frames annotated by humans (ground truth) and those where pointing gestures were detected by the automated detection pipeline (therefore comprising an end-to-end system with gesture detection and target selection in a single step). Maximum F1 score is indicated with the purple dot. The maximum F1 scores vary anywhere between 0.33 (Group 4) and 0.69 (Group 2). This range is likely due to variability in accuracy and style of pointing as they are used by each participant/group. In addition to human inaccuracy, pointing in such a small space is likely to return more than one object as the radii grow. Because of this, as the frustum size increases we have the potential to return more false positive targets. This is reflected in the increase in recall as the radii grow, but the eventual decline in precision and F1.

In most cases, except Group 4, using the end-to-end system, where frames were selected by the automated gesture pipeline, outperformed detection over human annotations. In Group 5 particularly, the gesture pipeline frames eventually overtook the human annotated frames by about 0.1 F1 overall and thereafter remained consistent. We hypothesize this may be because the automatically selected frames are ones that the static classification model recognizes as a point with the index finger. In Group 5, sometimes participants would point with pens, or would gesture at the blocks using their entire hand. Overcoming this limitation is another potential area for future work. In other groups the accuracy statistic of the human annotated frames more closely matches the automated frames, indicating that the participants were more likely to point using the index finger (as expected).

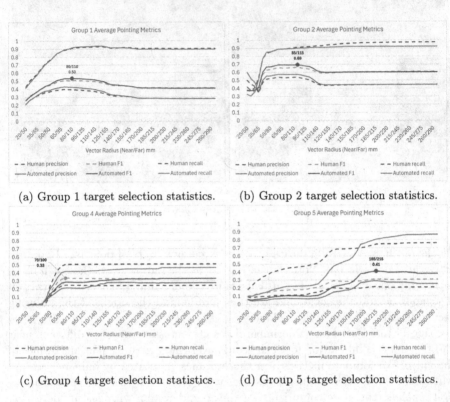

(a) Group 1 target selection statistics.   (b) Group 2 target selection statistics.

(c) Group 4 target selection statistics.   (d) Group 5 target selection statistics.

Fig. 15. Average precision, recall, and F1 for 4 test groups, averaged over all frames. Solid lines indicate where frame selection was performed using the robust gesture detection pipeline [26]. Dashed lines indicate where frame selection was performed by human annotation.

6   Conclusion and Future Work

Deictic gestures are common in small group communication as a means to indicate objects and referents in context. The ability to both identify deictic gestures, such as pointing, and to identify their denotata in context is a critical capability in interpreting multimodal communicative acts in situated physical shared tasks. In this paper we leveraged a previously-developed pipeline to help automatically detect semantically significant movement for a given gesture, and save off the "key frames" for future use [26]. Here we leveraged that pipeline as a means to automatically detect pointing gestures, and created a pointing frustum based on that information for target detection. The combination of our automated pointing detection and the pointing frustum showed promise as a means to detected the intended target of a participant. Our detection pipeline preformed similarly too, and in some situations better than, the human annotated ground truth annotation as a reliable and robust way of performing object selection via deixis in challenging, real-world data.

There is room for improvement when it comes to the overall accuracy of target detection, with the maximum F1 achieved across individual groups and a range of radius combinations being about 0.69. Future work includes leveraging additional context from other features, like speech, in a larger multimodal system to further aid in narrowing down the exact intended target in a small space. Speech can help provide a signal to select which of a set of objects is the true intended target. It is important to emphasize here that in this paper target selection is conducted using only deixis, and in the actual group task, pointing inaccuracies likely did not hinder participants' ability communicate with each other, as they relied on additional communicative modalities, such as speech and gaze, to provide additional context and information to each other. These additional features could be used as tools to help further signal the true intended target from a group of selected targets. For instance, this could be done by aligning the speech signal with gesture for disambiguation, such as using language to select one among a set of objects indicated through deixis, as done in [14, 15, 22–24].

Better accuracy in object selection using deixis may also be aided with the addition of other features. For instance, objects that were the anchor of recent actions (e.g., recently moved blocks) may be more likely to be a deictic target, because partial information about them is more likely to be known after the action. Therefore they may be more likely to be the denotatum of a spoken demonstrative, and thus singled out with deixis.

Furthermore, we relied on human object annotations as the ground truth against which to assess our performance. A true end-to-end system for target selection via deixis would not only perform pointing detection and frustum construction automatically, as we do, but also automatically detect the positions of the blocks in the video. Object detection via methods such as 6 degrees of freedom object pose would significantly reduce the preprocessing time required to leverage our pipeline, allowing us to experiment on more real world scenarios.

Finally, when humans engage in collaborative problem solving (CPS) tasks such as the Weights Task, multiple simultaneous communicative modalities are implicated. The ability to detect gestures and make inferences about their meanings is a critical capability for automated agents that support human-human collaboration, as in real-time project teams or classrooms. Approaches need to be lightweight and extensible to create tractable methods for interactive AI in supporting a wider range of CPS tasks [27].

Acknowledgements. This work was partially supported by the National Science Foundation under award DRL 2019805 to Colorado State University. The views expressed are those of the authors and do not reflect the official policy or position of the U.S. Government. All errors and mistakes are, of course, the responsibilities of the authors. Special thanks to Nathan Kampbell for the linear interpolation tool used in Sect. 3.1, and to Jade Collins and Carlos Mabrey for extensive data annotation.

References

1. Arnheim, R.: Hand and mind: what gestures reveal about thought by David McNeill. Leonardo **27**(4), 358–358 (1994), publisher: The MIT Press
2. Bradford, M., Khebour, I., Blanchard, N., Krishnaswamy, N.: Automatic detection of collaborative states in small groups using multimodal features. In: Proceedings of the 24th International Conference on Artificial Intelligence in Education (2023)
3. Brutti, R., Donatelli, L., Lai, K., Pustejovsky, J.: Abstract meaning representation for gesture. In: Proceedings of the Thirteenth Language Resources and Evaluation Conference. pp. 1576–1583. European Language Resources Association, Marseille, France (Jun 2022). https://aclanthology.org/2022.lrec-1.169
4. Clark, H.H., Schreuder, R., Buttrick, S.: Common ground at the understanding of demonstrative reference. J. Verbal Learn. Verbal Behav. **22**(2), 245–258 (1983)
5. Herbort, O., Krause, L.M.: The efficiency of augmented pointing with and without speech in a collaborative virtual environment. In: Duffy, V.G. (ed.) Digital Human Modeling and Applications in Health, Safety, Ergonomics and Risk Management. pp. 510–524. Lecture Notes in Computer Science, Springer Nature Switzerland, Cham (2023). https://doi.org/10.1007/978-3-031-35741-1_37
6. Hostetter, A.B., Alibali, M.W.: Visible embodiment: gestures as simulated action. Psych. Bull. Review **15**, 495–514 (2008)
7. Hu, Z., Xu, Y., Lin, W., Wang, Z., Sun, Z.: Augmented pointing gesture estimation for human-robot interaction. In: 2022 International Conference on Robotics and Automation (ICRA), pp. 6416–6422 (2022). https://doi.org/10.1109/ICRA46639.2022.9811617
8. Kandoi, C., et al.: Intentional microgesture recognition for extended human-computer interaction. In: Kurosu, M., Hashizume, A. (eds.) Human-Computer Interaction: Thematic Area, HCI 2023, Held as Part of the 25th HCI International Conference, HCII 2023, Copenhagen, Denmark, July 23–28, 2023, Proceedings, Part I, pp. 499–518. Springer Nature Switzerland, Cham (2023). https://doi.org/10.1007/978-3-031-35596-7_32
9. Kendon, A.: Gesticulation and speech: two aspects of the process of utterance. Relation. Verbal Nonverbal Commun. **25**(1980), 207–227 (1980)
10. Khebour, I., et al.: When text and speech are not enough: a multimodal dataset of collaboration in a situated task (2024)
11. Kita, S.: Pointing: a foundational building block of human communication. Pointing: Where language, culture, and cognition meet, pp. 1–8 (2003)
12. Kranstedt, A., Lücking, A., Pfeiffer, T., Rieser, H., Wachsmuth, I.: Deixis: how to determine demonstrated objects using a pointing cone. In: Gibet, S., Courty, N., Kamp, J.-F. (eds.) GW 2005. LNCS (LNAI), vol. 3881, pp. 300–311. Springer, Heidelberg (2006). https://doi.org/10.1007/11678816_34
13. Kranstedt, A., Wachsmuth, I.: Incremental generation of multimodal deixis referring to objects. In: Proceedings of the Tenth European Workshop on Natural Language Generation (ENLG-05) (2005)
14. Krishnaswamy, N., et al.: Diana's world: A situated multimodal interactive agent. In: Proceedings of the AAAI Conference on Artificial Intelligence. vol. 34, pp. 13618–13619 (2020)
15. Krishnaswamy, N., et al.: Communicating and acting: Understanding gesture in simulation semantics. In: IWCS 2017-12th International Conference on Computational Semantics-Short papers (2017)

16. Krishnaswamy, N., Pustejovsky, J.: Deictic adaptation in a virtual environment. In: Creem-Regehr, S., Schöning, J., Klippel, A. (eds.) Spatial Cognition 2018. LNCS (LNAI), vol. 11034, pp. 180–196. Springer, Cham (2018). https://doi.org/10.1007/978-3-319-96385-3_13

17. Lascarides, A., Stone, M.: Formal semantics for iconic gesture. Universität Potsdam (2006)

18. Lascarides, A., Stone, M.: A formal semantic analysis of gesture. J. Seman. **26**(4), 393–449 (2009), publisher: Oxford University Press

19. McNeill, D.: Language and gesture, vol. 2. Cambridge University Press (2000)

20. Moratz, R., Nebel, B., Freksa, C.: Qualitative spatial reasoning about relative position. In: Freksa, C., Brauer, W., Habel, C., Wender, K.F. (eds.) Spatial Cognition 2002. LNCS, vol. 2685, pp. 385–400. Springer, Heidelberg (2003). https://doi.org/10.1007/3-540-45004-1_22

21. Narayana, P., Beveridge, R., Draper, B.A.: Gesture recognition: focus on the hands. In: Proceedings of the IEEE Conference on Computer Vision and Pattern Recognition, pp. 5235–5244 (2018)

22. Pustejovsky, J., Krishnaswamy, N.: Embodied human-computer interactions through situated grounding. In: Proceedings of the 20th ACM International Conference on Intelligent Virtual Agents, pp. 1–3 (2020)

23. Pustejovsky, J., Krishnaswamy, N.: Situated meaning in multimodal dialogue: human-robot and human-computer interactions. Traitement Automatique des Langues **61**(3), 17–41 (2020)

24. Pustejovsky, J., Krishnaswamy, N.: Embodied human computer interaction. KI-Künstliche Intelligenz **35**(3–4), 307–327 (2021)

25. van der Sluis, I., Krahmer, E.: The influence of target size and distance on the production of speech and gesture in multimodal referring expressions. In: Proceedings of the 5th International Conference on Spoken Language Processing (ICSLP'04) (2004)

26. VanderHoeven, H., Blanchard, N., Krishnaswamy, N.: Robust motion recognition using gesture phase annotation. In: Digital Human Modeling and Applications in Health, Safety, Ergonomics and Risk Management: 14th International Conference, DHM 2023, Held as Part of the 25th HCI International Conference, HCII 2023, Copenhagen, Denmark, July 23-28, 2023, Proceedings, Part I,. pp. 592–608. Springer-Verlag, Berlin, Heidelberg (Jul 2023). https://doi.org/10.1007/978-3-031-35741-1_42

27. VanderHoeven, H., et al.: Multimodal design for interactive collaborative problem-solving support. In: Human-Computer Interaction. Theoretical Approaches and Design Methods: Thematic Area, HCI 2024, Held as Part of the 26th HCI International Conference, HCII 2024. Springer (2024)

28. Volterra, V., Caselli, M.C., Capirci, O., Pizzuto, E.: Gesture and the emergence and development of language. Beyond nature-nurture, pp. 53–90 (2004)

29. Zhang, F., et al.: Mediapipe hands: on-device real-time hand tracking. arXiv preprint arXiv:2006.10214 (2020)

Aging-Friendly Certification of Community Canteen Service for the Elderly in China: A Review of Literature

Yi Wu[1], Meng Li[1(✉)], and Haizhu Zhou[2]

[1] School of Design, South China University of Technology, Guangzhou, China
mengli@scut.edu.cn
[2] China Academy of Building Research, Beijing, China

Abstract. The aging of China's population has led to assisted feeding services becoming essential to community-based home care services. Service certification is a conformity assessment activity determining whether an organization's service capacity meets the relevant service standards. It can be used to regulate the level of service suitability of community canteens for the elderly by providing "aging-friendly" certification. This study undertook a systematic review method to investigate the necessity and feasibility of "aging-friendly" service certification for community canteens catering to the elderly. We explored the development trend of "aging-friendly" by investigating relevant standards for community canteen services for the elderly in China. The study found that while some aging-friendly factors were included in the standards, there was still insufficient consideration of the physical, psychological, and behavioral characteristics of the elderly. Therefore, we can conclude that proposing "aging-friendly" certification of services in community canteens for the elderly aligns with the domestic community development trend and promotes the development of multiple levels of certification of services in community canteens. This work could assist future community canteens in developing personalized and differentiated assisted feeding services that better meet the diverse needs of the elderly in accordance with local conditions.

Keywords: Community Canteen for the Elderly · Aging-friendly · Service Certification

1 Introduction

Service certification provides confidence to customers, regulators, industry, and other stakeholders that a service provider's services meet specific requirements [1]. Prescribed service requirements are typically found in service standards or other normative documents. These documents translate the intangibility of services into tangible elements that are applied to service processes, outcomes, and quality control. Most domestic service certifications promulgated for the restaurant food service industry [2, 3] and community senior care services [4, 5] are International Organization for Standardization (ISO) management system certifications. Although management system certification can provide some protection for the operation and management of the service industry, the intangibility, heterogeneity, indivisibility, and perishability of the service itself make it difficult to differentiate the characteristics of service industry and improve the competitiveness of certified organizations solely through ISO management system objectives [6].

The term "aging-friendly" was first introduced in Global Age-Friendly Cities, published by the World Health Organization in 2007. This guide identifies the characteristics of aging-friendly cities in eight areas: outdoor spaces and architecture for urban living, social participation, respect, social inclusion, and community support [7]. With the accelerating trend of global population aging, "aging-friendly" has become a keyword for developing community-based elderly care services. This term has formed different development trends and lists of elements in various countries and regions. Although there are multiple perspectives on "aging-friendly", they all essentially describe the dynamic interplay between functional adaptation and environmental change to maintain optimal physical functioning in older people [8]. Improving the aging-friendly level of community canteen services for the elderly will help build "age-friendly communities" and promote the realization of the "ageing in place" model in China. Elderly canteens' services focus on meeting the needs of the elderly can help address various challenges associated with aging. Aging-friendly services offer a supportive environment for a diverse group of older individuals, keeping their dietary health, independence, functional maintenance, and social integration to the maximum extent [9].

Therefore, this study analyzed the aging-friendly factors of domestic service certification standards and service standards of community canteen for the elderly from the ergonomics perspective of "Man-Machine-Environment" and considering the physiological, psychological, and behavioral characteristics of the elderly. This article explored the extent to which the supply of assisted feeding services matches the needs of the elderly. We suggested a trend towards incorporating aging-friendly certification in the certification of community canteen services for the elderly. The study was driven by three research questions: (RQ1) Is there a trend towards considering ageing-friendly in the current development of community service standards in China? (RQ2) Are there any standards related to the theme that have been promulgated in China meet the physiological, psychological and behavioral characteristics of the elderly in all aspects of the "Man-Machine-Environment"? (RQ3) Has China promulgated service certification standards for community elderly canteens? What are the main areas of focus in the content, if any? If the standard does not exist, what impact will this study have on its development?

2   Method

This study used a systematic review method to collect, identity, screen, and review related standards. Notably, unlike traditional review articles, we collected some service certification standards that have been promulgated in China, not research papers. In our research, we could not rely solely on a limited number of papers, as the field we are looking at is a relatively new one. Service certification standard is overseen by the national or provincial Market Regulatory Administration. Its development and review process are detailed and rigorous, making the standard more authoritative. The standards are streamlined, but the information we receive from them is more effective. Therefore, organizing service certification standards is more helpful for our research.

2.1 Identification

After conducting preliminary screening, it was found that although there are standards related to the elderly canteens in China, the overall number is relatively small. These standards are new and have only been formally implemented within the past two years. No relevant documents were found in the field of service certification. Meanwhile, we recognized that community services and services for the elderly also encompass assisted feeding service. Therefore, this study expanded on the existing service standards and service certification standards of community canteens for the elderly by analyzing the community assisted feeding service standards promulgated in China and the assisted feeding service link in the community service standards. Based on these studies, we suggest a direction for developing aging-friendly certification for community canteen services for the elderly.

The standards for this study should consist of two parts: "community canteens for the elderly" and "service certification", based on the conceptualization of the research theme. In this literature review, the term "elderly canteens" may have multiple variants (e.g. elderly dining tables, assisted feeding services, and elderly meal services) and these terms were used to conduct the search to ensure all related standards were include in this literature review. The primary keywords for community services are "community services" and "community services for the aged". As there are no promulgated standards for service certification standards related to canteens for the elderly in China, this study moderately expanded its scope to include a search for "service standards". Consequently, this study used the terms elderly canteens, elderly dining tables, assisted feeding services, elderly meal services, community services and community services for the aged as a selection criterion for the service (certification) standards to perform the initial search. We used the following three domestic websites for screening standards: National Public Service Platform for Standards Information [10], National Standard Information Inquiry Website [11], and Standard Website [12]. China National Knowledge Infrastructure (CNKI) and Google Scholar were secondary standards sources.

We captured an initial sample of 147 standards, including 10 national standards, 130 provincial standards, 2 professional standards, and 5 social organization standards.

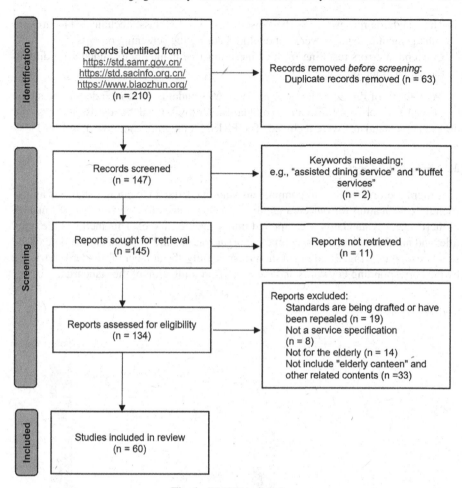

Fig. 1. PRISMA diagram

2.2 Screening and Included

Upon reviewing the standards' title and full text, it was discovered that some of the retrieved standards were not relevant to "community canteens for the elderly". Therefore, we screened the relevant service (certification) standards based on the following criteria:

a) The screening standards must be active and promulgated by December 20, 2023. Draft or defunct standards were not considered.

b) The standards must cover canteens and assisted feeding services for the elderly in Chinese communities. Service standards should consider the needs of older individuals, including their specific characteristics. The study did not cover catering and assisted feeding services for the general public.

c) Standards of community services and services for the elderly that do not include "assisted feeding services" in their content were excluded.

d) The standards retrieved must be those of the service class. Technical standards on management categories were not explored during the screening process.
e) Conceptual errors resulting from Chinese must be manually excluded according to the actual situation.

As a result of this selection process, only 60 standards were included in the study. 4 national standards, 49 provincial standards, 2 professional standards, and 5 social organization standards were included. The PRISMA diagram can be seen in Fig. 1.

2.3 Selected Papers

This literature review aims to comprehensively understand the current status of aging-friendly certification for our community canteen services for the elderly. Information of these selected standards was inputted into a sheet on Excel. This included the type, title, and number of standards, competent organization, and implementation date of the standards. Figures Fig. 2 and Fig. 3 show, respectively, the number of standards retrieved by the corresponding keywords and the date of promulgation of the standards.

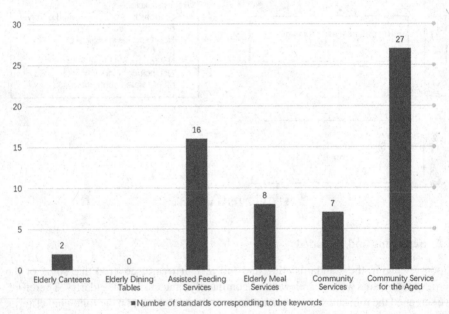

Fig. 2. Number of standards corresponding to the keywords

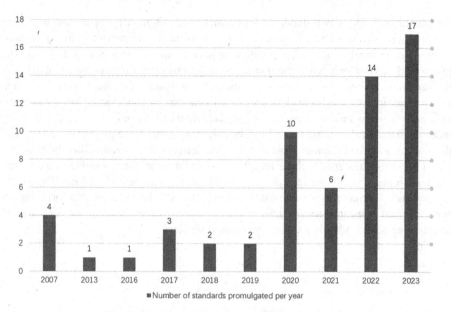

Fig. 3. Number of standards promulgated per year

3 Descriptive Analyses

In this section, this study provided a descriptive analysis of the selected standards through systematic literature review queries. The analysis was organized in three parts: year of promulgation of the standards, keywords and the type of standards.

3.1 Standards by Year

The present study investigated the temporal trends in research standards on the emergence of community canteens for the elderly from 2007 to 2023, as illustrated in Fig. 2. Our findings demonstrated the number of standards with relevant topics has increased significantly in the last 2 years. With the rapid changes in the aging process in China, the emergence of this trend may be related to the state's policy of vigorously promoting multi-level and high-quality healthy aging in the community and building a livable environment for the elderly. Additionally, we noted that service (certification) standards strongly related to community canteen services were implemented in 2022–2023. This situation illustrated the rapid development of community canteens for the elderly and assisted feeding services and the improvement of related support standards has become an inevitable trend.

3.2 Standards by Keyword

The standard distribution of different keywords is shown in Fig. 3. We found that only two standards have been promulgated in China on the subject of "community canteens for the elderly". These two standards set normative requirements for the environmental construction, facilities and equipment, service personnel, and service delivery of canteens. The keyword "elderly dining tables" appeared only in the topics of the domestic papers and was not included in the standard search. Among the 16 standards that include the keyword "assisted feeding services," there are provisions for dine-in services and a range of services such as home delivery of meals and feeding the elderly. Most standards related to "elderly meal services" focus on geriatric nutrition and introduce a variety of individualized meal configurations (e.g., liquid, semi-liquid, hyperglycemic, and special diets, etc.), with less content related to service delivery in canteens. The community-based services standards include requirements for accessibility of environments and services, some of which are relevant to assisted feeding services. The 27 standards with the keyword "community service for the aged" all cover the requirements for different types of meal assistance services, such as dine-in and home-delivered services, which are more aging-friendly than community-based services.

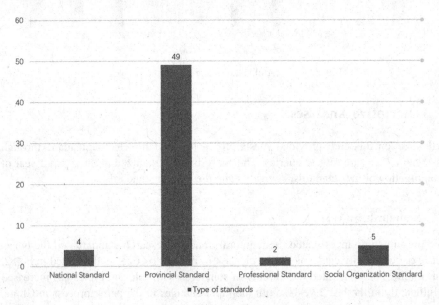

Fig. 4. Type of standards

3.3 Standards by Type

Figure 4 shows the number of types of the 60 selected standards. The four national standards are all related to community services, and there are currently no national standards related to assisted feeding services. The prominence of provincial standards in the figure is noteworthy. As the level of development of assisted feeding services varies from province to province, district to district, and city to city, the number and size of canteens for the elderly also vary, which has led to the setting of differentiated and diversified service standards. The data shows that Anhui Province has significantly more assisted feeding standards than the other provinces, with 8,330 senior canteens (meal assistance points) already built in the province [13]. In some areas, the number of standards of assisted feeding services does not match the level of development of local services. As early as December 2016, the municipal government of Guangzhou instructed all districts to set up community-level canteens for the elderly reasonably, according to the number of elderly people and the scope of their residence [14]. Nowadays, although there are many senior canteens in Guangzhou, the number of relevant standards is far less than the size of the local canteens, and the standardization construction still needs to be improved.

RQ1 Results. In this part of the study, we found that the aging-friendly trend of community services is increasingly significant. The service emphasizes more on "people-oriented" with the development of society. It will become an inevitable trend to provide more personalized and diversified community services for the elderly.

From the perspective of when the standard was promulgated, this section of the paper was developed. In 2006, the national standard [15] proposed the construction of "residential service facilities such as restaurants and bathrooms." In Part 2 [16], it specified that "Considering the needs of special groups (e.g. the elderly)." It emphasized the focus on "later life preventive services" for the aged in part 4 [17]. The requirement of "paying attention to the elderly" is a preliminary exploration of China's aging-friendly construction, but only the general direction has been standardized at the initial stage, and a comprehensive service system has not been formed. The standard for home care services promulgated in 2013 [18] began to include specific requirements for feeding services for the elderly, suggesting that the diverse eating habits of the elderly should be respected. The senior physiological characteristics were further taken into account in the standard for assisted feeding services [19] implemented in 2016. The standard emphasized the need to not only meet the dietary needs of the elderly due to their age, but also to take into account their individualized and diversified dietary needs. The aging-friendly considerations in the standards have grown richer over time. In the service standard promulgated in 2018 [20], it is suggested that the service staff should treat the elderly with care and consideration, and give them sufficient time to eat. Such a rule not only meets the physical needs, but also give the elderly psychological satisfaction of being respected. In the subsequent implementation of the standards, in addition to optimizing the existing aging-friendly elements of all aspects, more attention was paid to improving details. In addition to basic accessibility, the standard promulgated in 2020 [21] emphasized the livability of the dining environment. Another standard stated that dining venues should have natural lighting and ventilation [22]. The content required that the interior design of the canteen should be warm and uniform in color, simple and spacious, and the sign should be clearly visible. The standards implemented in 2022 [23] also requested the production of information materials on healthy nutrition for the elderly, to meet their growing spiritual needs. In 2023, the State Council of the People proposed to require local governments to actively develop assisted feeding services for the elderly, standardize the supply of services, and improve the satisfaction of the aged. The policy emphasized the service experience of the elderly and encouraged communities and organizations to support the development of community senior canteens. Districts [13] also encouraged qualified canteens to provide activities such as educational lectures, health counseling, and social interaction during non-dining hours.

RQ2 Results. It was found that the differences in the content of the standards were not significant as a result of this study. The three aspects of "Man-Machine-Environment" formed the basis of most standards. While the standards were all based on the above perspectives, the gap in ergonomic considerations for older people is very clear. Very few standards could cover aging-friendly factors from a physical, psychological, and behavioral perspective, and they are not comprehensive and adequate. Most standards satisfied only one of the three perspectives, and incomplete content remained the biggest problem. Table Table 1 shows the conformance content of standards related to the topics we categorized from the ergonomics perspective of the elderly.

Table 1. Conformance content of standards related to the topics

Ergonomics		Needs	Key Content	References
Man	Physiological	Dietary Nutrient	A light diet and avoiding high salt and fried foods	DB34/T 4458-2023 [24]
			Fresh vegetables, a combination of meat and vegetables, and appropriately supply of protein	RB/T 069-2021 [25]
		Individualized Diets	Regional characteristics, habits of the elderly, and religious culture	DB15/T 3022-2023 [26]
			The principle of keeping healthy in Chinese medicine	DB2303/T 010.2-2022 [27]
			Special diets for chronic diseases	DB4205/T 92-2022 [28]
		Diversified Diets	Texture, flavor, color, and aroma of dishes	DB4106/T 17-2020 [29]
		the Pirce	Publish recipes and prices and a budget meal holiday	DB12/T 488-2013 [18]

(continued)

Table 1. (*continued*)

Ergonomics		Needs	Key Content	References
		Quality of Ingredients	Food processing and preparation comply with regulations	DB21/T 2044-2023 [30]
			Transportation support, tableware disinfection, and after meal cleaning	DB4110/T 58-2023 [31]
		Health Status Assessment	Assess first, then make a meal plan	MZ/T 186-2021 [32]
	Psychological	Esteem	Provide meticulous, thoughtful and friendly service to the elderly	DB6101/T 3128-2022 [33]
			Respect the eating habits and ethnic habits of the aged	DB3601/T 4-2022 [34]
			Allow plenty of time for meals	DB4205/T 92-2022 [28]
		Independent Living Support	Encourage self-directed eating	DB15/T 3020-2023 [35]
			Encourage concentrate on dining in canteens	DB42/T 1939.1-2022 [36]
		Re-employment	Utilize the strengths of the elderly	GB/T 20647.1-2006 [15]
		Holiday Activities	Create an atmosphere of cultural activities	DB37/T 4631-2023 [37]
		Parties	Banquet hall and round table for parties	DB12/T 890-2019 [38]
		Transparency of Services	Public production of key links	DB37/T 4631-2023 [37]

(*continued*)

Table 1. (*continued*)

Ergonomics		Needs	Key Content	References
		Diversified services	Medical recreation, life care, psychological comfort, sports and entertainment, etc	DB4401/T 214-2023 [39]
		Service Feedback	Check the satisfaction of the elderly regularly	DB54/T 0196-2020 [40]
	Behavioral	Ease of movement	The dining point is close	DB3210/T 1149-2023 [41]
		Safety of eating	Pay attention to the dining situation	DB37/T 4631-2023 [37]
Machine	Intelligent Retirement Care	Intelligent Construction	Card swipe or face swipe payment devices connected to the smart information platform	DB4404/T 21-2022 [42]
Environment	Internal and External	Adjust Measures to Local Conditions	Consider the surrounding environment	DB3302/T 1139-2023 [43]
		Dining Environment	Plenty of light and good ventilation	DB3302/T 1139--2023 [43]
		Non-Slip Surface	Non-slip materials and safety auxiliary measures	DB22/T 2680-2017 [44]
		Signs	Service orientation and safety signs	DB37/T 4631-2023 [37]
	Facility and Equipment	Facilities	The number of equipment meets the demand	DB4403/T 69-2020 [22]
		Dining Tables and Chairs	Solid and stable single seat	DB4403/T 69-2020 [22]
			No sharp edges and corners	DB6105/T 150-2021 [45]

(*continued*)

Table 1. (*continued*)

Ergonomics		Needs	Key Content	References
		Dining Tableware	Easy to take food and prevent soup, water upset	DB1501/T 0025-2022 [46]
	Health Orientation	Health and Nutrition Education	Diet health education	DB22/T 2680-2017 [44]
			Nutrition knowledge lectures or salons	MZ/T 186-2021 [32]
			Put up health posters	DB42/T 1939.1-2022 [36]

RQ3 Results. We found only two standards were promulgated in China just for community canteens for the elderly. Both are service standards and there are no certification standards of their services. Notably, community-based aging services already have certification standards. As a key part of community elderly services, the development of service certification for elderly canteens is an inevitable requirement, as it is a fine-tuned guideline for elderly services.

Our study has clarified the direction of development of certification of elderly canteen services, with potential theoretical and practical references for future research. As can be seen in Table 1, each standard focuses on the consideration of aging-friendly content. Although the completeness of each standard needs to be improved, our summary of the content of the 60 standards showed a trend toward comprehensive coverage. This is a great help for our further research. Especially in the construction of community canteens for the elderly, the service standards related to the subject can be a rich source of reference. We found the aging-friendly factors mentioned in community services were not all covered by existing canteen standards. Therefore, by combining the aging-friendly content of existing standards and subsequent in-depth research on the ergonomics of the elderly, it is possible to develop certification standards for elderly canteen services from a more comprehensive perspective.

4   Conclusion

Service certification, as a means to guarantee the quality of service, is being accepted by various countries and regions in the world [47]. This study sought to explore the aging-friendly growing trend of service certification for community senior canteens in China in terms of subject-related standards. To this end, a systematic review method was employed to analyze the standards in three dimensions: Human-Machine-Environment. In the course of the study, we did not find any paper related to the service certification of elderly canteens, so we screened 60 service standards that are closely related to the topic. These standards cover the current situation of the aging-friendly level of assisted feeding services in different regions of China. We found that the aging-friendly degree of domestic elderly community service standards is becoming increasingly obvious. This lays a theoretical foundation for the development of service certification of elderly canteens in the direction of becoming more aging-friendly. Although the relevant standards of the subject have a certain degree of aging-friendly characteristics, they are still imperfect. In the future, based on the research, we will expand the in-depth study of the ergonomics of the elderly, and propose a more comprehensive service certification system from the physiological, psychological, and behavioral aspects. The proposed certification will also better guide the direction of service standards. The two are mutually reinforcing, and a more aging-friendly service is the goal we are striving for. Therefore, this study also provides important practical guidance for improving aging-friendly community canteens for the elderly.

The study aims to promote the level of aging-friendly service certification of community canteens for the elderly, to ensure the validity and satisfaction of the certification results, and to make the certification results more in line with the interests of the elderly. This effort can help the elderly to choose suitable and reliable community canteens and increase their confidence in the catering industry. At the same time, an increase in the aging-friendly level of elderly canteens will also promote the improvement of the overall quality level of community elderly services, and finally achieve the sustainable development goals of the community.

References

1. Conformity Assessment: GB/T 27205-2019. Conformity assessment — Guidelines and examples of a certification scheme for services. Standardization Administration of China, Beijing, China (2019)
2. National Certification and Acceditation Administration: RB/T 309-2017. Requirements for service certification of restaurant catering. National Certification and Acceditation Administration, Beijing, China (2017)
3. Shanghai Testing Inspection and Certification Associsation: T/STIC 130016-2023. Requirements for service certification of green restaurant catering. Shanghai Testing Inspection and Certification Associsation, Shanghai, China (2023)
4. National Certification and Acceditation Administration: RB/T 068-2021. Elderly care service in-home certification requirements — General. National Certification and Acceditation Administration, Beijing, China (2021)
5. China Certification & Accreditation Association: T/CCAA 37-2020. Requirements for service certification of community senior care. China Certification & Accreditation Association, Beijing, China (2020)
6. Sun, D., et al.: Research on the application status and development of service certification in China. In: Opportunities for Standardization Reform and Development — Proceedings of the 12th China Standardization Forum, pp. 1967–1973. China Association for Standardization, Beijing (2015)
7. World Health Organization.: Global age-friendly cities: a guide. World Health Organization, France (2007)
8. Plouffe, L.: Towards global age-friendly cities: determining urban features that promote active aging. J. Urban Health-Bull. N. Y. Acad. Med. 733–739 (2010)
9. Yu, Y.F.: The topic of this issue: age-friendly communities. Shanghai Urban Plan. Rev. (06), 5–6 (2020)

10. National Public Service Platform for Standards Information Homepage. https://std.samr. gov.cn/. Accessed 25 Dec 2023
11. National Standard Information Inquiry Website Homepage. https://std.sacinfo.org.cn/home. Accessed 25 Dec 2023
12. Standard Website Homepage. https://www.biaozhun.org. Accessed 25 Dec 2023
13. Unknown.: Anhui Province: diversified efforts to promote the sustainable development of assisted dining services for the elderly. China Social Work (29), 8–9 (2023)
14. Sun, H.H.: A survey on the satisfaction of the elderly with the elderly canteen in Guangzhou community. Reg. Gov. (43), 37 (2020)
15. China National Institute of Standardization: GB/T 20647.1-2006. Guideline for community service - Part 1: General. General Administration of Quality Supervision, Inspection and Quarantine of the People's Republic of China, Beiiing, China (2006)
16. China National Institute of Standardization: GB/T 20647.2-2006. Guidelines for community service - Part 2: Environment management. General Administration of Quality Supervision, Inspection and Quarantine of the People's Republic of China, Beiiing, China (2006)
17. China National Institute of Standardization: GB/T 20647.4-2006. Guideline for community services - Part 4: Healthcare service. General Administration of Quality Supervision, Inspection and Quarantine of the People's Republic of China, Beiiing, China (2006)
18. Tianjin Municipal Civil Affairs Bureau: DB12/T 488-2013. Home-based care - Community service specification. Tianjin Administration for Market Regulation, Tianjin, China (2013)
19. Department of Commerce of Jiangxi Province: DB36/T 899-2016. Elderly catering service as quality standards. Jiangxi Administration for Market Regulation, Jiangxi, China (2016)
20. Department of Civil Affairs of Shaanxi Province: DB61/T 1140-2018. Community home pension service code. Shaanxi Administration for Market Regulation, Shannxi, China (2018)
21. Department of Civil Affairs of Shandong Province: DB37/T 3776-2020. Evaluation standard of community home care service quality. Shandong Administration for Market Regulation, Shandong, China (2020)
22. Shenzhen Municipal Civil Affairs Bureau: DB4403/T 69-2020. Evaluation criterion for quality of community elderly care. Shenzhen Administration for Market Regulation, Shenzhen, China (2020)
23. Department of Civil Affairs of Guizhou Province: DB52/T 1649-2022. Standard for daily monitoring and evaluation of service quality of home-based community elderly care. Guizhou Administration for Market Regulation, Guizhou, China (2022)
24. Department of Civil Affairs of Anhui Province: DB34/T 4458-2023. Guidelines for dietary preparation of elderly meal assistance services. Anhui Administration for Market Regulation, Anhui, China (2023)
25. State Administration for Market Regulation: RB/T 069-2021. Elderly care service in-home certification requirements — Dietary service. State Administration for Market Regulation, Beijing, China (2021)
26. Department of Civil Affairs of Inner Mongolia Autonomous Region: DB15/T 3022-2023. Specification of home-based service for the elderly meal service. Inner Mongolia Autonomous Region Administration for Market Regulation, Inner Mongolia Autonomous Region, China (2023)
27. Jixi Municipal Civil Affairs Bureau: DB2303/T 010.2-2022. Elderly care - Part 2: Assisted meal service. Jixi Administration for Market Regulation, Heilongjiang, China (2022)
28. Yichang Municipal Civil Affairs Bureau: DB4205/T 92-2022. Service specification of home based for the elderly meal. Yichang Administration for Market Regulation, Hubei, China (2022)
29. Hebi Municipal Civil Affairs Bureau: DB4106/T 17-2020. Service standards for home and community assisted dining institutions for the aged. Yichang Administration for Market Regulation, Henan, China (2022)

30. Department of Civil Affairs of Liaoning Province: DB21/T 2044-2023.Specification for community elderly care service and management. Liaoning Administration for Market Regulation, Liaoning, China (2023)

31. Xuchang Municipal Civil Affairs Bureau: DB4110/T 58-2023. Home and community elderly care services door-to-door service specifications. Xuchang Administration for Market Regulation, Henan, China (2023)

32. Ministry of Civil Affairs of the People's Republic of China: MZ/T 186-2021. Basic specification for catering services in senior care organization. Ministry of Civil Affairs of the People's Republic of China, Beijing, China (2021)

33. Xi'an Municipal Civil Affairs Bureau: DB6101/T 3128-2022. Specification for elderly care services - Meal assistant service. Xi'an Administration for Market Regulation, Shaanxi, China (2022)

34. Nanchang Municipal Civil Affairs Bureau: DB3601/T 4-2022. Specification of meal service for old-age home service institutions. Jiangxi Administration for Market Regulation, Jiangxi, China (2022)

35. Department of Civil Affairs of Inner Mongolia Autonomous Region: DB15/T 3020-2023. Specification of daily monitoring and evaluation of the quality for home - based community elderly care service. Inner Mongolia Autonomous Region Administration for Market Regulation, Inner Mongolia Autonomous Region, China (2023)

36. Department of Civil Affairs of Hubei Province: DB42/T 1939.1-2022. Guidelines for improved nutrition services for the elderly - Part 1: Nutritional meals for the elderly. Hubei Administration for Market Regulation, Hubei, China (2022)

37. Department of Civil Affairs of Shandong Province: DB37/T 4631-2023. Construction and service requirements of community canteen for the elderly adults. Shandong Administration for Market Regulation, Shandong, China (2023)

38. Tianjin Municipal Civil Affairs Bureau: DB12/T 890-2019. Service specification for comprehensive old-age community. Tianjin Administration for Market Regulation, Tianjin, China (2019)

39. Guangzhou Municipal Civil Affairs Bureau: DB4401/T 214-2023. Specification of community & home care service for the elderly - catering service. Guangzhou Administration for Market Regulation, Guangdong, China (2019)

40. Tibet Autonomous Region Municipal Civil Affairs Bureau: DB54/T 0196-2020. Standard of meal service in pension institutions. Tibet Autonomous Region Administration for Market Regulation, Tibet Autonomous Region, China (2020)

41. Yangzhou Municipal Civil Affairs Bureau: DB3210/T 1149-2023. Specification for community elderly meal assistant service. Yangzhou Administration for Market Regulation, Jiangsu, China (2023)

42. Zhuhai Municipal Civil Affairs Bureau: DB4404/T 21-2022. Specifications of grade evaluation for community elderly care services. Zhuhai Administration for Market Regulation, Guangdong, China (2022)

43. Ningbo Municipal Civil Affairs Bureau: DB3302/T 1139-2023.The construction and service specification of the elderly canteen. Ningbo Administration for Market Regulation, Zhejiang, China (2023)

44. Department of Civil Affairs of Jilin Province: DB22/T 2680-2017. Specification of meal service for old-age home service institutions. Jilin Administration for Market Regulation, Jilin, China (2017)

45. Commerce Bereau of Weinan Municipality: DB6105/T 150-2021. Specification of nursing home meal service operation. Weinan Administration for Market Regulation, Shaanxi, China (2021)

46. Hohhot Municipal Civil Affairs Bureau: DB1501/T 0025-2022. Service specification of community home nursing and feeding institutions. Hohhot Administration for Market Regulation, Inner Mongolia Autonomous Region, China (2022)

47. Cao, L.L.: A review of service certification development at home and abroad. China Stand. **11**, 60–64 (2011)

A New Smart City Construction Performance Evaluation System from the Perspective of User Experience: An Empirical Study of Qingdao, China

Wenyu Yan[1], Liying Sun[2], Lianxin Ma[1], Lingxuan He[1], and Weilin Liu[1(✉)]

[1] School of Management Engineering, Qingdao University of Technology, Qingdao 266520, China
lwl0446@163.com
[2] School of Civil Engineering, Hengxing University, Qingdao 266100, China

Abstract. The concept of smart city development originated from the idea of 'Smart Earth' proposed by IBM in 2008. The Chinese government has been actively promoting the planning and construction of smart cities to address challenges such as traffic congestion, medical issues, and environmental pollution caused by rapid urbanization, with the aim of improving public welfare. Currently, countries worldwide are embracing the construction of smart cities, utilizing information and communication technologies like big data and cloud computing to achieve efficient management of cities in terms of public services, governance, and livability, thus promoting sustainable urban development and enhancing residents' convenience. As China's urbanization progresses and information technology advances, along with people's pursuit of a high-quality life, new concepts and requirements for smart cities have emerged, necessitating the timely development of new smart city concepts. The public, being the end users and evaluators of smart city construction outcomes, holds significant influence in assessing the quality of such construction. However, previous studies on smart cities have predominantly focused on technological advancements, neglecting the evaluation of smart city construction effectiveness from the perspective of citizens. Therefore, establishing a scientific and reasonable performance evaluation index system for new smart city construction is crucial to the construction of new smart cities, based on the public's direct experience and user perception.

This study introduces user perception as a key component in the evaluation system for new smart city construction and established a new smart city construction performance evaluation index system based on user perception. By doing so, it aims to provide a more comprehensive understanding of the actual impact of urban development on residents' lives. To establish the evaluation index system, the study combines research findings from relevant domestic literature and Chinese government documents, resulting in a set of 32 indicators. The membership degree analysis and reliability and validity tests were then conducted to determine the rating system for five first-level indicators, 12 second-level indicators, and 31 third-level indicators. These indicators include benefit to the people service, precise governance, ecological livability, intelligent facilities, and intelligent services relying on the platform. Finally, questionnaires were distributed to Qingdao

V. G. Duffy (Ed.): HCII 2024, LNCS 14709, pp. 390–404, 2024.
https://doi.org/10.1007/978-3-031-61060-8_27

citizens using snowball sampling through the questionnaire Star platform. The survey results were obtained from 390 valid questionnaires in Qingdao, Shandong province. The entropy method was applied to objectively assign weights to each evaluation index and determine their respective importance. The findings highlight the significance of benefit to the people service, index. The research results provide guidance for evaluating the impact of smart city construction in China and offer insights for future improvements and development directions in this field.

Keywords: Public perception perspective · New smart city · Construction performance

1 Introduce

In recent years, there has been a rapid influx of people into cities, leading to an accelerated pace of urbanization [1]. It is projected that by 2050, approximately 70% of the world's population will reside in urban areas [2]. This presents a significant challenge to the sustainable development of cities [3]. In response, the global initiative for smart cities has gained momentum, with smart city construction taking place worldwide [4]. Building smart cities has emerged as a key direction for urban development on a global scale.

According to statistics, by the end of 2019, China had over 500 cities engaged in the construction of smart cities, with a planned investment of approximately 327.4 billion yuan. This makes China the country with the highest number of smart city construction projects [5]. With the rapid urbanization in China, advancements in information technology, and the growing demand for a high-quality lifestyle, new concepts and requirements for smart cities have emerged. However, traditional smart city development faces challenges such as an excessive focus on technology rather than practical applications, poor user experience, and a lack of tangible benefits for users to perceive the achievements of smart city construction [6]. As end users and evaluators of the new smart city developments, users hold the highest authority in assessing the quality of these projects. Therefore, a new smart city development approach that prioritizes user experience has emerged.

In order to improve the construction of new smart cities in China and address issues such as poor user experience, it is crucial to establish a scientific and reasonable performance evaluation index system. This system will help assess users' perception of the achievements of new smart city construction in China. However, the current evaluation index system in China lacks a thorough investigation of user experience. Some systems only consider user experience as one of the indicators and fail to examine user satisfaction with the construction achievements of new smart cities from a user experience perspective. As a result, it becomes difficult to objectively evaluate public satisfaction with the effectiveness of new smart cities. To address this, it is essential for China to urgently establish a scientific and reasonable performance evaluation index system for new smart city construction. This system will enable a better evaluation of the construction effect of new smart cities and facilitate the timely identification of factors contributing to poor user perception.

This study aims to address the existing research gap by proposing a novel smart city construction performance evaluation system based on user perception. The effectiveness of this system will be verified through an empirical analysis conducted in Qingdao, China. The findings of this study will offer valuable guidance for the development of new smart cities in China.

2   Primary Selection and Testing of Evaluation Indicators

Due to the specific focus of this study on the Chinese region, international indicators may not provide an accurate reflection of the situation in this area. To address this, the paper utilizes Qingdao City, China as a case study and combines relevant Chinese literature research findings and government documents. The study conducts an initial screening of indicators and employs membership analysis, as well as reliability and validity analysis, to test them. Ultimately, the paper establishes an indicator system based on these analyses.

2.1   Primary Evaluation Index

Today, the development of smart cities in China faces the challenge of users not being able to perceive the results [7]. This paper aims to understand the concept and meaning of the new smart city by referring to representative Chinese literature and official documents listed in Table 1. It also examines the construction of new smart cities in China's prefecture-level cities. The paper selects performance indicators that are easily noticeable by users in their daily lives, based on the principles of science, representativeness, human nature, and operability. These indicators include people's services, accurate governance, ecological livability, and intelligent facilities, which serve as primary evaluation indicators. With the widespread use of mobile internet and smart mobile terminals, smart services provided through platforms such as websites, apps, and WeChat mini programs have become crucial for the public to perceive the achievements of new smart city construction. The level of construction directly impacts the public's perception of these achievements. Therefore, this paper integrates the intelligent service platform into the primary evaluation index system, which initially consists of 5 primary indicators, 12 secondary indicators, and 32 tertiary indicators, as shown in the first three columns of Table 2.

2.2   Testing of Evaluation Indicators

In order to ensure the reliability of sample data, this study utilizes the questionnaire star platform to distribute online questionnaires to experts and scholars in relevant fields of new smart cities in a snowball manner. The membership analysis is conducted to preliminarily screen the index system. Subsequently, the reliability test is performed to eliminate the indexes with low reliability, followed by a secondary screening of the remaining indexes. As a result, a representative and rational evaluation index system is established.

Table 1. Relevant representative research results

Author	Time	Document title	Primary index
National Development and Reform Commission [8]	2018	《New Smart City Evaluation Indicators (2018)》	Benefit to the people, precise governance, ecological livable, intelligent facilities, information resources, information security, innovative development, citizen experience
Shandong Big Data Bureau [9]	2020	《Shandong Provincial local standards New smart city construction indicators Part 1: municipal indicators》	Digital benefits, digital government, digital economy, infrastructure, safeguards, local characteristics
Wang Chaonan [10]	2019	《Construction and empirical research of smart city construction performance evaluation index system》	Public services, industrial modernization level, environmental livable level, urban economic development level, urban infrastructure
Sun Yuning [11]	2019	《Research on the evaluation of smart city construction level from the public perspective》	Infrastructure, public services, Social management, ecological livable, industrial system
Jiang Jun [12]	2019	《Construction of smart city construction maturity evaluation system from the public perspective》	Benefit the people service, accurate governance, intelligent facilities, network information management, service economy and security knowledge
Chen Weiqing [13]	2019	《Research on the construction of new smart city in Nanning based on principal component analysis》	Infrastructure, scientific and technological innovation, information industry, livelihood services, value realization
Du Delin [14]	2020	《Evaluation of China's smart city development status based on multi-source data》	Smart economy, smart transportation, smart medical care, smart education, smart management

Membership Analysis. To establish an indicator system and ensure rigor and readability, we designed an expert survey questionnaire around 32 primary indicators. The Likert five-point scale was used to measure the importance of each item, with '5' indicating high importance, '4' indicating moderate importance, '3' indicating neutral, '2' indicating low importance, and '1' indicating not important. The indicators were quantitatively analyzed. We distributed a total of 157 questionnaires to experts and scholars in the field of new smart city through the online platform SurveyStar, using the snowball sampling method. After excluding invalid questionnaires, we received 145 valid responses, resulting in an effective response rate of 92%. In the sample analysis, a significant proportion of respondents (43.4%) consisted of professors and associate senior researchers. The majority of respondents (46.2%) were affiliated with universities.

Assuming {X} is a fuzzy set composed of three-level indicators in the initial indicator system, each element (indicator) Xk in this set corresponds to a membership function value in the interval [0, 1]. The membership degree formula [15] for evaluating indicators is shown below:

$$R_k = \frac{D_1 + 0.75D_2 + 0.5D_3 + 0.25D_4 + 0D_5}{T} \tag{1}$$

Rk represents the membership degree of indicator Xk. D1 corresponds to the number of experts who consider Xk as extremely important, D2 corresponds to the number of experts who choose the option 'comparatively important,' D3 corresponds to the number of experts who choose the option 'moderately important,' D4 corresponds to the number of experts who choose the option 'less important,' D5 corresponds to the number of experts who choose the option 'not important,' and T is the total number of experts and scholars participating in this survey. The reference [10] uses a critical value of 0.5 as the membership degree to screen indicators. After conducting the membership degree analysis, it was found that only C13 had a membership degree lower than 0.5. Therefore, 5 first-level indicators, 12 second-level indicators, and 31 third-level indicators were retained (refer to Table 2).

Table 2. Membership degree of initial evaluation indicators

The first-level indicators	The second-level indicators	The third-level indicators	Membership degree
Benefit the people A1	Traffic service B1	The accuracy of real-time traffic information C1	0.986
		The convenience of online car rental and car booking C2	0.96
	Government affairs B2	Satisfaction with remote business networking C3	0.956
		Satisfaction with the speed of government affairs C4	0.95

(*continued*)

Table 2. (*continued*)

The first-level indicators	The second-level indicators	The third-level indicators	Membership degree
		Satisfaction with social openness level of public information resources C5	0.944
	Medical service B3	The convenience of online booking and registration C6	0.943
		The popularity of electronic medical records C7	0.935
	Educational service B4	The richness of online educational resources C8	0.944
		The rationality of the price of online learning resources C9	0.946
Precise governance A2	Urban management B5	Satisfaction with market order C10	0.992
		City appearance satisfaction C11	0.961
		Satisfaction with emergency response speed C12	0.94
		Ease of reporting, supervising urban management work, etc. C13	0.491
	Public safety B6	Food safety satisfaction C14	0.928
		Satisfaction with traffic safety C15	0.92
		Satisfaction with network security C16	0.93
		Satisfaction with the level of social security C17	0.948

(*continued*)

Table 2. (*continued*)

The first-level indicators	The second-level indicators	The third-level indicators	Membership degree
Ecological habitability A3	Green energy saving B7	Satisfaction with water environment quality C18	0.857
		Air quality satisfaction C19	0.934
		Satisfaction with surrounding greenery C20	0.818
		Public awareness of energy conservation and emission reduction C21	0.809
	Environmental monitoring B8	Accuracy of environmental monitoring C22	0.821
		Timeliness of environmental monitoring results announcement C23	0.821
		Satisfaction with the effect of environmental improvement C24	0.913
Intelligent facility A4	Broadband network facility B9	Satisfaction with home fiber access coverage C25	0.987
		Public WIFI service satisfaction C26	0.957
	Public infrastructure B10	Coverage rate C27	0.943
		Construction level C28	0.959
Intelligent services rely on the platform A5	Diversification B11	Service channel diversification C29	0.931
		Functional comprehensiveness C30	0.864

(*continued*)

Table 2. (*continued*)

The first-level indicators	The second-level indicators	The third-level indicators	Membership degree
	Specialization B12	Service completion rate C31	0.925
		User experience level C32	0.876

Reliability and Validity Assessment

1. Reliability analysis

SPSS 19.0 software was utilized to assess the reliability of the 31 chosen indicators. As shown in Table 3, the α coefficient for each dimension and the overall α coefficient of the new smart city construction performance evaluation index system, from the perspective of public perception, exceed the standard 0.7 [16]. This suggests a strong consistency among all items in the scale.

Table 3. Cronbach's α coefficients for each dimension

Each dimension	Benefit the people A1	Precise governance A2	Ecological habitability A3	Intelligent facility A4	Intelligent services rely on the platform A5	Entirety
Cronbach's α	0.925	0.982	0.933	0.896	0.970	0.955

2. Validity assessment

Factor analysis is commonly employed to assess the effectiveness of index system design. Prior to conducting factor analysis, it is necessary to perform KMO and Bartlett tests in order to determine its suitability. Table 4 shows that the KMO measure value is 0.863 and Sig = 0.000, indicating that factor analysis is appropriate [17].

Then, exploratory factor analysis was conducted using SPSS 19.0, followed by orthogonal rotation. The rotation component matrix, presented in Table 5, was analyzed to assess the effectiveness of the indicators. It is observed from Table 5 that all 31 indicators are valid [18].

Table 4. Examination of KMO and Bartlett

Sample the Kaiser-Meyer-Olkin measure of adequacy		0.872
Bartlett's sphericity test	Approximate chi-square	6427.184
	df	465
	Sig	0.000

3 Weight Calculation of Evaluation Index by Entropy Method

The entropy method calculates the weight based on the amount of information contained in the index data. It reflects the degree of dispersion of the index data, thus indicating the amount of information it contains. A smaller entropy value corresponds to a larger index weight when the index data contains a significant amount of information. This method helps minimize the influence of human factors and ensures a more objective and fair evaluation result.

3.1 Data Acquisition

Online questionnaires were distributed to residents of Qingdao city through the QuestionStar platform using the snowball sampling method. A total of 456 questionnaires were collected. After eliminating invalid ones, 390 questionnaires remained, resulting in a questionnaire validity rate of 85.5%. In the descriptive statistical analysis of the sample, males accounted for 50.77% while females accounted for 49.23%. The highest proportion was found in the age group 'under 20 years old,' which accounted for 40.77% of the sample. Among the sample, 58.21% identified as students, and an additional 30.77% were working professionals. Within the sample, 51.79% of the participants reported being unemployed and having no income, and over 50% of the sample had a residential duration of '3 years or more.' The results of the descriptive statistical analysis indicate that the sample of this study has a wide coverage and meets the basic requirements of the research, thus possessing a certain level of representativeness. Additionally, we employed the previously described method and conducted validity and reliability tests using SPSS 19.0, all of which yielded positive results.

3.2 Entropy Method of Index Weighting

1. Get the raw data matrix

There are m survey objects and n evaluation indicators, and the original data matrix $X = (x_{ij})_{mxn}$ is obtained:

$$X = \begin{bmatrix} x_{11} & x_{12} & \ldots & x_{1n} \\ x_{21} & x_{22} & \ldots & x_{2n} \\ \vdots & \vdots & \cdots & \vdots \\ x_{m1} & x_{m2} & \cdots & x_{mn} \end{bmatrix} \tag{2}$$

Table 5. Rotational component matrix a

The third-level indicators	Formulation				
	A1	A2	A3	A4	A5
C1	0.795	0.125	0.156	0.324	0.112
C2	0.796	0.103	0.181	0.317	0.143
C3	0.764	0.197	0.170	0.185	0.073
C4	0.724	0.105	0.186	-0.022	0.024
C5	0.733	0.163	0.164	0.161	0.139
C6	0.748	0.206	0.138	0.193	0.082
C7	0.675	0.055	0.184	0.061	0.124
C8	0.670	0.093	0.348	0.145	0.199
C9	0.663	0.061	0.188	0.253	0.249
C10	0.125	0.926	0.108	0.072	0.141
C11	0.165	0.905	0.108	0.095	0.059
C12	0.151	0.882	0.107	0.110	0.059
C13	0.080	0.936	0.088	0.084	0.127
C14	0.143	0.922	0.085	0.128	0.139
C15	0.140	0.930	0.116	0.097	0.162
C16	0.146	0.943	0.117	0.087	0.140
C17	0.316	0.121	0.712	0.010	0.056
C18	0.322	0.091	0.696	0.017	0.066
C19	0.154	0.092	0.827	0.216	0.260
C20	0.153	0.051	0.869	0.220	0.193
C21	0.184	0.205	0.647	0.109	0.108
C22	0.189	0.109	0.861	0.204	0.232
C23	0.177	0.067	0.863	0.208	0.185
C24	0.373	0.190	0.145	0.817	0.148
C25	0.354	0.199	0.146	0.792	0.164
C26	0.359	0.157	0.346	0.659	0.114
C27	0.200	0.103	0.319	0.676	0.158
C28	0.172	0.170	0.233	0.121	0.917
C29	0.183	0.177	0.220	0.095	0.907
C30	0.193	0.209	0.238	0.108	0.888
C31	0.271	0.221	0.263	0.285	0.755

Extraction method: principal component.

Rotating method: Orthogonal rotating method with Kaiser standardization.

A. Rotation converges after 5 iterations.

x_{ij} is the score of the i respondents on the j index.

2. Normalization of the original matrix

$$R = (r_{ij})mxn, \quad r_{ij} = \frac{x_{ij}}{\sum\limits_{i=1}^{m} x_{ij}} \tag{3}$$

3. Calculate the information entropy of the index

$$e_j = -\frac{1}{\ln m} \sum_{i=1}^{m} r_{ij} \ln r_{ij}, j = 1, 2, 3, \cdots, n \tag{4}$$

4. Calculate the utility value of the indicator

$$d_j = 1 - e_j \tag{5}$$

5. Calculate the weight of the indicator

$$o = \frac{d_j}{\sum\limits_{j=1}^{n} d_j} = \frac{1 - e_j}{n - \sum\limits_{j=1}^{n} e_j} = o_1, o_2, \cdots, o_n \tag{6}$$

Based on the solution steps of the entropy method and the 390 valid questionnaires obtained in Sect. 3.1, the objective weights of 31 tertiary indicators were determined using SPSS software. Subsequently, the original data matrix was constructed.

$$X = \begin{bmatrix} 5 & \cdots & 5 \\ \vdots & \ddots & \vdots \\ 5 & \cdots & 3 \end{bmatrix} * (390,31)$$

The raw data matrix should be imported into SPSSAU to calculate the information entropy (ej), utility values (dj), and weights (o) of each indicator, as demonstrated in Table 6.

Table 6. Information entropy, utility values, and weight values of the third-level indicators.

indicator	information entropy (physics)e_j	utility valued_j	proportion$o$	indicator	information entropy (physics)e_j	utility valued_j	Proportion o
C1	0.9951	0.0049	3.03%	C17	0.9947	0.0053	3.31%
C2	0.9953	0.0047	2.94%	C18	0.9949	0.0051	3.19%
C3	0.9953	0.0047	2.91%	C19	0.9948	0.0052	3.23%
C4	0.9951	0.0049	3.05%	C20	0.9953	0.0047	2.95%

(*continued*)

Table 6. (*continued*)

indicator	information entropy (physics)e_j	utility valued_j	proportion$o$	indicator	information entropy (physics)e_j	utility valued_j	Proportion o
C5	0.9952	0.0048	3.01%	C21	0.9949	0.0051	3.20%
C6	0.9953	0.0047	2.93%	C22	0.9953	0.0047	2.91%
C7	0.9951	0.0049	3.03%	C23	0.9949	0.0051	3.17%
C8	0.9952	0.0048	3.01%	C24	0.994	0.006	3.74%
C9	0.9953	0.0047	2.92%	C25	0.9939	0.0061	3.78%
C10	0.9943	0.0057	3.54%	C26	0.994	0.006	3.76%
C11	0.9943	0.0057	3.55%	C27	0.9942	0.0058	3.58%
C12	0.9943	0.0057	3.54%	C28	0.9952	0.0048	2.97%
C13	0.9944	0.0056	3.50%	C29	0.9954	0.0046	2.88%
C14	0.9945	0.0055	3.42%	C30	0.9951	0.0049	3.06%
C15	0.9943	0.0057	3.54%	C31	0.9955	0.0045	2.78%
C16	0.9943	0.0057	3.57%				

Table 7. Weights of the second-level indicators

indicator	proportion	indicator	proportion
B1	0.0597	B7	0.1268
B2	0.0897	B8	0.0928
B3	0.0596	B9	0.0752
B4	0.0593	B10	0.0734
B5	0.1063	B11	0.0585
B6	0.1403	B12	0.0584

The weights of the second-level indicators are equal to the sum of the weights of the corresponding third-level indicators. The weight values of the second-level indicators are shown in Table 7:

The weights of the first-level indicators are equal to the sum of the weights of the corresponding second-level indicators, as shown in Table 8.

The weights of the above-mentioned third-level and second-level indicators are normalized to obtain the weights of the final index system using the entropy method, as illustrated in Table 9.

Table 8. Weights of the first-level indicators

indicator	proportion
A1	0.2683
A2	0.2466
A3	0.2196
A4	0.1486
A5	0.1169

Table 9. Weightings of the final index system using the entropy method.

The first-level indicators	proportion	The second-level indicators	proportion	The third-level indicators	proportion
A1	0.2683	B1	0.2225	C1	0.5075
				C2	0.4925
		B2	0.3343	C3	0.3244
				C4	0.3400
				C5	0.3356
		B3	0.2221	C6	0.4916
				C7	0.5084
		B4	0.2210	C8	0.5076
				C9	0.4924
A2	0.2466	B5	0.4311	C10	0.3330
				C11	0.3340
				C12	0.3330
		B6	0.5689	C13	0.2495
				C14	0.2438
				C15	0.2523
				C16	0.2545
A3	0.2196	B7	0.5774	C17	0.2610
				C18	0.2516
				C19	0.2547
				C20	0.2326
		B8	0.4226	C21	0.3448

(*continued*)

Table 9. (*continued*)

The first-level indicators	proportion	The second-level indicators	proportion	The third-level indicators	proportion
				C22	0.3136
				C23	0.3416
A4	0.1486	B9	0.5061	C24	0.4973
				C25	0.5027
		B10	0.4939	C26	0.5123
				C27	0.4877
A5	0.1169	B11	0.5004	C28	0.5077
				C29	0.4923
		B12	0.4996	C30	0.5240
				C31	0.4760

4   Conclusion

From the perspective of user perception, this paper establishes the initial evaluation index system of smart city construction performance by taking Qingdao, Shandong Province as an example. The methodology involved sending out questionnaires to obtain expert opinions, conducting membership analysis and reliability and validity analysis to screen the data, and ultimately determining the evaluation index system. The paper calculates the objective weight of evaluation indicators using the entropy method and analyzes the importance of each indicator in China's smart city construction.

The research findings indicate that the weight of benefit the people service is 0.2683, making it the most significant weight among the first-level indicators. Precision governance follows with a weight of 0.2466, while the weight of intelligent service relying on the platform is the least. This suggests that benefit the people service and precise governance have the greatest impact on users' perception of the new smart city construction performance. Therefore, continuously improving the level of benefit the people service and precise governance is crucial for enhancing users' perception of the effectiveness of the new smart city.

The research framework proposed in this study for China's new smart city construction can serve as a methodological reference for evaluating the construction effect of new smart cities. It also provides insights for improving the level of new smart city construction and offers valuable guidance for the further development of new smart cities.

Acknowledgments. This study was funded by Undergraduate Teaching Reform and Research Project at Qingdao University of Technology (grant number F2023–012).

Disclosure of Interests. The authors have no competing interests to declare that are relevant to the content of this article.

References

1. Li, X., et al.: Response of the groundwater environment to rapid urbanization in Hohhot, the provincial capital of western China. J. Hydrol. **603**, 127033 (2021)
2. Yin, S., Zhang, N.: Prevention schemes for future pandemic cases: mathematical model and experience of interurban multi-agent COVID-19 epidemic prevention. Nonlinear Dyn. **104**, 2865–2900 (2021)
3. Abdullah, L., Rahim, N.: The use of fuzzy DEMATEL for urban sustainable development. In: Kahraman, C., Cebi, S., Cevik Onar, S., Oztaysi, B., Tolga, A.C., Sari, I.U. (eds.) INFUS 2019. AISC, vol. 1029, pp. 722–729. Springer, Cham (2020). https://doi.org/10.1007/978-3-030-23756-1_86
4. Gu, D., et al.: Tracking knowledge evolution in cloud health care research: knowledge map and common word analysis. J. Med. Internet Res. **22**(2), e15142 (2020). https://doi.org/10.2196/15142
5. China Investment Research Institute. "14th Five-Year Plan" data under the construction of China's smart City in-depth survey and investment prospects forecast report. (2019)
6. Iresearch. Long after the feast on: wisdom of China city development report 2019 [EB/OL]. http://report.iresearch.cn/report/201903/3350. SHTML, 25 Mar 2019
7. He, W., Li, W., Deng, P.: Legal governance in the smart cities of China: functions, problems, and solutions. Sustainability **14**, 9738 (2022). https://doi.org/10.3390/su14159738
8. National Development and Reform Commission, Cyberspace Administration of the CPC Central Committee. Notice on Continuing the Evaluation of New Smart City Construction and Further Promoting the Healthy and Rapid Development of New Smart City [EB/OL].(2018-12-19) [2020-06-22]
9. Shandong Big Data Bureau. Shandong Province New smart City construction index (municipal) [EB/OL]. http://bdb.shandong.gov.cn/art/2022/11/21/art_101017_10308764.html?eqid=d609ccb0000c11cf000000036460f82a&eqid=ebf7502600119120000000002648bb9ad
10. Wang, C.: Construction and Empirical Research of Smart City Construction Performance Evaluation Index System. Xiangtan University (2019)
11. Sun, Y.: Research on the evaluation of Smart City construction level from the public perspective. Beijing Univ. Civil Eng. Archit. (2019)
12. Jun, J., Yuning, S., Dongjun, W.: Construction of smart city construction maturity evaluation system from the public perspective. J. Beijing Univ. Archit. Archit. **35**(02), 7–15 (2019)
13. Weiqing, C., Wenchao, Z., Xueyao, Z.: Research on new smart city construction in Nanning based on principal component analysis. Ecol. Econ. **35**(04), 99–103 (2019). (in Chinese)
14. Du, D., Huang, J., Wang, J.: Evaluation of China's smart city development status based on multi-source data. J. Geo-Inf. Sci. **22**(6), 1294–1306 (2019). (in Chinese)
15. Cao, L.: Construction and application of performance evaluation index system for government purchase of community public cultural services [D]. Soochow University (2020)
16. Zhang, C., et al.: Reliability, validity, and measurement invariance of the general anxiety disorder scale among Chinese medical university students. Front. Psych. **12**, 648755 (2021)
17. Lu, T., Kong, L., Zhang, H.: Psychometric evaluation of the healthy aging activity engagement scale. Front. Public Health **10**, 986666 (2022)
18. Shen, Y.C., Chen, H.S.: Exploring consumers' purchase intention of an innovation of the agri-food industry: a case of artificial meat. Foods **9**(6), 745 (2020)

Evaluating the Effect of Adapting Virtual Humans Based on Individual Differences in Users

Mohan Zalake[1]([⊠]) [iD], Alexandre Gomes De Siqueira[2], Krishna Vaddiparti[2], Pavlo Antonenko[2], and Benjamin Lok[2]

[1] University of Illinois Chicago, Chicago, USA
zalake@uic.edu
[2] University of Florida, Gainesville, USA
{agomesdesiqueira,kvaddiparti}@ufl.edu, p.antonenko@coe.ufl.edu,
lok@cise.ufl.edu

Abstract. This paper investigates the effects of adapting a virtual human's persuasion strategy based on users' personalities and prior beliefs regarding recommended behavior in the context of promoting mental health coping skills among college students. The paper uses the Theory of Planned Behavior (TPB) as the theoretical model to study how a virtual human's persuasion strategies impact behavior change. The paper also employs Cialdini's six persuasion strategies - Reciprocity, Scarcity, Authority, Commitment, Likability, and Consensus - to manipulate the virtual human's dialog. The paper develops a user model that predicts the effectiveness of different persuasion strategies based on user data from a previous study. The paper then evaluates the user model in an empirical study with 292 undergraduate students, comparing three experimental conditions - a matched condition where the virtual human used a more effective persuasion strategy, a mismatched condition where the virtual human used a less effective persuasion strategy, and a control condition where the virtual human did not use any persuasion strategy. The paper finds that adapting the virtual human's persuasion strategy can positively influence users who have low self-efficacy to perform the recommended behavior, but can negatively influence users who already have high self-efficacy. The paper also finds that persuasion strategies may not be sufficient to induce behavior change, and suggests accounting for users' perceived barriers and benefits of the recommended behavior. The paper contributes to the Human-Computer Interaction research by providing evidence for the importance of individual differences in designing virtual human health interventions.

Keywords: Virtual humans · Health · Behavior change · Adaptive systems

1 Introduction

Prior studies have demonstrated that virtual humans can effectively employ various persuasion strategies to influence people's behavior related to health

V. G. Duffy (Ed.): HCII 2024, LNCS 14709, pp. 405–423, 2024.
https://doi.org/10.1007/978-3-031-61060-8_28

[17, 18, 20]. For instance, when virtual humans use empathic messages [17] or a positive tone [18], individuals are more likely to be motivated to alter their health-related behavior. Based on social psychology research [3, 22, 29], these persuasion strategies can be more effective when they are adapted to individual differences. Therefore, in this research, we investigate the effects of adapting a virtual human's persuasion strategy based on users' personalities and prior beliefs regarding recommended behavior in the context of promoting mental health coping skills among college students.

Around 30% of U.S. college students are reported to suffer from mental health issues [19]. These students are at a higher risk of dropping out, getting lower grades, and facing unemployment [30]. Prior work has suggested the use of coping skills to enhance the mental health of these students [6]. However, a significant number of students do not utilize these recommended coping skills [6]. To comprehend the factors that influence students' usage of coping skills, the Theory of Planned Behavior (TPB) has been identified as a reliable model in previous research [6]. Therefore, we use TPB as the theoretical model to study how a virtual human's persuasion strategies impact behavior change. According to TPB, a person's attitude, subjective norms, and perception of control over a behavior shape their intentions towards the behavior, which in turn predict the person's behavior.

In this research, a virtual human is used to advocate for a coping skill known as gratitude journaling. This involves individuals writing down events that evoke feelings of gratitude, a practice shown to alleviate symptoms of anxiety and depression [8]. To encourage students to adopt gratitude journaling, the virtual human utilizes one of the six persuasion strategies proposed by Cialdini [7] - Reciprocity, Scarcity, Authority, Commitment, Likability, and Consensus. While other taxonomies categorizing persuasion strategies exist, Cialdini's strategies were chosen due to their extensive application in previous studies on human-computer persuasion [11, 15, 29]. These strategies have also been evaluated in the context of virtual humans in our previous work [33], demonstrating that virtual humans can effectively implement Cialdini's persuasion strategies and can overcome the limitations of implementing Cialdini's strategies using computers. Our previous work has also identified the underlying mechanisms of how Cialdini's persuasion strategies used by a virtual human can influence users' intentions to perform gratitude journaling [32]. Moreover, the findings from our previous work indicate that the impact of persuasion strategies was influenced by the user's personality. This research goes beyond our previous work by examining if adapting a virtual human's persuasion techniques based on the underlying mechanisms identified in our previous work can enhance persuasion effectiveness.

To adapt virtual human's persuasion techniques, we modeled the relationship between individual differences in students and the effectiveness of various persuasion strategies employed by a virtual human based on the data from our previous study [32]. This user model was then employed to empirically evaluate the extent to which leveraging the relationship between the effectiveness of persuasion strategies and individual differences among users is beneficial. The study compared three experimental conditions - a matched condition where the virtual human used a Cialdini's persuasion strategy deemed more effective by the user model, a mismatched condition where the virtual human used a less effective Cialdini's persuasion strategy as recommended by the user model, and a third condition where the virtual human did not employ any of the Cialdini's persuasion strategies. The research question addressed was as follows:

RQ: Can a virtual human that employed a more effective Cialdini's verbal persuasion strategy recommended by the user model based on students' individual differences be more successful in persuading students to change health behavior than a virtual human that used a) a less effective Cialdini's verbal persuasion strategy recommended by the user model based on students' individual differences, and b) a virtual human that did not use a Cialdini's verbal persuasion strategy?

The study highlights the importance of accounting for users' individual differences when designing virtual human health interventions. The study contributes to the Human-Computer Interaction research by providing evidence that shows adapting a virtual human's persuasion strategy can positively influence users who have low self-efficacy to perform the recommended behavior. However, using a less effective strategy can negatively influence users who already have high self-efficacy to perform the recommended behavior. In addition, persuasion strategies may be effective in improving precursors to behavior change, such as user self-efficacy. However, improvement in precursors does not necessarily translate to behavior change.

2   Related Work

Our work builds upon prior works that have studied the use of verbal persuasion strategies by virtual humans for behavior change, health behavior models in the context of promoting coping skills among college students, and the use of Cialdini's persuasion strategies in health promotion.

2.1   The Use of Verbal Persuasion Strategies by Virtual Humans for Behavior Change

Virtual humans, capable of simulating human-like face-to-face interactions, have been studied for their ability to employ verbal persuasion strategies used by humans during health-related discussions [17,18,20]. For instance, research has explored the impact of various affective tones used by a virtual coach on a user's motivation to exercise [18]. It was found that users reported a higher motivation to exercise when the virtual human used positive language as opposed to negative language. Similarly, another study by Olafsson et al. investigated whether a virtual human's use of humor could inspire users to adopt healthy behaviors like exercising and increasing fruit and vegetable intake [20]. The study found that humor significantly boosted the motivation to engage in recommended healthy behaviors. In a related vein, previous research has also compared the effects of social dialogues and persuasive dialogues used by a virtual human [26]. It was discovered that persuasive dialogues used by a virtual human led to an increase in positive attitudes towards exercising compared to social dialogues. In summary, research consistently shows that virtual humans effectively use various verbal persuasion strategies to influence user behavior.

2.2 The Use of Cialdini's Persuasion Strategies in Health Promotion

Cialdini's persuasion strategies are among the most extensively studied in both social psychology and persuasion technology research [15,22]. Cialdini proposed that persuasion is achieved through six universal psychological principles:

1. Commitment: People can be persuaded by making them commit to a goal and later asking them to honor the commitment.
2. Consensus: People can be persuaded by showing them that several others have performed the same action.
3. Reciprocity: People can be persuaded by making them feel obligated to return favors.
4. Scarcity: People can be persuaded by increasing the desirability of a product due to its perceived scarcity.
5. Authority: People can be persuaded by having them interact with experts or persons who have authority.
6. Likability: People can be persuaded by increasing the liking of the person who is persuading them.

In the context of health promotion, previous research has assessed the application of Cialdini's persuasion strategies in developing persuasive text messages for users [15,29]. Prior work has found that among all of Cialdini's strategies, Commitment and Authority are the most effective [21,29]. However, the design of monologue text messages using Cialdini's persuasion strategies has posed challenges in fully implementing all of Cialdini's strategies effectively [15]. Strategies such as Reciprocity, which are centered around dialogue interactions, can be implemented using virtual humans [33]. Furthermore, prior work has consistently found that the effectiveness of Cialdini's persuasion strategies varies based on the user's personality [3,22,29]. For instance, our previous work suggested that the user personality influences the TPB factors and the effects of virtual humans' persuasion strategies [32]. We use this knowledge from our previous work to investigate whether adapting persuasion strategies to user personalities is beneficial.

2.3 The Use of TPB to Predict Coping Skills Use

Health interventions that are technology-based yield better results when they are grounded in behavioral models [9]. Previous research has leveraged such models, including the Transtheoretical Model, to design health interventions involving virtual humans [5,20]. These models provide insights into the fundamental factors that drive health behaviors. TPB has been used to predict the adoption of mental health coping skills among college students [6]. The TPB's concept of perceived control over behavior has been identified as a significant predictor of college students' use of coping skills both in prior work and in our previous work [6,32]. Given the reliability of the TPB in predicting students' use of coping skills, the current research employs the TPB to study the adoption of coping skills among college students.

3   System Design

A web-based platform [34] was used to develop and deliver the virtual human intervention to college students. The platform involved a client-side 3-D virtual human delivered using WebGL and a server-side dialog manager that used a conversational script written using an open-source Ink scripting language [13]. The Ink scripting language enabled writing interactive branching conversations. During the conversation, the virtual agent used dialog from the Ink script to converse with the user. The user responded to a virtual human using multiple-choice options or open-ended responses via text. The platform was embedded within the Canvas Learning Management System (LMS) used for the two undergraduate courses at the University of Florida. The virtual human intervention was delivered via LMS because prior work has found that students lack knowledge about the available services [27]. The delivery of the virtual human intervention via the course curriculum in LMS helped increase the visibility of the intervention to college students. A female virtual human was employed because female virtual humans are found to be more effective in influencing students' behavior than male virtual humans in prior work [23]. The virtual human was developed using Adobe Fuse (illustrated in Fig. 2). The virtual environment was developed using Unity3D. The virtual human used a Google Text-to-speech to generate speech. The virtual human was sitting in an idle position with a breathing animation for the duration of the conversation.

4   Method

The evidence from our previous work [32] suggested that, along with students' personalities, TPB factors influenced the effectiveness of persuasion strategies in promoting gratitude journaling. Thus, both students' personality types and students' reported scores on TPB questionnaires were used to identify the effectiveness of different persuasion strategies for a given student. To do so, a persuasion strategy prediction model was developed using the data from 208 participants generated from the previous study [32]. The development of the prediction model involved two stages: 1) implementation of a model to identify students' personality types based on their Big-5 personality dimensions, and 2) implementation of a prediction model that uses students' personality types derived from stage one and students' responses to TPB questionnaires to predict relative effectiveness of persuasion strategies. The following section describes two stages in detail.

4.1   Identifying Student Personality Type

Gaussian Mixture Modeling (GMM) was used to develop a model that can identify personality types in our student population. GMM models the data using
several Gaussian distributions, also called components. The goal of the modeling process is to identify the optimum number of Gaussian distributions that
are required to represent the data and determine the optimal values of Gaussian
parameters (e.g., covariance). Using the guidelines [14], user scores reported on
the personality questionnaire were aggregated and standardized around mean
into five personality dimensions - Intellect, Conscientiousness, Extroversion,
Agreeableness, and Emotional Stability. To estimate the parameters of Gaussian mixture distribution from the best-performing model, multiple models were
fit to the data with a different number of Gaussian components and covariance types using GaussianMixture class from the Scikit-learn machine learning
library [24]. The covariance type allows controlling the covariance matrix, which
determines the shape of Gaussian components [2]. The best-performing model
was selected based on the lowest BIC score [16]. The model with 2 Gaussian
components and spherical covariance type (i.e., variance same around all axes)
had the lowest BIC score and was chosen for predicting the personality types of
users. The model clustered students into two groups. The first group reported a
lower-than-average score on all five personality dimensions (illustrated in Fig. 1).
The second group reported a higher-than-average score on all five personality
dimensions. The resulting model was used to identify a student's personality
type.

4.2   Persuasion Strategy Prediction Model

The goal of the persuasion strategy prediction model was to identify the effectiveness of persuasion strategies in improving students' self-efficacy to perform
gratitude journaling. Students' self-efficacy was chosen as an outcome variable
because the findings from the previous study [32] showed that a change in students' self-efficacy determined the change in students' intentions to perform gratitude journaling. Therefore, using a more effective persuasion strategy to improve
students' self-efficacy could improve students' intentions to perform gratitude
journaling.

   To build a persuasion strategy prediction model, students' self-reported
scores on the TPB questionnaire before the virtual human intervention and
students' personality types generated from the personality model were used. For
building a prediction model, the following problem definition was established:

   *Problem definition: Given students' responses on the TPB questionnaire and
personality type, identify the effectiveness of persuasion strategies in maximizing
the students' self-efficacy to perform gratitude journaling after the virtual human
intervention.*

   The prediction model developed by Gentile et al. [10] was used to build the
persuasion prediction model as it was effective with sample sizes and enabled
training and using models with missing data. The proposed prediction model

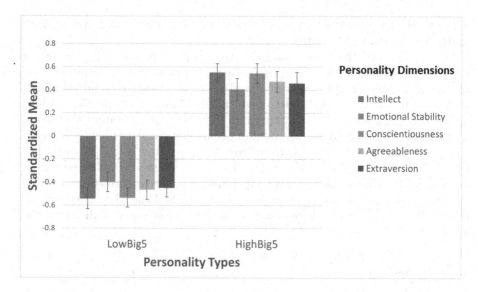

Fig. 1. Standardized means of user self-reported scores on Big-5 personality dimensions. The bars indicate how many standard deviations away users' scores were from means of each dimension. Error bars represent standard errors.

estimates the probability density function of the outcome variable given a set of input variables. Probability distributions were estimated using Gaussian mixtures. Input variables include - Persuasion Strategy, Personality type derived from the personality prediction model described in Sect. 4.1, Pre-intervention student responses on TPB questionnaire items - AttitudeGood, AttitudeBeneficial, SubjNormLikeMe, SubjNormApprove, ControlUpToMe, ControlEfficacy, and Intentions (refer to Table 1 for descriptions of TPB questionnaire items). The output variable was Post-intervention ControlEfficacy.

To identify significant features, Support Vector Regression with radial basis function was used to fit the data due to its similarity to Gaussian distribution among the available kernel functions in the Scikit-learn machine learning library and better performance [31]. To select significant features, a forward SequentialFeatureSelector was used with 10-fold cross-validation. Six features that led to an increase in R^2 score were included in the model - Persuasion Strategy, Personality type, Pre-intervention SubjNormApprove, Pre-intervention ControlUpToMe, Pre-intervention ControlEfficacy, and Pre-intervention Intentions.

To evaluate the performance of the developed persuasion strategy prediction model, Leave-One-Out cross-validation was used over 208 samples. The mean absolute error (MAE) was 1.144 and the standard deviation of MAE was 1.142. An additional analysis was performed to understand the distribution of persuasion strategies recommended by the model for 1647086 possible input combinations. The most effective strategy was the Authority strategy for all users. The Likability strategy is recommended the majority of the time as the second most effective strategy and the Commitment strategy is recommended the majority of the time as the least effective strategy.

The study used the second-most effective strategy predicted by the model because the adaptation was not possible with the most effective strategy. The most effective strategy was Authority for all users, independent of individual differences in users. Although the lack of dependence on the most effective Authority strategy on students' personalities may seem like the adaptation of strategy is unnecessary, this could be only valid in persuading students to practice gratitude journaling context. For other contexts, there may not be one strategy that is most effective for all users. In such contexts, researchers would benefit from understanding whether adapting a virtual human to use a more effective strategy based on individual differences in users would be beneficial. Therefore, in this study, we decided to use the second-most effective strategy predicted by the model.

4.3   Study Design

To evaluate the effect of adapting virtual humans based on individual differences in user, the users were assigned to one of the following conditions in a between-subject design study (refer to Table 3 for examples of dialogs in each condition):

- KernelMessage condition: The virtual human used kernel messages that provided the same information as other experimental conditions without using Cialdini's persuasion strategies. The condition was included to determine whether the virtual humans that used the second-most or least effective strategy performed any better than a virtual human that did not use Cialdini's persuasion strategies. The comparison also helped determine whether using the least effective strategy performed better or worse than using no Cialdini's persuasion strategy.
- Matched condition: The virtual human used the second-most effective Cialdini's persuasion strategy to manipulate kernel messages based on users' prior beliefs, attitudes, and personality type.
- Mismatched condition: The virtual human used the least effective Cialdini's persuasion strategy to manipulate kernel messages based on users' prior beliefs, attitudes, and personality type.

4.4   Metrics

To understand the effect of the intervention, the constructs defined in the TPB were measured pre-and post-intervention (refer Table 1). The pre-intervention survey included demographics (e.g., sex and race) and IPIP personality dimensions [12]. The post-intervention survey also included an item measuring the user's behavior based on whether the user practiced gratitude journaling after the intervention. An open-ended response was collected in the post-survey to understand why users chose or did not choose to practice gratitude journaling.

Table 1. TPB items

Item Name	Item
AttitudeGood	My writing down what I feel grateful about for the next week would be bad for my mental health/good for my mental health
AttitudeBeneficial	My writing down what I feel grateful about for the next week would be not beneficial/beneficial
SubjNormLikeMe	Most people like me write down what they feel grateful about every week
SubjNormApprove	Most people who are important to me approve of my writing down what I feel grateful about every week
ControlUpToMe	My writing down what I feel grateful about for next week is up to me
ControlEfficacy	I am confident that I can write down what I feel grateful about every week
Intentions	I intend to write down what I feel grateful about for the next week to have a good mental health

User Self-efficacy of Performing Gratitude Journaling. To evaluate the effectiveness of persuasion strategies, users' self-reported self-efficacy (ControlEfficacy) to practice gratitude journaling before interaction and after interaction with the virtual human was measured.

User Intentions of Performing Gratitude Journaling. We hypothesized improvement in users' ControlEfficacy would also positively influence user intentions to perform gratitude journaling. Therefore, users' self-reported intentions to practice gratitude journaling before and after the interaction with the virtual human were also measured.

User Behavior to Practice Gratitude Journaling. To evaluate if the experimental conditions influenced user behavior in performing gratitude journaling, users were given a chance to practice gratitude journaling after the intervention. Users were asked - "Would you like to practice gratitude journaling now?" If users agreed to practice gratitude journaling, they were asked to journal by textually responding to the following three prompts - "Tell me something that made you smile recently". "What did you enjoy the most today?", and "A favorite food you enjoy".

4.5   Participants

A total of 383 undergraduate students enrolled in computer science courses (during Fall 2021) at the University of Florida in the United States participated in the study. The study was approved by the institution review board. Among 383 participants, 30 chose not to include the data in the research, 25 failed the attention check, 4 had previously participated in the study the previous semester, and 3 had missing data due to errors in data storage. An additional 30 participants did not clear the minimum threshold time set by the researcher based on the visual analysis of histograms of completion times, indicating participants might have completed these surveys hastily without paying attention. The data from the remaining 292 students were analyzed. The students were provided extra course credits as compensation to participate in the research. Refer to Table 2 for the demographics of users.

Table 2. Demographics and distribution of users across different experimental conditions in the second study

	Study (N=291)
Age	M= 19.617 (SD= 2.641, Min.= 18, Max.=37)
Sex	195 Male, 96 Female
Race	157 White, 13 Black or African American, 94 Asian, 9 Other, 17 Mixed race, and 1 Not-specified
Experimental Conditions	96 in Matched, 94 in Mismatched, 101 in KernelMessage

4.6 Procedure

The students went through 4 stages: 1) Informed Consent, 2) Pre-survey, 3) Intervention, and 4) Post-survey. Consented participants completed the pre-survey that included user demographics (e.g., sex and race) and the IPIP personality scale. User self-reported responses for IPIP personality items and TPB questionnaires collected in pre-survey are sent to the virtual human system. Using the user self-reported IPIP scores and personality model developed in Sect. 4.1, the personality type of the user is determined. If the input data is incomplete, the user is not assigned any personality type. When the user starts the intervention, the system determines the effectiveness of different strategies by predicting the probability density function of post-intervention user self-efficacy. After the pre-survey, the students were randomly assigned to one of the 3 experimental conditions. The interaction involved 6 stages, as shown in Fig. 2. The participants were asked to complete the post-survey after the intervention.

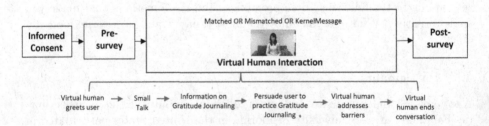

Fig. 2. Overview of the study design.

Table 3. Operational Definitions for Cialdini's persuasion strategies and examples

Persuasion Strategy (Operation definition)	Examples
Kernel Message (Informational message without using Cialdini's persuasion strategies)	Practicing gratitude journaling for 2 or 3 times a week can have profound positive effects on your mental well-being
Likability (Virtual human highlights similarity with user, compliments and establishes cooperative effort)	I can help you practice gratitude journaling. Practicing gratitude journaling for 2 or 3 times a week can have profound positive effects on your mental well-being. As your personal assistant, I want to do everything in my capabilities to help you succeed
Reciprocity (Virtual human performs a favor early in the conversation with the user and later asks the user to return the favor.)	Now that I have shared with you so much information about ensuring good mental health, you can maintain good mental health by simply practicing gratitude journaling for 2 or 3 times a week
Commitment (Virtual human asks for users to commit to their goal of having a good mental health)	You can work towards your commitment to having good mental health by simply practicing gratitude journaling for 2 or 3 times a week
Consensus (Virtual human highlights that others have benefited from performing the recommended behavior)	Many people have reported that practicing gratitude journaling for 2 or 3 times a week can have profound positive effects on their mental well-being
Authority (Virtual human highlights authorities agree with what virtual human is suggesting)	The scientists recommend practicing gratitude journaling for 2 or 3 times a week
Scarcity (Virtual human highlights the opportunity to use exclusive information)	You can benefit from this exclusive information by simply practicing gratitude journaling for 2 or 3 times a week.

5   Results

The primary goal of the analysis was to evaluate the effectiveness of an adaptive virtual human that uses a more effective verbal persuasion strategy based on students' responses to the TPB questionnaire and personality types to increase their self-efficacy. The dependent variables were the normalized change scores of the students' self-efficacy, normalized change scores of the students' user intentions, and behavior to perform gratitude journaling. The normalized change scores for self-efficacy and intentions were calculated based on pre- and post-intervention scores using the Eq. 1. All the statistical analyses were conducted using JASP v0.16.

$$\text{Normalized score} = \begin{cases} \frac{\text{post score} - \text{pre score}}{7 - \text{pre score}} & \text{if post score} > \text{pre score}, \\ \frac{\text{post score} - \text{pre score}}{\text{pre score}} & \text{if post score} < \text{pre score}. \end{cases} \tag{1}$$

5.1   User Self-efficacy to Practice Gratitude Journaling

A Kruskal-Wallis test was conducted to evaluate the effect of the experimental conditions on user self-efficacy as data did not meet parametric assumptions. In the analysis, the between-subject factor was experimental conditions and the dependent variable was normalized change scores for self-efficacy. The analysis showed that there was no significant difference in normalized change scores of students' self-efficacy between Matched, Mismatched, and KernelMessage conditions (Kruskal-Wallis H=4.151, p=0.126). Figure 3 shows descriptive plots of normalized change scores of students' self-efficacy across three experimental conditions. There was no overall effect of experimental conditions on normalized change in self-efficacy.

To further understand what factors contributed to this result, differences in students' self-efficacy scores before the intervention were investigated. In our experiment, some students might have had low or high self-efficacy in performing gratitude journaling before they started the intervention. So it was hypothesized that the effect of experimental conditions may vary for students with low self-efficacy in performing gratitude journaling. The data was divided into subgroups: 1) students who rated pre-intervention self-efficacy scores less than 4 (N=67) and 2) students who rated pre-intervention self-efficacy scores greater than or equal to 4 (N=222). For this analysis, a score of 4 was considered as the center based on prior work with semantic differential scales [25]. Therefore, scores below 4 were considered as low and scores equal to or above 4 were considered as high.

A Kruskal-Wallis test was conducted to evaluate the effect of experimental conditions on students who rated pre-intervention self-efficacy less than 4. The analysis showed that there was a significant effect of experimental conditions on normalized change scores in students' self-efficacy (H=8.742, p=0.013). Pairwise post-hoc comparisons using Dunn's test reveal that normalized change in students' self-efficacy scores was significantly higher for the Matched condition than the Mismatched condition (p=0.030, p-value corrected using Holm-Bonferroni method). Similarly, normalized change in students' self-efficacy scores was significantly higher for the Matched condition than the KernelMessage condition (p=0.007, p-value corrected using Holm-Bonferroni method). Whereas, there was no significant difference between KernelMessage and Mismatched condition with normalized change in students' self-efficacy scores (p=0.281, p-value corrected using Holm-Bonferroni method). Figure 4 shows a descriptive plot of normalized change scores in user self-efficacy for students whose pre-intervention self-efficacy scores were less than 4 across three experimental conditions. The findings suggest that the Matched condition performed significantly better than both the KernelMessage condition and Mismatched condition.

Similar to the previous analysis, a Kruskal-Wallis test was conducted to evaluate the effect of experimental conditions on students who rated pre-intervention self-efficacy equal or greater than 4. The analysis showed that there was a significant effect of experimental conditions on normalized change scores in students' self-efficacy at alpha level 0.1 (H=5.316, p=0.07). Pairwise post-hoc comparisons using Dunn's test reveal that normalized change in students' self-efficacy scores was significantly higher for the KernelMessage condition than the Mismatched condition (p=0.033, p-value corrected using Holm-Bonferroni method). There were no significant differences between KernelMessage and Matched condition (p=0.173) as well as Matched and Mismatched condition (p=0.176) with normalized change in students' self-efficacy scores. Figure 5 shows the descriptive

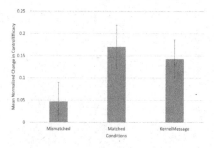

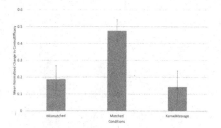

Fig. 3. Mean normalized change in students' self-efficacy across experimental conditions. Error bars represent standard errors.

Fig. 4. Mean normalized change in students' self-efficacy across experimental conditions for students who reported pre-intervention self-efficacy scores of below 4. Error bars represent standard errors.

plot of normalized change scores in students' self-efficacy for students whose pre-intervention self-efficacy scores were equal to or greater than 4 across three experimental conditions. These results show that the KernelMessage condition performed better than the Mismatched condition for students who already had relatively higher self-efficacy scores. The Mismatched condition on average led to no change in students' self-efficacy scores.

5.2   User Intentions to Practice Gratitude Journaling

A Kruskal-Wallis test was conducted to evaluate the effect of the experimental conditions on students' intentions as data did not meet parametric assumptions. In the Kruskal-Wallis analysis, the between-subject factor was experimental conditions and the dependent variable was the normalized change in intentions. The analysis showed that there was a significant difference in normalized change scores of students' intentions between Matched, Mismatched, and KernelMessage conditions at alpha 0.1 (Kruskal-Wallis H=5.531, p=0.063). Pairwise post-hoc comparisons using Dunn's test reveal that normalized change in students' intentions scores was significantly higher for the Matched condition than the KernelMessage condition (p=0.033, p-value corrected using Holm-Bonferroni method). No significant differences were found for KernelMessage versus Mismatched comparison and Mismatched versus Matched comparison. Figure 6 shows descriptive plots of normalized change scores of students' intentions across three experimental conditions.

There were no significant effects of experimental conditions on students' intentions for users who rated pre-intervention intentions low (less than 4) or high (equal or greater than 4).

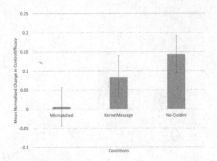

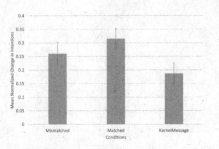

Fig. 5. Mean normalized change in students' self-efficacy across experimental conditions for students who reported pre-intervention self-efficacy scores of greater than or equal to 4. Error bars represent standard errors.

Fig. 6. Mean normalized change in students' intentions across experimental conditions. Error bars represent standard errors.

5.3   User Behavior of Practicing Gratitude Journaling

A total of 34 (33.66%) users practiced gratitude journaling in the KernelMessage condition, 42 (44.68%) in the Mismatched condition, and 39 (40.62%) in the Matched condition. To understand whether the experimental conditions influenced user behavior in practicing gratitude journaling after the intervention, a Pearson chi-square test was conducted. There was no significant association found between experimental conditions and whether or not users practiced gratitude journaling $\chi^2(2)=2.546$, p=0.280.

Qualitative Analysis of Open-Ended Responses To further understand what factors influenced students' decision to not practice gratitude journaling after the intervention, a preliminary qualitative analysis was performed on open-ended responses from students in the post-intervention survey for the statement - "Briefly describe the reasons for not choosing to practice gratitude journaling." A total of 173 responses were analyzed. To analyze the student responses and identify potential themes, an individual open coding was performed. The individual open coding led to an initial set of codes. The codes were then refined to remove ambiguities in the definition of identified codes. Examples of final codes used in the analysis included students having time constraints, students preferring to perform gratitude journaling later, and students prefer to use other coping skills than gratitude journaling (refer to Supplementary materials for the list of codes and their descriptions [1]. A total of 151 segments were coded and used for further analysis.

The most frequent theme that emerged among students' responses was the lack of time to practice gratitude journaling (59 out of 151 students, 39.1%). For example, one student said - "I am short on time and have other things to do shortly". Some students (27 out of 151 students, 9.2%) preferred practicing gratitude journaling later in their own time, as one said - "I will do it later in my own time."

Students also preferred using other coping skills than practicing gratitude journaling (31 out of 151 students, 20.5%). For example, one student said - "Personally, I have many hobbies/practices that I do to maintain good mental health, and I do not think that journaling would be very helpful for me personally". Among 31 students, 15 students preferred to practice gratitude journaling without writing down. One student commented - "I just like to reflect what I did and wish not spend any further time with journaling".

Students also believed that gratitude journaling is not beneficial or required for them (51 out of 151, 33.7%), as one student responded - "I do not believe it will help improve my mental health. I would rather have some school days off". A few students (4 out of 151) also commented that performing gratitude journaling was not an efficient use of their time to improve their mental health.

Three students preferred to not share personal information online or in a research study. While six students had already performed gratitude journaling before.

6 Discussion

The results suggest that there was no significant effect of experimental conditions on change in user self-efficacy. However, when the data were divided into subgroups based on users' pre-intervention scores of their self-efficacy, significant differences were found between the experimental conditions. The users with low self-efficacy reported significantly higher self-efficacy post-intervention scores in the matched condition than users in both KernelMessage and mismatched conditions. However, as described before, this partition led to a comparison between the Likability and Commitment strategies as they were found to be the second most effective and least effective strategy respectively (except for 1 user who was assigned the Consensus strategy in matched condition and excluding the data point did not affect results). Thus, the Likability strategy performed significantly better than the Commitment strategy in improving user self-efficacy for users who had low self-efficacy before the intervention. More importantly, the Likability strategy also performed better than the KernelMessage condition wherein the virtual human did not use Cialdini's persuasion strategy. These results suggest that using an effective Cialdini's persuasion strategy can improve user self-efficacy compared to not using a Cialdini's persuasion strategy. These results are similar to our previous work wherein the Likability strategy was more effective compared to other strategies [32]. The results extend our previous research by showing that using an effective Cialdini's strategy is better than not using a Cialdini's strategy for users with low self-efficacy scores.

For users who had relatively high pre-intervention scores, the results suggest that change in user self-efficacy was significantly low in the mismatched condition compared to the KernelMessage condition. However, no significant differences were observed between the KernelMessage and matched condition or matched and mismatched condition. The results suggest that for users who have relatively high pre-intervention self-efficacy, using no Cialdini's strategy (i.e., KernelMessage condition) was better in improving user self-efficacy than using the least effective strategy (i.e., mismatched condition).

Although differences in self-efficacy and intentions to perform gratitude journaling were observed in experimental conditions, no differences were observed in user behavior of gratitude journaling. To understand why users didn't perform gratitude journaling, a qualitative analysis was performed on users' open-ended responses. Users reported reasons such as lack of time for not practicing gratitude journaling. The barrier of lack of time was addressed by the virtual human during the interaction, by saying statements like - "You do not need a lot of time to practice gratitude journaling. You can just spend as-low-as 1 min to become happier and feel more grateful." However, users preferred to practice it later or use that time for other activities such as hobbies as they did not find gratitude journaling beneficial.

Considering both qualitative and quantitative analysis, the findings suggest that although persuasion strategies can be useful in improving users' self-efficacy to perform gratitude journaling, the improvement in users' self-efficacy is not sufficient for users to perform gratitude journaling. To increase users' likelihood of engaging in the recommended behavior, virtual human interventions should also address users' perceived barriers and improve users' perceived benefits of practicing the recommended behavior. These observations can be explained by the Health Belief Model [28] which suggests that, along with people's self-efficacy, people's perceived benefits of performing a behavior and barriers determine their likelihood to engage in health-promoting behavior. Thus, in addition to users' self-efficacy, virtual human interventions should also account for individual differences in users' perceived barriers and perceived benefits. One possible way to account for individual differences in perceived benefits is to personalize the health conversations to users' needs at a given moment rather than discussing health topics that users might not find useful at a given moment. For example, if a student is experiencing stress due to a lack of time to complete assignments, the virtual human should discuss coping skills that are more relevant to their needs (e.g., time-management skills) than other less-relevant coping skills (e.g., pursuing a hobby).

7 Limitations

Our study provides insights into how using a more or less effective persuasion strategy influences users' beliefs about performing the recommended behavior. However, the effectiveness of different persuasion strategies is limited to the context of promoting gratitude journaling among college students. Additional research is required to understand how the effectiveness of persuasion strategies varies in other contexts. Other limitations include: 1) The lack of virtual human's non-verbal behaviors during the conversation with the user, which can affect user perceptions [4]. 2) The study did not measure long-term user behavior in practicing gratitude journaling. Studying the long-term effects of persuasion strategies used by a virtual human may provide further insights into how to increase the effectiveness of virtual human health interventions.

8 Conclusion

The paper evaluated whether adapting a virtual human's dialog based on individual differences in users may improve the effectiveness of virtual human health intervention in promoting healthy behavior. To achieve this goal, a user model was developed that captured the relationship between virtual human's persuasion strategies and individual differences in users. The user model was then evaluated to understand whether the adaptation of a virtual human's dialog improved the effectiveness of the virtual human health intervention. The evidence suggests that, for college students who have low self-efficacy to perform gratitude journaling, the virtual human using a more effective Cialdini's persuasion strategy recommended by an adaptive system is better in improving college students' self-efficacy than the virtual humans that used the least effective Cialdini's persuasion strategy. Based on these findings, design implications were discussed to design effective virtual human health interventions.

References

1. OSF | Persuasion   Study   4.   https://osf.io/dnsca/?view_only=d86959f8364443c3bbbb6f5f8cb8696f
2. GMM covariances - scikit-learn 1.0.2 documentation (2022). https://scikit-learn.org/stable/auto_examples/mixture/plot_gmm_covariances.html#sphx-glr-auto-examples-mixture-plot-gmm-covariances-py
3. Alkiş, N., Taşkaya Temizel, T.: The impact of individual differences on influence strategies. Personality Individ. Differ. **87**, 147–152 (2015). https://doi.org/10.1016/j.paid.2015.07.037
4. Baylor, A.L., Kim, S.: Designing nonverbal communication for pedagogical agents: when less is more. Comput. Hum. Behav. **25**(2), 450–457 (2009)
5. Bickmore, T.W., Schulman, D., Sidner, C.L.: A reusable framework for health counseling dialogue systems based on a behavioral medicine ontology. J. Biomed. Inform. **44**(2), 183–197 (2011). https://doi.org/10.1016/j.jbi.2010.12.006
6. Bistricky, S.L., et al.: Understanding and promoting stress management practices among college students through an integrated health behavior model. Am. J. Health Educ. **49**(1), 12–27 (2018). https://doi.org/10.1080/19325037.2017.1377651
7. Cialdini, R.B.: Influence : science and practice (2001). https://www.amazon.com/Influence-Practice-Robert-B-Cialdini/dp/0205609996
8. Emmons, R.A., Stern, R.: Gratitude as a psychotherapeutic intervention. J. Clin. Psychol. Session **69**, 846–855 (2013). https://doi.org/10.1002/jclp.22020

9. Fanning, J., Mullen, S.P., Mcauley, E.: Increasing physical activity with mobile devices: a meta-analysis. J. Med. Internet Res. **14**(6), e2171 (2012). https://doi.org/10.2196/jmir.2171, https://www.jmir.org/2012/6/e161

10. Gentile, V., Khamis, M., Milazzo, F., Sorce, S., Malizia, A., Alt, F.: Predicting mid-air gestural interaction with public displays based on audience behaviour. Int. J. Hum. Comput. Stud. **144**, 102497 (2020). https://doi.org/10.1016/j.ijhcs.2020.102497, https://linkinghub.elsevier.com/retrieve/pii/S1071581920300999

11. Gkika, S., Lekakos, G.: The persuasive role of explanations in recommender systems. In: CEUR Workshop Proceedings, vol. 1153, pp. 59–68 (2014). https://citeseerx.ist.psu.edu/viewdoc/download?doi=10.1.1.663.7538&rep=rep1&type=pdf

12. Goldberg, L.R., Psychology, E.A.O.P.: A broad-bandwidth, public-domain, personality inventory measuring the lower-level facets of several Five-Factor models. In: European Conference on Personality, Tilburg University (1999). https://ipip.ori.org/Abroad-bandwidthinventory.pdf

13. Inkle: Ink: Inkle's open source scripting language for writing interactive narrative (2021). https://github.com/inkle/ink

14. ipip.ori.org: IPIP Scale Scoring Instructions (2014). https://ipip.ori.org/newScoringInstructions.htm

15. Kaptein, M.: Personalized persuasion in ambient intelligence. J. Ambient Intell. Smart Environ. **4**(3), 279–280 (2012). https://doi.org/10.3233/AIS-2012-0153

16. Lanza, S.T., Cooper, B.R.: Latent class analysis for developmental research. Child Dev. Perspect. **10**(1), 59–64 (2016). https://doi.org/10.1111/cdep.12163

17. Lisetti, C., Amini, R., Yasavur, U., On, N.R.: I can help you change! an empathic virtual agent delivers behavior change health interventions. In: ACM Transactions on Management Information Systems, pp. 1–28 (2014). https://doi.org/10.1145/2544103

18. Lucas, G.M., Krämer, N., Peters, C., Taesch, L.S., Mell, J., Gratch, J.: Effects of perceived agency and message tone in responding to a virtual personal trainer. In: Proceedings of the 18th International Conference on Intelligent Virtual Agents, pp. 247–254. IVA 2018, ACM, New York, NY, USA (2018). https://doi.org/10.1145/3267851.3267855

19. Morris, M.M.: A Parent's Guide to Mental Health for College Students | NAMI: National Alliance on Mental Illness (2018). https://www.nami.org/Blogs/NAMI-Blog/December-2018/A-Parent-s-Guide-to-Mental-Health-for-College-Students

20. Olafsson, S., O'Leary, T.K., Bickmore, T.W.: Motivating health behavior change with humorous virtual agents. In: Proceedings of the 20th ACM International Conference on Intelligent Virtual Agents, IVA 2020, pp. 1–8. Association for Computing Machinery, Inc, New York, NY, USA (2020). https://doi.org/10.1145/3383652.3423915

21. Orji, R., Mandryk, R.L., Vassileva, J.: Gender, age, and responsiveness to Cialdini's persuasion strategies. In: MacTavish, T., Basapur, S. (eds.) PERSUASIVE 2015. LNCS, vol. 9072, pp. 147–159. Springer, Cham (2015). https://doi.org/10.1007/978-3-319-20306-5_14

22. Oyibo, K., Orji, R., Vassileva, J.: Investigation of the influence of personality traits on Cialdini's persuasive strategies. In: CEUR Workshop Proceedings, vol. 1833, pp. 8–20 (2017). http://ceur-ws.org

23. Ozogul, G., Johnson, A.M., Atkinson, R.K., Reisslein, M.: Investigating the impact of pedagogical agent gender matching and learner choice on learning outcomes and perceptions. Comput. Educ. **67**, 36–50 (2013). https://doi.org/10.1016/j.compedu.2013.02.006

24. Pedregosa, F., et al.: Scikit-learn: machine learning in Python. J. Mach. Learn. Res.**12**(7), 2825–2830 (2011). https://scikit-learn.org/stable/, http://scikit-learn.sourceforge.net, http://jmlr.csail.mit.edu/papers/v12/pedregosa11a.html%5Cn, http://arxiv.org/abs/1201.0490

25. Ploder, A., Eder, A.: Semantic Differential. International Encyclopedia of the Social & Behavioral Sciences: 2nd (Edn.), pp. 563–571 (2015). https://doi.org/10.1016/B978-0-08-097086-8.03231-1

26. Schulman, D., Bickmore, T.: Persuading users through counseling dialogue with a conversational agent. In: Proceedings of the 4th International Conference on Persuasive Technology - Persuasive 2009, p. 1. ACM Press, New York, New York, USA (2009). https://doi.org/10.1145/1541948.1541983, http://portal.acm.org/citation.cfm?doid=1541948.1541983

27. Storrie, K., Ahern, K., Tuckett, A.: A systematic review: students with mental health problems-A growing problem. Int. J. Nurs. Pract. **16**(1), 1–6 (2010). https://doi.org/10.1111/j.1440-172X.2009.01813.x

28. Strecher, V.: Psychology, I.R.H.O., Health, U. The health belief model. books.google.com (1997). https://books.google.com/books?hl=en&lr=&id=zVh30FrAuDsC&oi=fnd&pg=PA113&dq=health+belief+model&ots=Im1MkCvIrv&sig=3PX7Av8SNdgTx3X4KhspesJA-_8

29. Thomas, R.J., Masthoff, J., Oren, N.: Personalising healthy eating messages to age, gender and personality: using Cialdini's principles and framing. In: International Conference on Intelligent User Interfaces, Proceedings IUI, pp. 81–84. Association for Computing Machinery, New York, New York, USA (2017). https://doi.org/10.1145/3030024.3040986, http://dl.acm.org/citation.cfm?doid=3030024.3040986

30. U.S. Government Accountability Office.: Young adults with serious mental illness: Some states and federal agencies are taking steps to address their transition challenges. (2008). https://www.gao.gov/new.items/d08678.pdf

31. Way, T.W., Sahiner, B., Hadjiiski, L.M., Chan, H.P.: Effect of finite sample size on feature selection and classification: a simulation study. Med. Phys. **37**(2), 907–920 (2010)

32. Zalake, M., Gomes De Siqueira, A., Vaddiparti, K., Antonenko, P., Lok, B.: Towards understanding how virtual human's verbal persuasion strategies influence user intentions to perform health behavior. In: Proceedings of the 21th ACM International Conference on Intelligent Virtual Agents (2021). https://doi.org/10.1145/3472306

33. Zalake, M., Siqueira, A.G.D., Vaddiparti, K., Lok, B.: The effects of virtual human's verbal persuasion strategies on user intention and behavior. Int. J. Hum.-Comput. Stud. **156**, 102708 (2021). https://doi.org/10.1016/J.IJHCS.2021.102708

34. Zalake, M., Vaddiparti, K., Antonenko, P., Lok, B.: Towards understanding how virtual human's verbal persuasion strategies influence user intentions to perform health behavior. In: Proceedings of the 21st ACM International Conference on Intelligent Virtual Agents, IVA 2021, pp. 216–223 (2021). https://doi.org/10.1145/3472306.3478345

Author Index

V. G. Duffy (Ed.): HCII 2024, LNCS 14709, pp. 425–428, 2024.
https://doi.org/10.1007/978-3-031-61060-8

by Baker & Taylor Publisher Services

Printed in the United States
by Baker & Taylor Publisher Services